THE AGE OF REASONS

The Age of Reasons reads Don Quixote as a parodic example of eighteenth-century "reason." Reason was supposed to be universally compelling, yet it was also thought to be empirically derived. Quixotic figures satirize these assumptions by appearing to be utterly insane, while reproducing the conditions of universal rationality: they staunchly believe that reason is universal, that it can be confirmed by experience, and that they themselves are rational. Quixotism is a rational madness. It challenges reason's presumed authority as the neutral arbiter of all controversy by turning the definition of reason itself into an object of political controversy.

"The Age of Reason" was actually an Age of Reasons, Motooka contends. Joining imaginative literature, moral philosophy and the emerging discourse of the new science, she seeks to historicize the meaning of eighteenth-century "reason" and its supposed opposites, quixotism and sentimentalism. Reading novels by the Fieldings, Lennox and Sterne alongside the works of Adam Smith, Motooka argues that the legacy of sentimentalism is the social sciences. *The Age of Reasons* raises our understanding of eighteenth-century British culture and its relation to the "rational" culture of economics that is growing ever more pervasive today.

Wendy Motooka is Assistant Professor of English at Oberlin College, USA.

ROUTLEDGE STUDIES IN SOCIAL AND POLITICAL THOUGHT

THE AGE OF REASONS

Quixotism, sentimentalism and political
economy in eighteenth-century Britain

Wendy Motooka

London and New York

First published 1998
by Routledge
11 New Fetter Lane, London EC4P 4EE

Simultaneously published in the USA and Canada
by Routledge
29 West 35th Street, New York, NY 10001

© 1998 Wendy Motooka

Typeset in Garamond by Routledge
Printed and bound in Great Britain by Biddles Ltd, Guildford and
King's Lynn

British Library Cataloguing in Publication Data
A catalogue record for this book is available from the British Library

Library of Congress Cataloguing in Publication Data
Motooka, Wendy, 1964–
The age of reasons : quixotism, sentimentalism and political
economy in eighteenth-century Britain / Wendy Motooka.
p. cm.
Includes bibliographical references and index.
1. English fiction–18th century–History and criticism.
2. Economics–Great Britain–History–18th century. 3. Cervantes
Saavedra, Miguel de, 1547–1616. Don Quixote. 4. Cervantes
Saavedra, Miguel de, 1547–1616–Influence. 5. Great
Britain–Civilization–18th century. 6. Satire, British–History and
criticism. 7. Philosophy, Modern–18th century. 8. Sentimentalism in
literature. 9. Rationalism in literature. 10. Smith, Adam,
1723–1790. I. Title.
PR858.E37M68   1998
823'.509355–dc21   97–45073
                                                             CIP

ISBN 0–415–17941–6

FOR MY PARENTS,
PHILIP AND JANET MOTOOKA

CONTENTS

ACKNOWLEDGMENTS

A project such as this one would not have been manageable, bearable, or any fun without the support and assistance of others. I would like to express my deep gratitude to James A. Winn, for his guidance and inspiration over the years, and to thank James G. Turner, Julie Ellison and Don Herzog for their wise counsel and warm encouragement. Anne K. Krook has been both a friend and a mentor, as well as a savvy and generous critic. I would also like to thank Leo Damrosch, Jim Engell and Marc Shell for their intellectual and practical advice. In its various forms and fragments, this book has benefited from the kindness and critical acumen of many other friends and colleagues, who have added rigor as well as pleasure to the undertaking. My thanks to Peter Webb and his noontime symposia, Robin Ikegami, Christine Blouch, Katie Conrad, Anne Cheng, Carol Barash, Jan Thaddeus, Sylvia Watanabe, Joe Won, Rafia Zafar, and the ever-witty and convivial 1996–7 junior faculty reading group of the Harvard English department: Lynn Wardley, Shannon Jackson, Jonah Siegel, Bill Handley, Jeffrey Masten, Barbara Claire Freeman, Nick Jenkins, Jesse Matz and Jed Esty. My debt to David M. Levy's generous erudition and indefatigable intelligence is incalculable. Scott Karambis and Laura Yim not only read the entire manuscript, they also made revision enjoyable. I am grateful also to Rob Hur, Hisayo Suzuki and especially Simone Sandy, for their help in tracking down research materials.

I have also been very fortunate to have had liberal institutional support. The Hyder E. Rollins Fund, Fred N. Robinson Publication Fund and the Clark Fund at Harvard generously subsidized the research and writing of this book. Thanks to Anne Sudbay Furbush for her able and friendly administration. For their kind assistance, I would also like to thank the staffs at several libraries: the University of Michigan Rare Book Room, the Newberry Library, the Houghton Library, the British Library, the University of London Library and the Public Record Office at Kew.

On a more personal note, I would like to acknowledge the loved ones who have sustained me, and put up with me, through this long process. I thank my parents, who were always there with encouragement and support; my Boston *ohana*, especially Anae Merseburgh, who took me to testosterone flicks whenever I really just needed to see things being blown up, Manu Aluli Meyer, who would remind me of what is important, and Melissa Lukin, who showed me the ropes; Leigh Motooka; Harumi Kuno and Dan Muntz. I am deeply grateful to Yuri Kimura, whose vital energy and affection kept me buoyant. And though it feels like too little too late, my sad thanks to Tofu, who was there at the beginning, but who did not live to celebrate the end.

An earlier version of Chapter 3, "Coming to a bad end," appeared in *Eighteenth-Century Fiction*, 8, 1996. I thank the editors for granting me permission to republish this essay in its revised form.

ABBREVIATIONS

ADM   Admiralty Records, Public Record Office at Kew.

Amelia   Fielding, Henry, *Amelia*, ed. Martin C. Battestin, Middletown CT: Wesleyan University Press, 1983.

Antiquixotus   Antiquixotus, Philonauticus, *The Rule of Two to One: Or, the Difference betwixt Courage and Quixotism*, London, 1745.

Astell   Astell, Mary, *Some Reflections Upon Marriage*, 1730, New York: Source Book Press, 1970.

"Astronomy"   Smith, Adam, "History of astronomy," *Essays on Philosophical Subjects*, eds W.P.D. Wightman and J.C. Bryce, 1980, Indianapolis IN: Liberty Classics, 1982.

Behn   Behn, Aphra, *The Rover and Other Plays*, ed. Jane Spencer, Oxford: Oxford University Press, 1995.

Berkeley   Berkeley, George, *The Works of George Berkeley Bishop of Cloyne*, eds. A.A. Luce and T.E. Jessop, 9 vols, London: Thomas Nelson and Sons, 1953.

Boswell   Boswell, James, *Life of Johnson*, ed. R. W. Chapman, Oxford: Oxford University Press, 1985.

Burnet   Burnet, Thomas, *Remarks on John Locke, with Locke's Replies*, ed. George Watson, Doncaster: Brynmill, 1989.

Challenge   *The Challenge, Sent by a Young Lady to Sir Thomas: Or, the Female War*, London, 1697.

CGJ   Fielding, Henry, *The Covent-Garden Journal*, ed. Gerard Edward Jensen, 2 vols, 1915, New York: Russell and Russell, 1964.

DQ   Cervantes, Miguel de, *Don Quixote*, trans. Peter Motteux, rev Ozell, New York: Modern Library, 1950.

Drake   Drake, Judith, *An Essay in Defence of the Female Sex*, London, 1696.

DS   Fielding, Sarah, *The Adventures of David Simple*, ed. Malcolm Kelsall, Oxford: Oxford University Press, 1973.

Enquiry   *An Enquiry into the Conduct of Capt. M—n*, London, 1745.

Essay	Locke, John, *An Essay Concerning Human Understanding*, ed. Peter H. Nidditch, Oxford: Clarendon Press, 1975.
Fielding, Works	Fielding, Henry, *The Works of Henry Fielding*, ed. Leslie Stephen, 10 vols, London, 1882.
FQ	Lennox, Charlotte, *The Female Quixote*, ed. Margaret Dalziel, Oxford: Oxford University Press, 1973.
Gerard	Gerard, Alexander, *An Essay on Taste*, facsimile reproduction of the 3rd edn, 1780, by Walter J. Hipple Jr, Gainesville FL: Scholars' Facsimiles & Reprints, 1963.
Glanvill	Glanvill, Joseph, "The vanity of dogmatizing," in *The Vanity of Dogmatizing: The Three "Versions,"* Hove: Harvester Press, 1970.
HS	Lennox, Charlotte, *The Life of Harriot Stuart. Written by Herself*, 2 vols, London, 1751.
Hume, Essays	Hume, David, *Essays Moral, Political, and Literary*, ed. Eugene F. Miller, rev. edn, Indianapolis IN: Liberty Classics, 1985.
Hume, Treatise	Hume, David, *A Treatise of Human Nature*, ed. L.A. Selby-Bigge, 2nd ed. rev. P.H. Nidditch, Oxford: Clarendon Press, 1978.
Hutcheson	Hutcheson, Francis, *The Collected Works of Francis Hutcheson*, facsimile edn prepared by Bernhard Fabian, 7 vols, Hildesheim: Georg Olms, 1971.
JA	Fielding, Henry, *Joseph Andrews*, ed. Martin C. Battestin, Boston MA: Houghton Mifflin, 1961.
Law	Law, William, *Remarks upon the Fable of the Bees*, introduction by F.D. Maurice, Cambridge, 1844.
Mandeville	Mandeville, Bernard, *The Fable of the Bees*, ed. F.B. Kaye, 2 vols, 1924, Indianapolis IN: Liberty Classics, 1988.
Miscellanies	Fielding, Henry, *Miscellanies by Henry Fielding, Esq*, ed. Henry Knight Miller, 2 vols, Oxford: Wesleyan University Press, 1972.
Prior	Prior, Matthew, *The Literary Works of Matthew Prior*, eds H. Bunker Wright and Monroe K. Spears, 2 vols, Oxford: Clarendon Press, 1959.
Shaftesbury	Shaftesbury, Anthony Ashley Cooper, Third Earl, *Characteristics of Men, Manners, Opinions, Times*, ed. John M. Robertson, 2 vols, Gloucester MA: Peter Smith, 1963.
Sophia	Sophia, *Woman Not Inferior to Man*, 1739, London: Brentham Press, 1975.
Spectator	Addison, Joseph and Richard Steele, *The Spectator*, ed. Donald F. Bond, 5 vols, Oxford: Clarendon Press, 1965.

Sprat	Sprat, Thomas, *The History of the Royal Society*, eds Jackson I. Cope and Harold Whitmore Jones, St Louis MO: Washington University Studies, 1958.
Swift	Swift, Jonathan, *The Prose Works of Jonathan Swift*, ed. Herbert Davis, 14 vols, Oxford: Blackwell, 1939–68.
Tatler	Steele, Richard, *The Tatler*, ed. Donald F. Bond, 3 vols, Oxford: Clarendon Press, 1987.
Temple	Temple, William, *Essays on Ancient and Modern Learning and Poetry*, ed. J.E. Spingarn, Oxford: Clarendon Press, 1909.
TJ	Fielding, Henry, *Tom Jones*, ed. Fredson Bowers, Middletown CT: Wesleyan University Press, 1975.
TMS	Smith, Adam, *The Theory of Moral Sentiments*, eds D.D. Raphael and A.L. Macfie, 1976, Indianapolis IN: Liberty Classics, 1982.
True Patriot	Fielding, Henry, *The True Patriot and Related Writings*, ed. W.B. Coley, *The Wesleyan Edition of the Works of Henry Fielding*, Middletown CT: Wesleyan University Press, 1987.
TS	Sterne, Laurence, *The Life and Opinions of Tristram Shandy*, ed. Ian Campbell Ross, Oxford: Oxford University Press, 1983.
TT	Locke, John, *Two Treatises of Government*, ed. Peter Laslett, student edn, Cambridge: Cambridge University Press, 1988.
Vindication	*A Vindication of the Conduct of Capt. M—N and of the Court-Martial*, London, 1745.
WN	Smith Adam, The Wealth of Nations, eds R.H. Campbell, A.S. Skinner and W.B. Todd, 2 vols, 1976, Indianapolis IN: Liberty Classics, 1981.

INTRODUCTION

The quixotic problem: questioning the self-evident

> About this time, the knight of the mirrours came to himself, and Don Quixote perceiving he had recovered the use of his senses, clapped the point of his naked sword to his throat, saying, "Knight, you are a dead man, if you do not instantly confess that the peerless Dulcinea del Toboso excels your Casildea de Vandalia in beauty." ... "I confess, judge and perceive in all respects, as you believe, judge and perceive," answered the discomfited knight.
>
> Cervantes, *Don Quixote*, II, xiv[1]

Most post-Romantic discussions of quixotism focus on the inherent dignity and beloved idealism of the quixotic figure. This study does not. For it is self-evident that Don Quixote *is* generally admired, and recent studies by Alexander Welsh and Eric Ziolkowski have done much to illuminate the particular reasons why we admire this figure, with his passion for justice and dedicated pursuit of virtue.[2] Instead, I am interested in considering the implications of Don Quixote's self-evident heroism, and the power of self-evidence in general. My discussion focuses on the historically specific period of Restoration and eighteenth-century Britain through the 1770s, when Don Quixote was not always benevolent or heroic.[3] Though my topic is culturally specific, I believe that its broader themes reach out to present-day concerns, from multiculturalism to economic theory.

The act of self-authorization, disguised as deference to established rules, is the central trope of *Don Quixote*. I therefore read eighteenth-century Britain as an age of quixotism. My purpose in doing so is to rethink the meaning of the "rational," particularly in its relation to the "sentimental," for I contend that it is a mistake to hold these terms in opposition. The dichotomy of rational and sentimental comes in many familiar forms: the presumption that men are rational, while women are sentimental; or that economics is rational, while the humanities are sentimental; or that objectivity is rational, while resistance to it is sentimental. In these pairings, "rational" designates order, authority and

1

generality, while "sentimental" describes arbitrariness, triviality and particularity. Yet eighteenth-century Britain is remembered both as an "Age of Reason" and as an "Age of Sentiment." To disentangle this apparent contradiction and the assumptions behind it, I focus on three well-known features of the period: Cervantic imitations, or quixotic madness; sentimentalism, or overpowering feeling, usually of a moral nature; and the emergence of classical political economy, or the triumph of dispassionate rationality. My argument does not seek to refute any particular theories of reason or of sentiment, but instead proposes a historically supported reimagining of the relation between rationality and sentimentality.

My premise is that quixotism, sentimentalism, and reason—though apparently quite different—may be seen as facets of the same cultural problem, which I will call the quixotic problem. The quixotic problem is political and epistemological in nature, resulting from the coexistence of two conflicting cultural assumptions about the nature of rational authority: the first being that reason is universal, and therefore compelling to all rational people (a tautology); the second being that experience and the empirical method are the means through which individuals acquire this universal reason or general view. The first assumption (universal reason) limits the diversity of credible ways of thought, even as the second assumption (the importance of individual experience) frequently defies general principles. Simply stated, rationality can be at odds with individuality. I call this the quixotic problem because eighteenth-century quixotic figures embody individual madness, while reproducing the conditions of universal rationality: they staunchly believe that reason is universal, that it can be confirmed by experience, and that they themselves already have it. Quixotism is a parody of reason, satirizing rational authority as a political fiction only as rational as the authority of Don Quixote's lance. The quixotic problem turns the definition of reason itself into an object of political controversy, thereby challenging reason's presumed authority as the neutral arbiter of all controversy. The discomfort surrounding "multiculturalism" and "diversity," most acute in education and politics, is a modern version of this problem. As I hope to show in the following pages, an examination of quixotism, situated within the political and epistemological controversies of eighteenth-century Britain, can offer a critical window into Enlightenment assumptions that still powerfully shape our thinking about the role of reason in public life.

Defining the quixotic

Don Quixote was everywhere in eighteenth-century England.[4] In addition to numerous English translations of Cervantes' novel, the nation saw a parade of indigenous successors, such as Steele's quixotic political upholsterer, Addison's Will Honeycombe, Fielding's Parson Adams, Charlotte Lennox's Arabella, George Coleman's Polly Honeycombe, Sterne's Yorick, Smollett's

Launcelot Greaves, Richard Graves' Geoffrey Wildgoose, and a host of other quixotic figures in plays, poems, novels, periodical essays and pamphlets throughout the century. One early, anonymous translation acknowledges the English affinity for the mad knight's humor by naturalizing Don Quixote in an introductory poem, "Don Quixote de la Mancha, To the English Reader". "So, forgetting Spanish, I'm your own," the poem's Don Quixote proclaims,

> To find the Country Mirth, and please the Town.
> Me as a Stranger then no longer hold,
> But with me as a Native now make bold.[5]

Why is Don Quixote so natural an English subject? Because in England, "there are thousands full as mad as I," the Don Quixote of the poem explains: "Men that have Wind-mills in their Pates like mine," who "Bustle and Sweat, with endless Toil and Care,/To frame at last strange Castles in the Air." This Don Quixote recognizes his brethren. He sees in England a nation full of quixotes.

This allusion to universal quixotism waggishly reverses the assumption of universal reason prevalent in early eighteenth-century political thought. The Revolution of 1688, an event that itself conjured older memories of the Civil Wars, had left many people on edge, fearful of more disorder and violence, and wondering how political stability could be restored. Hobbes' absolutist solution was anathema, for in articulating a basis for law and order, it confirmed what many refused to accept: that moral and positive law were both arbitrary—unsupported by reason, revelation, or nature. A Hobbesian monarch was an arbitrary power, an authority maintained by the threat of brute force.[6] For a nation already involved in civil disputes—a nation without a strong monarch—Hobbesian politics seemed to augur only more violence, for no authority could bring about peace without resorting to force. Could civil society prosper if, as Locke phrases it, "all Government in the World is the product only of Force and Violence, and . . . Men live together by no other Rules but that of Beasts, where the strongest carries it"? No, Locke warns, legitimating arbitrary power would merely lay "a Foundation of perpetual Disorder and Mischief, Tumult, Sedition and Rebellion."[7] Locke repels this incipient chaos by invoking reason as the powerful opposite of arbitrary power. Defining the "*Word Reason* in the *English* Language" as "[t]hat Faculty in Man, whereby Man is supposed to be distinguished from Beasts,"[8] Locke distances himself from Hobbes' leviathan. Reason as a non-arbitrary power constitutes the crucial difference between legitimate government and the law of the stronger practiced by beasts. Its universality guarantees its validity. "The *State of Nature* has a Law of Nature to govern it, which obliges every one: And Reason is . . . that Law," Locke asserts (*TT* 271). Unlike the authority of tyrannical monarchs and overly zealous parliaments, the law of reason compels universal consent: it "obliges every one." Reason transcends political interests, and thus may be trusted to govern even a divided populace.

Locke's argument is attractive, but for one complication: reason in the eighteenth century did not really appear to be universal, and its authority could not always be clearly distinguished from the law of the stronger. "Success qualifies the Action," Matthew Prior (1664–1721), poet and diplomat, explains: "If ALEXANDER had lost the Day at Arbella, he had been Consigned by History for a Madman."[9] Because the winners write the histories, Prior intimates, history tends to rationalize the actions of the victors. Prior inverts Locke's theory of rational authority by suggesting that politics transcends reason. Far from being the master of arbitrary power, reason is its creature. The ubiquity of Don Quixote may be understood within this context of unreliable rational standards and the doubtful legitimacy of authority, for Don Quixote is a madman who had the misfortune to lose the day. He is the lunatic who is neither sane enough to be credible, nor insane enough to be easily dismissed. He ranges from the mad to the romantic, drawing fear, scorn, pity and admiration.[10] In other words, he is an embodiment of radical political difference. The term "quixotic," therefore, can be regarded as descriptive rather than evaluative. Eighteenth-century quixotes function within empirically derived rational systems, but those systems are not shared by those around them. Quixotes appear to be crazy because their rationale rests on peculiar, not general, experiences, yet they nonetheless forcefully insist on the universal validity of their own authority. Implicitly mocking the purportedly non-political, non-violent nature of Lockean reason, quixotism describes epistemological problems that become political problems, or political problems that turn out to have their basis in epistemological divisions.

The problem with Don Quixote's epistemology is his peculiar belief in the historical veracity of romances: "all the Fables and fantastical Tales which he read, seem'd to him now as true as the most authentick Histories."[11] Authorized by the events set down in these "Histories," Don Quixote follows their example, imagining his own imperial sway not too far off (DQ 4). This odd way of thinking soon translates into a political problem, for Don Quixote's romantic aspirations supersede civil authority. One adventure pits the errant knight, resolved to "relieve the Distress'd, and free suffering Weakness from the Tyranny of Oppression," against the king's own officers, as they transport a shackled group of his majesty's prisoners to the galleys. When an officer resists Don Quixote's demand for the prisoners' release, Quixote strikes the man down, "dangerously wounded with his Lance" (DQ 158–9). In his zeal, Don Quixote threatens both universal reason and the public peace; he is a madman with weapons that work, a man whose delusions make him act upon an authority that others refuse to credit, a man whose deeds look like exercises in arbitrary power. Yet as the above epigraph reminds us, the quixote's success will qualify his actions. "I confess, judge and perceive in all respects, as you believe, judge and perceive," the battered Knight of the

4

Mirrors concedes, compelled to amend his thinking by the brilliant logic of Don Quixote's naked sword. Don Quixote persuades by the force of his arm. To the Knight of the Mirrors (the bachelor Carrasco in disguise), Don Quixote's reason *is* his arbitrary power. Nonetheless, Don Quixote believes himself to be quite orderly, legalistically assuring the Knight of the Mirrors that "These Conditions are conformable to our Agreement before the Combat, and do not transgress the Rules of Knight-Errantry" (*DQ* 533).

The trope of the quixotic thus prompts serious questions about the uniqueness and universality of reason. For if reason is unique to individuals (such as Don Quixote or John Locke) or to specific communities of individuals (such as knights-errant or Whigs) rather than unique in nature, then by what standard and in what meaningful way can reason be called universal? Does reason oblige everyone, or is everyone merely obliged to come to terms with reason, as is the Knight of the Mirrors? In the context of the Revolution of 1688, Locke's opinions about reason's political transcendence—recall that these opinions vigorously defend revolution as a rational action of the people—sound suspiciously like the tale as told by a successful revolutionary (as indeed it was, and was perceived to be). The vanquished King James' supporters were urged to come to terms with the new rationale, for their doctrine of passive obedience and non-resistance to supreme authority was dismissed as insane. Locke himself conveys his scorn for this doctrine by speculating on what might occur "if *Don Quixot* had taught his Squire to Govern with Supreme Authority" (*TT* 201). Here, quixotism is not incomprehensible lunacy, but a trope to disparage those who adhere to a different set of political values, supported by a different political rationale. The "ridiculous" and the "reasonable" are unstable categories, particularly in the context of revolution. Chapter 1 will expand on this argument, illustrating the prominence of menacing quixotes, such as the Pretender and his supporters, or feminist writers like Judith Drake and Mary Astell, in early eighteenth-century British political writing.

I should mention, however, that by eighteenth-century standards, Cervantes' Don Quixote was indeed insane. Within eighteenth-century empiricist epistemology, sensation—believed to be common to everyone—served as the foundation of universal rational thought; according to Michael DePorte, the "ability to separate impulses originating from within from those originating from without was, in fact, a common criterion for sanity."[12] As a rational system, empiricism can account for the lunacy of Cervantes' Don Quixote in a way that distinguishes his antics from reasonable authority: the knight must be consigned to madness because his senses are unreliable. As Cervantes describes him, "the poor Gentleman's obstinate Folly had so infatuated his outward Sense, that his Feeling and his Smell could not in the least undeceive him" (*DQ* 100). Don Quixote is quite literally out of his senses. Unable to distinguish between impulses originating from within and those originating from without, he is, by empirical standards, really crazy.

It is therefore all the more significant that English quixotic characters are not insane by empiricist standards. The senses of English quixotes are always reliable.[13] Their unusual views cannot be dismissed as the raving results of faulty perception. Rather, English quixotes are characterized by their uncommon ways of interpreting the findings of common sense. For example, when Arabella, the female quixote of Lennox's novel, sees "Three or Four Men of a genteel Appearance, on horseback" riding up to her coach, she concludes that they are knights mistakenly intent upon delivering her. Her companions, of course, recognize the gallant riders to be highwaymen. Arabella sees exactly what everyone else sees: four men genteelly clad. She does not see armor where there is no armor; she sees the riders as they are. Yet she interprets their appearance in such an odd way that her companions look upon her "as one who [is] out of her Senses."[14] Likewise, Walter Shandy can see a nose or hear the syllables of a Christian name as accurately as anyone else, but he understands noses and names in a peculiar manner.[15] To Walter, noses and names are true indicators of human character: small-nosed men with unworthy names like "Tristram" can never be anything but unfortunate within Walter's rational system, for "like all systematic reasoners," Walter "would move both heaven and earth, and twist and torture every thing in nature to support his hypothesis" (*TS* 38). Neither can empirical evidence do anything to alter Arabella's singular beliefs: "she had such a strange Facility in reconciling every Incident to her own fantastic Ideas, that every new Object added Strength to the fatal Deception she laboured under" (*FQ* 340). As Walter's and Arabella's comic, self-fulfilling expectations suggest, English quixotism criticizes empirical method by exposing its potential circularity. The rational authority of empiricism can do little to intervene in the tautological circuit formed when experience produces the reason that is in turn used to rationalize experience, and the record of experience, history. Taken to its logical extreme, this critique of empirical rationality implies that universal reason exists only in the wake of a uniform history of uniform experience, a ridiculous precondition in the eighteenth century, and probably so in any century. If histories are contestable fictions, as Matthew Prior's observation about Alexander the Great suggests, then can Don Quixote be crazy for contending that fictions are histories?

The quixotic case of Captain Mostyn

To establish the plausibility of the quixotic problem in lived experience, I turn now to the notorious case of Captain Savage Mostyn. I will discuss this case at some length, for in its elaborate detail, the incident illustrates how intertwined the concepts of reason, arbitrary power and quixotism were in the eighteenth century, and how deeply they reached into practical thinking. The Mostyn trial posed a challenge to the fiction of rational authority, for the case turned on many arcane particulars, the larger meanings of which could be assessed only by those knowledgeable in the specialized occupation of maritime combat. General knowledge and common experience could not be relied upon as the basis for sound judgment. Particular knowledge and special experience were required, qualifications that could be found only in Mostyn's fellow officers. Their judgments, however, were suspected to be biased, due to the structures of command and the power of interest within the Navy itself. There was, therefore, no single rational view from which to judge this case. Rather, there were only various conflicting views, each claiming to be rational. The case of Captain Mostyn reveals the hopelessness of trying to resolve conflicts rationally, when the rules of reason are diversely—not universally—understood. Illuminating the fluid relation between experience, history and rational authority, Captain Mostyn's case shows reason shading imperceptibly into quixotism.

In early January of 1745, Captain Mostyn was in command of an English seventy-gun ship, *Hampton Court*, cruising off Ushant. Sailing with *Hampton Court* were three other warships: *Captain*, *Dreadnought* and *Sunderland*. When they spotted three French vessels—*Neptune*, *Fleuron* and *Mars*—the English gave chase. *Captain* veered off, following the French ship *Mars*, and by evening had captured her. *Sunderland* lost a mast and fell behind the action, while *Hampton Court* and *Dreadnought* continued to pursue *Neptune* and *Fleuron*. Mostyn's ship closed in on the enemy vessels and was able to pull up to *Neptune*, out of gunshot range on her windward side. *Dreadnought*, however, lagged several hours behind. Unwilling to attack alone, Mostyn waited for *Dreadnought*'s approach. A night and a day passed, but *Dreadnought* gained no ground. Finally, Mostyn gave up, fearing that he was already too close to French shores, and *Neptune* and *Fleuron* escaped.[16]

Upon returning to England, Mostyn submitted a detailed account to the Admiralty, carefully explaining the incident and the circumstances that prevented him from attacking. The weather had been squally and the seas choppy, Mostyn reported, and the enemy vessels sat higher and more upright in the water than *Hampton Court*, which heeled too far over to engage effectively in battle (the gun ports on the lee side were below the waterline, while those to windward inclined at so sharp an angle that they too were unserviceable). Hence Mostyn would not attack without *Dreadnought*'s assistance, for fear that his ship would have been too easily outgunned. The Admiralty accepted this explanation, and all might have passed quietly except that Mostyn then wrote to the Navy Office to request that his ship be refitted with smaller masts. The Navy Office's reply makes a great show of humoring the captain, but in effect tells him that no changes will be made to *Hampton Court*, for the Office believes that "as there has never been any Complaint, of her before, that She will do very well."[17] The letter thus impudently hints to Mostyn that the Navy Office suspects him to be inventing problems with the ship's design in order to excuse his recent embarrassment. Signed "Your affectionate Friends," the letter was probably written in fun, meant to tease and torment a fellow officer who showed signs, at least later in life, of excessive seriousness.[18] Mostyn was not amused at the Navy Office's imputation. Upon receiving the letter, he immediately petitioned the Admiralty Board for a court martial, so that, as he phrases it, "the truth of my Conduct may be publickly known to the world."[19]

The court martial was convened and Captain Mostyn acquitted, the court being "unanimously of Opinion that Captain Mostyn did his Duty as an experienced good Officer, and as a Man of Courage and Conduct."[20] Mostyn had comported himself reasonably in the eyes of the Admiralty. Yet the case did not end here, for an anonymous "Sea-Officer," now identified as Admiral Edward Vernon (1684–1757), distrusted the court's proceedings and its judgment. In a pamphlet entitled *An Enquiry into the Conduct of Capt. M—n* (1745), addressed to the House of Commons, Vernon reopens the case, bringing both Mostyn and his judges before the court of public opinion. "I shall now consider the Evidence in due order," Vernon promises,

> which are all of a Tone, and to a Court-Martial not willing, or perhaps able to ask any other Questions, but such as a prepar'd Evidence were instructed to answer, their Determination, at first Sight, seems well enough; but examined into, it will, I conceive, appear, that the Court-Martial either knew, or desired to know, as little as the Delinquent did to act.[21]

The trial was not legitimate, Vernon charges. The outcome initially looks "well enough," only because the witnesses were coached, the cross-examination too weak, and the court martial unwilling to inquire further. The findings of his own inquiry, Vernon pledges, will be quite different, for they will prove to the public that Mostyn's judges were as "Delinquent" as Mostyn himself. Vernon rejects the authority of the court martial itself. In his pamphlet, the trial is on trial.

What reason had Vernon, or anyone, to question the authority of the court martial's verdict? The answer may be found in Mostyn's family tree. Daniel, Earl of Winchilsea (1689–1769), First Lord of the Admiralty from 1742 to 1744 and then again in 1757, was Savage Mostyn's maternal uncle. This family connection was no doubt on Vernon's mind, for he taunts an allegedly perjured witness: "You will well deserve a Ship, if no Body goes beyond you, and a certain Noble L—d resumes his former Dignity; for sure St. *James*'s never bred so consummate a Courtier" (*Enquiry* 9). The "certain Noble L[or]d" is probably Winchilsea, who had stepped down from his "former Dignity" as First Lord in December of 1744, just a few weeks prior to Mostyn's trial. As Winchilsea did resume the First Lordship in 1757, Vernon's suspicions about the earl's continuing influence were not unfounded.

In rejecting the judgment of the naval court martial, Vernon confronts the fictiveness of rational authority. Naval authority usually regulated itself,[22] but in this case could not be trusted to do so in an impartial way, due—in Vernon's opinion—to the arbitrary power of an influential uncle. The "Great and Powerful," Vernon explains, "using all their Art and Interest to protect Delinquents," can and will legitimate arbitrary fictions to cover their crimes (*Enquiry* 25). Unable to trust such interested authority, Vernon must take his case to the disinterested public. Yet in leaping beyond the grasp of bias, Vernon lands in the embrace of ignorance. As he well recognizes, the propriety of a naval officer's conduct cannot be determined by appeals to common sense, for sea-fighting is a specialized business requiring specialized knowledge and experience. "One is under a good deal of Disadvantage in writing Tracts of this Nature," Vernon confesses,

> for if one enters into too nice a Disquisition, notwithstanding most People think themselves capable of judging on the Science of Sea-fighting, yet very few even amongst Mariners, know much of the matter, and therefore to define it too nicely, by Lines and Angles, would be writing to the Satisfaction of a very few, else would it more plainly appear why Mr. *M—n* ought to have fought the *French*.
>
> (*Enquiry* 17)

Vernon's "Disadvantage" is the inexpertise of his audience; he does not fully trust his case to their opinion, for he fears that to civilians, "even amongst Mariners," Mostyn will not look guilty. A civilian audience will "think themselves capable of judging," but will most probably be mistaken, Vernon anticipates. Therefore he attempts to override his readers' judgment before it has even been rendered, by assuring them that if they knew better, they would conclude just as he does: were civilian readers truly knowledgeable about the "Science of Sea-fighting," Vernon postulates, he would then be able to write a precise, technical explanation ("too nice a Disquisition" for the present lay audience) in which Mostyn's misconduct would "more plainly appear." The evaluation of Mostyn's behavior, Vernon acknowledges, is an assessment best left to his peers, for only his fellow naval officers understand sea-fighting well enough to ascertain the appropriateness of his actions. Of course, this line of argument leaves Vernon defending a contradictory and embarrassed position, since Mostyn's peers in the Navy already *had* passed judgment: they found him not guilty. Caught between the partiality of a knowledgeable audience and the impartiality of an ignorant one, Vernon's only standard is himself. In effect, he assures his audience that if they thought like him, he could convince them to think even more like him.

Vernon quickly realizes that his effectiveness depends on his ability to reproduce his own subjectivity within the minds of his readers. Naval customs and habits of reasoning differ from civilian common sense, he insists, and Mostyn should be judged by the standards of the former. Because the lay audience would not know what these standards are, Vernon summarizes them:

It has been said to be a Rule in the Navy, that one of our Ships of War, should not refuse fighting two of her equal Force, but might run from three; this Rule has no Establishment in our Laws, but is very well established in Honour and Reason, it being well understood by every experienced Seaman, that two Ships against one, are not the great Odds, which at first Sight they seem to be, the single Ship being thrown into a proper Disposition, and being sufficiently mann'd. To explain this here, would not only be leading the Reader away from the main Point, but also be too Prolix to be included in these Sheets.

(*Enquiry* 2)

As Vernon admits, the rules by which he condemns Mostyn have no legal standing. They are the unwritten laws of custom, established in "Honour" and "Reason," too complicated to explain to landlubbers, but "well understood by every experienced Seaman." Despite acknowledging widespread misunderstanding between civilians and seamen, Vernon nonetheless maintains that within the ranks of the Navy, "Reason" is still universal. Rather optimistically, the admiral presumes that all disinterested sailors, experienced in the ways of the service, must conclude as he does. In Vernon's court, there can be no honorable diversity of opinion. Imagining himself in Mostyn's situation, Vernon concludes that "Honour" and "Reason" must direct all competent officers to attack under the circumstances, simply because he himself would have attacked under those circumstances. Admiral Vernon's standard of rational conduct is himself. The admiral had, in fact, demonstrated his own unusual courage and skill in fighting against odds at Porto Bello in 1739. Success qualified his bold actions there, and he emerged from the victory a much celebrated national hero; more commemorative medals were struck for Admiral Vernon than for any other person in the eighteenth century, which in turn indicates that his conduct was perceived to be exceptional rather than standard.[23]

Undaunted by the implicit complications of his own singularity, Vernon presses onward, determined to prove that "Reason" must find Mostyn guilty. "[T]hat Officer makes a wretched Defence, who has only to say that his Ship Heels more than the Enemy," Vernon instructs his lay audience, for "when our Ships meet with those of the Enemy at Sea, the Weather is very probably as good for one as the other" (*Enquiry* 3–4). As Vernon sees it, Mostyn could have easily improved his situation by taking in his sails. *Hampton Court* would then have righted herself in the water, and, being a lighter and cleaner ship, could have still kept pace with the heavily laden, fouler French vessels: "a light Ship will, for very obvious Reasons," Vernon adamantly asserts, "make as good way as a loaded Ship, though she carries but two thirds the Quantity of Canvass" (*Enquiry* 3). Vernon can find absolutely no reason why Mostyn should not have at least attempted to fire, since his ship, windward to the enemy, had the advantage of the wind:

for the *French* being to the Leeward durst not have engaged with their lower Sails standing, for this single Reason, that on firing their weather Guns, part of the Wads, with variety of Sparks of Fire, would have blown back into the Ships, and hazarded the setting of them on Fire, which is the true Reason why even Ships in a running Fight, and to Leeward of the Enemy, either fire no Guns at all, or are obliged to haul up their Courses, and fight running under their upper Sails; it will follow that either they would have haul'd up their Courses, or not have fir'd at all; if they had haul'd up their Courses, then the *Dreadnought* and *Sunderland* would have come up; If they had not, then would the *Hampton-Court* have had sufficient Advantage of them, by employing her Guns towards disabling them, without any hazard of being disabled by them.

(Enquiry 15)

The "obvious Reasons" pointing to Mostyn's guilt are the suppositions of Vernon's imagination. Bringing to the situation his own understanding of cause, effect and probability, Vernon dismisses Mostyn's concerns about being outgunned. Ships will not shoot into the wind, the admiral maintains, for they fear that the sparks could blow back and ignite their own sails. Therefore the French vessels either would not have fired at all, or they would have fired only after raising their lower sails to avoid the sparks of their own guns. In the first case, *Hampton Court* would have been in no danger; in the second case, the chase would have slowed, enabling the other English ships to catch up. Mostyn should have imagined this chain of events just as Vernon has: "for this single Reason," "which is the true Reason," "it will follow," "if they had . . . then," "If they had not . . . then," Vernon's rhetoric presents its own conclusions as the only logical ones that can be drawn. Indeed, as the argument wears on, Vernon grows increasingly impatient at having to account for all of Mostyn's detailed, extenuating circumstances. At one point the admiral explodes:

all Formality . . . as Matters are circumstanced, only tends to keep the main Point out of the Question, and to give Knaves and Fools an Opportunity to justify themselves on the Credit of Jargon and Nonsense, whereby they think to perplex Superiors, and get acquitted with Honour, for what they deserve to be hang'd. The plain Question is only this, if their Ships meet others of equal Force, as the Weather is the same for both, Did you fight or did you not?

(Enquiry 23)

Contradicting his earlier assertion that Mostyn's guilt would "more plainly" appear to experienced seamen, Vernon now insists that technical expertise ("the Credit of Jargon and Nonsense") interferes with proper judgment. The "plain Question" of reasonable inquiry should concern itself only with the "main Point," as Vernon understands it. Once again, the standard of rationality is Vernon himself.

Soon after the *Enquiry*, two more pamphlets were published, both engaging directly with Vernon's arguments in order to defend Captain Mostyn's actions. Interestingly, the pamphlets claim to represent opinions from each of Vernon's supposed inadequate audiences; one purports to contain the views of a naval commander, while the other identifies its author as a landsman. *A Vindication of the Conduct of Capt. M—N and of the Court-Martial* (1745) by a "SEA-OFFICER," picks up on Vernon's dilemma by recognizing that Mostyn's case hinges on the elusiveness of proper rational standards:

> The chief Matter upon which all depends, falls within a very narrow Compass; it is whether Captain *M—n* ought in common Prudence to have engag'd the *French* alone, in the Situation he found them? how could he have been seconded by the *Dreadnought*? and what would in the Reason and common Sense of things have consequently followed?[24]

For this sea-officer, the crux of the matter is "common Prudence" within a specified context. Was Mostyn's conduct appropriate "in the Situation," considering what "Reason and common Sense" should have anticipated? The question is straightforward enough, except that common prudence, reason and common sense, with respect to Mostyn's situation, were not common. Like Vernon, the sea-officer worries that a lay public will have difficulty understanding the intricacies of a case that

> is in itself of so nice a Nature, and generally so little understood, and consists of such a variety of Matter, so abstracted from any such certain Tests which usually determine Men in their Judgments, and subject to Ideas and Calculations, so very uncommon and little known.
>
> (*Vindication* 6)

The *Vindication* seriously undermines Vernon's argument simply by evidencing that not all sea-officers think alike. Vernon's rhetorical stance had conflated rationality and expertise in himself. The *Vindication* exposes this triple identification as a fallacy, by offering a different expert opinion on the technicalities of Mostyn's case. For example, the sea-officer agrees that Mostyn may have indeed been able to right his ship by pulling in the sails, but argues that the heeling of *Hampton Court* was not really the cause of Mostyn's inability to fight. Rather, it was the ship's "disorder'd Motion, occasion'd by a swelling Sea" that rendered her guns useless, for under such conditions—as "every Seaman" knows—the lower-deck ports would have been subject to dangerous submersion at "uncertain Intervals," while the upper-deck guns would have been too unsteady to take a proper aim. Going to the heart of Vernon's argument—his "plain Question"—the sea-officer rebuts:

> The Reader will from hence naturally infer, that as to this Matter, both the *Hampton-Court* and the Enemy's Ships were equally affected by the rowling of the Sea; but this will appear to be no such matter, when the Evidence, join'd to common Experience, shews, that Ships who sail more steady and upright, are not liable to be equally convuls'd, with such as lye more along, with the same Pressure of Sail.
>
> (*Vindication* 8–9)

Pitching his argument to those uninitiated in maritime affairs, the sea-officer encourages them to substitute an easy experiment for "common Experience":

> Any Landman may comprehend the Theory immediately . . . by only taking two small Tubs, the one a little ballasted, the other empty, and committing them in a good Gale of Wind to the Mercy of such little Waves as the Canal in St. *James*'s *Park* is capable of producing, when the Wind blows right up or down it.
>
> (*Vindication* 12)

The sea-officer expects that this exercise will prove to his readers the truth of his arguments by illustrating conditions at sea. His deeper assumption is that "common Experience" must lead to consensus. Thus, in order to explain why he and "the Enquirist" (his name for Vernon)—both of whom are experienced seamen—disagree, the sea-officer maintains that the Enquirist is "bias'd," whereas he himself is "absolutely disinterested in the Affair" (*Vindication* 6, 9).

A greater challenge to Vernon's *Enquiry*, however, comes from the landsman's pamphlet, for presumably he speaks from the perspective of those whom Vernon most needs to convince. *The Rule of Two to One: Or, the Difference betwixt Courage and Quixotism* (1745), written by a layman who styles himself "Philonauticus Antiquixotus," levels Vernon's argument by refusing to defer to his expertise. "I shall now make some Reflections on a Rule the *Enquirer* tells us is said to be in the Navy," Antiquixotus announces, citing Vernon's rule of two-to-one, the very rule Vernon had declined to explain for fear of "leading the Reader away from the main Point." Comfortable with the strength of his own uninitiated conclusions, Antiquixotus charges:

> To have explain'd this would be leading the Reader away from his, the *Enquirer*'s, main Point (I readily grant) which is to impose an implicit Belief on him, that *two to one* in Sea-fighting is no great Odds; I am sure it is allowed to be so at Foot-Ball, and I take it to be so in all Cases; but he tells you that the single Ship is to be thrown into a

proper Disposition. Tho' I am no Seaman, and therefore don't pretend to understand the proper Disposition of Ships, yet I can conceive as well as any Seamen of them all, that the *two* Ships may be thrown into a proper Disposition as well as the single *one*, and I believe it won't be deny'd, that the Enemy knows how to do so as well as we.[25]

To Antiquixotus, the rational rule of two-to-one should apply "in all Cases." Reason is universal; the attempt by anyone to confine it to a particular profession, situation, or nationality should be rejected as a ridiculous imposition of "implicit Belief." Thus the pamphleteer demands that Mostyn's case be considered in light of a model readily accessible to everyone's understanding, "Foot-Ball."[26] Complicated explanations, experience on the high seas, and tiny models of ships are all unnecessary, for the Navy does not hold the monopoly on reason. People do not have to think like sailors in order to evaluate Mostyn's situation rationally. As his name suggests, Antiquixotus rejects as ridiculous the special naval customs, unknown to landsmen, yet so important to Vernon in evaluating Mostyn's conduct. To Antiquixotus, the Enquirer's rule of two to one—alleged by Vernon to be "very well established in Honour and Reason"—is simply fantastic "Quixotism":

> The *Quixot* who is a sort of Enthusiast in Honour . . . is actuated by a distemper'd Brain, never meddles with any but military Men, and tho' he may do some Injury to a good Name, among the unthinking, yet he cannot entirely blast it, his Notions being too romantick and chimerical.
>
> (Antiquixotus 4)

The "romantick and chimerical" aspects of Vernon's "Notions," however, like Don Quixote's, can be exposed only against a compelling set of counternotions. Because Vernon invokes history to establish the validity of the rule of two-to-one, a common understanding of history and historiography becomes essential to reaching consensus about Mostyn's conduct. "THERE was a time, though it be somewhat beyond the Reach of most of our Memories," Vernon enthuses,

> when a *British* Ship of War would have refused almost no Odds; when our Fleets, numerous or few, never refused to engage with the Enemy, was the Difference never so great, the Weather never so boisterous, the Reason of the thing at first sight never so disadvantageous; we, as *Caesar* phrases it, came, saw and conquered; the Honour of *England* then distended itself like the Light of the Sun, and equally influenced the Politicks of the Earth, as the Sun its Products. We were in those Days so far from refusing to fight an Enemy at Odds, when we met

them, that it was but to know, there were such to be found, and at all
Events to engage them.

(*Enquiry* 1)

Against this shining past standard, which places England on a par with
Imperial Rome, there can be no doubt of Mostyn's failure. Vernon urges his
readers to consult the record of history, where they will see the danger of
allowing Mostyn to go unpunished. "Sir *Edward Howard*'s Thoughts of these
Things were, That nothing is to be effected in Maritime Affairs, but where the
Officers Courage rises even to Madness," Vernon argues: "successive Times
have convinc'd us how well he understood what he said. The *Dutch* Wars
display'd it in all its bloody Colours; and since then we can hardly ever be said
to have fought in Earnest" (*Enquiry* 22). The decline of England may be
charged to the disappearance of this martial spirit. Vernon's understanding of
history convinces him that for the sake of national security, Mostyn must be
disciplined.

Yet Mostyn's defenders maintain that Vernon's understanding of history is
as questionable as his condemnation of the captain. In fact, they argue, Vernon
misjudges Mostyn precisely because the admiral does not know how to interpret history correctly. "I would beg leave to ask the *Enquirer*," Antiquixotus
responds after considering Vernon's historical representations,

> whether such Commanders, if any such there were, who acted
> contrary to Reason, yet were happly successful, did not deserve
> Censure for their Rashness? And whether himself (should he ever
> have the Honour to command a Squadron) which by the like Conduct
> should be taken or destroyed by the Enemy, notwithstanding he
> might plead his being work'd up to Sir *Edward Howard*'s Courage, a
> Courage even to Madness[,] would not well deserve to be H[ange]d?
>
> (Antiquixotus 7)

Antiquixotus remains skeptical not only about the authenticity of Vernon's
heroes ("if any such there were"), but also about their appropriateness as examples ("did [they] not deserve Censure for their Rashness?"). "Reason,"
Antiquixotus trenchantly maintains, should be distinguished from the happy
success of madmen. The former is reliable, a rule by which commanders
should conduct themselves, while the latter is merely a rash commitment to
the arbitrary power of fortune. With history celebrating only the successes,
Antiquixotus implies, Vernon's historical analysis glorifies not reason, but
merely the law of the luckier.

Likewise, the sea-officer's *Vindication* devotes several pages to evaluating
Vernon's understanding of history, arguing that his nostalgic sympathy with
the heroic past critically ignores historical difference:

As to that Branch of the Enquirist's Argument how others have behav'd heretofore? and how we ought to imitate them now? are not Points so easily settled, as at first Sight may be imagin'd; the way of making War at different Ages, is as much a Fashion as that of our Apparel, and it therefore is not always which way, or in what Disposition this or that Fleet or Army are put into, but likewise by what Disposition the Enemy form themselves, which the other side must in some measure fall in with and pursue.

(Vindication 17)

Disagreements over the correct lessons of history "are not Points so easily settled," because historical representation ("how others have behav'd heretofore?") and interpretation ("how we ought to imitate them now?") involve the same complicated processes of rational inquiry that led to the escalating controversy over Mostyn in the first place. The sea-officer's doubts about the veracity and applicability of history reflect a wider eighteenth-century skepticism toward the lessons of the past. Lord Bolingbroke, for example, writing in the 1730s and still regarded as an authority on the "*uses* of history" in the 1760s,[27] will not praise the enlightening powers of history without reservation. "THERE are certain general principles, and rules of life and conduct, which must always be true, because they are conformable to the invariable nature of things," Bolingbroke asserts:

He who would study history as he would study philosophy will soon distinguish and collect them, and by doing so will soon form himself a general system of ethics and politics on the surest foundations, on the trial of these principles and rules in all ages, and on the confirmation of them by universal experience.[28]

Yet these "general principles" and this "general system of ethics and politics" must be carefully distinguished from the "particular modes of actions, and measures of conduct" found in history, for to follow particular modes too closely "is always ridiculous, or imprudent and dangerous" (Bolingbroke 64–5). For example, Bolingbroke explains:

In the early days of the Athenian and Roman government, when the credit of oracles and all kind of superstition prevailed . . . even human blood was shed under wild notions of atonement, propitiation, purgation, expiation, and satisfaction; they who set such examples as these acted an heroical and a rational part too. But if a general should act the same part now . . . he might pass for an hero, but I am sure he would pass for a madman.

(Bolingbroke 63)

The complications within Bolingbroke's theory of history are clear. Though history should reveal the "invariable nature of things," much of what it records is "particular examples" that should not, in Bolingbroke's words, be "translated servilely into our conduct" (Bolingbroke 62). Allowing that the "heroical," and even the "rational," varies so wildly across time and place that heroism may become indistinguishable from madness, Bolingbroke urges that history be swallowed only with a good dose of skepticism. "DON QUIXOTE believed," he solemnly pronounces, "but even SANCHO doubted" (Bolingbroke 120).

In the quixotic case of Captain Mostyn, rational standards falter at the troubled confluence of individual experience, "Interest," historical understanding, and the desire for a general system of ethics and politics. Mostyn's case illustrates the futility of appealing to reason, when the definition of reason is itself the very subject of contention. In fact, even 250 years later, no consensus has yet been reached on Mostyn's case: the *Dictionary of National Biography* finds the court's decision "palpably absurd"; Clowes finds it "difficult to believe that this decision was come to without bias"; Charnock, however, will only circumspectly state that Mostyn's conduct, "being investigated before a court-martial, was perfectly approved of"; Rodger regards Mostyn's hesitancy as "perhaps prudent"; and Daniel Baugh, following H. W. Richmond, credits Mostyn's claim that his ship's design was at fault.[29] It should offer no surprise, then, that Vernon's assumption of the voice of reason looked to Antiquixotus like something else. Dismissing "the *Enquirer*" as a "*Quixot*," Antiquixotus explains: "He is only angry, despises and reviles you, because you don't, like himself, take a Windmill for a Man, and engage it till you are convinced of you[r] Error by your Bones being broke. And this is the only Way as I conceive," Antiquixotus ominously adds, "to bring one of this Cast to his Senses" (Antiquixotus 4). Antiquixotus here, perhaps unwittingly, articulates the paradoxical problem associated with quixotism: if the only way to make quixotes see reason is to break their bones, what then distinguishes rational authority from arbitrary power?

Quixotism, feeling and sentimentalism

As the Mostyn case illustrates, the absurdity of quixotism can be used to describe serious political, moral and epistemological concerns. The strict sanity of English quixotes by the empiricist standards of the eighteenth century deviates from Cervantes' original, emphasizing the rationality of quixotism over its madness. (Vernon was not disparaged for misperceiving the material world; he was ridiculed for misinterpreting history.) This curious conflation of the rational and the quixotic highlights their fundamental similarity, as the representatives of each category seek in their own way to regularize experiential difference. Vernon would not allow that Mostyn's assessment of *Hampton Court*'s situation might have been both different from his own *and* acceptable. Likewise Antiquixotus, by holding "Quixotism" in diametrical opposition to reason, only replicates from another perspective the admiral's strident demand for uniformity of judgment. Each man subscribes to the dubious proposition that individual experience will translate into common belief. The trope of the quixotic parodies this fiction of universal reason by mischievously suggesting a more plausible, perhaps even inevitable alternative: namely, that if rationality derives from the vagaries and diversity of experience, then universal quixotism should be a far more likely outcome than universal reason.

"All mankind are mad, 'tis plain," concludes the final song in Fielding's play, *Don Quixote in England* (1733):

> Since your madness is so plain,
>   Each spectator
>   Of good-nature,
> With applause will entertain,
> His brother of La Mancha:
> With applause will entertain
> Don Quixote and squire Sancho.[30]

The "good-nature" mentioned in Fielding's song explicitly draws moral philosophy into the discussion of the quixotic, for Fielding understood "good-nature" to comprehend all the social and sympathetic virtues:

> What by this Name, then, shall be understood?
> What? but the glorious Lust of doing Good?
> The Heart that finds it Happiness to please,
> Can feel another's Pain, and taste his Ease.
> The Cheek that with another's Joy can glow,
> Turn pale, and sicken with another's Woe;
> Free from Contempt and Envy, he who deems
> Justly of Life's two opposite Extremes.
> Who to make all and each Man truly blest,
> Doth all he can, and wishes all the rest?[31]

Fielding's definition of "good-nature" here—the desire to promote another's happiness, aided by the ability to identify with another's "Pain," "Ease," "Joy" and "Woe"—describes what Adam Smith would later call "sympathy": "our fellow-feeling with any passion whatsoever," prompted by the "principles in [man's] nature, which interest him in the fortune of others, and render their happiness necessary to him."[32] This tradition of universal benevolence, which imagines a community firmly united in sympathy, if not in reason, softens quixotic difference by maintaining the uniformity of human passion, sensation, and interest in the welfare of others. The tradition's roots in the religious controversies and anti-Hobbesian hysteria of the seventeenth century are a further reminder of quixotism's particular political resonances; Fielding appeals to "good-nature" to rescue communal harmony from quixotism at the end of the comedy, just as the latitudinarian divines promoted it against internecine conflict at the end of the seventeenth century.[33]

Yet Fielding's song does not entirely elide the differences that have been the subject of his play. In seeking applause only from "Each spectator/Of good-nature," rather than from all spectators, the song undercuts the play's concluding salute to the comprehensive moral concord promised by sympathy. It also cleverly obstructs criticism by preemptively attributing disapprobation to the bad nature of the critic, rather than the badness of the play. The reconciliatory "good-nature" of Fielding's closing song divides the audience into two kinds of people—those who are of good nature and those who are not—and offers the prospect of sympathetic community only to the former. Thus, though the play gestures toward the restoration of moral uniformity, it does so by simultaneously presupposing, and then excluding, the existence of moral difference. This concurrent presupposition and dismissal of moral diversity is a distinguishing feature of sentimentalism. *Don Quixote in England* offers sentimental consensus as the corrective to quixotic conflict.

In some ways, sentimental consensus was indeed the corrective for quixotic conflict, though the larger relation between sentimentalism and quixotism is much more involved. Like the meanings of quixotism, the meanings of sentimentalism are variable. The term "sentimental" is now often used casually and pejoratively to describe effete, excessive, or untrustworthy emotionalism. It still bears a more neutral sense, however: "sentimental," when used to describe moral philosophy, refers to the belief that knowledge of moral ideas springs not from human thought, as does mathematics, but "from ordinary sensation in one way or another."[34] This sense of "sentimental" reminds us that the "feeling" long associated with sentimentalism should be understood within the context of empiricism and its consequences for the idea of rational authority. Sentimentalism is a form of empiricism.

As R. F. Brissenden explains: "Sentimental ideas . . . all derive from one basic notion . . . that the source of all knowledge and all values is human experience," an epistemology that renders the "process of moral judgment . . . essentially private and subjective."[35] Applying empirical method to the study of "moral judgment," sentimentalists are engaged in science. David Hume would be an example of this kind of sentimentalist, as he announces his "science of Man" in *A Treatise of Human Nature* (1739) by proclaiming on the title page: "BEING An Attempt to introduce the experimental Method of Reasoning into MORAL SUBJECTS."[36] Hume's sentimentalism aspires to "render all our principles as universal as possible, by tracing up our experiments to the utmost, and explaining all effects from the simplest and fewest causes"; he desires no less than "to establish . . . a science, which will not be inferior in certainty, and will be much superior in utility to any other of human comprehension" (Hume, *Treatise* xvii, xix). What Hume's science of man most famously discovers, however, are the limits of rationality: "Reason is, and ought only to be the slave of the passions, and can never pretend to any other office than to serve and obey them" (Hume, *Treatise* 415). As Hume recognizes, the problem with his science—the empirical study of morals—is that it is private and subjective, "that we can give no reason for our most general and most refined principles, beside our experience of their reality; which is the reason of the mere vulgar" (Hume, *Treatise* xviii). The universal authority of "Reason" splinters under the pressure of what Brissenden describes as a distinguishing feature of sentimentalists, "their belief in the sanctity and authority of their private judgments."[37] Though sentimentalists may envision a universal knowledge of mankind, their method contrarily ratifies diverse particularity of individual feeling instead, for moral experience is absolute: "essentially private and subjective." Hume's persistent skepticism seems to have resulted from his recognition of the paradox inherent in trying to establish moral authority through empirical means.[38] In a diverse world, the empirical quest for universal knowledge can quickly devolve into individual "sanctity and authority," for one person's experience cannot disprove another's; one person's feeling does not invalidate another's; and thus one person's process of moral judgment can hardly be ranked above another's. How, then, can anyone rationally justify the imposition of any moral authority over any other?

Sentimentalism reveals that the empirical model of rational authority, with its ideal of gradually emerging consensus,[39] ultimately and ironically justifies the persistence of irreducible difference too. Hence, as Martin Price observes, "the age of sensibility" explores the implications of "relativism," the suspension of authority that comes of "seeing man as a natural creature, a product in large measure of his peculiar climate, and of seeing the exotic and subject peoples as having their own cultural rightness."[40] In this light, what Brissenden points to as the sentimentalists' trait—"their belief in the sanctity and authority of their private judgments"—can be recognized as quixotism, for sentimentalism *becomes* quixotism when the "cultural rightness" of other people militates against the "sanctity and authority" of the observer's "private judgments"; when relativism disrupts the stable hierarchy of views necessary to the scientific and the sentimental modes; when "subject peoples" and objective observers flatten into an undifferentiated plane of subjective people. The sentimental gesture of presupposing and dismissing moral diversity emerges because moral difference, once recognized, cannot be disproved: it can only be excluded, devalued, discounted.

At this point, a definition of sentimentalism that incorporates both the pejorative and the philosophical senses of the term can be articulated: sentimentalism is a mode of representation, reading, and/or understanding that assumes—in the face of plausible alternatives—the empirical existence of an empirically unverified moral truth that can be denied only by those willing to be excluded from the community that testifies to this moral truth. Sentimentalists translate private feeling into universal truth, urging moral uniformity to advance a new fiction of empirical, rational authority. The fact that moral truth is not empirically accessible—the fact that it must go empirically unverified, allowing plausible alternatives to flourish and multiply—gives rise to sentimentalism's pejorative sense, as well as its tendency to ground itself by locating superior sensibility in particular communities. Sentimentalism (in the pejorative sense) is an effect of moral diversity, for moral ideas can be recognized as "sentimental" (pejoratively) only in the context of plausible alternatives. Moral ideas in the absence of such alternatives are never dismissed as sentimental; rather, they are accepted as self-evident truths. Incidentally, the contingency of sentimentalism helps to account for a curious phenomenon in the reception history of sentimental fiction: namely, the frequency with which readers feel compelled to debate whether a given sentimental work is really sentimental, or whether it is in fact a parody of the sentimental.[41] This indeterminacy arises because moral diversity exists among the readership.

Chapter 2 will discuss in detail the mercurial relation between eighteenth-century sentimentalism, empiricism and moral diversity, beginning with an account of the Royal Society's promotion of empirical method as an anti-quixotic, politically peaceful means to restore universal authority. As I will argue, however, the new philosopher's opponents were able to redefine empiricism as quixotism, because that most important topic of study—moral truth—is not empirically accessible. The task of showing that moral truth can be empirically derived was taken up by sentimental philosophy and literary sentimentalism, a point the chapter will develop through discussions of Francis Hutcheson, his nemesis Bernard Mandeville, and Sarah Fielding's sentimental novel *David Simple* (1744). But for now, two critiques of Lockean empiricism, one from Thomas Burnet (1635?–1715) in the 1690s, the other from Matthew Prior in the early 1720s, should serve to illustrate the epistemological and political difficulties that surround sentimentalism, the empirical approach to moral knowledge.

Locke's *Essay Concerning Human Understanding* (1690) had unnerved Thomas Burnet, a clergyman most famous for his *Theory of the Earth* (1684–90) by declaring that in addition to there being no innate ideas, there are also no innate *"practical Principles,"* that is, no innate moral rules. Locke regards universal assent as the gauge of innateness. Therefore, noting that moral rules *"come short of an universal Reception,"* Locke concludes that they must all be acquired after birth. "I appeal to any, who have been but moderately conversant in the History of Mankind, and look'd abroad beyond the Smoak of their own Chimneys," he writes: "Where is that practical Truth, that is universally received without doubt or question, as it must be if innate?" (*Essay* 66). Locke quickly adds, however, that his observations in no way assail the truth of moral principles, for though not innate, "these moral Rules are

21

capable of Demonstration: and therefore it is our own faults, if we come not to a certain Knowledge of them" (*Essay* 66). How we can be expected to come to "a certain Knowledge of them" when they are not innate, not universally accepted and not supported by "the History of Mankind," Locke does not say. His muteness on so important a topic incited Burnet's agitated response.[42]

In a series of three "Remarks," Burnet affects to elicit from Locke a stronger articulation of "a sure foundation for morality, revealed religion and a future life," all the while hinting at the ungodliness of Locke's system.[43] He rejects Locke's empirical approach to moral knowledge as dangerously uncertain. "As to morality," Burnet crisply observes,

> we think the great foundation of it is the distinction between good and evil, virtue and vice—*turpis et honesti*, as they are usually called; and I do not find that my eyes, ears, nostrils or any other outward sense make any distinction of these things, as they do of sounds, colours, scents or other outward objects; nor from any ideas taken in from them, or from their reports, am I conscious that I do conclude, or can conclude that there is such a distinction in the nature of things.
>
> (Burnet 24)

The truth of moral rules, Burnet recognizes, cannot be empirically determined by the five senses. Nor is he satisfied with Locke's vague reassurances that moral truths may be rationally demonstrated. "I think the illiterate part of mankind, which is far the greatest part, must have more compendious ways to know their duty than by long and obscure deductions," Burnet urges, fearful that such rational demonstration would be beyond the abilities of the vast majority of men.

The sure foundation to which Burnet subscribes, and for which he seeks Locke's public endorsement, is the "natural conscience," or—as it has later come to be discussed—the "moral sense" (Burnet 66).[44] Due to the natural conscience, Burnet believes that there can be no uncertainty about the distinction between good and evil. "This I am sure of," he proclaims:

> that the distinction, suppose of gratitude and ingratitude, fidelity and infidelity, justice and injustice and such others, is as sudden and without any ratiocination, and as sensible and piercing as the difference I feel from the scent of a rose and of assafoetida. 'Tis not like a theorem which we come to know by the help of precedent demonstrations and postulatums, but it rises quick as any of our passions, or as laughter at the sight of a ridiculous object. But I will leave this to your farther explication . . . you having signified in several parts of your treatise that you think morality as capable of demonstration as mathematics.
>
> (Burnet 24–5)

Moral certainty cannot be based on rational proofs, Burnet argues, for such "ratiocination," "precedent demonstrations" and "postulatums" are too abstract and slow. In fact, in the only formal reply Locke ever made to Burnet's *Remarks*, the philosopher confirms Burnet's suspicions about the inaccessibility of mathematical demonstration. "I have said indeed in my book that I thought morality capable of demonstration as well as mathematics," Locke peevishly professes: "But I do not remember where I promised this gentleman to demonstrate it to him" (Burnet 34). Burnet's natural conscience, functioning as a moral sense, alleviates all such rational difficulties by making moral distinctions as immediate and as obvious as sensation itself—"as sensible and piercing," Burnet writes, "as the difference I feel from the scent of a rose and of assafoetida," and as quick to rise "as laughter at the sight of a ridiculous object." Burnet's sure foundation of moral knowledge, patterned after empirical method, rests on the rule of the obvious, the logic of the self-evident. Burnet is a man of feeling. His moral judgments rise "sudden without any ratiocination," as "quick as any of our passions." Because his convictions come from within, he shares a key characteristic with the heroes and heroines of sentimental novels written long after his death: "their belief," to borrow Brissenden's phrase, "in the sanctity and authority of their private judgments." Ironically, Burnet's sentimental impulse relies on the very thing it rejects: the authority of experience. Basing his sure moral foundation on the empirical criterion of his own feeling, Burnet can allow no credible person to feel any differently. He therefore defines the moral variations of cultural diversity as criminality.

"[Y]ou seem to make account that, if conscience was an innate principle, it should be invincible and inextinguishable, and universally received without doubt or question," Burnet reminds Locke in his *Third Remarks*:

> Then, to prove that it is not so, you bring in several barbarous or semi-barbarous people as your witnesses: Mengrelians, Tonoupinambos and such others—gentlemen that are not of my acquaintance. These are witnesses to prove that there are no practical innate principles or natural conscience in mankind. This is like searching gaols and prisons to find witnesses for a bad cause.
>
> But I except against your witnesses as *personae infames* whose testimony is of no force or validity.
>
> (Burnet 66–7)

Firmly maintaining the self-evidence of his own feelings against all challenges, Burnet denies similar authority to others. Like Fielding's appeal only to his good-natured spectators, Burnet here appeals only to the privileged sensibilities of the already like-minded, entirely rejecting the possibility that cultural difference could provide anything of empirical value. Locke's response, in the form of marginalia scribbled into his copy of the *Third Remarks*, maintains,

> This author mistakes what I say, B[ook] I, c[hapter] iii. 9, which is that moral rules are not innate, for if they were they would be in all men; and if they were in the minds of men, they could not without all touch of conscience be transgressed, as many instances shew they are.
>
> (Burnet 66)

The difference between Burnet's reading of Locke and Locke's correction of this reading is subtle, but significant. Burnet presumes that Locke speaks of "conscience"—"a spring and motive of our actions" (Burnet 66)—whereas Locke maintains that he discusses "moral rules" and the ease and frequency with which they are transgressed. Burnet speaks of motives directly, whereas Locke focuses on what may be inferred about them through the empirically accessible medium of human behavior. The two disputants disagree over what constitutes valid empirical evidence; Locke overrides Burnet's sure feeling with the testimony of "gentlemen" not of Burnet's acquaintance, while Burnet dismisses Locke's anthropological anecdotes as being "of no force or validity." Burnet rejects the experience of Locke's "witnesses," while Locke discounts the experience of Burnet. This quixotic dispute points to the methodological flaw of expecting experiential ways of knowing to lead to universal conclusions about humankind. As Tristram Shandy, a famous sentimental quixote, Lockean follower, and hobby-horsical devotee extraordinaire, still felt necessary to observe at mid-century, "our minds shine not through the body . . . if we would come to the specifick characters of them, we must go some other way to work" (*TS* 52–3).

The irreducible diversity of mind, fortified by the sensibility of opaque bodies, is a theme picked up by Matthew Prior as well. Prior's critique of Lockean rational empiricism, like Burnet's, comes in the form of an attempted conversation, an effort to interrogate Locke directly, as if he otherwise remains too inaccessible. Locke, of course, was inaccessible by the time Prior wrote (probably) in the early 1720s; Locke had died in 1704. Prior removes this impediment by writing "A Dialogue between Mr: John Lock and Seigneur de Montaigne," a dialogue of the dead in which Prior imagines a conversation taking place between the shades of these two famous authors.[45] Debating the merits and faults of their respective works, Prior's Montaigne dismisses Locke's "close way of reasoning" as too solipsistic and peculiar to be applicable to mankind in general. "All the while you wrote you were only thinking that You thought: You, and Your understanding are the *Personae Dramatis*, and the whole amounts to no more than a Dialogue between John and Locke," Montaigne charges, summarizing Locke's *Essay* as an example of particular experience masquerading as universal knowledge. For Montaigne, Locke's way of reasoning is not so much a clear and distinct articulation of rational method

24

as it is a private hobby-horse for Locke's own amusement. "You seem, in my poor apprehension," Montaigne remarks, "to go to and fro upon a Philosophical Swing like a Child upon a wooden Horse always in motion but without any Progress" (Prior 1: 620–1). Montaigne's most devastating critique of Locke's epistemology, however, lingers over the disruptive political consequences that Montaigne envisions, should the *Essay*'s teachings ever indeed become universal. As an exemplary warning, Montaigne imagines what would happen if Locke's own servant, also named John, were to spend his leisure hours "dabling" in Locke's book.

According to Montaigne, John's head would soon be turned by reading too deeply in the *Essay Concerning Human Understanding*, a transformation that would render him ill-suited to his function in Locke's house. John would now begin to analyze even the simplest commands, reasoning so closely that the thoughts required to make sense of his master's simple instructions, "John . . . You may go down and Sup, Shut the Door," could form a short treatise:

> John . . . reasons thus upon the matter . . . John You may go down and Sup; Shut the door. Now *John* has been a common Appellative to Millions of Men, thrô many Ages, from Apostles, Emperors, Doctors and Philosophers, down to Butlers 'and Valets de Chambre and Persons of my Quality; some of whom however Christened John, are commonly called Jack, but pass for that; Now to none of these could my Master Speak, for they are either Dead or Absent; it must there-fore be to me; doubtful again: for my Masters own name is John, and being a Whimsical Person, he may probably talk to himself. No that cant be neither, for if he had Commanded himself, why did he not obey himself: If he would go down why does he sit stil in the Elbow-chair, 'twas certainly therefore meant to me *John*, not to him *John*.
>
> (Prior 1: 635–6)

John's new analytical style finds difficulties and complications where none should exist, where the logic of the self-evident should prevail. More impor-tantly, however, John's close way of reasoning does not promote human understanding. On the contrary, it obstructs communication, rendering John incompatible with his fellow servants, and introducing dissension and hostility into the household. As Montaigne describes it to Locke:

> Let us now imagine . . . John safely arrived in the Kitching, Margaret the Cook Maid sets the cold Beef before Him, Robin the Butler gives Him a Bottle of Strong Beer, and they proceed Amicably to the News of the Day, If the Regent is at Madrid, or the King of Spain upon the Coast of Scotland. If Digwell the Gardiner Stole two of Sir Thomas's Spoones, or the Match holds between my Lord Truemadams Coachman and Prue the Dairy maid. All this goes on

the best in the World from point to point till John Stroking Trip, the
Grehound, says, to Margaret, do You think, Child, that a Dog, thô he
can retain several Combinations of simple Ideas, can ever compound
enlarge or make complex Idea's? Truly John, says Margrett I neither
Know nor care.

(Prior 1: 637–8)

As John persists in questionings of this kind, he causes misunderstandings to
multiply and tempers to warm, for his fellow servants can make no sense of his
ramblings about reason. Finally, when Margaret misinterprets as drunken
bawdry John's discussion of "Body," "Motion" and "Extension of parts," an
irritated Robin cries out with asperity, "that's e'en too true, John always was
and will be a pragmatical Puppey."

Puppy says John, in what Predicament do you place the human
Species? Sirrah Robin Answers in great Anger I scorn your words, I
am neither Predicament nor Species any more than your Self; But I
won't Stand by and see my fellow Servant affronted. Here, Mr: Lock
[Montaigne observes,] you find, Bella plus quam Civilia. John and
Margaret form their different Aliances, the whole Family is set into a
flame by three leaves of Your own Book, and you may knock Your
heart out for Your Boyled Chicken, and Your Roasted Apples.

(Prior 1: 638)

Montaigne's whimsical sketch refutes Locke's new articulation of rational
authority, his "close way of reasoning," as divisive rather than universal,
conducive to discord rather than harmony. With the family "set into a flame
by three leaves of [Locke's] own Book," Locke's reason can hardly be distinguished from quixotism. Locke's reason does not "oblige every one," as the
increasing belligerence of Robin the Butler indicates. Far from transcending
internecine conflict, Locke's reason creates it, for the authority of individual
experience does not readily coalesce into the natural law of universal reason.
Montaigne presses the point against empirical authority:

probably neither Robin, John, Margrate You or I, or any other five
Persons alive have either the same Idea's of the same thing, or the
same way of Expressing them. The difference of Temperament in the
Body, Hot, Cold, Phlegmatic or hasty create as Manifest a Variety in
the Operations of our hands and the Conduct of our Lives; and our
Conceptions may be as various as our faces, Bodies and Senses, or
Sensations as you call them. If I like Assafetida I say it has a good
smell, If you can't endure a Rose you complain it Stinks . . . If so it
may happen I say, that if no Mans Ideas be perfectly the same Locks
Human Understanding may be fit only for the Meditation of Lock

26

himself, nay further that those very Ideas changing, Lock may be led into a new Laberinth, or Sucked into another Vortex, and may write a Second Book in order to disprove the first.

(Prior 1: 639)

Skeptical about the general relevance of empirically derived knowledge, Prior's Montaigne belittles both Locke's reason and Burnet's feeling by denying the commensurability of sensation across individuals. The "proof" of Burnet's natural conscience—the sudden and piercing difference he feels "from the scent of a rose and of assafoetida"—here becomes evidence of human diversity. "If I like Assafetida I say it has a good smell, If you can't endure a Rose you complain it Stinks," Montaigne observes, reversing the common olfactory opinions associated with the two plants. Differences in sensation will render common understanding improbable if not impossible, even without the added difficulty of achieving a common means of expression. If "a good smell" can describe both the scent of a rose to one person and a whiff of assafetida to another, while "Stinks" may be said both of assafetida's pungency to one and the aromatic pain of a rose to another, what common ideas, practical principles, or standards of conduct—not to mention universal knowledge—can empirical method be trusted to yield? Locke's careful reflections upon his own reasoning faculty may be just that: "a Meditation of Lock himself," not an essay on human understanding.

"Pray, Sir, in all the reading which you have ever read, did you ever read such a book as Locke's Essay upon the Human Understanding?" the quixotic Tristram Shandy asks:

as I write to instruct, I will tell you in three words what the book is.—It is a history.—A history! of who? what? where? when? Don't hurry yourself.—It is a history-book, Sir, (which may possibly recommend it to the world) of what passes in a man's own mind.

(TS 70)

As Tristram's narrative is itself a history of what passes in a man's own mind—though unlike Locke's Essay, it does not pretend to sameness with any man, but instead revels in its singularity—Locke's rationality, by comparison, looks like a less entertaining version of Sterne's whimsicality. If a quixote is one who attempts to universalize his or her own peculiar way of thinking, then Locke is more quixotic than Tristram Shandy. By the end of Prior's dialogue, Locke and Montaigne can finally agree: reason based on experience has not the authority to oblige everyone, for things may pass through people's minds with such uniqueness—so many different feelings, so many different histories—that an essay on human understanding may amount to no more than a meditation upon oneself, leading not to the placid realms of reasonable society, but to "another Vortex," a "Second Book" full of peculiar knowledge, spinning ever inward yet pretending to universality. "Aye now Sir I like You," Locke admits at last, happily contemplating the world's need for his next authoritative book: "We are come to the very State of the Question."

Sentimentalism and the "science of man"

In the eighteenth century, as the foregoing discussion suggests, literature, moral philosophy and the "science of man" had not yet solidified into the distinct disciplines that they have since become. What linked them was their sentimentalism, their attempt to discover natural order in human societies through the empirical study of moral knowledge. Not surprisingly, given this methodology, the exact nature of orderly systems—political, intellectual and moral—was controversial. Is order really natural and rational, moral empiricists had to wonder, or arbitrarily imposed by the perceiver? Sentimentalism promotes the former idea, while quixotic imitation plays with the latter. Eighteenth-century fiction explores both possibilities extensively. Chapters 3, 4 and 5, therefore, will focus on three mid-century novels, Charlotte Lennox's *The Female Quixote* (1752), Henry Fielding's *Tom Jones* (1749) and Laurence Sterne's *Tristram Shandy* (1759–67). In each of these sentimental quixotic novels, the instability of rational, empirical standards constitutes a prominent thematic element.

Chapter 3 argues that the issues at stake in the problematic ending of *The Female Quixote* can be redefined once we acknowledge the non-oppositional nature of reason and quixotism in the period. Recent discussions of *The Female Quixote*, which often regard the work as feminist, have had difficulty recuperating the novel's seemingly anti-feminist conclusion, because they equate reason with masculinity and quixotism with femininity. The book's sudden sentimental ending makes more sense, I suggest, when quixotism is recognized as the parodic parallel of masculine reason, rather than its feminine opposite.

Chapter 4 discusses Henry Fielding, a writer long recognized to belong to the Cervantic tradition. I argue that Fielding's fascination with quixotism goes beyond direct allusion and overt imitation. Focusing on *Tom Jones*, I show that Fielding, like his contemporaries, associates quixotism with specific political and intellectual conflicts—women's equality, empirical method, social diversity, Jacobitism—and that he responds to these conflicts by embracing sentimentalism. He complicates quixotism, however, by representing it not just as a malady of readers, but as an affliction of authors as well. Fielding tries to mock quixotism as feminine, irrational and peculiar, and to applaud rational authority as masculine, cerebral and general. Yet because he approaches this task already committed to moral empiricism—the empirical study of invisible things—he finds himself unable to represent his own authority as non-quixotic.

Chapter 5 reads Sterne's *Tristram Shandy* as the epitome of the sentimental quixotic tradition. Sterne, I argue, celebrates those aspects of quixotism that

Fielding most resists: its perceived impotency, effeminacy and particularity. Through the characters of the Shandy men, Sterne satirizes the relentless desire for rational explanation as being the most quixotic of all quixotisms. His satire aims especially at those moral empiricists who purport to be able to see directly into the human heart. Merrily emphasizing the peculiarity of all opinions, Sterne's novel tweaks all efforts—be they rational or sentimental—to establish their own universal importance, relevance and authority.

The question of whether order is naturally inherent or artificially imposed also pervades eighteenth-century economic theory, so my final chapter turns to Adam Smith. The economist's function, according to Smith, is to study invisible things empirically—to observe what cannot be readily seen or proven—a fact implicit in his famous metaphor of the "invisible hand." The subject of Chapter 6 is Smith's epistemological difficulties in articulating a general view of moral knowledge and economic activity in *The Theory of Moral Sentiments* (1759) and *The Wealth of Nations* (1776). Smith's earlier writing on the "History of Astronomy" shows his awareness of the quixotic problem associated with empirically derived rational authority, and his *Theory of Moral Sentiments* begins cautiously by asserting the limited—because empirical—nature of all moral knowledge. Over the course of his treatise, however, Smith's "impartial spectator" gradually and inexplicably acquires godlike omniscience. I compare this impartial super-spectator to "the philosopher" of *The Wealth of Nations*, who alone of all "tradesmen" is able to comprehend the complex workings of a diversified economy. The "peculiar trade" of "philosophers or men of speculation," according to Smith, is to view the economic whole, to see the connections that other workers, confined by the horizons of their own specialized trades, cannot. (The philosopher, as Smith imagines him, would have been an adequate judge in the Mostyn trial, capable of seeing through interest and beyond ignorance.) Yet despite this figure of the comprehensive philosopher, Smith still cannot entirely shake his suspicion that division of labor will ultimately undermine rational authority, for in a diversified economy, not everyone can be the philosopher. In fact, Smith surmises, the majority of people will not be philosophers, but narrow-minded specialists incapable of understanding the general view or of sympathizing with their fellows. This recognition puts Smith's "philosopher" in a position parallel to that of Tristram Shandy: both spend their lives offering rational explanations and describing general views that most other people, consulting their own experience, would find peculiar, even quixotic.

Smith was himself a man of broad interests, whose career combined literary study, moral philosophy and political economy; he gave his first public lectures on English literature and criticism in 1748–50, published on moral philosophy in 1759, and established the modern field of economics in 1776.[46] Unresolved questions that pervade his work—concerning the role of the observer, the scope of rationality, occupational hierarchies, the standards and authority of scientific understanding, and of course, the meaning and credibility of the invisible hand—have come to define important (politicized) disciplinary boundaries between literary study, economics and other social disciplines. Modern economists, who acclaim Smith as an unbiased scientific authority and the founding father of their field, while making public policy prescriptions in his name, have pushed him to the center of the controversy. Adam Smith rules much of the Western world, or so it is perceived, especially by those who recall the Reagan and Thatcher years.[47] Thus the politicized intellectual resistance to the expanding authority of economic thought often comes in the form of critical examination of Adam Smith's writings.

Donald Winch, for instance, historically contextualizes Smith in order to reassert the unavoidable importance of politics within Smith's economic "science," a strategy also adopted by Patricia Werhane. Vivienne Brown, on the other hand, invokes Bakhtinian narrative theory to sift Smith's ethics from his political economy, arguing that economists misread Smith by not recognizing in his work a hierarchy of discourse that keeps the realm of ethics distinct from that of worldly outcomes.[48] The resistances to the "economic" reading of Smith have at least one feature in common: a deep dissatisfaction with the reductiveness of surrendering morals, aesthetics and human motivation to the "scientific" explanations of economics and rational choice theory. Asserting the importance of political science, Winch rejects the suggestion that Smith "constructed an intellectual system in which politics is epiphenomenal to the more profound economic forces at work in modern commercial society." He bristles at the disciplinary hierarchy implied by this presumption that politics is "a mere derivative (the discarded husk?)" of economics.[49] Brown's work, seeking to spare moral philosophy from the ever-encroaching influence of economics, declares a different disciplinary hierarchy, arguing that *The Theory of Moral Sentiments* functions at a higher discursive level for Smith than does *The Wealth of Nations*. Jonas Barish, David Marshall and Jean-Christophe Agnew, in finding "theatricality" at the heart of Smith's thought, subvert the authority of scientific objectivity by emphasizing the pervasive uncertainties of subjectivity.[50] All of these critiques, to a greater or lesser extent, challenge economic logic by re-situating economic ideas within disciplines whose methodologies diverge from that of economics.

In the epilogue, my own re-situation of Smith and twentieth-century economic theory within the context of eighteenth-century quixotism and sentimentalism, questions not only the disciplinary hierarchy at stake in the quarrels between modern economics and its related fields, but also the critical hierarchy implicit in the "obvious" triviality of the quixotic and the sentimental. Quixotism, sentimentalism and political economy share common methodological ground. I hope thus far to have shown at least that they belong together in one discussion. Curiously, however, the first two in this triumvirate have come to be dismissed as madness, frivolity and irrational hypersensitivity, while the last has been elevated to a science whose teachings now frequently determine both the means and the ends of government and public policy. Though the distinction seems to be arbitrary, it is not inconsequential, for it prescribes what counts as "rational" choice. In other words, by uncritically accepting the customary distinctions between quixotism, sentimentalism and rationality, we may be perpetuating a system of thought that forecloses the possibility of an equal and rational voice to those—such as women, minorities, scholars of the humanities, and other embodiments of "softer" understandings—who have had the historical misfortune of being lumped with the quixotic and the sentimental, rather than with the scientific.[51] To rethink "Reason" for a diverse world, we must be willing to question the self-evident.

1

TURNING AUTHORITY INTO JEST

Tyrants, pedants, quixotes and enthusiasts in the early eighteenth century

> If still our reason runs another way,
> That private reason 'tis more just to curb
> Than by disputes the public peace disturb,
> For points obscure are of small use to learn:
> But common quiet is mankind's concern.
> Dryden, *Religio Laici*, ll. 446–50

In the early eighteenth century, quixotism was not entirely a laughing matter. Quixotism conjured images of innovation, cultural change and revolution. Describing alternate political and intellectual systems, yet authorizing them in terms strikingly similar to those used in support of the *status quo*, quixotism parodied the very form of rational discourse. It turned authority into jest, and made reason look like madness, by reimagining nature as art and art as nature. Quixotism's competing claims to reason and authority drew attention to the fictional underpinnings of the social and political world. If Don Quixote was mad for relying on fictions to authorize his beliefs and actions, then who was not just as mad as the errant knight? "*EVery man has something of* Don Quixote *in his Humor, some darling* Dulcinea *of his Thoughts, that sets him very often upon mad Adventures,*" observes Peter Motteux, one of *Don Quixote*'s early translators. "*What* Quixotes *dos not every Age produce in Politics and Religion,*" he asks, "*who fancying themselves to be in the right of something, which all the World tells 'em is wrong, make very good sport to the Public, and shew that they themselves need the chiefest Amendment?*"[1] Motteux here suggests that quixotism is universal. Twentieth-century readers may be inclined to regard this universal quixotism as eccentric but harmless idealism, for over the past three centuries Don Quixote has grown increasingly benign and benevolent.[2] Motteux's eighteenth-century audience, however, would have seen universal quixotism as a disturbing social nuisance, even a menace. For during Motteux's time, quixotism characterized the actions of those political and religious innovators who, forcefully *"fancying"* their own rectitude, impose their "private reason"—to borrow a phrase from Dryden—on everyone else, much to the detriment of "the public peace" and "common quiet." Quixotism was the shadow of civil unrest, sometimes traveling before, sometimes lagging behind, but always nearby.

This chapter will discuss the idea of universal quixotism and its associations in the period just following the Revolution of 1688, arguing that quixotism (despite its humor) often described an urgent political threat, one rendered all the more serious (and all the more humorous) by the challenges quixotism posed to the rational structures meant to contain it. Quixotism was a political problem because it was an intellectual problem. Motteux was not unusual in believing quixotes to be themselves in need of the *"chiefest Amendment."* Yet by what impartial standard could this need for correction be assessed, and by what just method might this correction be achieved? In a world of universal quixotism, little consensus can be reached on what constitutes the absurd, the ridiculous or the rational. And without consensus, efforts to correct errancy look like political oppression—tyranny, as it was commonly called in the eighteenth century. When correction cannot be distinguished from tyranny, there can be no obvious difference between reason and quixotism. In such a world, the dignity of authority dwindles into the menacing posturings of tyrants, pedants, quixotes and enthusiasts.

Ridicule, reason and revolution

Anthony Ashley Cooper, Third Earl of Shaftesbury, thought that the relation between reason and ridicule must be obvious. In his *Letter Concerning Enthusiasm* (1708), celebrating the power of ridicule to restore reason, Shaftesbury advocates giving "liberty to wit." The ancients thrived, he contends, by tolerating "visionaries and enthusiasts of all kinds," who in turn were kept in check by "the force of wit" and the raillery of others. "And thus matters were happily balanced," Shaftesbury reports,

> reason had fair play; learning and science flourished. Wonderful was the harmony and temper which arose from all these contrarieties. Thus superstition and enthusiasm were mildly treated, and being let alone they never raged to that degree as to occasion bloodshed, wars, persecutions, and devastation in the world.[3]

Ridicule, according to Shaftesbury, not only regulates "contrarieties," it is also self-regulating. It preserves the peace and gives reason "fair play," keeping enthusiasms reined in by "the force of wit" rather than by the violent force of "bloodshed, wars, persecutions, and devastation." For Shaftesbury, political intervention always obstructs rational outcomes; reason has "fair play" only when the coercive power of the state leaves it alone. The earl subscribes to a kind of intellectual *laissez faire*; the "freedom of raillery" alone, he maintains, will be sufficient to expose ridiculous systems of thought.

Illustrating this point, Shaftesbury contrasts the decline of various manifestations of enthusiasm with the persistence of its religious form. Religious enthusiasm, he argues, endures beyond the rest because it alone is handled without mirth:

> We may treat other enthusiasms as we please. We may ridicule love, or gallantry, or knight-errantry to the utmost; and we find that in these latter days of wit, the humour of this kind, which was once so prevalent, is pretty well declined. The crusades, the rescuing of the holy lands, and such devout gallantries, are in less request than formerly: but if something of this militant religion, something of this soul-rescuing spirit and saint-errantry prevails still, we need not wonder, when we consider in how solemn a manner we treat this distemper, and how preposterously we go about to cure enthusiasm.
> (Shaftesbury 1: 16)

Enthusiasms, when freely ridiculed, peacefully depart. And for Shaftesbury, the epitome of successful ridicule is *Don Quixote*; the three enthusiasms he describes as "once so prevalent" though now "pretty well declined"—"love, or gallantry, or knight-errantry"—are all targets of Cervantes' satire. Religious enthusiasm remains, however, because it has been taken too seriously, a condition Shaftesbury seeks to rectify by ridiculing such fanaticism as a kind of quixotism: "saint-errantry." The alternate policy, that of invoking the full force and official power of government to curb enthusiasm, Shaftesbury dismisses as a preposterous approach that would serve only to perpetuate the enthusiast's challenge. To persecute rather than ridicule enthusiasts only solemnizes their authority; to oppose them with the full force of the state is to recognize their power. Thus, for Shaftesbury, laughter can be the only appropriate response to quixotism, for only through spontaneous ridicule can rational balance be maintained. "Whatever humour has got the start," he affirms, "if it be unnatural, it cannot hold; and the ridicule, if ill-placed at first, will certainly fall at last where it deserves" (Shaftesbury 1: 10). Trusting to nature's self-correcting powers, Shaftesbury has no fear that unchecked quixotism could ever triumph. Confident in himself, he shows no concern that his own proposals could be dismissed as quixotic.

In contrast, William Temple regards the objects and outcomes of raillery with less assurance, noting that ridicule may have unintended casualties. By way of illustration, he recalls the account of an "Ingenious *Spaniard* at *Brussels*," who argued that "the History of *Don Quixot* had ruined the *Spanish* Monarchy: For before that time Love and Valour were all Romance among them." But,

[a]fter *Don Quixot* appeared, and with that inimitable Wit and Humour turned all this Romantick Honour and Love into Ridicule, the *Spaniards* . . . began to grow ashamed of both, and to laugh at Fighting and Loving . . . and the consequences of this . . . this *Spaniard* would needs have pass for a great Cause of the Ruin of *Spain*, or of its Greatness and Power.[4]

Cervantes' wit, Temple's story relates, banished not only foolish knight-errantry, but Spain's "Greatness and Power" as well. In this case, ridicule caused ruin rather than improvement. Though Temple seems somewhat skeptical of this history of Spanish decline, he does not doubt the power of ridicule to undermine pre-eminence. As a defender of ancient learning against the innovative claims of modern scholars,[5] Temple reads the Spaniard's tale specifically as a warning to learned authority. "Whatever effect the Ridicule of Knight-Errantry might have had upon that Monarchy," Temple asserts, "I believe that of Pedantry has had a very ill one upon the Commonwealth of Learning" (Temple 42). In fact, Temple blames the slow progress of "Learning" on ridicule,

the scorn of pedantry, which the shallow, the superficial, and the sufficient among scholars first drew upon themselves, and very justly, by pretending to more than they had, or to more esteem than what they could deserve, by broaching it in all places, at all times, upon all occasions, and by living so much among themselves, or in their Closets and Cells, as to make them unfit for all other business, and ridiculous in all other Conversations.

(Temple 40–1)

Pedants, Temple laments, erode the dignity of all scholars by making far grander claims than they are able to meet. Not recognizing the limits of their own authority, they render themselves ridiculous by fanatically promoting their cloistered understandings as universally relevant. "[U]nfit for all other business" except conversing "among themselves," so "sufficient" as to remain entirely unaware of their own ignorance, pedants are scholarly quixotes who sally boldly forth, confidently enforcing their opinions upon everyone else. They are such easy targets for mockery that Temple, himself a learned man, worries that the free play of ridicule would be insufficiently discriminating—that under its influence, people would begin to grow ashamed of learning (rather than pedantry), and to laugh at scholarship (rather than sufficiency). Ridicule may have unintended, undesired casualties. Unlike Shaftesbury, Temple can imagine his own authority, through the broad force of ridicule, dwindling into the quixotic.

Temple's understanding of the quixotic captures the fragility and uncertainty of rational authority. Temple's pedants, like Shaftesbury's enthusiasts, are quixotic precisely because they aggressively innovate upon reason, zealously imposing their knowledge upon others "in all places, at all times, upon all occasions." Self-sufficiently reducing the entire world to fit within the compass of their own partial and fixed understandings, pedants, quixotes and enthusiasts embody intellectual tyranny. Though their condition may be unnatural, it is quite common, Swift's Hack observes in *A Tale of a Tub* (1704). "For, what Man in the natural State, or Course of Thinking, did ever conceive it in his Power, to reduce the Notions of Mankind, exactly to the same Length, and Breadth, and Heighth of his own?" asks the Hack in his digression on madness: "Yet this is the first humble and civil Design of all Innovators in the Empire of Reason."[6] Innovating upon reason is, of course, neither "humble" nor "civil"; it is violent, tyrannical, and revolutionary:

> For, if we take a Survey of the greatest Actions that have been performed in the World, under the Influence of Single Men; which are, *The Establishment of New Empires by Conquest: The Advance and Progress of New Schemes in Philosophy; and the contriving, as well as the propagating of New Religions*: We shall find the Authors of them all, to have been Persons, whose natural Reason hath admitted great Revolutions from their Dyet, their Education, the Prevalency of some certain Temper, together with the particular Influence of Air and Climate.
>
> (Swift 1: 102)

Attributing history's profoundest events to individuals' "particular" influences—diet, education, temper, climate—Swift creates an ironic distance between the grand sweep of history and the absurdly arbitrary motivations of history's great men. With the universal importance of "the greatest Actions" thus revealed to be the product of "particular Influence," history's notables begin to resemble Temple's pedants: ridiculous little fellows who force their own ludicrously narrow interests on the public at large. The authors of all great revolutions, the Hack suggests, are either tyrants, who establish new empires by conquest; pedants, who advance new schemes in philosophy; or enthusiasts, who contrive and propagate new religions. And all three of these types the Hack insouciantly believes to be highly unnatural: "For, the Brain, in its natural Position and State of Serenity, disposeth its Owner to pass his Life in the common Forms, without any Thought of subduing Multitudes to his own *Power*, his *Reasons* or his *Visions*" (Swift 1: 108).

Like his benefactor Temple, the satiric Swift recognizes that reason may not be naturally self-correcting. Instead, he strongly hints that reason—far from correcting the delusions of tyrants, pedants, quixotes and enthusiasts—has itself over the course of history been corrected by their "*Power*," "*Reasons*" and "*Visions*." The devastating irony of Swift's observations reverberates off the idea of "the common Forms" which, given the "mighty Revolutions, that have happened in *Empire*, in *Philosophy*, and in *Religion*" (Swift 1: 108), can no longer be considered synonymous with any constant state of reason or nature. The arbitrary events of history create the "common Forms," glorifying, rationalizing, and naturalizing the happy victories of madmen. "Success qualifies the Action," writes Matthew Prior: "If ALEXANDER had lost the Day at Arbella, he had been Consigned by History for a Madman." Like Prior, who in subsequent years would become his literary collaborator, Swift here ironically insinuates that history serves to celebrate the numerous triumphs of quixotism throughout the ages. "Thus one Man," the Hack sagely observes,

> chusing a proper Juncture, leaps into a Gulph, from thence proceeds a Hero, and is called the Saver of his Country; Another atchieves the same Enterprise, but unluckily timing it, has left the Brand of *Madness*, fixt as a Reproach upon his Memory; Upon so nice a Distinction are we taught to repeat the Name of *Curtius* with Reverence and Love; that of *Empedocles*, with Hatred and Contempt.
> (Swift 1: 110–11)[7]

Contrary to Shaftesbury's belief that "[w]hatever humour has got the start, if it be unnatural it cannot hold," Swift strongly suspects that the unnatural can and does hold, that nature has disappeared behind the nice distinctions of history, that quixotism may pass for reason, because reason and quixotism are now indistinguishable.

To question the natural basis of the common forms, however, is to doubt the rational foundations of the social, political and moral world. It is a revolutionary act. Thus John Locke's efforts to draw a distinction between the rationale for the "Glorious Revolution" and mere enthusiasm—between reason and arbitrary power—must take up the question of foundations, nature and the common forms. Enthusiasm, according to Locke, has no foundation. He dismisses it, in the *Essay Concerning Human Understanding* (1690), on the grounds that it has no grounds. "Whatsoever credit or Authority we give to any Proposition more than it receives from the Principles and Proofs it supports itself upon, is owing to our Inclinations that way," Locke asserts (*Essay* 697–8). Enthusiasm is a condition wherein the mind allows "ungrounded Fancies" or "groundless Opinion" to be "an Illumination from the Spirit of GOD, and presently of divine Authority" (*Essay* 699). With the only limit to enthusiastic claims thus being the zealot's own inclinations and ambitions, Locke reasons that such unchecked zeal must necessarily eventuate in a tyranny of understanding:

> The assuming an Authority of Dictating to others, and a forwardness to prescribe their Opinions, is a constant concomitant of this bias and corruption of our Judgments. For how almost can it be otherwise, but that he should be ready to impose on others Belief, who has already imposed on his own? Who can reasonably expect Arguments and

Conviction from him, in dealing with others, whose Understanding is not accustomed to them in his dealing with himself? Who does Violence to his own Faculties, Tyrannizes over his own Mind, and usurps the Prerogative that belongs to Truth alone.

(*Essay* 698)

Enthusiasts can be identified by their deviation from the natural and common forms of conduct. Having been "imposed on" by themselves, they exhibit "bias," "corruption" and a general departure from reasonable "Arguments and Conviction." The foundation from which they derive their authority is assumed, usurped and tyrannical. Most striking in this passage is the slippage between the language of truth and the language of politics. Like Swift, Locke sees in enthusiasm the precursor of political revolution. The kingdom Locke describes here exists only in the mind, but it plays out the turmoil of the unruly, unreasonable rabble's rising up to "prescribe their Opinions," doing "Violence," tyrannizing and usurping the place of the legitimate monarch, "Truth." Political disturbances, Locke intimates, may be traced to epistemological flaws, "[f]or how almost can it be otherwise, but that he should be ready to impose on others Belief, who has already imposed on his own?" Yet with irrationality thus identified as the root of revolution, what could justify the Revolution of 1688, other than its success? In other words, on what legitimate grounds—as opposed to arbitrary, political ones—could the Revolution be said to stand?

Reason in context: quixotism and arbitrary power

How could the events of 1688 be construed as a legitimate revolution rather than a rebellion? Locke answers this question by presenting the Revolution as a *recovery* of reason and nature, not as an innovation upon them. "The *State of Nature* has a Law of Nature to govern it, which obliges every one: And Reason . . . is that Law," he writes, articulating what would become known as "Revolution Principles," the rights whereby the people may dissolve their compacts with oppressive governments (*TT* 271).[8] By enthroning the rule of reason as eternal and universal law, Locke defines rationality as an arbiter independent of political faction, as a natural authority above that of parliaments and kings. By definition, rational authority will oblige everyone; it will naturally command consent. Significantly, included in the law of nature is a person's obligation to self-preservation, which Locke interprets as an injunction against tyranny. "*Freedom* from Absolute, Arbitrary Power," he argues, "is so necessary to, and closely joyned with a Man's Preservation, that he cannot part with it" (*TT* 284). Through this abstract discussion of self-preservation, Locke slyly inoculates readers against the themes of his loyalist Jacobite and Tory opponents, who, advocating the doctrines of passive obedience and non-resistance to "supreme power," urged, in opposition to Revolution Principles, that the people had no right to resist the monarch, even should he prove tyrannical.[9] As Locke interprets nature, reasonable people cannot adhere to the doctrines of passive obedience and non-resistance, for those who would choose to live passively under a tyrant "are not a Society of Rational Creatures entred into a Community for their mutual good" (*TT* 376). Rather, they are offenders against the law of nature, which is the law of reason.

The "Glorious Revolution" was a specific application of this general argument. Within Whig ideology, James II had been a tyrant, a circumstance that entitled the people—in fact, obliged them by the law of reason—to remove him. A tyrant, Locke explains, is a prince who, having set up a "distinct and separate Interest" from the public good, "makes all give way to his own Will and Appetite"; a tyrant is a prince who, sacrificing the common good to act upon his own personal interest, rules with arbitrary power (*TT* 376, 400). Therefore, Locke argues, in defying James, the people had not "*incroach'd upon the Prerogative*"—they had not rebelled—for a king is not authorized to have an interest distinct from that of the people, and "[i]n whatsoever he has *no Authority*, there he is no *King*, and may be *resisted*: For *wheresoever the Authority ceases, the King ceases too*, and becomes like other Men who have no Authority" (*TT* 424). Contrary to the original sense of the word "interest," which had been used by princes to designate their secret prerogative,[10] authority and interest are now opposed. "For though the Law of Nature be plain and intelligible to all rational Creatures; yet Men being biassed by their Interest . . . are not apt to allow of it as a Law binding to them," Locke observes (*TT* 351). Interested princes will govern irrationally, tyrannically believing, like other interested men, that the law of nature does not bind them. For the sake of peaceful society, then, such princes must be disregarded, for they violate the compact with the people by exercising arbitrary power, and those "introducing a Power, which the People have not authoriz'd . . . actually *introduce a State of War*, which is that of Force without Authority" (*TT* 416). Interested princes will be tyrannical princes, and tyrannical princes are by definition at war with the state. In arguing the rectitude of his own politics, Locke represents James as the offending interest; it was James, not the people, who had rebelled.

The opposition between reason and arbitrary power thus emerges as a key support of post-Revolution Whig rational authority. By Locke's definition, no reasonable man would live under arbitrary power, for resistance to arbitrary power constitutes one of the very expressions of reason. Moreover, only reasonable men can make meaningful political decisions. "*Lunaticks*," "*Ideots*" and "*Madmen*," Locke asserts, "or anyone who comes not to such a degree of Reason, wherein he might be supposed incapable of knowing the Law," cannot be allowed to reason for themselves; they must be guided by that reason which guides the men in authority over them (*TT* 307–8). Locke's law of reason, then, has an ironic and important corollary: the Tories and the Jacobites, who uphold passive obedience and non-resistance, cannot be considered reasonable, and therefore their political choices must be disallowed. By definition, only Whigs are reasonable, for only Whigs accept Revolution Principles, which conform to the law of nature, which is the law of reason.

The opponents of Revolution Principles acquire a quixotic character within Locke's analysis. Attacking the political philosophy of Sir Robert Filmer, whose arguments in favor of passive obedience loyally proclaim that "to make anyone *properly a King*, needs no more but *Governing by Supreme Power*" (*TT* 200), Locke satirically counters:

> By this notable way, our A[uthor] may make *Oliver* as *properly a King*, as any one else he could think of: And had he had the Happiness to live under *Massanello's* Government, he could not by this his own Rule have forborn to have done Homage to him, with *O King live for ever*, since the Manner of his Government by Supreme Power, made him *properly* King, who was but the Day before *properly* a Fisherman. And if *Don Quixot* had taught his Squire to Govern with Supreme Authority, our A[uthor] no doubt could have made a most Loyal Subject in *Sancho Pancha's Island*: and he must needs have deserved some Preferment in such Governments, since I think he is the first Politician, who, pretending to settle Government upon its true Basis, and to establish the Thrones of lawful Princes, ever told the World, That he was *properly a King, whose Manner of Government was by Supreme Power*, that Regal and Supreme Power is properly and truly his, who can by any Means seize upon it: and if this be, to be *properly a King*, I wonder how he came to think of, or where he will find, an *Usurper*.[11]
>
> (*TT* 200–1)

With his sarcastic repetition of the phrase, "*properly a King*," Locke makes clear that his contempt for Filmer's political theory lies in its inability to distinguish between proper and improper authority. Filmer's arguments, Locke implies, rest on intellectually uncompelling definitions by fiat, quixotic pretensions that merely pronounce usurpers to be proper kings and squires to be proper governors. Filmer's "*Supreme Power*" is arbitrary, merely "a product of Force and Violence," and hence a "Foundation for perpetual Disorder and Mischief," Locke insists (*TT* 267–8), shrewdly linking Filmer's authority to Masaniello's bloody rabble-rousing in Naples, and Oliver Cromwell's brutality in England. "The same arts that did gain/A power, must it maintain," Andrew Marvell had ominously warned of England's Lord Protector.[12] Indistinguishable from arbitrary power, Filmer's "*Supreme Power*" is unreasonable to Locke: "our A[uthor] no doubt could have made a most Loyal Subject in *Sancho Pancha's Island*." Under the doctrine of passive obedience, reason is whimsy, for rational behavior and right conduct have no measure beyond the shifting and fickle standards imposed by the monarch's arbitrary will. Passive obedience is irrational, and all those who subscribe to it—that is, all those who are not Whigs—are quixotes, madmen whose opinions and causes, being groundlessly based upon no more than caprice, pose a violent threat to the "Society of Rational Creatures entred into a Community for their mutual good." Locke uses the trope of quixotism to smear his political opponents with the taint of enthusiasm, tyranny and violence. Quixotism's conflation of reason and force is both horrifying and ridiculous, collapsing Shaftesbury's opposition between "bloodshed" and "ridicule." The ridiculous becomes violent, and violence becomes ridiculous, for ridicule begins where reason reaches its limits—where we confront, in Foucault's words, "the stark impossibility of thinking *that*."[13]

Locke was not alone in relegating the Whigs' political opponents to the quixotic realm of absurd impossibility. For as a madman with weapons that worked, Don Quixote was readily seen as a political threat—as a pretender to authority—like the Stuart Pretenders, plotting their return to power from French exile. The Old Pretender, said to be "raving like *Don Quixote* . . . about Kingdoms, and the Government of imaginary Islands" during the '15,[14] drew serious political attention. Government propagandists reacted to him hysterically, vividly detailing how miserable life would be under his arbitrary power: "brown husky Bread, and Herbs, and Rot-gut Soop" instead of "substantial Beef and Pudding"; "course tatter'd Jackets" for Sunday clothes; crushing taxes; bloody persecution of Protestants; English wives and daughters prostituted to the Jacobite army.[15] The Pretender's quixotic refusal to relinquish his claims to the throne led one "Jack Catch" to revoke from him even the common civic status of "other Men who have no Authority." Instead, he was

> one *James Stuart*, alias *Oglethorp*, alias *Tiler*, alias *George*, alias *Chevalier*, alias *Pretender,* alias *King*, alias *No-King*; neither *Cesar* nor *Nullus*, neither a Man nor a Mouse, neither a Man's Man, nor a Woman's Man, nor a States-man nor a little Man, nor a great Man; neither *English*-Man, nor *French*-Man, but a *Mungrelian*, between both; neither Wise nor otherwise; neither Soldier nor Sailer, nor Cardinal; without Father or Mother; without Friend or Foe, without Foresight or Aftersight, without Brains or Bravery, without House or Home.[16]

Reduced to a string of aliases and identifications by negation, the Pretender becomes a spurious and woeful figure, wandering about like a knight-errant with no connections to any place or anyone, yet nonetheless insisting upon his own importance and authority in the world. The metaphor remained current as the years wore by. In 1727, "a great Number of Knights Errant," like "*Don Quixotte*," were reported to be launching "an Expedition in favour of the *Pretender*."[17] The nickname, "Chevalier de St George," which James Francis Edward Stuart had earned for courageous military service in the War of the Spanish Succession, stuck to his son Charles as well, perhaps because it conveniently conduced to the Stuarts' image as quixotic tyrants. The fictitious

Chevalier's Declaration, probably of 1745, reveals Prince Charles Edward to be just as tyrannical as his grandfather was said to have been. Pronouncing the laws to be "totally void and abrogated," the *Declaration's* Young Pretender plans to replace them with new legislation taking the form, "*Be it enacted by the King's most Excellent Majesty, with himself, and by himself, of his own meer will and Pleasure.*"[18] According to Henry Fielding, Prince Charlie's arbitrary reign would be no bonnier than what was fearfully imagined of his father's. Fielding's *True Patriot* (1745–6) describes what the Young Pretender would have done for England had he triumphed in the '45: "Houses burnt, dead bodies of men, women and children strewn every where," Protestants burned, estates confiscated, women raped, promises to non-jurors broken, people seized and tried without juries by chief justices who speak in broken English.[19] In the popular imagination, the Young Pretender would be as unreasonable and tyrannical as his forebears.

The terms associated with arbitrary power—"tyranny," "inclination," "distinct and separate Interest," "Will and Appetite," "bias," "mere pleasure"—all serve to magnify the disparities between personal and universal interests, describing as arbitrary, unreasonable and politically untenable, those actions or ideas that too hastily collapse or ignore the divide between particular opinions and universal truth. Yet just about anyone can be dismissed for seeking to impose their ideas on the rest of the world, for too readily reducing "the notions of mankind exactly to the same length, and breadth, and height of his own." Locke himself was guilty of as much, according to Matthew Prior, who, as discussed above, criticized the philosopher's *Essay* as irrelevant to everyone except Locke himself: "All the while you wrote you were only thinking that You thought: You, and Your understanding are the *Personae Dramatis*, and the whole amounts to no more than a Dialogue between John and Locke" (Prior 1: 620). As Prior's critique indicates, Locke's insistence on the universality of reason promotes an ideal of consensus that seems unobtainable in any actual open political debate.

Writing from the position Locke dismisses as quixotic, George Berkeley's *Passive Obedience* (1712) ponders the contested relation between reason and universal obligation, seeing clearly how elusive rational consensus is:

> Though it be a point agreed amongst all wise men, that there are certain moral rules or laws of nature, which carry with them an eternal and indispensable obligation; yet, concerning the proper methods for discovering those laws, and distinguishing them from others dependent on the humour and discretion of men, there are various opinions. Some direct us to look for them in divine ideas; others in the natural inscriptions on the mind: some derive them from the authority of learned men, and the universal agreement and consent of nations. Lastly others hold that they are only to be discovered by the deductions of reason. The three first methods must be

acknowledged to labour under very great difficulties; and the last has not, that I know, been anywhere distinctly explained, or treated so fully as the importance of the subject doth deserve.[20]

While Locke assumes the universality of reason, Berkeley dwells upon the disputes that would appear to disprove such a claim. The agreement of wise men, Berkeley allows, should lead them to "certain moral rules or laws of nature," which, carrying with them "an eternal and indispensable obligation," will in turn reinforce the concord of the wise. Yet men do not agree, he observes. Instead, they quarrel over methodology out of fear that some rules and laws, biased by a dependence on "the humour and discretion of men," will be wrongly advanced as universal. The confusion, contention and diversity of opinion respecting the "laws of nature," Berkeley emphasizes by retreating to mere catalogue: some men argue for revelation, some for innate ideas, others for learned authority and prevalent opinion. Finally, he notes, some call for reason, which unfortunately has yet to be distinctly explained. Berkeley thus recognizes the need to constitute his political essay as a forum in which to address the epistemology of ethics:

> I hope therefore it will be pardoned if, in a discourse of passive obedience, in order to lay the foundation of that duty the deeper, we make some inquiry into the origin, nature, and obligation of moral duties in general, and the criteria whereby they are to be known.
>
> (Berkeley 6: 19)

For Berkeley, politics and epistemology cannot be discussed independently.

The preservation of civil society, according to Berkeley, requires not Lockean reason, but consent to supreme power. His argument rests on the desirability of certainty: to obey the supreme power is to follow "certain universal rules of morality," whereas the alternative—"obliging every one upon each particular occasion to consult the public good, and always to do that which to him shall seem, in the present time and circumstances, most to conduce to it"—would provide "no sure standard" (Berkeley 6: 21). "[T]here can be no harmony or agreement between the actions of good men . . . no adhering to principles" if "the measure and rule of every good man's actions is supposed to be nothing else but his own private disinterested opinion of what makes for the public good at that juncture," Berkeley insists (Berkeley 6: 22). Because opinion must unavoidably be different in different men, due to their "particular views and circumstances," as well as different in the same man as he changes over time, a civil society governed by these opinions—disinterested though they may be—could never settle upon universal rules. Rather, there would ensue "the most horrible confusion of vice and virtue, sin and duty, that can possibly be imagined" (Berkeley 6: 22). For Berkeley, political stability requires eternal, universal moral principles. A common epistemology of ethics must unite the polity, or different understandings of moral rules will lead to civil war: "there [will be] no politeness, no order, no peace, among men." The world will be "one great heap of misery and confusion," the bishop warns, unless the "'laws of nature' . . . are universal, and do not derive their obligation from any civil sanction, but immediately from the Author of nature himself" (Berkeley 6: 25, 23). These "'laws of nature'"—"termed 'eternal rules of reason'"—include: "'Thou shalt not resist the supreme power'" (Berkeley 6: 23, 25). By Berkeley's definition of reason, Locke's definition is unreasonable; it is Revolution Principles, not passive obedience, that threaten civil society with perpetual disorder and mischief.

At the heart of the dispute over reason and supreme power is the meaning of arbitrariness. Though Locke and his fellow Whigs could argue that supreme power was arbitrarily designated, their opponents could easily counter that so too was any concept of reason not founded on clearly defined, eternal rules. By what standards could one determine whether the Revolution and its principles were enthusiastic *innovations* upon nature, or simply reasonable and timely *corrections* made to a society that had already, through the happy success of madmen, long since departed from any correspondence to nature? Berkeley accepts supreme power at face value, while Locke reinterprets it as an arbitrary imposition upon true nature. To Locke's mind, Berkeley's laws of nature are the product of past political arts. To Berkeley's thinking, Locke's laws of nature are recent political art. The conflict is thus a quixotic one, the two sides at odds over assumptions, unable to agree even on how to distinguish nature from art. With the rage of party spirit magnifying such differences, quixotism in the early eighteenth century—not reason—appeared to be the universal. The famous trial of Dr Sacheverell in 1710 offers a good illustration of how commonly, and in what manner, the rhetoric of universal quixotism was employed in public debates about Revolution Principles, passive obedience and monarchical authority.

Quixotism and the Sacheverell affair

The high-flying Anglican divine, Dr Henry Sacheverell, commenced a quixote with a sermon delivered at St Paul's Cathedral on 5 November 1709.[21] Sacheverell's sermon, *The Perils of False Brethren, both in Church and State*, stirred the ire of the reigning Whigs by flagrantly preaching the Tory doctrines of passive obedience and non-resistance, thereby impugning Revolution Principles and the current Whig administration.

> The *Grand Security* of our *Government*, and the very *Pillar* upon which it *stands*, is founded upon the *steady Belief* of the *Subject's Obligation* to *Absolute*, and *Unconditional Obedience* to the *Supream Power*, in *All* Things *Lawful*, and the utter *Illegality* of *Resistance* upon any *Pretence* whatsoever.[22]

Sacheverell had boomed from the pulpit. Unabashedly, the doctor preached that the Church was endangered by "false brethren," the Whigs with their Revolution Principles, especially the Lord Treasurer Godolphin.[23] And the Church in danger meant the State in danger, too. As Sacheverell's sermon asserts:

> 'tis hard to say, whether the *Doctrins* of the *Church of England* contribute *more* to *Authorize*, and *Enforce* Our *Civil Laws*, or Our *Laws* to *Maintain*, and *Defend* the *Doctrins* of Our *Church* . . . 'tis almost impossible to offer a *Violation* to the *One*, without *Breaking* in upon the *Body* of the *Other*.
>
> (Sacheverell 11–12)

Whigs and Tories could at least agree that the security of Church and State were interdependent; Whigs thus championed toleration for dissenters and promoted the contract theory of government, while Tories defended the exclusive authority of the Anglican Church and urged the divine right of monarchic authority.[24] If the Tories were right, then "Revolution Principles" were a foundation of air, with the Revolution of 1688 resting upon it.

In effect, Sacheverell's sermon had accused the Whigs of sedition. Whether or not Godolphin, as it is sometimes alleged, initially stirred up the proceedings in a fit of rage,[25] the administration had good cause to take action once the sermon reached the booksellers. Printed without authorization, 50,000 copies of the work were being borrowed, read and loaned by the middle of December, a figure that rose to 100,000 by March.[26] The administration's reaction to Sacheverell's assumption of authority, both in his preaching the sermon and in his allowing it to be illicitly printed, shows how seriously the Whigs regarded the matter. Meeting his challenge with the full force of the law, the Whig leaders impeached the doctor for "high crimes and misdemeanors."

Sacheverell's trial was a highly publicized event,[27] a spectacle quintessentially quixotic in its fusion of humor and violence, arbitrariness and reason. Because popular sentiment was against them, the Whig lords who initiated the proceedings hoped to make quick work of the doctor in a quiet trial at their own bar, for publicity would only favor the doctor and his Tory supporters. The Tories, however, managed to circumvent these plans by demanding that the entire House of Commons be present for the trial, as was allowed by precedent.[28] The situation inspired one wit to verse:

> HOW? At the other B[ar] to try a Priest?
> What, is your own Authority a Jest?
> Try him your selves, like th'Rump, without more Words;
> They that can make their K[ing]s, can make their Lords.[29]

Entitled "Said to be dropt in the House of C[ommon]s," the poem reminds readers of the Rump Parliament in order to satirize the Commons as a body of upstarts who rule tyrannically, overriding all opposition by creating and installing their own fictions of authority whenever convenient: "They that can make their K[ing]s, can make their Lords." Humor and violence fuse in these verses as the poem's wit turns on the ridiculous image of the Commons defending its authority by exercising arbitrary power—in the context of the allusion to the Rump Parliament, to "make" a king means, of course, to kill a king. The poem mocks the Commons' authority as tyrannical, reinterpreting the Commons' objection to the Lords' bar as evidence of their complicity in Sacheverell's assault upon established authority. From the very beginning, the trial was about authority turned into jest, the legitimacy of government, and civil war.[30] As one rhyming Sacheverell supporter warns: "O A[nn]a! see the Prelude is begun,/Again they play the Game of Forty One,"[31] while a Sacheverell detractor, drawing a parallel between the present times and the tense situation of 1666, follows Dryden's lead by writing a new "Age of Wonders":

> *Sachev'rell* like, with double Face,
>   We pray for our Defender;
> To good Queen *Anne* make vile Grimace,
>   But drink to the Pretender.[32]

As these mentions of "the Game of Forty One" and toasts to the Pretender indicate, the Sacheverell affair was regarded as a pivotal moment in a long history of national political struggle. The doctor's impeachment was of grave concern, for the constitution of post-Revolution England was on trial with Sacheverell.

Two poems occasioned by the trial compactly spell out the constitutional differences between those for and those against the doctor. "Fair Warning," a Whig production, reminds the Queen that her reign depends upon Revolution Principles, that Sacheverell's advocating of non-resistance only aids the Pretender, and that Sacheverell thereby impeaches the Queen's own authority:

> MAdam, look out, your Title is arraign'd;
> *Sacheverell* saps the Ground whereon you stand.
> 'Tis Revolution that upholds your Throne.
> Let Non-Resistance thrive, and you're undone.
> If passive Doctrines boldly are reviv'd,
> Your Crown's precarious, and your Reign short-liv'd.
> Such Notions with Impunity profest,
> Will make the Pow'r of Parliaments a Jest.
> Their Acts of Settlement are Ropes of Sand,
> And *Hannover* may rule his native Land.

> When Pulpits sound no Limitation's good,
> No Right, but in Proximity of Blood,
> Who sees not the Pretender's understood?
> Impatient for their darling Chevalier,
> You're in their Mercy for another Year:
> Tho' Loyalty and Church are their Pretence,
> Inherent Birthright is their secret Sense,
> And Restoration is the Consequence.[33]

The "Fair Warning" traces Anne's power back only as far as 1688, where "Revolution" upheld her throne. By preaching non-resistance and passive obedience, Sacheverell turns the basis of political authority, "the Pow'r of Parliaments," into "a Jest." Sacheverell's "secret Sense," the poem warns, is "Inherent Birthright"—hereditary and indefeasible right—which can only validate the claims of the Pretender. If Parliament is denied the power to authorize "Acts of Settlement," then "Restoration" must be the logical "Consequence." Sacheverell's "secret Sense" makes Queen Anne the real pretender.

In reply to the "Fair Warning," came the Tory retort, "An Answer to the Fair Warning." Obedience, the "Answer" argues, upholds the throne, while resistance overturns it. The Queen's true entitlement comes not from Parliament, but from Divine Right:

> MOnarchs, beware, your Titles they disown,
> Who say Obedience undermines the Throne.
> 'Tis Non-Resistance that upholds the Crown;
> Let bold Resistance thrive, 'twill tumble down.
> If Whiggish Maxims saucily are taught,
> Your Crowns are Baubles, and your Titles nought.
> Such prophane Notions impudently prest,
> Will make supream Prerogative a Jest.
> All divine Rights are then like Spiders Nets,
> And Church Decrees and Homilies are Cheats.
> When Tub-Dissenters eagerly are bent
> Against Monarchical-Establishment,
> Who sees not *Cromwell* is expressly meant?
> Impatient for their darling Common-wealth,
> Which they promote by Violence or Stealth,
> Tho' Laws and Constitution's their Pretence,
> Inherent Anarchy's their secret Sense,
> And Decollation is the Consequence.[34]

The "Answer to the Fair Warning" reads the meaning of the Sacheverell controversy against an historical context earlier than 1688, comparing Anne to her grandfather Charles I. Resistance, not obedience, makes "supream Prerogative a Jest," taking down both "Church Decrees" and "Monarchical-Establishment." The Whigs' "secret Sense," the poem warns, is "Inherent Anarchy"—the violent or stealthy exercise of individual arbitrary power—which turns all "Crowns" and "Titles" into "nought." If "bold Resistance" is allowed to thrive, then "Decollation" may well be the "Consequence." The Whigs' "secret Sense" offers the chilling prospect of another royal decapitation.

The elision of violence and jest—revolution and the ridiculous—pervades the atmosphere surrounding the Sacheverell case. With the prospect of revolutionary change rendering the "ridiculous" a serious possibility, few could indulge in the comforting practice of dismissing the ridiculous as entirely silly and unthreatening. One poem, hoping to distract the nation from its "*in-bred Jars*," tries to argue that Sacheverell is unimportant, that his cries of "The *Church* is sore opprest" should not be seriously heeded, for "ev'ry Man of common Sense/Knows that is but a Jest."[35] This rhetorical appeal to the common sense, and the common sense of humor, of "ev'ry Man" greatly overstates, however, what men could be presumed to know in common. The sentiments it slights as "but a Jest" were controversial enough to cause rioting in London after the third day of Sacheverell's trial. Thousands of the doctor's supporters cavorted through the city for eight hours that night, crying "High Church and Sacheverell," harassing passers-by and destroying property. Yet the mass disorder was not the most frightening feature of the riots. More terrible to the Whig administration was the *order*. The destruction of property was not random, as the rioters systematically attacked famous meeting houses of dissenters. Crowds assembled with the proper tools for the job (crowbars, axes, pick-axes, hammers) already in hand. The rioters then methodically dismantled the conventicles, using division of labor to make their rioting more efficient: some rioters were responsible for pulling the meeting houses down, others for carrying the pieces away, and still others for overseeing the bonfire. The mobs carefully avoided damaging neighboring structures, sometimes lugging rubble from the conventicles several hundred yards before igniting it. Witnesses reported that early in the evening, gentlemen had directed the proceedings, while some of the rioters themselves later confessed to having been paid for their participation. The rioting crowds were dispersed only after Queen Anne, "seized with a paleness and trembling" upon hearing of the disturbance, dispatched her personal guard (leaving herself unprotected) to quell the commotion.[36] Inspired by the fuss caused by Sacheverell, one ballad proclaimed:

> THE Nation had always some Token
> Of *Madness*, by Turns and by Fits;
> Their Sense was both shatter'd and broken,
> But now they are out of their Wits.[37]

48

But if the people of London had gone mad over Sacheverell, there was a method to their madness. Nicholas Lechmere, one of the prosecutors in the case, identified it, calling the night's activities "rebellion" and "high treason."[38] Sacheverell's claim that the Church was in danger, a "Jest" that all men of common sense should recognize, easily passed for "the Game of Forty One."

Clearly, in the Sacheverell case, jesting with authority was not always a joke. It could be as grim as a prelude to civil war. The level of complacency necessary to dismiss such jests as mere ridiculous froth requiring no further attention, was not characteristic of the early eighteenth century. Doctor Sacheverell was perceived to be in league with the Pretender. His ideas threatened social and political change. As jester, tyrant, madman and revolutionary, the doctor had all the ridiculous and ominous associations of a quixote. Several political pamphlets occasioned by the trial make Sacheverell's quixotism explicit by depicting him as a modern-day knight-errant.

Before the trial had even begun, John Dunton was calling Sacheverell a "*Bully-Errant . . . a great Pretender to Courage*," and chastising him for his "most *malicious Slanders* in the Face of Authority":

> I call him *Errant*, because he wanders about, like the Crack-brain'd *Don of Mancha*, in *Quest of Imaginary Giants*, and Monsters that wou'd ravish, or eat up his *Dulcinea*, his Ideal Mistress (what he calls) the CHURCH, and runs raving mad about he knows not what.[39]

A later pamphlet, by the pseudonymous Jack Touchwood, identifies Sacheverell's "*Imaginary Giants*" as "the Church," "*Tolleration*," the "*Administration* of the *present Government*" and "*the Late Revolution*."[40] Dubbing the doctor "DON HENRICO FURIOSO *de* SACHEVERELLO, *Knight of the Fire-brand*," Touchwood lampoons Sacheverell as a "*Spiritual Kt. Errant*" and the great-grandson of Don Quixote. With arms bearing the *fleur-de-lis*, a mitre for a helmet, and the mighty steed "FACTION" for a mount, Sacheverello "racks a Text to make it confess a *meaning it never dream'd of*." He brandishes a sword that "makes no more of a Minister of State, than it would of a *Magpye*, and slices a *Constitution* as it would a *Cucumber*." This famous weapon can allegedly "at one blow shred all the *Separatists* in *Great Britain* and *Ireland* like so many *Shallots*, let *blood* a *Comprehension*, cleave a *Tolleration*, *murther* a *Succession*, and knock *down a Church*." Like the frenzy of the Sacheverell rioters, the doctor's madness has a method: Touchwood reinterprets Sacheverello's excessive concern for the Church's safety as a disguised plot to betray the nation to France, the Pope, and the Pretender. As Don Henrico's helmet and *fleur-de-lis* arms suggest, the horrors of popery, tyranny and foreign subjugation cannot be distinguished from his quixotism. Signifying the long reach of the dreaded Inquisition, the spiritual knight-errant "racks" a text to make it "confess" what it had never before dreamed of. As this image of textual torture makes plain, quixotism is a tyranny over meaning, a conflation of reason and force embodied in the figure of Sacheverello as inquisitor.

Touchwood was not unique in identifying Sacheverell's quixotism with Jacobitism. Dunton had suggested as much when he spoke of Sacheverell's "*Brethren of* Rome, *and his Master the* Pretender."[41] Other pamphlets also proclaimed the alliance between Sacheverell and the Pretender, including Defoe's *Instructions from Rome In Favour of the Pretender, Inscrib'd to the most Elevated Don Sacheverellio, and his Brother Don Higginisco* (1710), which portrays High Church Tories as tools of a demonic Rome, fellow-questers in the company of that other errant knight, "little *George* the *Chevalier*," James Francis Edward Stuart.[42] Read alongside these charges of sedition, Sacheverell's alleged madness—his ridiculous quixotism—is not so much lunacy as political difference. The Whigs confirmed this when they refused to accept the doctor's supposed insanity as his defense; despite the rhetoric about Sacheverell's madness, he was thought competent enough to be politically culpable. Tory admissions that Sacheverell was guilty of "folly, madness and the greatest extravagance in the world," but not of high crimes and misdemeanors, did not sway the doctor's prosecutors.[43] To them, Sacheverell was as crazed and dangerous as James Stuart. He was a pretender to authority, and "Force without Authority" is a state of war.

The quixotic figure of Sacheverell is thus a bundle of contradictions. He is crazy yet calculating, ridiculous yet dangerous, errant yet methodical. As a quixote, he embodies the very conflation of rational thought and political interestedness that the Whig theory of reason had tried to minimize. Quixotism serves as a recurring reminder that reason may not be disinterested, for under the law of the stronger, the victorious always have the resources with which to rationalize their conduct. Tellingly, while impugning Sacheverell's rationality, Touchwood rehearses the following anecdote:

> Once upon a time a certain Doctor, a Man of great Brawn and Muscle, Large, Tall and Termagant, hapned to Preach before King *Charles* the IId. being heated with his Subject, much warm'd by Proofs, and impatient of Contradiction, even in the looks of an Audience, on a sudden he stript up, and shew'd the amazed Congregation a most thundring Arm, with which he strook the Cushion, and was heard to cry out—*And dares any Body here deny this?*—The King shrunk back, and mutter'd to himself: *No Body in his senses,* Doctor, *within reach of You.*[44]

In this story, the monarch's peril before the preacher's vehemence parallels the dangers that the Whigs saw in the Sacheverell affair. The threat to the monarch comes in the form of a reasoned articulation that, when confronted with resistance, swiftly and naturally shades into violence: "heated with his Subject," "warm'd by Proofs," "impatient of Contradiction," the doctor resorts to belligerent display. For the force of reason, he substitutes reason by force. As an obvious barb thrown Sacheverell's way, Touchwood satirically remarks that this doctor's forceful, argumentative style "is proving the present existence of *Giants* [and *H]obgoblins* with a Vengeance, 'tis a pithy way of deciding a [C]ontroversy, and very much practiced in our *Modern Church Chivalry*."[45] As chivalry is an institution under which controversies are decided by might of arms, Sacheverell and all his brother firebrand high-flyers, Touchwood suggests, are guilty not only of treasonous behavior against the state, but also of subverting the rule of reason. Their arguments not only endanger the present government, but their style of arguing—their method—jeopardizes the idea of reason as a rule that "obliges every one," as an authority that neither succumbs to, nor exercises, arbitrary power.

Thus, despite its comedy, quixotism raises as a serious concern the difficulty of distinguishing between rational and irrational rules. The notion that "all Government . . . is the product only of Force and Violence, and that Men live together by no other Rules but that of Beasts, where the strongest carries it," Locke had argued, would lay "a Foundation of perpetual Disorder and Mischief, Tumult, Sedition and Rebellion" (*TT* 267–8). Reason, he had claimed, should provide these other "Rules" of conduct, thereby ensuring the uncontested good order of a secure and peaceful state. The behavior of the quixotic Sacheverell upset this reassuring model by confronting its adherents with a much publicized, alternate rationality. Because of the doctor's popularity and influence, Sacheverell's enemies had to respond to him as though he were sane, yet could hardly admit that he was so, for to admit his sanity would be to confess that he came to valid rational conclusions different from their own. A sane Sacheverell would require inquiry into the much more complicated political and epistemological problem of rational diversity—an oxymoronic term by Locke's universalist standards. The idea of rational diversity supplants reason with mere reasons, making rational authority, like political power, an object of contention rather than a disinterested, ethical guide. Under Revolution Principles, rational diversity must be shunned as a sort of Jacobitism of the mind, where the rule of reason is perpetually threatened, like the Protestant succession, by dangerous pretenders plotting close to home.

The "Age of Reason" in England, I would argue, was actually an "Age of Reasons," a world feared by its inhabitants to be universally quixotic. No party appeared to represent universal reason in the Sacheverell controversy. "The History of the Imp[eachme]nt: OR, The Nation's gone mad" ridicules the absurdity of Sacheverell's Tory rioters, "by force of Arms they would prove,/That they had no *Right* to rebel,"[46] while "The Age of Riddles: Or, A True list of certain extraordinary Positions, formerly call'd Contradictions, but now distinguish'd by no Names at all, Faithfully extracted from several Modern Doctrines and Practices" reasons slyly against the Whigs: "I. ALL Government is overturn'd by Obedience, and establish'd by being resisted. Therefore, II. The most eminent Instance of Loyalty, is, to condemn

Subjection; and he is the greatest Rebel that preaches against Rebellion."[47] Doctor Sacheverell committed high crimes and misdemeanors against the rule of reason because his views compelled others to confront their own inconsistencies. A party that had deposed a monarch for being interested (and therefore tyrannical) had to rationalize why its own power was not likewise interested (and therefore tyrannical). As one critic fumed against Revolution Principles, "To cure the *tyranny* of a *king*, by setting up the *people*, is setting 10000 *tyrants* over us instead of *one*."[48] The puzzle before Revolution apologists was how to legitimate their own authority, how to avoid appearing quixotic. "THE true Spirit of *Quixotism*, or *Martial Lunacy*," wrote the Tory *Examiner* (1710–16), chiding Whig alarmists in 1714, "consists in forming strong Ideas of imaginary Dangers and Adventures, and in violent fits of a Romantick Rage or Impulse, work'd up to such a Height, that every thing, which comes in the way, is taken for an Enemy." Don Quixote, in the "Extremities of his Distemper," the *Examiner* pointedly reminds the Whigs, "mistook *Windmills* for *Giants*, *Puppets* for *Knights-Errant*, *Flocks of Sheep* for *Armies*, *Inn-keepers* for *Magicians*," and—in an amazing parallel to the practices of Whig propagandists—"almost every think [*sic*] he met upon the Road, was call'd *Chevalier*." Quixotism is everywhere, the *Examiner* warns:

> Instead of touching here and there a weak Head, or reaching only to a few frolicksome Individuals, it has Infected whole Bodies and Societies of Warlike *Enthusiasts*: . . . our *Romantick Madmen* march up and down in Troops and Squadrons: The Regularity and Resemblance of their Frenzy creates Order and Discipline.[49]

To Tory observers, Whig madness too had a method.

Beginning with a "dangerous" text, promoting assaults on authority, and resulting in absurd and violent conflict that made reason look like arbitrary power, the Sacheverell affair added quixotic emphasis to an already quixotic time. The Duke of Buckingham's announcement during Sacheverell's trial— namely, that he "was more desireous to know which was the stronger party than which of them had the juster and better cause"[50]—captures the uncertainty and discomfort entailed by quixotism. In the end, the accused quixote triumphed in the Sacheverell case; Whig authority was turned into jest as the administration managed to gain a conviction but was unable to follow through with a respectably severe sentence. Sacheverell emerged from the proceedings a wealthy national hero, as numerous admirers showered him with gifts and entertainments during the glorious progress he staged just after the trial. Moreover, with the help of the trial's publicity, the Tory party soundly defeated the Whigs in the general election of 1710.[51] When all was said and done, Sacheverell's prosecutors themselves appeared to have been the real quixotes, bustling and sweating with endless toil and care to build at last strange castles in the air.

Universal quixotism

Quixotism, as the Whigs learned to their cost, is a relative condition. Seen as an aberration—as an errancy—quixotism takes shape only against an agreed-upon alternative. It exists in contrast to common understanding and common principles, the commonness of which can be modified through political arts—as Sacheverell attempted to do by delivering and publishing his sermon, which the Whig administration then attempted to counter by putting him on trial for it. If universal reason springs from nature, quixotism springs from art. And art, in politics and ideas, is much more ubiquitous than nature, for "nature" can always be invented, denied, and reinvented again by anyone with an interest in doing so. The authority to concoct these systematic fictions of universal nature, when exercised by everyone, is universal quixotism—a bewildering explosion of rational political difference that depicts reason as always already arbitrary and artificial. Replacing reason with a plethora of reasons, universal quixotism parodies the comprehensive pretensions of disinterested rational authority, mocking as quixotic and tyrannical those who would demand that their own particular notions be recognized as reason itself. Universal quixotism denies reason its status as universal, unbiased and above politics, instead substituting a vision of intellectual and political life in which no rational standards are stable, no histories impartial and no authority disinterested. The final two sections of this chapter will explore the epistemology of quixotism, focusing in particular on the vertiginously disconcerting interdependence of artful contrivance, learned authority and the arbitrariness of "principles."

Locke himself acknowledges the means by which quixotism can eclipse reason. His epistemology, in contrast to his political theory, readily concedes the artificiality of most people's understandings.[52] Lacking innate ideas, a person's mind can be imposed upon arbitrarily, a process that Locke holds responsible for political difference. "[H]owever strange it may seem," Locke asserts,

> it may really come to pass, that *Doctrines*, that have been derived from no better original, than the Superstition of a Nurse, or the Authority of an old Woman; may, by length of time, and consent of Neighbours, *grow up to the dignity of Principles* in Religion and Morality. For such, who are careful (as they call it) to principle Children well, (and few there be who have not a set of those Principles for them, which they believe in) instil into the unwary, and as yet, unprejudiced Understanding, (for white Paper receives any Characters) those Doctrines they would have them retain and profess.
>
> (*Essay* 81)

Principles are wondrously malleable because people are so easily imposed upon by art: "white Paper receives any Characters." Even the spurious tales of that most unreasonable of populations—nurses and old women—may through custom and consent *"grow up to the dignity of Principles."* Raised in these principles, men grow zealous for *"Absurdities and Errors,"* and will "contend . . . fight, and die in defence of their Opinions," Locke warns (*Essay* 83). Their reason looks like madness to those raised with different principles—their heroism appears quixotic—for there is little structural difference between the two conditions. "[M]*ad Men* . . . do not appear to me to have lost the Faculty of Reasoning," Locke concedes:

> but having joined together some *Ideas* wrongly, they mistake them for Truths; and they err as Men do, that argue right from wrong Principles. For by the violence of their Imaginations, having taken their Fancies for Realities, they make right deductions from them.
>
> (*Essay* 161)

With an act of "violence" causing them to take "Fancies for Realities," madmen reason rightly but proceed from "wrong Principles." Theirs is a rational madness: they pursue, with rigor and consistency, principles that they believe to be right, but that others believe to be wrong. Their logic is flawless—their assumptions, however, unfortunately mistaken. Committed to what others ridicule as *"Absurdities and Errors,"* rational madmen bear a striking resemblance to proponents of political opposition.

With the difference between reason and quixotism thus hanging on controversial distinctions between right and wrong principles, Revolution apologists can hardly be faulted for the urgency with which they sought to establish and defend Revolution Principles. The disputants in the politicized intellectual debates of the early eighteenth century sensed that historical interpretation and the principles it conveyed might be as arbitrary as arbitrary power. "Success qualifies the Action," as Prior insists. Bringing the notion home to England, Prior elaborates:

> WE need not go from our own Country, or our own Memory for Instances of this Kind; the DUKE of MONMOUTH came to England with Liberty and Property, and the Protestant Religion on his Standard: He was beaten and Beheaded, his Honors were taken from his Family. The Prince of Orange does the same thing, he is Successfull, is Crowned King of England, transmits an Imortal Memory to Posterity; Gives us a new Epoche of Time, and a different Sett of Principles from the Revolution.
>
> (Prior 1: 598–9)

Not the least of William's advantages now is his ability to transmit an "Imortal Memory," a history to exalt and perpetuate the "different Sett of Principles" that will define rational belief and conduct in the new epoch. Genre, in this case, has immense political significance, for what passes as authentic history will determine what must be relegated to romance, fable, seditious ravings and pretty poetic lies. History, Prior intimates, rationalizes the law of the stronger.

Fancifully expanding upon this insight, Prior presents "A Dialogue between Charles the Emperour and Clenard the Grammarian," which directly compares the arbitrary power of tyrant and historian. In this dialogue of the dead, Charles V (1500–58), Holy Roman Emperor (1519–56) and suspected quixote,[53] argues with the scholar Nicolas Clenard (c. 1493–1542) over "which of Us Two had most Power" (Prior 1: 601). "Facts, Clenard, real visible Facts are on my side," Charles expostulates, insisting that he, as monarch, had the greater power in life. "Thy Glory is only Speculative, Meer imagination," Charles informs Clenard: "To alter the Constitution of Provinces, to raise or Depose Princes, to give War or Peace as I pleased. This has laid the foundation of a lasting renown for me and a Monument upon which Fame must sit for ever" (Prior 1: 607). Charles' deeds, however, leave Clenard unawed, for the scholar quickly dismisses Charles' accomplishments as mere puerile mischief:

> Suppose I should walk my Children over other Mens Gardens, let 'em pull down the Hedges, root up the Melons, and Rob the Orchard, what would People say, but that I was a Senseless Creature, and a Drunken Sott. But yet when one of You Princes take a Fancy to Burn whole Towns, and lay the Provinces round them Desolate You seem Satisfyed when You Answer it was for your Glory.
>
> (Prior 1: 607)

Trespass, destruction, theft and wanton violence have been glorified in princes though rebuked in children, Clenard observes, hinting at the arbitrariness of the distinction. "Take this as a Maxim," he continues,

> Facts depend upon Words, The greatest Monarch and most Fortunate Captain, allowing his Cause to be strictly just, and the Event equally Fortunate is obliged for the Recital to a dealer either in Syntax or Prosodia. The out lines and drawings are only seen in the bare Action of the hero, But 'tis the Scholar that adds the heightnings and Colorings that gives the Beauty, nay faith, in great measure the very life and Substance to the Picture. So that this lasting Monument of which You seem so fond is founded upon the Pleasure of us Gramarians.
>
> (Prior 1: 608)

Seizing upon the very proof of Charles' power—his ability to do as he pleased—Clenard reveals it to belong more properly to "us Gramarians," thereby effectively relieving Charles of his vaunted agency. The whim, will and pleasure of Charles can never outlive the pleasure of scholars, Clenard boasts: "Age and Accident deface the Tomb, And, it is only one of Us Scholars that must take an Account of Your true Worth, and transmit it safe to succeeding Generations" (Prior 1: 608). Clenard thus argues that there is little difference between his scholarship—Charles calls it "Pedantry"—and the emperor's "Princely way of thinking" (Prior 1: 599). The power of the hero to change history is not so great as the power of the historian to do the same. The Hack in Swift's *Tale* invokes a related privilege, boldly asserting "I claim an absolute Authority in Right, as the *freshest Modern*, which gives me a Despotick Power over all Authors before me" (Swift 1: 81). As the *"freshest Modern"*—that is, as the author who is still writing—the Hack may freely indulge his despotic imagination, tyrannizing over all previous authors in order to rewrite history.[54]

Prior's satiric theory of history conflates knowledge with power, thereby denying the disinterestedness of learned authority. Critical pronouncements, Prior complains in 1710, are the edicts of tyrants, pedants and madmen, who govern taste and set standards arbitrarily. The occasion for Prior's disgust was a Whig panegyrical poem by Dr Samuel Garth, published in honor of the Lord Treasurer Godolphin, whose fortunes not improving since the Sacheverell trial, had been forced to resign the following August.[55] "THE *Collective* Body of the Whigs have already engross'd our Riches; and their *Representative* the *Kit cat*, have pretended to make a Monopoly of our Sense," Prior fulminates:

> 'Tis the Misfortune of our *Athens*, like that of Ancient *Greece*, to be govern'd by a set number of Tyrants: The Works of Learned Men are weigh'd here by the unerring Balance of Party; and he is sure to be most Ingenious in his Writings, who is, in their Phrase, most *thorough-pac'd* in his Politicks.
>
> (Prior 1: 389)

For Prior, the Whig domination over material and intellectual culture is seamless and all-encompassing, engrossing riches, monopolizing sense and exercising the learned in *"thorough-pac'd"* politics. Addison's Kit Cat Club, where *"Cato"* gives "his little Senate laws,"[56] imperiously decrees critical standards, forcing genius to submit to the "unerring Balance of Party." Under this critical despotism, "unerring" because tyrannically self-justifying, the "Works of Learned Men" dwindle into arbitrary instruments of political control, becoming chains and encumbrances rather than enlightening and liberating ideas.

Addison, of course, disagreed. He twice responded angrily to Prior's essay, at one point belittling it for having "so much of the Pedant" about it.[57] In attacking Prior's position, however, Addison was not entirely denying his opponent's disgruntled assessment of the relation between politics and good judgment. "A furious Party Spirit, when it rages in its full Violence, exerts it self in Civil War and Blood-shed," Addison warns in 1711: "It fills a Nation with Spleen and Rancour, and extinguishes all the Seeds of Good-nature, Compassion and Humanity." Not only is fellow-feeling lost, but rational evaluation, too:

> If this Party Spirit has so ill an Effect on our Morals, it has likewise a very great one upon our Judgments. We often hear a poor insipid Paper or Pamphlet cryed up, and sometimes a noble Piece depreciated by those who are of a different Principle from the Author. One who is actuated by this Spirit is almost under an Incapacity of discerning either real Blemishes or Beauties. A Man of Merit in a different Principle, is like an Object seen in two different Mediums, that appears crooked or broken, however streight and entire it may be in it self . . . As Men formerly became eminent in learned Societies by their Parts and Acquisitions, they now distinguish themselves by the Warmth and Violence with which they espouse their respective Parties. Books are valued upon the like Considerations: An Abusive, Scurrilous Style passes for Satyr, and a dull Scheme of Party Notions is called fine Writing.[58]

Like Prior, Addison too laments the scarcity of neutral standards. Yet whereas Prior seems willing to impute party spirit to interest, ambition and the desire to monopolize, Addison finds it harder to disentangle ambitious interest from the honest intentions of politically committed men. Party spirit, he argues, goes beyond hypocrisy, for hypocrisy requires a common standard against which actions are to be measured. Factionalism, on the contrary, imposes a limitation on judgment, fundamentally altering one's ability to perceive and evaluate: "One who is actuated by this Spirit is almost under an Incapacity of discerning either real Blemishes or Beauties." Comparing intellectual and aesthetic evaluation to the empirical verification of knowledge promoted by the new philosophy, Addison speculates that party spirit distorts the very process of observation. "Principle," he suggests, is like a refracting medium that causes misperception even in an observer dedicated to the most exacting impartiality. Under the influence of differing principles, men of merit can rationally, deliberately and violently disagree, each as thoroughly unwitting of his own bias as a man who, unaware of the presence of the refracting medium in the example above, would insist that the object he saw was in fact crooked or broken. This "dreadful Spirit of Division . . . destroys even Common Sense," Addison complains, recognizing that not even facts can be trusted to speak for themselves when they must first be filtered through "Principle." In response to this escalating political and intellectual fragmentation, Addison calls for "an honest Body of Neutral Forces" to band together in order to eliminate faction. Regrettably, he leaves no instructions on how this honest neutrality might be recognized or agreed upon.

Conspicuously absent from Addison's analysis is any direct consideration of his own paper's political intent, and the role of his own interests as an author within the system of "Neutral Forces" he promotes. As a self-proclaimed arbiter of intellectual standards, Addison deplores the incapacitating bias of other arbiters, yet offers little reassurance that his own judgment is not similarly limited. John Barrell has discussed how increasing occupational specialization over the course of the eighteenth century exacerbated this sense of intellectual limitation. If society's "unity was defined as being produced out of the competing but cooperative labours of different occupational groups," Barrell argues, "then to be a member of such a group was to have only a partial view of the organization of society as a whole."[59] The disinterested or general view became increasingly difficult to identify as the economy diversified and occupational specialties multiplied, Barrell contends, a development particularly challenging to laborers who supposedly trade, like the periodical essayist, in common sense, common judgment, common morals—in short, in common principles. Prior's complaint that Addison and the Kit Cats "make a Monopoly of our Sense" shrewdly stirs suspicions of authorial interestedness by comparing Addison's intellectual motives to economic greed. If Addison is confined by his interests, yet claims the voice of universal authority, then he speaks the language of quixotes and tyrants. Barrell has noted how Addison, alert to such criticism, sought to prop up the authority of Mr Spectator by positioning the persona as a disinterested and neutral (non-laboring) gentleman.[60] Addison's elusive irony further reveals his discomfort with the slippery ground he and his fellow authors occupy as individuals who vend their particular notions as general knowledge. As an authorial strategy, the selfconscious, ironic style of the eighteenth-century periodical essay defends against charges of quixotism by anticipating them.

Steele, for example, archly exposes his own quixotism in the sly self-satire of *Tatler* no. 178, an essay that begins by ridiculing Mr Bickerstaff's quixotic friend the political upholsterer. Don Quixote, Bickerstaff reminds his readers in this essay, lost his wits by trying too diligently to "unravel . . . Sense" from difficult sentences such as *"The Reason of the Unreasonableness, which against my Reason is wrought, doth so weaken my Reason, as with all Reason I do justly complain on your Beauty."*[61] The ironic aptness of so much *"Reason"* in one sentence causing quixotic madness is particularly sharp when seen against the period's political problem of universal reason. As ridiculous as Don Quixote is, Bickerstaff assures his audience, "it is very certain we have Crowds among us as far gone in as visible a Madness as his, tho' they are not observed to be in that Condition" (*Tatler* 2: 468). Numbering among this crowd is Bickerstaff's friend the upholsterer, whose madness manifests itself as a passion for politics. Making his appearance in four *Tatler* essays in 1710,[62] the quixotic upholsterer's political mania coincides with the publicity of the Sacheverell trial. "I have . . . with the utmost Care and Pains applied my self to the reading all Writings and Pamphlets which have come out since the Tryal, and have studied Night and Day in order to be Master of the whole Controversy," the upholsterer writes to Bickerstaff. "But the Authors are so numerous, and the State of Affairs alters so very fast," the studious upholsterer complains, "that I am now a Fortnight behind-hand in my Reading, and know only how Things stood Twelve Days ago. I wish you would enter into those useful Subjects; for, if I may be allowed to say so, these are not Times to jest in" (*Tatler* 3: 200). Busily absorbed by his readings, the upholsterer betrays a complete misunderstanding of his own relation to the very problems he laments. With authors "so numerous" and developments coming "so very fast" that he cannot keep up with his reading, the upholsterer foolishly exacerbates his own difficulties by urging Bickerstaff to add to the already overwhelming volume of literature. His earnest request for Bickerstaff's authoritative assistance—because "these are not Times to jest in"—is itself an unwitting jest, for Bickerstaff, as *Tatler* no. 178 clearly shows, is himself quixotic. In appealing to Bickerstaff as a serious and competent judge, the upholsterer turns jest into authority.

Bickerstaff's own quixotism begins to show as he settles into the magisterial role of disinterested critic. Lunacy of the upholsterer's sort plagues the entire nation, he observes, his analysis at first sounding eminently rational:

> This Touch in the Brain of the *British* Subject, is as certainly owing to the reading News-Papers, as that of the *Spanish* Worthy above-mention'd to the reading Works of Chivalry. My Contemporaries the Novelists have, for the better spinning out Paragraphs, and working down to the End of the Columns, a most happy Art in saying and unsaying, giving Hints of Intelligence, and Interpretations of indifferent Actions, to the great Disturbance of the Brains of ordinary Readers. This Way of going on in the Words, and making no Progress in the Sense, is more particularly the Excellence of my most ingenious and renowned Fellow-Labourer the *Post-Man*; and it is to this Talent in him that I impute the Loss of my Upholsterer's Intellects.
>
> (*Tatler* 2: 469)

A generic style that obscures meaning, rather than rendering it plain, addled Don Quixote's brains, Bickerstaff alleges, and now this same prose style—the language of ridiculous romances and rival newspapers—diverts British subjects to distraction as they try to tease out its meanings. Disapprovingly, Bickerstaff remarks that the political economy of Britain cannot help but languish in the throes of such an epistemological disturbance: "The Tautology, the Contradictions, the Doubts, and Wants of Confirmations, are what keep up imaginary Entertainments in empty Heads, and produce Neglect of their own Affairs, Poverty, and Bankruptcy, in many of the Shop-Statesmen" (*Tatler*

2: 471). Bickerstaff regards the upholsterer's "Intellects" as disordered precisely because the tradesman attempts to imagine things beyond his "own Affairs"; he tries to comprehend the general view, to understand the organization of society as a whole, to meddle in interests more properly reserved for politicians, gentlemen and especially newspaper writers. By indulging themselves in the "imaginary Entertainments" encouraged by profit-seeking newspaper authors, the upholsterer and his like-minded friends become a hybrid creation, "Shop-Statesmen," who perform the function of neither.

As the analysis unfolds, Bickerstaff implicates himself as a periodical writer in the production of the quixotic, by blaming periodicals for the strange madness that besets the nation. His care to identify a rival paper as the prime subverter of British intellects only emphasizes the doubtfulness of Bickerstaff's own claims; Steele presents a persona too obviously interested in the matter to be a credible authority. Bickerstaff's attempt to portray his rival as quixotic—the *Post-Man*, like Don Quixote, is "most ingenious and renowned"—eventually backfires as Bickerstaff's account of the "Touch in the Brain of the *British* Subject" too nearly resembles the reports it maligns. Bickerstaff's own prose—"it is very certain we have Crowds among us far gone in as visible a Madness as his [Don Quixote's], tho' they are not observed to be in that Condition"—mimics "the Contradictions, the Doubts, and Wants of Confirmations" that "keep up imaginary Entertainments in empty Heads," for in effect, Bickerstaff here ludicrously reports that very certainly, we have crowds *visibly* mad though *no one sees* them. Supposedly inveighing against quixotism and its meaningless style, Bickerstaff succeeds only in replicating them. Neither Bickerstaff nor the upholsterer appear very trustworthy by the end of the essay, for paradoxically, the upholsterer's credibility is rendered suspect by his interest in matters far from his own affairs, while Bickerstaff's authority is thoroughly compromised by his interest in matters near to his own affairs. As in the case of Captain Mostyn, the neutral reader must determine whether ignorance or interestedness is the better guide.

I should stress, however, that though Bickerstaff's quixotism appears self-interested, it should not be automatically equated with calculated self-interest. Rather, like Dr Drench and Mr Brief in Henry Fielding's play *Don Quixote in England*, Bickerstaff looks quixotic precisely because his self-aggrandizement seems so unwitting. In Fielding's play, Don Quixote travels to England, where his behavior is observed by the keen professional eyes of a doctor, Drench, and a lawyer, Brief. "Poor Man! poor man! he must be put to bed," Dr Drench exclaims, "His frenzy is very high; but I hope we shall be able to take it off." To which Mr Brief counters: "His frenzy! his roguery. The fellow's a rogue; he is no more mad than I am; and the coachman and landlord both have very good actions at law against him" (Fielding, *Works* 3: 96). To the doctor, Don Quixote must be ailing, while to the lawyer, he must be criminal. Thinking only in terms of their own spheres, Dr Drench and Mr Brief find patients and rogues respectively, as readily as Don Quixote, in his sphere of knight-errantry, finds giants, caitiff knights and damsels in distress. Drench and Brief are as singularly focused as the mad knight, each interpreting the world in a way that drums up business for himself: if Don Quixote is frenzied, then he needs the services of a doctor; if he is a rogue, then someone needs a lawyer. Drench's and Brief's analyses argue the importance of the respective professions of Drench and Brief. The comedy of the incident, however, arises less from this self-aggrandizement than from the fact that it might be wholly unselfconscious. Drench and Brief may honestly believe in the disinterested-ness of their own assessments, for their professional interests cannot be easily disarticulated from their sincere, reasoned opinions. After all, doctors meet many who ail, while lawyers meet many who cheat. The two professionals can hardly be faulted for discovering in Don Quixote what their experience and training have taught them to find. The scene's full humor comes with recog-nizing that Don Quixote's madness parallels Drench's and Brief's considered, professional judgments—that his quixotism is very much like their reason. Ironically, Brief's assertion about Don Quixote—"he is no more mad than I am"—appears to be true, and the play concludes with a song, "All mankind are mad, 'tis plain" (Fielding, *Works* 3: 118).

The universal quixotism that Fielding comically dramatizes and Steele archly inhabits turns authority into jest by skewering intellect that too facilely presumes disinterested credibility and general relevance for itself. Grudgingly, even Addison concedes the difficulty of maintaining intellectual dignity, though trying gallantly to salvage his own authority as a learned man. "A Man who has been brought up among Books, and is able to talk of nothing else, is a very indifferent Companion, and what we call a Pedant," Addison allows. "But, methinks," he adds, shielding men of letters from being singled out for derision, "that we should enlarge the Title, and give it every one that does not know how to think out of his Profession, and particular way of Life." What Steele describes as quixotism—unselfconscious circumscription within one's own trifling interests—Addison represents as a kind of pedantry, one which produces numerous examples: "the meer Man of the Town," whose narrow knowledge does not exceed "the Verge of the Court," yet who prides himself on his "Exemption from the Pedantry of the Colleges"; "the Military Pedant," who, "if you take away his Artillery . . . has not a Word to say for himself"; the "State-Pedant," like Steele's upholsterer, "wrapt up in News, and lost in Politicks" (*Spectator* 1: 437–8). "In short," Addison concludes, "a meer Courtier, a meer Soldier, a meer Scholar, a meer any thing, is an insipid Pedantick Character, and equally ridiculous." Having thus leveled all profes-sions by universalizing the ridicule, Addison at last recuperates the value of scholars:

> Of all the Species of Pedants, which I have mentioned, the Book-Pedant is much the most supportable; he has at least an exercised Understanding, and a Head which is full though confused, so that a

Man who converses with him may often receive from him hints of his
own Advantage, tho' they are of little use to the Owner.

(Spectator 1: 438)

Significantly, Addison's "most supportable" kind of pedant still lacks awareness of the wider relevance of his learning. His knowledge is a repository of
"little use" to himself, because he does not know what to do with it, but which
"a Man who converses with him" may mine to "his own Advantage." The
book-pedant is the most supportable kind of pedant because his knowledge, at
least, can be salvaged by the only reliable mind to emerge from Addison's
teeming metropolis of universal pedantry: the elusive, unspecified "Man who
converses" with the book-pedant. This vague character, in his anonymity and
presumed (rather than demonstrated) authoritative disinterestedness, is much
like Mr Spectator himself: the observer, not the observed; the representer, not
the represented; the reporter, not the reported. He controls interpretation by
avoiding being interpreted.

Yet Mr Spectator's presumed neutrality, however honestly believed by
himself, is the essence of quixotism. It is precisely the lack of self-scrutiny—
disavowal of alternative interpretations of one's own ideas and actions, the
confidence in one's authority to control meaning and monopolize sense—that
is the quixote's hallmark. Quixotism draws attention to the multiplicity of
perspectives, interpretations and rationales that can coexist in the world; it
explores rational diversity. Quixotes, tyrants, pedants and enthusiasts
ominously parody the idea of universal reason by insisting on the general relevance of their own systems of thought. Reason is universal, Locke had
proclaimed. Tyrants, pedants, quixotes and enthusiasts would be among the
very first to agree. Read against the proliferation of these character types, the
natural law of reason—imagined as an impartial control on the whims of arbitrary power—itself appears to be out of control, the result of impertinent
behavior, particular interests and grandiose ambitions, not their justification.
Little distinguishes the rational man from the tyrant, pedant, quixote or
enthusiast. Quixotes act tyrannically, pedants strut quixotically, and a meaningful contrast between the enthusiast (a man who forms parties after his own
particular notions and brings about revolutions based upon ungrounded
beliefs) and Locke's rational political agent (a man who forms parties after
Locke's own particular notions in order to uphold Revolution Principles)
appears tenuous at best. When the law of reason is effectively challenged as
being mere fiction rather than nature, Locke's reason dwindles into quixotism.

Rebellious subjects: gender, arbitrary power and the natural order

One final example of the serious meanings attached to quixotism during the
period can be found in the witty controversy surrounding the custom of

gender hierarchy. Quixotism, as I have argued above, rests on artifice, not nature; it describes an arbitrary order that creates, rather than reflects, the natural world. By raising doubts about the natural foundations of rational conduct, quixotism obscures the difference between absurd radicalism and simple logic. The dispute over gender hierarchy was fundamentally quixotic in this regard, for the controversy turned on whether male supremacy expressed a rational order ordained by nature, or merely imposed an arbitrary one contrived by artful men. Proponents of gender equality used the rhetoric of Revolution Principles and empiricist epistemology to argue the second point. They undermined the venerable cultural practice of male dominance by recasting it as an arbitrary innovation—a deviation from nature invented by ambitious men. In the context of Lockean epistemology and Revolution Principles, the absurd radicalism of women's equality becomes simple logic.[63]

In the *Two Treatises*, Locke is primarily concerned with conflicts between men, not conflicts between men and women. Accordingly, he gives little attention to antagonisms of the latter kind. Where he does explicitly address how to mediate disagreements between husbands and wives, he makes short work of the matter by glibly sacrificing the interests of the wife to the couple's collective good, that is, to her husband's preferences:

> the Husband and the Wife, though they have but one common Concern, yet having different understandings, will unavoidably sometimes have different wills too; it therefore being necessary, that the last Determination, *i.e.* the Rule, should be placed somewhere, it naturally falls to the Man's share, as the abler and the stronger.
>
> (*TT* 321)

For the sake of their "common Concern," the disputes born of "different understandings" and "different wills" between men and women ultimately require that someone be given the final word—"the last Determination"—"the Rule." Reasoning that this right to rule "naturally" falls to men "as the abler and the stronger," Locke conflates men's and women's "different understandings" with their physical differences, in order to give the upper hand to men. The apparent arbitrariness of this masculine advantage—the rule "should be placed somewhere," anywhere, simply because it is necessary to override unavoidable differences—is thus barely glimpsed before being quickly, conveniently and "naturally" denied. In deference to the "common Concern," women should naturally obey men.

As many post-Revolution writers recognized, however, this logic of natural obedience runs counter to Locke's epistemology and his Revolution Principles. For if, as Locke surmises, it is possible for men to receive "*Doctrines*, that have been derived from no better original, than the Superstition of a Nurse, or the Authority of an old Woman," and to elevate these "*Absurdities and Errors*" into the "*dignity of Principles*" (*Essay* 81), then it is also possible that the principle of man's superior rational ability is itself one of these absurdities. Locke's smooth elision of man as "the abler and the stronger" need not be assumed. Yet if man is thought to be only the stronger, not also the abler, he has insufficient grounds to rule over woman under Revolution Principles, for "Force without Authority"—strength without reason—is arbitrary power, mere tyranny. Gender equality would therefore appear eminently more reasonable than gender inequality, turning radicalism into simple logic. "To endeavour refuting an Opinion of so long standing as that of *the Superiority of the Men over the Women, with respect to Genius and Abilities*," writes "a Lady," the anonymous author of *Female Rights Vindicated* (1758), "must appear to many a strange and impracticable Attempt; and Numbers, even of Women, misled by Prejudice and Custom, may believe no one would be so *Quixotic* as to list herself Champion of the Sex upon this Occasion."[64] Quixotism, this author suggests, is actually true reason rendered unfamiliar by the impositions of "Custom."

Other writers agreed, challenging the logic of the rationale given for male supremacy.[65] "The Men by Interest and Inclination," writes Judith Drake in 1696,

> are so generally engag'd against us, that it is not to be expected, that any one Man of Wit should arise so generous as to engage in our Quarrel, and be the Champion of our Sex against the Injuries and Oppressions of his own. Those Romantick days are over, and there is not so much as a *Don Quixot* of the Quill left to succour the distressed Damsels.[66]

With the "Interest and Inclination" of men determining the standards of reason, a defense of women's equality against these interests must appear quixotic. The fact that no man will come forward to be "Champion of our Sex against the Injuries and Oppressions of his own" argues not the weakness of the cause, Drake intimates, only the thorough and pervasive extent of male bias. Drake must therefore become her own "*Don Quixot* of the Quill," confronting Locke's giant, uncritical conflation of men's supposedly greater ability and strength. She sallies forth philosophically, arguing,

> if we [women] be naturally defective, the Defect must be either in Soul or Body. In the Soul it can't be, if what I have hear'd some learned Men maintain, be true, that all Souls are equal, and alike, and that consequently there is no such distinction, as Male and Female Souls; that there are no innate *Idea's*, but that all the Notions we have, are deriv'd from our External Senses, either immediately, or by Reflection.

> (Drake 11–12)

In Drake's interpretation of Locke's empiricist epistemology, the gendered soul must be banished along with all other innate ideas. Male advantage would then exist only in "Body," making men superior to women only in strength. Drake's mock modesty—evident in her arch conditional phrase, "if what I have hear'd some learned Men maintain, be true"—highlights the potential absurdities and errors of sexist understanding: the weakness of her own argument, if any, Drake suggests, is its willingness to rely upon the opinions of "learned Men." To deny Drake's conclusion that "Male and Female Souls" are equal would be to confess the error of man's learned opinion. Yet to accept the authority of such "learned Men" would be to admit the political irrelevance of man's superior physical strength, for as Drake points out, still in keeping with Locke's teachings, a stronger body should not command greater authority in a rational society. Acknowledging man's superior physical power, Drake's logic is satirically impeccable. She shows proper respect for this greater power by proposing that women be educated in "Arithmetick, and other Arts which require not much bodily strength," so that

> they might supply the places of abundance of lusty Men now employ'd in sedentary Business; which would be a mighty profit to the Nation by sending those Men to Employments, where hands and strength are more requir'd, especially at this time when we are in such want of People.
>
> (Drake 17)

This "want of People" probably refers to the soldiers England needed for its war on the Continent, hence the more masculine employments Drake alludes to here are those of military service. The superiority of male physical strength, she pointedly suggests, earns men the right to be killed by other men, not the right to dominate women. Her analysis falls wholly in line with Locke's own critique of tyranny. Superior force, without the authority of superior reason, is a state of war; so men, whose superiority resides in body only, should be sent to the front.

Satirical arguments like Drake's continued throughout the century. "Strength of Mind goes along with Strength of Body," Mary Astell mockingly remarks, "and 'tis only for some odd Accidents which Philosophers have not yet thought worth while to enquire into, that the sturdiest Porter is not the wisest Man!"[67] Likewise, the pseudonymous Sophia at mid-century maintains that "bare strength intitles the *Men* to no superiority above *us*."[68] "What has greatly help'd to confirm the *Men* in the prejudiced notion of *Women*'s natural weakness, is the common manner of expression which this very vulgar error gave birth too," she explains:

> When they mean to stigmatise a *Man* with want of courage they call him *effeminate*, and when they would praise a *Woman* for her courage

they call her *manly*. But as these, and such like expressions, are merely arbitrary and but a fulsome compliment which the *Men* pass on themselves, they establish no truth.

(Sophia 51)

The "arbitrary" grounds of gendered praise, Sophia reasons, "establish no truth," for they persist merely as self-serving fictions in men's brains. Moreover, even if man's greater strength renders him more fit for military service, it still does not prove his greater social worth. "With regard . . . to warlike employments, it seems to be a disposition of *Providence* that custom has exempted us from them," Sophia concedes, only to follow with a scathing reinterpretation of the meaning of this natural fact: "As sailors in a storm throw overboard their more useless lumber, so it is but fit that the *Men* shou'd be exposed to the dangers and hardships of war, while we remain in safety at home" (Sophia 55–6). Male supremacy in a rational society cannot logically be deduced from man's superior physical strength. By Revolution Principles, such governance is tyrannical and should be resisted.

Resistance to this tyranny was indeed expressed, often in terms borrowed from the rhetoric of the Glorious Revolution. "Tyrant Man," as Lady Mary Chudleigh calls him, is a usurper who deserves to be toppled by lawful rebellion. What men will not suffer themselves, she protests, they hypocritically inflict upon women:

> Passive Obedience you've to us transferr'd,
> And we must drudge in Paths where you have err'd:
> That antiquated Doctrine you disown;
> 'Tis now your Scorn, and fit for us alone.[69]

No longer quixotically imposing that "antiquated Doctrine" upon everyone, "Tyrant Man" now arbitrarily applies it only to women. Astell concurs. "If the Authority of the Husband, so far as it extends, is sacred and inalienable," she inquires, laying a trap for post-Revolutionaries, "why not that of the Prince?" As it must now be confessed, under the new government, that the prince's authority is not sacred and inalienable, Astell can freely assail men with their own rhetoric:

> is not then partial in Men to the last Degree, to contend for, and practise that Arbitrary Dominion in their Families, which they abhor and exclaim against in the State? For if Arbitrary Power is evil in it self, and an improper Method of Governing Rational and Free Agents, it ought not to be practis'd any where; nor is it less, but rather more mischievous in Families than in Kingdoms, by how much 100,000 Tyrants are worse than one.

(Astell 106–7)

As Whigs spoke frequently of "Governing Rational and Free Agents" while Tories bemoaned the certain danger that numerous tyrants (usually in some multiple of ten[70]) would be "worse than one," Astell here lampoons both parties in one passage.[71] By invoking the rational standards of the Glorious Revolution, she compels defenders of male dominance to recognize their irrationality:

> He who has Sovereign Power does not value the Provocations of a Rebellious Subject; he knows how to subdue him with Ease, and will make himself obey'd: But Patience and Submission are the only Comforts that are left to a poor People, who groan under Tyranny, unless they are Strong enough to break the Yoke, to Depose and Abdicate, which, I doubt, would not be allow'd of here. For whatever may be said against Passive-Obedience in another Case, I suppose there's no Man but likes it very well in this; how much soever Arbitrary Power may be dislik'd on a Throne, not *Milton* nor B[enjamin] H[oadly], nor any of the Advocates of Resistance, would cry up Liberty to poor *Female Slaves*, or plead for the Lawfulness of Resisting a private Tyranny.
>
> (Astell 34–5)

The rhetorical bluster of men like the poet John Milton, the Low Churchman Dr Benjamin Hoadly (1676–1761), and other "Advocates of Resistance" who loudly revile tyranny, reverts absurdly into dogmatic espousals of passive obedience when confronted by women seeking relief from "a private Tyranny," Astell drily observes. Locke's law of nature "would not be allow'd of here," it seems, where masculine rule is maintained not for reason's sake, but because men like it this way. Incisively, Astell suggests that society, in its traditional state, is already irrational, arbitrary and tyrannical. "And if meer Power give a Right to Rule," she persists, echoing Locke's disdain for Filmer's quixotism, "there can be no such Thing as Usurpation" (Astell 106). Revolution Principles, if reasonably applied, support women's liberty.

Analyzed in these terms, the system of gender hierarchy becomes an unreasonable practice, a form of quixotism that has been afflicting entire societies for centuries, an absurdity and error raised to the dignity of principle. The spurious stories from which it draws its origin, however, are the histories of men, not the superstitious tales of nurses and old women. By way of example, Judith Drake points to the relation between "history" and the Salic Law, that institution devised to exclude women from sovereign rule. Purporting to offer the true history of this law, Drake describes the restriction as an innovation dreamed up by tyrannical men in order to rationalize and legalize the unnatural power they had usurped from women. The framers of the law, Drake writes, were suspicious, that if the Regal Power shou'd fall often into the hands of Women, they would favour their own Sex, and might in time restore 'em to their Primitive Liberty and Equality with the Men, and so break the neck of that unreasonable Authority they so much affect over us; and therefore made this Law to prevent it. The Historians indeed tell us other Reasons, but they can't agree among themselves, and as Men are Parties against us . . . therefore their Evidence may justly be rejected. To say the truth Madam, I can't tell how to prove all this from Ancient Records; for if any Histories were anciently written by Women, Time, and the Malice of Men have effectually conspir'd to suppress 'em; and it is not reasonable to think that Men shou'd transmit, or suffer to be transmitted to Posterity, any thing that might shew the weakness and illegality of their Title to a Power they still exercise so arbitrarily, and are so fond of.

(Drake 22–3)

Drake's history reiterates the conjectural history told to authorize the Glorious Revolution, copying its language, but introducing gendered terms: men's "unreasonable Authority" and arbitrary power have encroached upon women's "Primitive Liberty and Equality," and therefore should be resisted by rational agents. Undermining the epistemological supports of gender hierarchy, Drake argues that traditional political and institutional arrangements (like the Salic Law) must be rejected, or at least critically re-evaluated as products of the male interests that usurped women's power in the first place. Men and women are of different parties, she alleges, thus calling into doubt all male-authored histories as party propaganda—as interest, not reason. "Historians indeed tell us other Reasons" than her own, Drake concedes, but she quickly dismisses them as uncompelling because not universal: "they can't agree among themselves." Like Bishop Berkeley over a decade later, Drake recognizes the interdependence of political and epistemological standards of truth. Though unable to document her own assertions from "Ancient Records," she can and does point to the foolishness of expecting to find such proofs in these records: "it is not reasonable to think" that men, promoting their partisan interests, would allow the survival of histories that detail "the weakness and illegality" of men's "Title" to power. The historical record is vulnerable to the contrivances of those in power, Drake intimates, thus challenging the very value of history as a rational justification for current cultural forms. With no authoritative history to refer back to, all appeals to history may be mere quixotism.

"[P]ray, what Infallible Rule can your Wisdoms give us, whereby we may distinguish Truth from Falshood in the *Gravest Historians?*" asks one Madam Godfrey in a debate over the respective merits of romance and history in 1697. Her opponent in this quarrel is one "Sir Thomas," who complains that romances render women politically unmanageable.[72] Comparing female romance readers to "*Modern Regicides*," Sir Thomas subordinates women by disparaging their intellect, characterizing them as "great Children" who never outgrew romances. This continued interest in romances, he sarcastically concludes, addressing uppity women directly, is

> [a]n Infallible Proof of what has bin often asserted by *your humble Dotards*, that you have *equal Capacity* with those whom Nature has justly made your Masters, and who leave you to take up with those Exercises, when you come to what shou'd be your Years of Discretion, which they soon after their Infancy learnt to despise, leaving the reading of *Romances*, the making *Dirt-Pyes*, and *playing* with *your Sex* altogether.
>
> (*Challenge* 96)

Like Locke, Sir Thomas associates irrationality with spurious ideas introduced during childhood. Because women never leave this childhood, according to Sir Thomas, women have no right to claim an "*equal Capacity*" with men, whose superior "Nature" causes men to advance beyond romances "soon after their Infancy." Madam Godfrey's rebuttal thus swiftly cuts the legs out from under Sir Thomas' argument by suggesting that men are just as susceptible to arrant fictions, only they are too foolish to realize it. By what "Infallible Rule" can truth be recognized even in the "*Gravest Historians*"?

"I think you rekon *Livy* none of the meanest," Madam Godfrey satirically recalls, using the romance convention of litotes to hint at the fabulousness of the Roman historian's own works. If Livy numbers among the "*Gravest Historians*," then absurdity must be a common characteristic of serious history as well as of fanciful romance, Godfrey reasons. "[W]ou'd you," she asks incredulously,

> have us be such very Oafs as to believe *Mutius Scevola* ever spoke that fine Oration, when his Fist was broyling, which he [Livy] has made for him? No,—I'll as soon believe all *Clelia* as one Word on't, any more than that his Generals had nothing else in their heads just before Engagements, than to make fine Orations, which it is not likely the thousandth part of their Army cou'd ever hear.[73]
>
> (*Challenge* 99–100)

The behavior of characters depicted in men's "*Solid History*," as Godfrey witheringly styles it, is no more plausible to rational, intelligent people—those who are not "very Oafs"—than the romance depictions that Sir Thomas faults women for reading. The primary difference between history and romance, she explains, is that "[a]n Historian relates things as they really are, or at least ought to do so; but a fine *Romance* gives 'em us as they ought to be, or as the Reader wou'd wish 'em" (*Challenge* 99). Embellishing his narrative with fine though unlikely speeches, Livy is evidently a bad writer of history, or a good writer of romance. It would seem he has done what Prior's pedant Clenard boasts of, adding the "heightenings and the Colorings," giving "the very life and Substance to the Picture" based solely upon his own imagination, interests and pleasure. "*Solid History*" such as Livy's, Godfrey insinuates, is the romance that men believe, though men are too profoundly deluded even to suspect their mistake. "WE never had yet, a shee-*Quixote*, that I read or heard of," Godfrey observes, "and therefore it seems, make not such an ill use of *Romances*, as you your selves who have Compos'd 'em" (*Challenge* 97). On the other hand, he-quixotes (quixotes unmodified?) like Sir Thomas abound, calling themselves rational men.

Astell and Sophia later reiterate Godfrey's critique of history as male romance. " '[T]is Men who dispute for Truth, as well as Men who argue against it: Histories are writ by them; they recount each other's great Exploits, and have always done so," Astell writes (Astell 87), while Sophia explains,

> the Men, bias'd by custom, prejudice, and interest, have heretofore presumed boldly to pronounce sentence in their own favour, because possession empower'd them to make violence take place of justice. And the Men of our times, without trial or examination, have taken the same liberty from the report of other Men. Whereas to judge soundly whether their sex has received from nature any real supereminence beyond ours, they should entirely divest themselves of all interest and partiality, and suffer no bare reports to fill the place of argument, especially if the reporter be a party immediately concern'd.
>
> (Sophia 7–8)

Like Astell, Sophia here questions the relation between the histories men tell themselves and the nature these histories purportedly describe, namely "whether their sex has received from nature any real supereminence beyond ours." Men know nothing of nature, Sophia contends, for they credulously defer to the fancied authority of one another, "without trial or examination." Their "interest" and "partiality" reduce all their stories and all their reasoning into a self-perpetuating, self-justifying, closed system that rationalizes and is rationalized by violent possession. What passes for rational thought currently is corrupt, gender-biased fiction, Sophia maintains, urging the remedy of "*rectified reason* . . . a pure intellectual faculty, elevated above the consideration of any sex, and equally concerned in the welfare of the whole rational species" (Sophia 8–9). Like Drake, Sophia presents an alternative, gendered history of the natural order, promoting the belief that men's "unjust usurpation" is a tyrannical encroachment upon the "state of equality *nature* first placed us in" (Sophia 9). To read and believe this alternative history is to recognize male supremacy as arbitrary, unreasonable and unnatural—a mere romance.

In this reversal of the usual arguments, the romance's pejorative association with women falls away, attaching instead to men's education, learning and ideas about nature.[74] Pursuing this reversal, Drake provocatively recasts romances as an educational genre, and the women who read them as society's most valuable educators. A "Girl of Fifteen is reckon'd as ripe as a Boy of One and Twenty," she observes, but rather than resort to the logic of inherent gender inequality by attributing this superior development in girls to "natural forwardness of Maturity," Drake generously suggests that educational differences may account for it. Specifically, "not teaching Women Latin and Greek" is "an advantage to them," for with no time-consuming languages to study, girls may be "furnish'd . . . with Books, such as *Romances, Novels, Plays* and *Poems*; which though they read carelessly only for Diversion, yet unawares to them, give 'em very early a considerable Command both of Words and Sense" (Drake 57–8). This reading, combined with the excellent example of their mothers upon social visits, teaches young girls conversational skills, "the manner, and address of elder Persons," while boys "drudge away the vigour of their Memories at Words, useless ever after to most of them" (Drake 58).

There is more to learning than the narrow knowledge closely monitored by the "Correction of Pedants," Drake disdainfully asserts (Drake 47). Romances teach women sociable converse, a worthwhile skill that ultimately ennobles men, too, for conversation with women gives talented men the refinement and inspiration needed to achieve "great things." As evidence for this claim, Drake cites the success of three prominent male authors: " 'tis my Opinion, that we owe the Neat, Gentile Raillery in Sir *George Etheredge*, and Sir *Charles Sedley's* Plays, and the Gallant Verses of Mr. *Waller* to their Conversing much with Ladies." The costs of undervaluing women's "Words and Sense" Drake documents by retelling William Temple's anecdote about the waning of Spanish glory: "I remember an Opinion of a very Ingenious Person, who ascribes the Ruine of the *Spanish Grandeur* in great measure, to the ridiculing in the person of *Don Quixot*, the *Gallantry* of that *Nation* toward their *Ladies*" (Drake 146). Citing the same "history" as Temple, yet attending to the category of gender, Drake glosses the tale not as a warning against pedantry, but as an indictment of male arrogance and self-sufficiency: ridicule ruined Spain by undermining the status of women. Drake revalidates romance patterns of behavior by ascribing national greatness to them. Her reading of history traces causal relations and unintended effects that run counter to common expectations, just as her analysis of gendered educational practices yields the astonishing discovery that slow male development is attributable not to nature, but to the curriculum foisted upon boys. Determined to unsettle complacent assumptions, Drake redraws the line between natural and acquired qualities, emphasizing the artificiality of "nature," and the systematic credulousness of those who too readily take the acquired for the natural.

In an age of universal quixotism, the authority of nature recedes into a distant, mediated, assumed and therefore controversial past. Breaking out of the hermeneutic circles that contrive and perpetuate this fictive nature, Sophia argues, should be the object of real (as opposed to merely rhetorical) reason.

"[W]hat a wretched circle this poor way of reasoning among the *Men* draws them insensibly into. Why is *learning* useless to us?" she contemptuously demands: "Because we have no share in public offices. And why have we no share in public offices? Because we have no *learning*" (Sophia 27). To liberate their understandings from the narrow, repetitious and quixotically unthinking constraints of past authority and precedent, men must open their minds to the vast possibilities before them, and recognize that what might seem absurd and unnatural is really no more bizarre than many of the fictions they currently live by. Men will cling to these old fictions, Sophia suspects, because

> so weak are their intellectuals, and so untuned are their organs to the voice of reason, that custom makes more absolute slaves of their senses than they can make of us. They are so accustom'd to see things as they now are, that they cannot represent to themselves how they can be otherwise. It wou'd be extremely odd they think to see a *Woman* at the head of an army giving battle, or at the helm of a nation giving laws; pleading causes in quality of counsel; administring justice in a court of judicature; preceded in the street with sword, mace, and other ensigns of authority; as magistrates; or teaching rhetoric, medicine, philosophy, and divinity, in quality of university professors.
>
> (Sophia 36)

Lacking in vision, enslaved by custom, and untuned to the voice of reason, men remain stubbornly faithful to the romance of male supremacy, revealing their ridiculous arrogance and ignorance by unselfconsciously regarding women in positions of authority as "extremely odd." Masculinist rational authority is quixotism in power.

The political rhetoric of reason in the early eighteenth century was thus a rhetoric of instability and opportunity. Drawing attention to the already crafted nature of the "state of nature," it could ridicule venerable ideas as anti-quated maxims, justify innovation as precedent and laugh at the quixotism of reason. It could turn authority into jest by scrutinizing learning. As one anonymous writer argues in a brief biography of Susannah Centlivre (1669–1723), an effective way to overcome the tyranny of old authority is to be the freshest modern—to write more books. Gladly this author observes that the old tyranny already begins to crumble:

> that bold Assertion, that Female Minds are not capable of producing literary Works, equal even to those of *Pope*, now loses Ground, and probably the next Age may be taught by our Pens that our Geniuses have been hitherto cramped and smothered, but not extinguished, and that the Sovereignty which the male Part of the Creation have,

until now, usurped over us, is unreasonably arbitrary; And further, that our natural Abilities entitle us to a larger Share, not only in Literary Decisions, but that, with the present Directors, we are equally intitled to Power both in Church and State.[75]

Once the "usurped" and "unreasonably arbitrary" power of men has been revised by women's "Pens," women will be restored to their "natural" share "in Literary Decisions" and in "Power both in Church and State." They will have Clenard's power to make history known to "the next Age." Women will then occupy recognized positions of authority, forming young minds and instilling in them rational principles derived from no better original than what Locke had regarded as an obvious source of "*Absurdities and Errors*": "the Authority of an old Woman." Or perhaps, more to the point, the authority of an old woman, seemingly unreasonable to men, might then set the standard by which reason would be distinguished from quixotism. The revolution would then have succeeded beyond Locke's wildest imagination, and Shaftesbury's followers could pine for the days when people knew what was really ridiculous, and what was not.

2

COMMON SENSE, MORAL SENSE AND NONSENSE

Sentimentalism and the empirical study of invisible things

> There he often found passages like *"the reason of the unreason with which my reason is afflicted so weakens my reason that with reason I complain of your beauty"* . . . Over this sort of folderol the poor gentleman lost his wits, and he used to lie awake striving to understand it and worm out its meaning.
>
> Cervantes, *Don Quixote*, I, i

> *Reasonable*, signifies the Result of employing *Reason*. *Thinking* according to this Result, is called *Thinking Reasonably*: And *Acting* according to it, *Acting Reasonably*. Sometimes indeed the Word *Reason* is used to signify the *Faculty of Reasoning*, or of employing *Reason*. But this is in a less proper and strict Sense. When again the Word *Reason* is used *to denote a Collection of Propositions already known to be true*, it is likewise improperly and figuratively used, and means no more than *Reasonable*, or the Result of *Reasoning*.
>
> Gilbert Burnet, *Letters Between the Late Mr. Gilbert Burnet and Mr. Hutchinson* (1735)

The adjective "sentimental" is much like the epithet "quixotic," a glib transition to disparagement, dismissal and ridicule. It too, however, can be read more rigorously. Eighteenth-century ethical theorists are traditionally divided into two schools, the rationalists and the sentimentalists, the difference being that the former regard "reason" as the source of moral knowledge, while the latter attribute moral ideas to sensation.[1] Eighteenth-century sentimentalism is fundamentally empirical in outlook, an effort to escape controversial metaphysical speculation by remodeling moral inquiry along the lines of the new science. For sentimentalists, as the above epigraphs suggest, the self-sufficiency of philosophical rationalism was uncomfortably close to quixotism. Taken from a public correspondence between Gilbert Burnet (1690–1726) and Francis Hutcheson (1694–1746), who debated the respective merits of rationalism and sentimentalism in the pages of the *London Journal* in 1725, the second of the two epigraphs reproduces a small portion of Burnet's rationalist argument. Here, in its effort to defend *"Reason"* as the foundation of moral action, Burnet's rationalism sounds disconcertingly similar to the first epigraph, which describes Don Quixote's descent into madness. Eighteenth-century sentimentalism recognized the quixotism of rationalism, and purported to offer a serious alternative to it.

Tracing the relations between empiricism, rational authority and moral diversity, this chapter will discuss eighteenth-century sentimentalism as a form of anti-quixotism. The chapter begins with the Royal Society's efforts to restore rational authority in the wake of civil war, a program that led its members to reject the traditional study of moral topics in favor of empirical inquiry into natural philosophy. Moral studies required speculation, not experiment, and they were therefore eschewed by the Society's early apologists as a dangerous form of quixotism, incompatible with the group's ideology of consensus, latitudinarianism and toleration. The Society could not easily sustain this position with dignity, however, for with nothing to say about moral truth, its initial program for the advancement of knowledge seemed absurdly incomplete, while its chosen method appeared to bar it forever from making up the deficiency: moral truth, after all, is invisible to the five senses. The new philosophy faced a choice between pedantry and quixotism: for they were pedants if they confined their studies only to the material world— "Flowers, Plants, Minerals, Mosses, Shells, Pebbles, Fossils, Beetles, Butterflies, Caterpillars, Grashoppers, and Vermin not above specified" (*Tatler* 3: 135); but they were quixotes if they expanded their scope to apply empirical method to the study of moral ideas—to view the political arts as though they were simple nature. Through the eyes of the new philosophy's critics, the Royal Society's empirical anti-quixotism looked like empiricism *as* quixotism, for the Royal Society's method—their way of reading the world—seemed unable to differentiate between art and nature.

Sentimental philosophers of the early eighteenth century were more successful in reconciling moral inquiry and empirical method. The chapter's second section will discuss some of these efforts, particularly those of Hutcheson, to articulate a rational, moral empiricism in opposition to the apparent amorality of Bernard Mandeville's egoistic philosophy. The controversy here, once again, turns on which ideas are really natural, which are the impositions of art, and by what means they can be distinguished. The twist is that Mandeville and Hutcheson both claim to be empiricists. Because moral virtues are invisible, Mandeville concludes that they do not exist. Hutcheson must prove that they do, an undertaking most readily achieved by rhetorical means, through conventions of interpretation that sustain the fiction of unmediated understanding, of minds shining out through the body. These conventions find their most unabashed expression in the world of sentimental literature. With its "fixation upon tears, sighs, and meanings beyond words," sentimental fiction habitually represents inner character as immediately legible on the body—as empirically accessible—reassuring readers that inner states do correspond to outer forms, that moral empiricism works.[2] For sentimental readers, sentimental fiction achieves the dream of sentimental philosophy; it naturalizes literary language, making moral truth visible as literary form. For unsentimental readers (readers who, in light of plausible alternatives, do not wholeheartedly embrace this moral truth), sentimental fiction will feel contrived, sanctimonious and effete—"sentimental" in the pejorative sense. To illustrate this connection between moral empiricism, moral diversity and the meanings of sentimental fiction, the chapter will close with a reading of Sarah Fielding's sentimental quixotic novel *The Adventures of David Simple* (1744).

Authority, romance and the Royal Society

Autority, which did a Body boast,
Though 'twas but Air condens'd, and stalk'd about,
Like some old Giants more Gigantic Ghost,

was chased from the groves of the learned by Sir Francis Bacon's new philosophy, Abraham Cowley recounts in his "Ode to the Royal Society."[3] The image captures the ambition at the heart of the Society's Restoration endeavors. Like the political restoration that gave the group its charter, the Society sought to banish an old authority—as if it were a bad dream, a ghostly fiction—and to replace it with a renewed, brighter and more substantial incarnation. Drawing on the prejudice against romance, Cowley's figure depicts the old authority of scholasticism as an absurd imposition upon rational thought. In philosophical terms, *"Body"* should be characterized by solidity, not as *"Air condens'd,"* a metaphor the poet may have drawn from Joseph Glanvill's empiricist manifesto *The Vanity of Dogmatizing* (1661). There Glanvill defines a *"Schoolman"* as "the Ghost of the *Stagirite*, in a Body of condensed Air."[4] Cowley's ode despises the old *"Autority"* as nonsense, representing it not as the fabulous, romantic figure of a tyrannizing giant, but as the even more incredible, empirically unsubstantiated ghost of this giant. The departure of this hulking, brooding, insubstantial bogey of *"Autority,"* however, left a much bigger void than one might expect from so airy a body. In trying to fill this vacancy—to make their new authority visible by giving it a real body, or at least a body of *"Real Knowledge"* more substantial and credible than the previous boasted body—the new philosophers found themselves embarked upon a quixotic cultural quest.[5] For in their attempts to defend their undertaking as a serious intellectual endeavor, the new philosophers created impossible expectations for their own authority, rendering themselves ridiculous in the eyes of numerous contemporaries.

Thomas Sprat's *History of the Royal Society* (1667) offers an apology for the new science.[6] Begun just two years after the Society's founding, and published five years later, Sprat's is a preemptive history, an attempt to account for the Society in a friendly, official manner before others less hospitable take up the task. Sprat's tone throughout the piece is inconsistent—careening between scornful confidence and nervous diffidence—a sign of the slippery and uncertain terms through which he must define the Society's project. He negotiates between ghosts and bodies, between the invisible and the real, between tyranny and pedantry, between relevance and triviality, between laughable grandeur and ridiculous modesty. At issue is the definition of authority itself. Is authority necessarily a frightful giant who terrorizes universally, or can it be reimagined as a joint venture of "the modest, humble, friendly Vertues" (Sprat 33)? Must authority be comprehensive, coherent and imperious, or can it be fragmented, partial and cooperative? The question is as much political as intellectual.

As Shapin and Schaffer have argued, the politics of Restoration science were closely related to the problem of Restoration social order: "The experimental philosophers aimed to show those who looked at their community an idealized reflection of the Restoration settlement. Here was a functioning example of how to organize and sustain a peaceable society between the extremes of tyranny and radical individualism."[7] The political and intellectual danger of tyrannical, overweening individualism emerges as a clear theme in the first part of Sprat's *History*. Containing comparative views of previous efforts to advance learning, Sprat's *History* documents a series of philosophical failures caused by scholarly self-aggrandizement and ambition. The "Philosophy of the East" suffered because their "Wise men" kept their knowledge "from the apprehensions of the vulgar," so as "to beget a Reverence in the Peoples Hearts toward *themselves*" (Sprat 5). The "Philosophy of Greece" was stunted by Athens' role as an imperial finishing school, whose purpose was to educate scholars to "go home satisfied with a belief in their own Proficience, and their Teachers Wisdom" (Sprat 7). After the death of Socrates, philosophical sects proliferated, causing much dissension and bickering as the various factions vied for power (Sprat 8), a scenario repeated in the "Warrs of the Tongue" conducted by "The Philosophy of the Primitive Church" (Sprat 10–12). Few advancements in learning were made under the Roman Church, for the churchmen consolidated their influence by keeping others ignorant: "the Laity being kept blind, were forc'd in all things to depend on the Lips of the *Roman Clergy*" (Sprat 14). In each case, according to Sprat, philosophy faltered when the learned put their own importance over the importance of learning. "[L]et them not over-spread all sorts of knowledge," Sprat chides: "That would be as ridiculous, as if, because we see, that Thorns, and Briers, by reason of their sharpness, are fit to stop a gap, and keep out wild Beasts; we should therefore think, they deserv'd to be planted all over every Field" (Sprat 21). The one exception to this imperialistic tendency of the learned comes during the Roman Empire, whose philosophy Sprat dismisses as derivative and useless, a mere comfort of retirement (Sprat 10). Sprat's comparative history thus conveys the two extremes to be avoided: philosophers should not swell into insubstantial giants by insisting on the universal relevance of their peculiar thoughts, nor should they dwindle into triviality by regarding learning as a modest, leisurely activity. Sprat's account suggests that philosophical authority always comes at a political cost—either the tyranny of a universal system, or the factionalism of competing sects— because philosophy, as traditionally understood, *compels* assent.[8] Learned authority constitutes itself by conquering its rivals. The Royal Society's *History*, resonating with the fear of this politicization of intellect, characterizes its own rational endeavors as different.

According to Sprat's *History*, the new philosophers pursued their studies out of a desire to avoid the pressures of politics. Mid-seventeenth-century enthusiasm, faction and civil war drove the founders of Gresham College together, where they could breathe "a freer air" and enjoy learned conversation "without being ingag'd in the passions, and madness of that dismal Age" (Sprat 53). Natural science appealed to them because political affairs were too disheartening:

> To have been eternally musing on *Civil business*, and the distresses of their Country, was too melancholy a reflexion: It was *Nature* alone, which could pleasantly entertain them, in that estate. The contemplation of that, draws our minds off from past, or present misfortunes, and makes them conquerers over things, in the greatest publick unhappiness: while the consideration of *Men*, and *humane affairs*, may affect us, with a thousand various disquiets; *that* never separates us into mortal Factions; *that* gives us room to differ, without animosity; and permits us, to raise contrary imaginations upon it, without any danger of *Civil War*.
>
> (Sprat 56)

The experimentalists fled to the study of nature because of its remoteness from the more politicized studies ("the consideration of *Men*, and *humane affairs*") believed to have caused the "madness of that dismal Age." In the natural sciences, everyone works together, for men become "conquerors over things," whereas in *"Civil business,"* men strive to be conquerors over other men, leading to "mortal Factions," "animosity" and *"Civil War."* Natural philosophy was attractive to the founders of Gresham College not because it resolved civil disputes, but because it ignored them. Natural philosophy allowed for latitudinarian tolerance by eschewing *"humane affairs."* Focusing their studies solely on natural things, and not on the human arts, the new philosophers proclaimed political distinctions irrelevant: "they openly profess, not to lay the Foundation of an *English, Scotch, Irish, Popish*, or *Protestant* Philosophy; but a Philosophy of *Mankind"* (Sprat 63).

The Society's conscious retreat from *"humane affairs"* into their famed embrace of empirical method was meant to encourage political harmony and intellectual modesty. Empiricism, as Sprat explains it, logically requires its practitioners to refrain from certain kinds of study, thereby limiting the range of subjects open to their inquiries. Sprat delineates the new philosophers' intellectual boundaries as follows:

> In men, may be consider'd the *Faculties*, and operations of their *Souls*; The *constitutions of their Bodies*, and the *works of their Hands*. Of these, the *first* they omit: both because the knowledg and direction of them have been before undertaken, by some *Arts*, on which they have no mind to intrench, as the *Politicks*, *Morality*, and *Oratory*: and also because the *Reason*, the *Understanding*, the *Tempers*, the *Will*, the *Passions* of Men, are so hard to be reduc'd to any certain observation of the *senses*; and afford so much room to the *observers* to falsifie or counterfeit: that if such discourses should be once entertain'd; they would be in danger of falling into *talking*, instead of *working*, which they carefully avoid. Such subjects therefore as these, they have hitherto kept out.
>
> > (Sprat 82)

Bodies not souls, works not words, and observations not interpretations fill the domain of the new philosophy, for empirical method attends to the visible, not the speculative. Politics, morality, oratory, reason, the understanding, tempers, the will and passions—all subjects that dwell on souls, words and interpretations—cannot be studied as *"Real Knowledge"* because they "are so hard to be reduc'd to any certain observation of the *senses*." Existing only as speculation, these subjects are essentially invisible to sensation; they cannot be brought down to empirical demonstration, for they are too easy to "falsifie or counterfeit." As Thomas Burnet would complain of Locke's empiricism: "the distinction between good and evil, virtue and vice . . . I do not find that my eyes, ears, nostrils or any other outward sense make any distinction of these things" (Burnet 24). Moral philosophy lies beyond the reach of empirical method—a truth, according to Sprat, that made empiricism attractive to the Royal Society in the first place. The promise of empirical method was its impotence in "the consideration of *Men*, and *humane affairs*."

Boasting of their limitations, apologists for the new philosophy made a virtue out of weakness. Their rhetoric frequently invokes the trope of the quixotic, through which they define their method as a rational practice open to all men of common sense, while ridiculing their more metaphysically inclined opponents as mad. For example, the goal of the new science, Joseph Glanvill asserts, is "to free *Philosophy* from the vain *Images* and *Compositions* of *Phansie*, by making it *palpable*, and bringing it down to the *plain objects* of the *Senses*" in order "to erect a well-grounded *Natural History*."[9] Figuring the old learning of scholasticism as "vain *Images* and *Compositions* of *Phansie*"—as a tyranny of imagination from which philosophy must be made "free"—Glanvill regards the old learning as a romance, the opposite of "a well-grounded *Natural History.*" The "*palpable*" evidence of common sense will ensure that the new philosophy always refers to something that can be commonly identified, investigated and understood; it puts observation before interpretation—something that the singular and fanciful Don Quixote never did. Like Glanvill, Sprat too promises that the new science will examine visible things rather than imaginary flights, that it will arm young men "against all the inchantments of *Enthusiasm*" by "bringing *Philosophy* down again to mens sight, and practice, from whence it was flown away so high."[10] Sprat also associates this improved visibility with well-grounded history. The new philosophers' "purpose is, in short," Sprat writes, "to make faithful *Records*, of all the Works of *Nature*, or *Art*, which can come within their reach: that so the present Age, and posterity, may be able to put a mark on the Errors, which have been strengthned by long prescription" (Sprat 61). The new philosophers will travel the world, or consult with those who have,[11] collecting data that will yield "solid *Histories* of Nature," unlike the numerous "*Romances*" of ancient lore, which exceed "all shadow of *probability*" and amount to "nothing else but *vain*, and *ridiculous Knight-Errantry*" (Sprat 214–15). Sprat promises that these natural histories will supplant the "pretty Tales, and fine monstrous Stories" of the ancients, whose accounts, when compared to those of the moderns, read "like *Romances, in respect of True History*" (Sprat 90–1). Representing the tyrannous grasp of the old philosophy as a kind of romance, the Society touts its own work—"for the Benefit of humane life, by the Advancement of *Real Knowledge*" (Sprat 2)— as the restoration of rational thought. The learned quixotism of philosophical speculation must be cured by bringing its practitioners, quite literally, back to their senses.

Through such metaphors, the experimentalists portray empiricism as the reasonable antidote to philosophical quixotism. Their rhetoric transforms the demonstrative certainty of the old philosophy into tyrannous, irrational dogma credible only to self-sufficient enthusiasts. In contrast, the new philosophy's empirical, probabilistic collectivism is the pattern of free and rational, modest yet solid inquiry. Substituting probabilism for demonstration, the experimentalists reconstitute the very meaning of philosophical authority.[12] "[I]t is not enough, that the *Tyrant* be chang'd; but the *Tyranny* it self must be wholy taken away," Sprat insists (Sprat 35). Under the new philosophy, no new tyrant can succeed, for knowledge must be a collective endeavor, no longer the province of a single great mind. "[T]he *Art* of *Experiments* . . . can never be finish'd by the perpetual *labours* of any one man, nay scarce by the successive force of the greatest *Assembly*," Sprat advises (Sprat 343). Likewise Cowley's ode warns:

> *Yet still, methinks, we fain would be*

> *Catching at the Forbidden Tree,*
> *We would be like the Deitie,*
> *When Truth and Falshood, Good and Evil, we*
> *Without the Sences aid within our selves would see;*
> *For 'tis God only who can find*
> *All Nature in his Mind.*

The new philosophical authority is partial and shared, acknowledging that no single individual can possibly comprehend nature in its entirety. The *"Sences aid"* must be relied upon to disclose individual difference, to reveal facets of *"Nature"* not *"within our selves."* Under the new philosophy, individual knowledge must always be regarded as small and imperfect, *"For 'tis God only who can find/All Nature in his Mind."*

Those who refuse to recognize their experiential limitations, Sprat ridicules as pedants. "It is natural to all Ranks of men," he writes, describing pedantry in much the same way as Addison would do almost fifty years later:

> to have some Darling, upon which their care is chiefly fix'd. If *Mechanicks* alone were to make a Philosophy, they would bring it all into their Shops; and force it wholly to consist of Springs and Wheels, and Weights: if *Physicians*, they would not depart farr from their Art; scarce any thing would be consider'd, besides the *Body* of *Man*, the *Causes, Signs*, and *Cures* of Diseases. So much is to be found in Men of all conditions, of that which is call'd *Pedantry* in Scholars: which is nothing else but an obstinate addiction, to the forms of some private life, and not regarding general things enough.
>
> (Sprat 66–7)

Characterizing demonstrative philosophy as "an obstinate addiction, to the forms of some private life," Sprat reduces the grandeur of great metaphysical minds to the paltry, pedantic, besotted puppets of some "Darling . . . care." His choice of examples—mechanics fixated on springs, wheels and weights; physicians narrowly attuned to "the *Body* of *Man*"—further deflates intellectual self-sufficiency by hinting at its mechanical origin. Far from being intellectual masters, pedants have become mechanical slaves of their professions. Only collective effort can transcend the confines of limited experience:

> By this *union* of *eyes*, and *hands* there . . . will be a full *comprehension* of the object in *all* its appearances; and so there will be a mutual communication of the light of one *Science* to another: whereas *single labours* can be but as a prospect taken upon one side.
>
> (Sprat 85)

By creating an ideal of universal authority that can be attained by individuals only partially, the new philosophy's empiricism banishes intellectual tyranny. Since only universal experience can produce the universal knowledge necessary to promote "the Universal Interest of the whole *Kingdom*" (Sprat 323), no individual can claim godlike knowledge and the authority it confers; to pretend to do so would be "*Catching at the Forbidden Tree*," making the "*Oracle*" speak only a "*privat* sence" (Sprat 66), usurping the prerogative of the deity.

Scorning the old philosophy for its quixotic, enthusiastic, tyrannical and pedantic blend of single-mindedness and extravagance, the new science offers an alternative model of authority, reimagining learned philosophers as modest, humble toilers in a world so vast as to be incomprehensible to any one mind. This posture, however, could not be perpetually sustained, nor was it intended to be. As Barbara Shapiro has argued, the ultimate goal of Baconian science was to achieve a sounder metaphysics through careful attention to nature.[13] The new philosophy's humility was tactical; it modified rhetoric more than ideology. For instance, Sprat's attack on pedants as "not regarding general things enough" betrays a continuing belief that true philosophers must have command over a vast scope. Though Sprat honors the "modest, humble, friendly Vertues" of those "willing to be taught, and to give way to the Judgement of others"; though he praises the patience of those who can endure "a long and a tedious doubting" in the search for truth; and though he warns against the "immoveable," "imperious" and "impatient" inclination that makes men "prone to undervalue other mens labours . . . least they should seem to darken their own glory" (Sprat 32–4), Sprat still does not reject the expectation that genuine authority must exude greatness and attract universal veneration, in a godlike manner. "*What Reverence all* Antiquity *had for the* Authors *of* Natural Discoveries, *is evident by the Diviner sort of Honor they conferr'd on them*," Sprat exults in the *History*'s Epistle Dedicatory to King Charles:

> *Their Founders of* Philosophical Opinions *were only admir'd by their own* Sects, *Their* Valiant Men *and* Generals *did seldome rise higher than to* Demy-Gods *and* Heros. *But the* Gods *they Worshipp'd with* Temples *and* Altars, *were those who instructed the World to* Plow, *to* Sow, *to* Plant, *to* Spin, *to* build Houses, *and to find out* New Countries.

By this account, philosophers were admired only partially, within "*their own* Sects," while generals and soldiers likewise enjoyed only limited respect as "Demy-Gods *and* Heros." On the other hand, the non-combative, unassuming, practical experimentalists became "*the* Gods" worshipped by all antiquity. Universal and enduring reverence is the reward Sprat dangles to encourage support for the new science: "*Your* Majesty *will certainly obtain* Immortal Fame, *for having establish'd a perpetual Succession of* Inventors."

Sprat's eagerness to portray the ancient experimentalists' ascendancy to godhead undoes his supposed distinction between the new philosophical authority and enthusiasm. If the old *"Autority"* erred in seeking to *"be like the Deitie,"* then its replacement appears to commit the same overreaching mistake. The new philosophy's new authority looks very much like the same old authority—a universal principle that masterfully transcends apparent differences, establishing uniformity of opinion: *"all* Antiquity," not just a few avid sectarians, reverenced *"the* Authors *of* Natural Discoveries," Sprat boasts. The new authority, like the old, must ultimately be comprehensive and almighty, not partial, limited and doubting. As Sprat's rhetoric makes clear, universal authority—nothing less—is what the new philosophers expect their empirical method eventually to discover. The Royal Society thus begins as a paradox, with the new philosophers disregarding their recent *experience* of pervasive social conflict, in order to pursue, via empirical method, an empirically suspect universalist ideal. What empirical evidence suggests that universal authority is even there to be found? Dryden's proposed epic poem, had it been written, would have taken up this empiricist paradox as the theme of the age:

> 'Tis a Doctrine almost Universally receiv'd by Christians, as well Protestants as Catholicks, that there are Guardian Angels, appointed by God Almighty, as his Vicegerents, for the Protection and Government of Cities, Provinces, Kingdoms, and Monarchies . . . But 'tis an undoubted Truth, that for Ends best known to the Almighty Majesty of Heaven, his Providential Designs for the benefit of his Creatures, for the Debasing and Punishing of some Nations, and the Exaltation and Temporal Reward of others, were not wholly known to these his Ministers; else why those Factious Quarrels, Controversies, and Battels amongst themselves, when they were all United in the same Design, the Service and Honour of their common Master?[14]

The management of these controversies would have been the action of the epic, a heroic story of struggles unfolding in a divine plan "not wholly known" to God's ministers. In this epic narrative, complete knowledge would have been God's knowledge of "his Providential Designs for the benefit of his Creatures," just as in the new philosophy, *"Real Knowledge"* is knowledge discovered "for the Benefit of humane life" (Sprat 2). Dryden's angelic "ministers" (and Dryden himself, had he ever written the poem) would have faced the same daunting task as Sprat's new philosophers, who labor under the burden of incomplete knowledge, trying to discover an unseen, universal order. The heroism of such a quest—of searching for this "common Master" amid "Factious Quarrels, Controversies, and Battels"—would have had special resonance for men of Dryden's and the new philosophers' generation, who matured during the civil wars.[15] Unable to escape their longing for a "common

Master," the new philosophers imagine their discourse becoming this master.[16] Ultimately, authority is supposed to be *"like the Deitie"*; if it is not, it does not appear to be authority. After all is said and done, conflict should cease as it does in Dryden's *Absalom and Achitophel*: "Once more the Godlike *David* was Restor'd,/And willing Nations knew their Lawfull Lord."[17]

In the face of "Factious Quarrels," and under the expectation that true authority mimics godhead by inspiring consensual obedience, the Royal Society's efforts begin to ring hollow. For if authority is not true unless it compels universal consent, then the Society can aspire to nothing better than mere travesty or new tyranny. "Thus by the one party, it is censur'd, for stooping too low," Sprat complains, "by the other, for soaring too high" (Sprat 27). In any event, the critical opposition to experimentalism could represent the new philosophy as quixotic—as travesty, as tyranny, or as both at once. For instance, Henry Stubbe (1632–76), one of the new science's earliest and most vehement critics, finds secret tyrannical designs in the Society's apparent triflings.[18] Attacking Sprat's *History*, Stubbe fulminates: "these *men* have no way answered *their expectation*, since the *relations* and *Experiments*, are so *trivial, defective,* and *false*, since that the *Authors of this fatal History* have more in them of *Campanella*, than of Mr. *Boyl*."[19] Stubbe's comparison between the Royal Society and the Dominican philosopher Tommaso Campanella (1568–1639) is well calculated to plant fears of lurking tyranny. For Campanella was a known resister of Aristotle, like the fellows of the Royal Society, but also an infamous proposer of a plan to expedite the conversion of the Protestant states back to Rome. His plan recommended that Protestants be encouraged in mathematics and natural philosophy, leaving theology to the uncontested authority of the Church.[20] Stubbe draws a parallel between Campanella's scheme and the Royal Society's projects, contrasting these deep designs with his own "principal motive" of supporting the English monarchy "against all such intendments as may either introduce *Popery* on the one side" or "*Anarchical projects*, or *Democratical* contrivances" on the other.[21] Stubbe scoffs at the Society's professed impartiality. Its self-proclaimed political disengagement harbors covert intentions, he charges, dismissing as a mere ruse Sprat's distinction between the Society's (neutral) natural histories and the (politicized) civil histories that the group purportedly eschews. Stubbe is correct, of course, in that Sprat's *History* is itself a (politicized) civil history, with its Epistle Dedicatory offering an account of antiquity tailored to glorify experimentalism.

Sprat creates a perfect opportunity for Stubbe to turn the Society's rhetoric of anti-quixotism back upon itself. Stubbe responds by meticulously dismantling the history contained in the Epistle Dedicatory, and declaring Sprat to be a poor historian, "little acquainted with the condition of *Europe*," and ignorant of "*Philology* and humane Learning" (Stubbe 3–13). The virtuosi who believe Sprat's history are, in Stubbe's opinion, ridiculous quixotes. "In fine," Stubbe announces, summarizing his lengthy and vitriolic review of Sprat's poor history,

> from the days that *Sparta* flourished to the Empire of the *Mancha* under the ingenious Author of the *Experimental* History of *Don Quixote*, I do not find that the *little inventors* of *trivial* and *useless toys*, though *improvements of reall knowledge*, and of the *powers of all mankind*, have had that honor which Mr. *Sprat* intimates.
>
> (Stubbe 9)

The Royal Society's chaotic experiments, like Don Quixote's picaresque adventures, strike Stubbe as nonsensical, trivial and comic—unless, of course, secretly tyrannical—because there appears to be no innocent universal principle directing their actions. Comparing the virtuosi's exploits to Don Quixote's misadventures, Stubbe refers to Cervantes' novel as "the *Manchegal Experiments*," giving special attention to the author's preface of the novel's second part. The preface recounts the story of the man of Seville "who was esteemed as *mad* by his Neighbors, though he did those feats that that [*sic*] might have rendred him considerable to some of the *Society*, and gained him an *immortal fame* in *Philosophical* transactions" (Stubbe 10). One of these feats was none other than to blow up dogs "*round as a Ball*" with "*a hollow Cane, small at one end . . . fitted to the Dog's Back-side*" (DQ 442). Stubbe may have been reminded of this trick by Robert Hooke's "Account of a Dog dissected," which appears in the second part of Sprat's *History*, and describes an experiment in which a dog's respiratory system was examined with the aid of "*a pair of bellows, and a certain Pipe thrust into the Wind pipe of the Creature*" (Sprat 232). The madman of Seville, of course, inflates his dog by inserting a hollow reed at the animal's other end, a variation that only adds ludic emphasis to Stubbe's accusation: the Royal Society's experiments—though unique and perhaps even difficult achievements—are ultimately meritless; they accomplish nothing significant unless their goal is to divert.[22]

Stubbe's critique of the Royal Society's quixotism thus recognizes two possible interpretations of the new philosophy: it is either politically innocent as it claims to be, and therefore irrelevant and ridiculous, engaged merely in diverting antics; or it deliberately dissembles, and is therefore sinister and significant, engaging in diversionary tactics. In suspecting the latter, however, Stubbe was in the minority. Attacks aimed at the Society's irrelevance were far more common. It was not simply that the Society's work failed to produce domestic improvements, though this disappointment was one sore spot exploited by the "terrible men" of wit Sprat so feared.[23] What made the Society especially vulnerable to attacks of this second sort was the widespread cultural belief that knowledge of humankind ("*Civil Business*") is more valuable than knowledge of things ("*Nature*"). Under this hierarchy of learning, the Society's chosen sphere of influence—no matter how successful—must always be of small importance. The fellows' professed disengagement from "humane affairs," if taken at face value, is precisely the source of their triviality.[24] Thomas Shadwell's *The Virtuoso* (1671), for instance, lampoons the new philosopher as one "who never cares for understanding mankind." " 'Tis below a virtuoso to trouble himself with men and manners," announces Shadwell's Nicholas Gimcrack: "I study insects."[25] Similarly, a stern Judith Drake observes that there is a "sort of Impertinents,"

> who, as they mind not the Business of other Men where it concerns 'em not, neglect it likewise where it does, and amuse themselves continually with the Contemplation of those things, which the rest of the World slight as useless, and below their Regard. Of these, the most egregious is the *Virtuoso*, who is one that has sold an Estate in Land, to purchase one in *Scallop, Conch, Muscle, Cockle-Shells, Periwinkles, Sea Shrubs, Weeds, Mosses, Sponges, Corals, Coralines, Sea-Fans, Pebbles, Marchasites,* and *Flint-Stones*; and has abandon'd the Acquaintance and Society of Men, for that of Insects, *Worms, Grubs, Maggots, Flies, Moths, Locusts, Beetles, Spiders, Grasshoppers, Snails, Lizards* and *Tortoises.*[26]

Not meddling in civil affairs, the new philosophers commit the graver error of neglecting their own social and economic business. Under the critical scrutiny of Drake, their perverse preference for natural studies over "human affairs" translates into the absurd practice of trading estates away for trifles, and leaving the society of men for a roomful of curios.

This stereotype of the new philosophers as triflers, who are unable to manage even their own household affairs, runs counter to their stated ambitions of advancing knowledge "for the Benefit of humane life." Frequent portrayals of the virtuosi's moral and social ineptness mock the new philosophy as detrimental to human life. Ned Ward's London Spy discovers at Gresham College "a topping virtuoso and Member of the Royal Society" who "is a joiner of sexes,"

> and will learnedly prove, upon such occasions, that generation was the main end of our creation. Whatever match he makes, he seldom fails of his double reward, that is, to get money on one side, and curses on t'other, for he is a man of such conscience and consideration that he generally takes care to couple those who are worth money to such as want it.[27]

In Ward's account, the Society's promiscuous pursuit of natural knowledge is literalized, stigmatized and satirized as a promiscuous approach to carnal knowledge, a mixing of rich and poor that threatens the stable reproduction of orderly social boundaries. Like Stubbe, Ward distrusts the virtuosi's motives, and is wary of self-interested designs that can hide behind the appearance of "conscience and consideration." Yet the new philosophers' mismanagement of human affairs, even if not the deliberate deception that Stubbe and Ward suspect, may still wreak social havoc. On a miniature scale, this confusion occurs routinely in satiric depictions of the virtuosi's inability to see through romantic intrigue. Shadwell's Gimcrack loses his nieces to a pair of wits who pretend to be philosophers themselves, while Mr Periwinkle, the virtuoso guardian of Mrs Ann Lovely in Centlivre's *A Bold Stroke for a Wife* (1718), is no match for the deceptions of Colonel Fainwell. Fainwell, doing what his name suggests, impersonates a new philosopher, grandly proclaiming that he pursues Mrs Lovely less for himself than "for the benefit of mankind."[28] In these portrayals, the virtuosi's obtuseness to human affairs arises directly from their misguided separation of *"Nature"* from *"Civil Business,"* and their foolish preoccupation with the novelties of the former.

Aphra Behn's Dr Baliardo in *The Emperor of the Moon* (1687), with "his microscope, his horoscope, his telescope, and all his scopes," most strikingly exhibits the errors of the new philosophy's social vision.[29] Described as "a little whimsical, romantic, or Don Quick-sottish, or so" (Behn 280), Baliardo spends his energies observing the world in the moon, rather than monitoring the romantic exploits of his daughter and niece, Elaria and Bellemante. His Don Quick-sottishness manifests itself as an utter inability to see, despite the aid of all his "scopes," the difference between nature and art, truth and imposture. With Baliardo so oblivious, Elaria and Bellemante, under the doctor's own roof and in collusion with his own servants, manage an intrigue with Don Cinthio and Don Charmante, suitors who feign to be dignitaries from the world in the moon. The essence of the doctor's folly is staged in Act 2, when he unexpectedly returns home and surprises the lovers, who hide from him by pretending to be figures in a hanging tapestry. Unable to recognize these figures as living creatures, Baliardo praises the tapestry as "a stately piece of work," mistaking nature for art (Behn 302). In Behn's farce, the new philosophy cannot keep *"Nature"* and *"Civil Business"* separate, because Baliardo's empiricism cannot distinguish between natural knowledge and social imposture. Cinthio's and Charmante's easy duping of the doctor—their ability to represent themselves as wonders of nature—argues Baliardo's need to attend more closely to the study of men and manners, to learn the difference between natural discoveries and "Ridiculous inventions" (Behn 333). "No emperor of the moon; and no moon world!" Baliardo marvels when finally informed of his mistakes. "Burn all my books, and let my study blaze," he cries, renouncing his quixotism: "Burn to ashes, and be sure the wind/Scatter the vile contagious monstrous lies" (Behn 334).

Satires on the virtuosi illuminate the absurd conflict inherent in the new philosophical project. The experimentalists urge empirical method as the antidote to quixotism—as a means toward *"Real Knowledge"* that will dispel "all the inchantments of *Enthusiasm"*—while their detractors, such as Stubbe and Behn, counter that the new philosophy's empiricism does not, in fact, oppose quixotism. "[O]*ur Modern Philosophers in the Abyss of Knowledg seem as fairly enchanted as the Knight in* Montesino's *Cave . . . and the Virtuoso's Perpetual Motion has very much of the Windmill*," writes Peter Motteux, in the preface to his translation of *Don Quixote*.[30] The Scriblerus Club members join in with their celebrated depiction of the extraordinary Martinus Scriblerus, a natural philosopher engaged in many "Projects for the benefit of mankind," who "by the Gravity of his Deportment and Habit, was generally taken for a decay'd Gentleman of Spain."[31] In its failure to recognize the proper limits of its own authority, empirical method *is* quixotism. As late as 1782, the anonymously written *Philosophical Quixote; Or, Memoirs of Mr. David Wilkins* builds its comedy around a foolish man who "most values himself upon . . . his knowledge in natural philosophy," and whose greatest foible is described as "*an ungovernable passion for discovering the useful*, which indeed is capable of leading men into the most glaring and ridiculous absurdities."[32] As the new philosophers were frequently reminded, "bringing *Philosophy* down again to mens sight" is a quixotic endeavor, because the subjects of philosophical study are often invisible. "Yea, the most common *Phaenomena* can be neither known, nor improved, without insight into the more *hidden* frame," writes Joseph Glanvill, a hundred years before Adam Smith: "For *Nature* works by an *Invisible Hand* in all things" (Glanvill 180). The unenviable, epic task of the new philosophy is to make this "*Invisible Hand*" a common sight, to reveal to all the "common Master" that Dryden could only hope to imagine for his poetic universe.

The human "*Arts*" ("*Politicks, Morality*, and *Oratory*") and their foundations ("the *Reason*, the *Understanding*, the *Tempers*, the *Will*, the *Passions* of Men") are the main example of invisible things—"so hard to be reduc'd to any certain observation of the *senses*"—that the new science cannot quite comprehend. In the hierarchy of knowledge, however, these are the subjects worthy of study. These "*Arts*" do more for the benefit of mankind than do the Society's trifling natural discoveries. Accordingly, Sprat concedes that these "*Arts*" are what the Royal Society's humble natural knowledge boldly aspires to become. Sprat dreams of a day when the invisible things that constitute human affairs, being rendered visible by advancements in empirical inquiry, will no longer mark the limits of the Society's intellectual domain: "when they shall have made more progress, in *material* things," Sprat earnestly proposes, "they will be in a condition, of pronouncing more boldly" on human affairs;

> For . . . by long studying of the *Spirits*, of the *Bloud*, of the *Nourishment*, of the parts, of the *Diseases*, of the *Advantages*, of the accidents which belong to *humane bodies* (all which come within their Province) there, without question, be very neer ghesses made, even at the more *exalted*, and *immediate* Actions of the *Soul*.
>
> (Sprat 82–3)

88

Looking toward that bright someday when empirical method will open a window on the "*immediate* Actions of the *Soul*," Sprat rejoices in the belief that his successors might one day be happily engaged in the empirical study of invisible things. It is this ludicrous scheme to study human interiority directly, via the external and therefore always indirect methods of empiricism, that Stubbe and Behn ridicule as the new philosophical quixotism. How could an examination of material things illuminate the spirit? What reliable inter-pretive principles could turn even the most careful bodily inspection into a revelation of the soul? As Don Quixote's romances ill-prepared him for the world he was to encounter beyond his library, so too do the Royal Society's materialist studies seem a radically inappropriate guide to the moral universe the new philosophers dream of governing.

Sprat can offer no convincing argument as to why the study of material things should be trusted in its "ghesses . . . at the more *exalted*, and *immediate* Actions of the *Soul*." In fact, materialist explanations need not recognize the importance of "the *Soul*" at all, a trajectory of thought that inevitably associ-ated materialism with atheism and immorality.[33] Confronting these accusations, Sprat can only doggedly assert that empirical study proves, rather than disproves, the existence of spirit:

> there can be no just reason assign'd, why an *Experimenter* should be prone to deny the essence, and properties of *God*, the universal Sovereignty of his *Dominion*, and his *Providence* over the *Creation*. . . . In every thing that he tryes, he believes, that this is enough for him to rest on, if he finds, that not only his own but the *universal Observations* of men of all times and places, without any mutual conspiracy have consented in the same *conclusion*. How can he then refrain from embracing this common *Truth*, which is witness'd by the unanimous approbation of all *Countries*, the agreement of *Nations*, and the secret acknowledgement of every mans breast?
>
> 'Tis true his *employment* is about *material things*. But this is so far from drawing him to oppose invisible *Beings*, that it rather puts his thoughts into an excellent good capacity to believe them. . . . If (as the *Apostle* says) the invisible things of *God* are manifested by the visible; then how much stronger Arguments has he for his belief, in the *eternal power*, and *Godhead*, from the vast number of Creatures, that are invisible to others, but are expos'd to his view by the help of his *Experiments*?.
>
> (Sprat 347–8)

Contrary to Sprat's assertions here, there is just cause to suspect that an exper-imenter might be prone to deny the essence of God: spirit is not a plain object of the senses, and therefore, by Sprat's earlier arguments, should not count as "*Real Knowledge*." To dodge this straightforward conclusion, Sprat speciously equates universal opinion with *"universal Observations."* The *"universal Observations* of men of all times and places, without any mutual conspiracy have consented in the same *conclusion,"* he writes, incorrectly implying that similar conclusions must derive from similar observations, and therefore that empirical study yields a "common *Truth*" about invisible things. A closer inspection of the passage, however, reveals that this "common *Truth*" has no human observers: it is "witness'd" by "approbation," not by any human agent; agreed upon, though not observed by, entire nations of people; and—when finally acknowledged by actual men—is so acknowledged only in "secret." This "common *Truth*" is thus not an empirical truth at all, though Sprat's rhetoric tries valiantly to disguise it as one. Sprat's defense of the empirical study of invisible things can only limp along on the dubious assumption that the presupposed "secret acknowledgement of every mans breast" counts as actual empirical data. How something "secret" could serve as empirical evidence of anything remains mysterious.

Certainly, a perplexed Bishop Berkeley in *Passive Obedience* (1712) finds no reassurance in this sort of empirical moral proof. Morality is invisible to the public eye, Berkeley worries:

> since the measure and rule of every good man's actions is supposed to be nothing else but his own private disinterested opinion of what makes most for the public good at that juncture; and since this opinion must unavoidably in different men, from their particular views and circumstances, be very different: it is impossible to know whether any one instance of parricide or perjury, for example, be criminal. The man may have had his reasons for it, and that which in me would have been a heinous sin may be in him a duty. Every man's particular rule is buried in his own breast, invisible to all but himself, who therefore can only tell whether he observes it or no.
>
> (Berkeley 6: 22)

Even "disinterested opinion" is deeply private and diverse, differing according to individual experience and circumstance, Berkeley reasons. Morality as an objective, universal "measure and rule" of good action is "impossible to know," for "particular views" vary so greatly that the same moral act may be applauded by some as "duty," while reviled by others as "heinous sin." Sprat's "secret acknowledgement of every mans breast," which he depends upon to identify and uphold "common *Truth*," is—unfortunately—secret. As a set of particular rules invisible to the public, moral ideas are not naturally universal, Berkeley argues. On the contrary, they are radically subjective.

Seen against Berkeley's sober considerations on the subject, Sprat's utopian confidence in the universality of moral opinion appears more quixotic than realistic, more wishful than rational. Certainly, no such universal concord reigned prior to the founding of the Royal Society. In fact, as Sprat himself relates, the group first began its meetings in order to escape universal conflict—"the passions, and madness of that dismal Age." Nor should the new philosophy be trusted to guarantee greater future accord, for as critics countered, the foundation and principles of empirical method appear more likely to lead to discord than consensus. Common sense may not be common, as Matthew Prior argued against Locke's empiricism:

> The difference in Temperament in the Body, Hot, Cold, Phlegmatic or hasty create as Manifest a Variety in the Operations of our hands and the Conduct of our Lives; and our Conceptions may be as various as your faces, Bodies and Senses, or Sensations as you call them. If I like Assafetida I say it has a good smell, If you can't endure a Rose you complain it Stinks. In our Taste, may not I nauseate the Food which You Covet, and is it not even a Proverb that what is Meat to one Man is Poyson to another. If we consider even the Fabric of the Eye and the Rules of Optic, It can hardly be thought we see the same; And yet no Words can express this Diversity.
>
> (Prior 1: 639)

By this account, empiricism promises—if anything—to inaugurate even more intractable disagreements, for it must accept on equal footing any opinion that can be shown to derive from sensation, despite the fact that individual variations in temperament, taste, conduct and perspective may be so great as to render one person's perceptions wholly unnatural and incredible to another. With subjective experience varying so radically, there is no common sense, nor any way even to discuss the differences: "It can hardly be thought we see the same; And yet no Words can express this Diversity." Similarly, Samuel Butler (1613–80), famed for his quixotic depiction of the English Civil Wars in *Hudibras* (1663–80), derides the Society's faith in empiricism as a means toward universal understanding:

> But still the narrower they pried,
> The more they were unsatisfied,
> In no one thing they saw agreeing,
> As if they'd several faiths of seeing.[34]

Natural knowledge ("seeing") cannot be separated from the human arts of interpretation ("faiths"). By caricaturing the Society's learned disputes as sectarian conflicts between "faiths of seeing," Butler rudely collapses the distinction drawn by the new philosophers between their empiricism and others' enthusiasm.

In other words, even if common sense really were common, interpretive differences would still remain, because there are "faiths of seeing." Facts are not independently significant; their meaning is contingent upon the prior experiences and conventions through which they are understood. Berkeley makes this point when he discusses the power of "particular views" to transform "heinous sin" into "duty" and vice versa. This relativism, as Michael McKeon has argued, owes some of its vigor to the Royal Society's own scornful oppositions between "romance" and "history." "The danger of speculative comparisons like these," McKeon writes, "is that they tend to relativize absolute notions of 'history' and 'romance,' showing them to be matters of degree and dependent upon one's comparative context."[35] In the late seventeenth century, radical uncertainty accompanied the emergence of epistemological probability—that aspect of probability, in Ian Hacking's words, "dedicated to assessing reasonable degrees of belief."[36] In the evaluation of this reasonable belief, history (the record of experience), in contrast to romance (the record of imagination), served as the general truth against which to measure the reasonableness of one's own particular beliefs: hence the Society's hopes that by carefully compiling "a well-grounded *Natural History*" they could bring about rational consensus. Yet the ambiguity of "history" and "romance," exacerbated by the Royal Society's empiricist progressivism, encouraged "the historicizing insight that what seems strange to one age may be revealed as true to its inheritors."[37] If reasonable assessments of probability vary with historical contexts—if what looks grossly improbable in one age may have been quite routine in another—then how can "history" be the measure of reasonable belief? Historical relativism can make history look like romance, romance look like history, reasonable conduct look like quixotism, and quixotism look like reasonable conduct. A parallel case may be made with respect to individual relativism. For in a diverse society, who can know enough about another's circumstances in order to deny the reasonableness of that person's beliefs, in proper context? Berkeley makes precisely this point. "The man may have had his reasons for it," is all the bishop need say to excuse the parricide or perjurer.

It should not be surprising that Berkeley's belief in radically diverse rational(ized) morality accompanies his endorsement of passive obedience as a political tenet superior to Lockean reason. Locke's reason, filtered through his empiricism, cannot produce the universal conformity desired as the *sine qua non* of a peaceful and orderly state. Rational belief is contingent upon particular circumstance, Berkeley maintains, and is therefore more likely to generate irreconcilable (because equally "rational") differences. As argued in the previous chapter, the extreme example of such rational diversity is the madness of Don Quixote—he too had his reasons for it. The similarities between empiricism and quixotism resonate more forcefully given the curiously consistent fact that eighteenth-century English quixotes, unlike Cervantes' own Don Quixote, never err in their sensations (they never mistake burlap for silk, or garlicky breath for Arabian perfume); they err only in their judgments about the empirical evidence before them. Their "seeing" is fine, but their "faiths" are questionable. With the haleness of their five senses testifying to their fundamental sanity by empirical standards, English quixotes serve as a critique of empirical method itself, displaying how differing interpretive principles can make one person's experientially derived probabilities look like another person's madness. Swift's Hack, looking "into the Fountains of *Enthusiasm*," sees to the bottom of the matter when he equates madness with diversity of belief:

> Of such great Emolument, is a Tincture of this *Vapour*, which the World calls *Madness*, that without its Help, the World would not only be deprived of those two great Blessings, *Conquests* and *Systems*, but even all Mankind would happily be reduced to the same Belief in Things Invisible.
>
> (Swift 1: 107)

Without madness—that is, without diversity—"*Conquests* and *Systems*" would be unnecessary and unknown, for everyone would already believe in the same "Things Invisible." The ubiquity of quixotes attests to the eighteenth century's fascination with rational madness, the fate of good empiricists who study invisible things in a diverse society.

The threat of interpretive diversity was no surprise to the Royal Society's founders. They recognized its problems in language, and thus arose their famed plans for linguistic improvement, whereby language would be returned to its "primitive purity, and shortness, when men deliver'd so many *things*, almost in an equal number of *words*" (Sprat 113).[38] If, as Foucault argues, *Don Quixote* is "the first work of modern literature . . . because in it language breaks off its old kinship with things,"[39] then the Royal Society's much discussed interest in "real characters" and universal language schemes—its effort to wed words to things—can be seen as yet another instance of the group's attempt to define itself in opposition to the quixotic. It was yet another effort whose outcome was dubious, prey to the witticisms of those gifted in the arts of ridicule. Swift memorably satirizes the Society's dreams of reducing words to things in his portrayal of the Grand Academy of Lagado in *Gulliver's Travels*. There, at "the School of Languages," the professors reason "that since Words are only Names for *Things*, it would be more convenient for all Men to carry about them, such *Things* as were necessary to express the particular Business they are to discourse on" (Swift 11: 169). Accordingly, these sages, often "sinking under the Weight of their Packs," converse in the purest, shortest (albeit the heaviest) form of language, omitting words altogether, and delivering so many "*Things*" in exactly an equal number of "*Things*."

In short, as these numerous critiques of the new philosophy make clear, the Royal Society's empirical study of "*Things*" did not restore rational authority, as it promised it would. On the contrary, the new philosophers' distinction between sober empiricism and quixotic excess was easily collapsed into empiricism *as* quixotism. With no single mind able to comprehend all nature, the gap between individual experience and the ideal of rational authority as universal is so large that almost any opinion can be made to look quixotic. Limited by their necessarily partial views, individuals can achieve rational authority only through enthusiasm, by asserting reason without empirical evidence; through pedantry, by basing reason on too narrow a range of empirical evidence; or through tyranny, by denying that reason requires any empirical evidence whatsoever. By far the most fantastic aspect of the empirical study of things, however, is its application to things invisible, such as moral rules and the "Actions of the *Soul*." Though crucial to the new philosophy's larger cultural goal of restoring intellectual and political authority, the invisible rules of the breast remain stubbornly resistant to empirical inquiry. Those who would study these invisible things would have to devise methods much subtler than the ones hitherto known, or else they would simply have to claim to see, with quixotic persistence, what others do not.

Seeing the "invisible union": empirical method, moral virtue and sentimental quixotism

The empirical study of invisible things flourishes in sentimentalism, as does the quixotism associated with the practice. Histories of sentimentalism record that men of feeling descend from the Spanish knight. According to John K. Sheriff, "the cervantic depiction of quixotic obsessions with ideas [was] part of the literary tradition that influenced the portrayal of the Good-Natured Man," while Janet Todd asserts: "The novels of the sentimental man are offsprings of *Don Quixote*, with its portrait of the idealistic *ingénu*."[40] Yet eighteenth-century sentimentalism also managed to redefine quixotism, as evidenced by Todd's conclusion that "the man of feeling" was "ultimately . . . unthreatening and required no deep engagement or ideological involvement."[41] Sentimentalism transformed Don Quixote from the very symbol of menacing ideological difference into the benign, unthreatening and ideologically uninvolved hero of whom Todd speaks.[42] Though often remembered as effete and silly, sentimentalism was a powerful system of thought. It offered extra-rational remedies for the problem of quixotic difference, and was, in Richard Voitle's words, "a patently successful attempt to evade [the] limitations" of Enlightenment reason.[43] Modeled on the new philosophy, sentimentalism was a serious and ambitious response to the problem of moral diversity, a fulfillment of Sprat's promise that moral truth and empirical method could be reconciled. The method of sentimentalism was primarily rhetorical. It established a "faith of seeing" that gave meaning to the mute signs of human nature, and subordinated all other interpretations to its own. Sentimentalism upheld the fiction of universal authority by celebrating exclusive communities of like-minded individuals, whose rectitude was ensured by their ability to identify, discount and expel diversity from their ranks. A discussion of the antagonism between egoistic and sentimental philosophy will illustrate this rhetorical strategy and its relation to the shifting meanings of quixotism.

Upon publishing his *Fable of the Bees* (1714, 1723),[44] Bernard Mandeville (1670–1733), as F. B. Kaye memorably states, succeeded to "the office of Lord High Bogy-man, which Hobbes had held in the preceding century."[45] Arguing that the "Moral Virtues" exist as no more than "the Political Offspring which Flattery begot upon Pride," Mandeville articulates a view of human nature devoid of real social feeling.[46] As Mandeville sees it, human beings are fundamentally selfish, devoted to their "private Interest," and unwilling to place the public good above their own appetites. Societies would never have formed, he reasons, had not politicians invented a system of fictive rewards with which to fool selfish individuals into social behavior: "being unable to give so many real Rewards as would satisfy all Persons for every individual Action, they were forc'd to contrive an imaginary one, that as a general Equivalent for the trouble of Self-denial should serve on all Occasions" (Mandeville 1: 42). Moral virtue was this imaginary reward. By this account, moral rectitude is a form of quixotic madness, a reverent devotion to fictitious virtue promulgated by dubious authority. Skeptical of Shaftesbury's belief in "the natural sense of right and wrong,"[47] Mandeville reinterprets moral principles as the nominal and fictive, arbitrary rationalizations of self-interested desire. Social feeling, he asserts, is not natural but artificial, and as such, subject to all the uncertainties, mutabilities and innovations of art. Explicitly drawing out the differences between his system and Shaftesbury's, Mandeville dismisses Shaftesbury's virtue by revealing it to be an effect not of nature, but of quixotism.

"This Noble Writer (for it is the Lord *Shaftesbury* that I mean in his Characteristicks) Fancies," Mandeville explains,

> that as Man is made for Society, so he ought to be born with a kind Affection to the whole, of which he is a part, and a Propensity to seek the Welfare of it. In pursuance of this Supposition, he calls every Action perform'd with regard to the Publick Good, Virtuous; and all Selfishness, wholly excluding such a Regard, Vice. In respect to our Species he looks upon Virtue and Vice as permanent Realities that must ever be the same in all Countries and all Ages, and imagines that a Man of sound Understanding, by following the Rules of good sense, may not only find out that *Pulchrum & Honestum* both in Morality and the Works of Art and Nature, but likewise govern himself by his Reason with as much Ease and Readiness as a good Rider manages a well-taught Horse by the Bridle.

The attentive Reader, who perused the foregoing part of this Book, will soon perceive that two Systems cannot be more opposite than his Lordship's and mine. His Notions I confess are generous and refined: They are a high Compliment to Human-kind, and capable by the

help of a little Enthusiasm of Inspiring us with the most Noble
Sentiments concerning the Dignity of our exalted Nature: What Pity
it is that they are not true: I would not advance thus much if I had not
already demonstrated in almost every Page of this Treatise, that the
Solidity of them is inconsistent with our daily Experience.

(Mandeville 1: 323–4)

Mandeville dismisses Shaftesbury's beliefs as quixotic, describing the noble
philosopher's principles as "Fancies," and criticizing the system built upon
them as absurdly tautological. Shaftesbury *supposes* that "Man is made for
Society" and "ought to be born with a kind Affection to the whole," and in
"pursuance of this Supposition," conveniently *defines* public-spirited actions as
"Virtuous" and selfish actions as "Vice." Wedded to an ideal of unchanging
social nature, Shaftesbury must remain frozen in a timeless world of "permanent Realities" that universally encompass "all Countries and all Ages."
Regarding "the Works of Art and Nature" as both subject to the very same
"Rules of good sense," Shaftesbury quixotically draws no distinction between
the rules of art and the rules of nature, all the while believing this lack of
discrimination to be "Reason." So commanding is this "Reason" that
Shaftesbury presumes it will govern men as easily as a skilled rider manages a
well-trained horse. The metaphor of a rider on horseback, however, suggests
the precariousness of reason as well. Swift, for example, had employed it to
depict enthusiasm:

when a man's fancy gets *astride* on his reason, when imagination is at
cuffs with the senses, and common understanding as well as common
sense, is kicked out of doors; then the first proselyte he makes is
himself, and when that is once compassed the difficulty is not so great
in bringing over others.

(Swift 1: 108)

Shaftesbury's "Fancies" are astride his reason, Mandeville implies, a condition
that bestirs in the chivalrous earl "generous and refined" notions, which
through "the help of a little Enthusiasm," inspire others with "the most Noble
Sentiments." In short, the first proselyte Shaftesbury made was himself, and
now he seeks to bring over others. Shaftesbury and his benevolist followers,
Mandeville suggests, are sentimental quixotes. They ignore the weight of
empirical evidence to persist in beliefs "inconsistent with our daily
Experience."

By mocking Shaftesbury's system as empirically unsound, Mandeville
exposes the methodological equivocation now famous as the "natural moral
sense" (Shaftesbury 262). Reasoning by analogy, Shaftesbury maintains that
moral ideas are empirically derived: "The case is the same in the mental and
moral subjects as in the ordinary bodies or common subjects of sense," he

affirms (Shaftesbury 251). Mandeville gleefully explodes such ponderous appeals to the authority of nature, simply by denying the existence of the moral sense in his own experience. Like Prior's and Butler's critiques of empiricism in general, Mandeville's satire of moral empiricism casts doubt upon the commonness of common sense. By regarding the allegedly natural feelings of the moral sense as finely contrived artifice (like the excellent figures Dr Baliardo so admires in his tapestry), Mandeville's system challenges defenders of Shaftesburian natural goodness either to prove the existence of the moral sense, or to admit that their ideas lack the "Solidity" of a true empirical foundation. His irreverent analysis of two virtues, "reason" and "honour" (the very two which made Admiral Vernon appear so quixotic in the Mostyn controversy), will serve to illustrate the implications of Mandeville's critique.

Reason, Mandeville argues, is not a natural faculty of mankind. Rather, it is an artful self-delusion encouraged by manipulative politicians who, having "thoroughly examin'd all the Strength and Frailties of our Nature," determined that "Flattery must be the most powerful Argument that could be used to Human Creatures":

> Making use of this bewitching Engine, they extoll'd the Excellency of our Nature above other Animals, and setting forth with unbounded Praises the Wonders of our Sagacity and Vastness of Understanding, bestow'd a thousand Encomiums on the Rationality of our Souls, by the Help of which we were capable of performing the most noble Atchievements. Having by this artful way of Flattery insinuated themselves into the Hearts of Men, they began to instruct them in the Notions of Honour and Shame; representing the one as the worst of all Evils, and the other as the highest Good to which Mortals could aspire.
>
> (Mandeville 1: 43)

Rationality, in Mandeville's conjectural history, is merely a Dulcinea, a "bewitching" and imaginary ideal whose putative excellence inspires "noble Atchievements." The dictates of "the Hearts of Men," he maintains, speak not with the true voice of nature, but unselfconsciously with the clichés of art. Rational men are those so thoroughly duped by "the artful way of Flattery" that they proudly conform to political convention, naturalizing custom, embodying platitudes—becoming a genre—just as Don Quixote did. To emphasize the artifice of virtue, Mandeville often makes a great show of testing the so-called natural virtues against empirical method. What method could better be trusted to distinguish *"Real Knowledge"* of nature from "pretty Tales, and fine monstrous Stories"? To the embarrassment of the new science, Mandeville's demand for empirical verification invariably discovers that our "exalted Nature" is purely imaginary—just a pretty tale, not real knowledge at all.

For example, "Remark (P)" of the *Fable* recounts the story of a shipwrecked merchant who, confronted by an enormous lion, must plead for his life. The lion uses the meeting to question the natural hierarchy that places men above beasts. "And if the Gods have given you a Superiority over all Creatures," the fierce brute asks, "then why must you beg of an Inferior?" The merchant can only respond with a pretty tale about divine favor:

> *Our Superiority . . . consists not in bodily force but strength of Understanding; the Gods have endued us with a Rational Soul, which, tho' invisible, is much the better part of us.*
>
> (Mandeville 1: 177)

The superiority that the gods have given man cannot be empirically shown, for the "*Rational Soul*" is "*invisible*." The merchant must hope that the lion will, without any hard evidence at all, choose to swallow this mysterious story, rather than chew upon something more substantial, like the merchant himself. The skeptical lion, however, quickly rejects the merchant's claim as fanciful: "Man never acknowledg'd Superiority without Power, and why should I? The Excellence I boast of is visible, all Animals tremble at the sight of the Lion" (Mandeville 1: 180). With no empirical evidence to support his claim, the merchant's assertions look no better than pretensions; the "exalted Nature" of his "*Rational Soul*" appears to exist only as enthusiastic self-delusion—imaginary, impermanent and insubstantial—having no solid basis in nature. The lion's skepticism toward the merchant's claims conveys Mandeville's amusement at the empirical logic that always mercilessly ridicules the imaginary, until it becomes inconvenient to do so. Far from being a natural and universal constant, "the Rationality of our Souls," Mandeville asserts, is a cleverly imagined inconstant: "we are ever pushing our Reason which way soever we feel Passion to draw it, and Self-love pleads to all human Creatures for their different Views, still furnishing every Individual with Arguments to justify their Inclinations" (Mandeville 1: 333). To Mandeville, Shaftesbury's "Reason" is delusion.

The moral virtue of "honour" is similarly imaginary. "HOnour in its Figurative Sense," Mandeville explains in "Remark (R)" of the *Fable*, "is a Chimera without Truth or Being,"

> an Invention of Moralists and Politicians, and signifies a certain Principle of Virtue not related to Religion, found in some Men that keeps 'em close to their Duty and Engagements whatever they be, as for Example, a Man of Honour enters into a Conspiracy with others to murder a King; he is obliged to go thorough Stitch with it; and if overcome by Remorse or Good-nature he startles at the Enormity of his Purpose, discovers the Plot, and turns a Witness against his

Accomplices, he then forfeits his Honour, at least among the Party he belonged to.

(Mandeville 1: 198)

Mandeville makes himself deliberately obnoxious to Shaftesburians by selecting regicide as the example of a principle to which "Honour" must remain true. Shaftesbury's moral sense theory, after all, seeks to reduce the significance of factional antagonism by positing that virtue naturally precedes and transcends politics. In contrast, Mandeville's blunt discussion of regicide here speaks loudly of the political differences moral sense theory tries to downplay. Salting the wound Shaftesbury had hoped to see healed, Mandeville illustrates how a virtue like honor actually helps to perpetuate political rancor and partisan loyalty at the expense of "Good-nature." If honor is natural and real—more than just a "Name," "the Aerial Coin of Praise" (Mandeville 1: 48, 55)—then how can it support the ambitions and actions of both regicides and loyalists? It can serve so diversely because it is neither natural nor real, Mandeville triumphantly concludes. "Honour" is simply a name, "an Invention of Moralists and Politicians," a fiction used to rationalize self-interested political distinctions.

These self-interested distinctions include class divisions as well. Mandeville's irreverent analysis of the principle of "Honour" continues: "The Excellency of this Principle is, that the Vulgar are destitute of it, and it is only to be met with in People of the better sort, as some Oranges have Kernels, and others not, tho' the out-side be the same" (Mandeville 1: 199). Once again, by stressing the empirical inaccessibility of virtue and merit, Mandeville challenges "natural" hierarchy itself as arbitrary and unnatural. Though trusted as a marker of class distinction between the "Vulgar" and the "better sort," honor proves to be empirically elusive, perhaps even illusory; from the "out-side," those with it and those without it look the same. The recognition of social quality, Mandeville implies, can never count as *Real Knowledge* in the Royal Society's natural sense, because honor is an "invisible Ornament." When translated into empirical terms, honor at once loses all its vaunted dignity: "In great Families it is like the Gout, generally counted as Hereditary, and all Lords Children are born with it," Mandeville writes, comparing this virtue to a disease; "[i]n some that never felt any thing of it, it is acquired by Conversation and Reading, (especially of Romances) in others by Preferment," he continues, dispassionately analyzing honor as an affectation born of quixotic reading and upstart pretensions; "but," he concludes, "there is nothing that encourages the Growth of it more than a Sword, and upon the first wearing of one, some People have felt considerable Shoots of it in four and twenty Hours" (Mandeville 1: 199). For Mandeville, "Honour," like the other moral virtues, is hubristic delusion—bold self-aggrandizement that mistakes itself for a public service. The last great practitioner of "ancient Honour," Mandeville reminds his readers, was *Don Quixote* (Mandeville 1: 199).

The differences between Mandeville's rational egoism and Shaftesbury's sentimentalism are sharp, but result from their mutual empiricism. Mandeville acknowledges that social truth is invisible, which leads him to regard moral virtue as an artful mystification. Shaftesbury assumes that social truth can be empirically apprehended through the "moral sense," which allows him to regard moral virtue as a natural phenomenon. For Mandeville, empiricism demystifies moral truth by relentlessly reducing it to a matter of common sense. While Sprat concedes that morals "are so hard to be reduc'd to any certain observation of the senses," and Thomas Burnet warns that "outward sense" can make no moral distinctions at all, Mandeville concludes that moral truths have no existence beyond their ever-changing signs. Virtue is not a permanent reality, an immutable quality of soul that shines through the body unmistakably. Rather, it is a social fiction substantiated only by a set of conventional behaviors available to anyone artful enough to mimic them. For Mandeville, these conventions do not *reflect* moral truths; on the contrary, they *create* them. Hence a gesture, such as wearing a sword, suddenly causes "considerable Shoots" of honor. By Mandeville's standards, Shaftesbury's moral sense is quixotic, for it bases its authority upon a "nature" that Mandeville derides as art. In mocking the moral sense, Mandeville makes the same arguments still used against sentimentalism today, namely, that it is naively optimistic about human sociability; that it foolishly reveres highly contrived, idealized fictions as natural truths; and that it remains blithely, perhaps even sanctimoniously, oblivious to how things work in the "real" world. Of course, the main issue between Mandeville's egoism and sentimental philosophy—the main issue driving any quixotic conflict or sentimental argument—is precisely the ambiguity of what constitutes natural truth and the real world.

Unsurprisingly, opponents of Mandeville responded by dismissing his reality as fantasy. They argued, in effect, that Mandeville's world is already quixotic, only he does not realize it. As Steele's Isaac Bickerstaff had argued about his quixotic friend, the political upholsterer: "it is very certain we have Crowds among us as far gone in as visible a Madness as his, tho' they are not observed to be in that Condition" (*Tatler* 2: 468). If quixotism is now already so universal that it goes unseen, passing for reason and nature, then what Mandeville and his followers do see as quixotism must not really be quixotism. By this head-turning critical principle of reverse logic, good readers can recognize the quixotic as its opposite. Don Quixote ceases to be a public menace, and becomes a noble hero. In their refutations of Mandeville, both William Law (1686–1761) and Francis Hutcheson incorporate this shift into their interpretations of Don Quixote's "madness."

Law and Hutcheson each refute Mandeville while trying to retain the validity of moral empiricism itself. Law's *Remarks upon a late Book, entitled, 'The Fable of the Bees'* (1723) asserts the reality of virtue by discussing moral knowledge as though it were the product of simple sensation: "let me tell you, sir," he lectures Mandeville,

> *moral virtue* came amongst men in the same manner as *seeing* and *hearing* came amongst them. . . . Were not the first principles and reasons of morality connatural to us, and essential to our minds, there would have been nothing for the moral philosophers to have improved upon.[48]

Law's rhetoric hints at the language of innate ideas—"principles . . . connatural to us" and "essential to our minds"—yet ultimately identifies itself as empiricist by comparing these fixed ideas to "*seeing* and *hearing*." The parallel does not quite work (seeing and hearing are processes while moral virtue exists as the processed), but Law later revises it somewhat, arguing that virtue has "that natural fitness to a rational soul that fine sights have to the eye, or harmonious sounds to the ear" (Law 29–30). In this instance, he again adopts rationalist language—"natural fitness to a rational soul"—while portraying it as empiricism. Law's "rational soul," receptive to virtue, functions as an additional sense. The dispute between Mandeville and Law, therefore, turns less on their methodological differences than on their unshared assumptions about what constitutes the full range of sensation. Mandeville limits himself to the five external senses, while Law maintains the presence of the "rational soul," which functions as a sixth sense. At this impasse, the two disputants may remain forever, as the authority of experience legitimates both equally. Mandeville's experience, limited to the five senses, denies the reality of the rational soul, for the "*Rational Soul*," as his merchant had to admit to the lion, is "*invisible*," a mere chimera to skeptical empiricists. Yet Law, feeling the promptings of his own rational soul, can claim them as proof of the rational soul's reality. He has as much reason to affirm as Mandeville has to deny. In fact, Law has a slight advantage, because Mandeville holds the weaker position in denying the existence of a thing because he has found no evidence for it, while Law holds the stronger position of asserting its existence based on perception.[49] Still, the problem remains that Mandeville can never accept Law's evidence as evidence, because he denies the natural validity of Law's sensory apparatus. Their conflict is quixotic; it occurs at the level of assumptions, and resists empirical resolution even though both men represent themselves as empiricists.

At such rational disjunctions, the attraction of Shaftesbury's "freedom of raillery" becomes apparent. His confidence in the corrective powers of ridicule promise that such disputes can be peacefully resolved, with reasonable systems of thought always triumphing over ridiculous ones. The idea would indeed be deeply reassuring, if only it could be believed. Law, however, doubts the efficacy of the earl's *laissez-faire* intellectualism, believing instead that raillery and wit can make any idea—even the most serious ones—seem ridiculous. For example, Law warns:

> Religion requires a serious and wise use of our reason, and can only recommend itself to us, when we are in a disposition to reason and think soberly; it preserves its power over our minds no longer than whilst we consider it as the most serious, important, and sacred thing in the world.
>
> Hence it appears why we are generally so little affected with religion, because we are seldom in a state of sober thinking.
>
> (Law 64)

Whereas Shaftesbury's "freedom of raillery" presumes that unchecked wit will eventually ridicule people back into sensible thought, Law fears that too much wit leads only to too much wit—to a universal lack of "sober thinking" that makes the "serious and wise use of our reason" an aberration rather than the norm. For Law, ridicule offers not the best defense against falsehood, but the worst assault on truth:

> they who only *laugh* at religion, may be said to have used the strongest argument against it, for there is no coming at it any other way; it is only to be attacked by little jests, lewd flings of wit, and such as may betray the mind into levity, and corrupt the imagination.
>
> (Law 64–5)

Rational authority, Law complains, can too easily be turned into jest: "a poor inflamed wretch, who never had the use of his reason in his life, may easily call religion a *Dulcinea del Tobosa*, and all who would procure any regard to it, *Saint Errants*" (Law 66). In an age "generally so little affected by religion" and its accompanying sober state of thinking, individuals stand out as quixotic not because they are mad, but because they are reasonable. True reason is called quixotism because true quixotism passes for reason. Law's argument begins to transform quixotism-as-wrong-headedness into quixotism-as-rightness.

While Law only suggests that modern-day quixotes are the happy, rational and virtuous few, Hutcheson backs up the claim with a fully articulated philosophy. Hutcheson's *Inquiry into the Origin of Our Ideas of Beauty and Virtue* (1725), "IN WHICH," the title-page boasts, "The Principles of the late Earl of SHAFTESBURY are Explain'd and Defended, against the Author of the *Fable of the Bees*," and later, his *Essay on the Nature and Conduct of the Passions and Affections* (1728), defend the reality of the moral virtues by affirming their status as objects of natural sensation. "We must . . . certainly have other Perceptions of *moral Actions* than those of *Advantage*," he maintains, denying the primacy of Mandevillean self-interest: "And that Power of receiving these Perceptions may be call'd a MORAL SENSE, since the Definition agrees to it,

102

viz. a Determination of the Mind, to receive any Idea from the Presence of an Object, which occurs to us, independently on our Will."[50] To Hutcheson, the moral sense literally is a sense, albeit an *internal* one; it perceives moral ideas passively, as the eye perceives light and the ear perceives sound.[51] As an internal sense, it is overlooked, he believes, because the Baconian revolution has not yet gone far enough. Philosophical tyranny, that old romance so reprehensible to Sprat for subjugating the authority of the external senses, still holds sway over the internal ones, Hutcheson contends:

> WHATEVER Confusion the *Schoolmen* introduced into Philosophy, some of their keenest *Adversaries* seem to threaten it with a worse kind of Confusion, by attempting to take away some of the most *immediate simple Perceptions*, and to explain all *Approbation, Condemnation, Pleasure* and *Pain*, by some intricate Relations to the Perceptions of the *External Senses*.[52]

The empiricists themselves, though the "keenest *Adversaries*" of the schoolmen, reproduce scholastic folly by refusing to trust the full range of their senses, Hutcheson argues. They hobble their knowledge by limiting it only to the perceptions of the five commonly recognized external senses. "SOME strange Love of *Simplicity* in the Structure of human Nature, or Attachment to some favourite *Hypothesis*, has engag'd many *Writers* to pass over a great many *simple Perceptions*, which we may find in our selves," he muses, hinting at the quixotism, "or Attachment to some favourite *Hypothesis*," at work behind narrow views of empirical evidence. "We have got the Number *Five* fixed for our *external Senses*, tho *Seven* or *Ten* might as easily be defended," and in addition, "[w]e have Multitudes of Perceptions which have no relation to any *external Sensation*," he maintains (Hutcheson 2: x). By regarding moral virtue as the natural object of internal sensation, Hutcheson makes moral ideas a matter of simple perception, in effect reinventing morality as a subject perfectly accessible to empirical method.

Hutcheson's sentimentalism—his belief in sensation as the source of moral knowledge—is an intellectual descendant of the new philosophy. It strives to make moral knowledge palpable, bringing it down to the plain objects of the moral senses. By stressing the importance of *feeling*, sentimentalism seeks to place rational thought about moral subjects on a more solid foundation. Hutcheson's public correspondence with Gilbert Burnet in 1725, debating the respective merits of sentimentalist and rationalist philosophy, illuminates the motives behind Hutcheson's reasoned sentimentalism. He opposes Burnet's rationalism out of concern that it cannot effectively combat Mandevillean egoism. By rationalist standards, Hutcheson warns, one can be both selfish and rational at the same time. Burnet, however, opposes Hutcheson's sentimentalism, because it does not guarantee universal moral understanding; rather, it often retreats from universalism, into the rhetoric of exclusivity characteristic of sentimental heroes and sentimental communities in the eighteenth-century novel.

Hutcheson's sentimental system lacks *"a sufficient Foundation,"* Burnet worries, because it anchors itself in sensation, not reason. *"Reason"* alone "discovers and delivers us to the *proper* Rule and Measure of *Action*" and "lays the *proper*, and indeed, strictly speaking, the *only Obligation* upon us to act in a certain manner," Burnet posits (Hutcheson 7: 5, 53).[53] Hutcheson's attempt to establish morality upon sensation will undermine the universality of moral truth guaranteed by reason, Burnet argues, fearing that the senses are too often mistaken. Left uncorrected by reason, the senses would discover no common truth:

> We judge any *Sense* to be wrong, or vitiated, when it represents Things otherwise than we know it would do, if we were in a right State of Body. And, even in our best State, our *Senses* often deceive us; and are, or may be rectified by our *Reason*. . . . In the same manner the *Moral Sense* must be esteemed wrong, or vitiated, where it contradicts our Reason . . . without this Standard of *Reason* to recur to, all *Senses* would be equally *Right*, merely because they were *Senses*; which we know to be contrary to fact.
>
> (Hutcheson 7: 76–7)

Because of the diversity inherent in empirical knowledge, Burnet rejects the suggestion that moral ideas spring from sensation. The final authority of *"Reason"* is necessary to prevent the incoherence of a world in which "all *Senses*" are "equally *Right*." Comparing moral truths to mathematical ones, Burnet rests his argument on the adamant foundation of self-evidence. What reason can be given for "why the Whole is equal to all its Parts" or "a Part is less than the Whole"?

> No Reason can be ever given for a self-evident Axiom: For all Reasoning is only an Appeal to some self-evident Principle or other. And if I could find a Man of so different a Make of Understanding from mine, that what was self-evident to me was not so to him, I should have no Medium by which I could argue with him any longer on that Head; but we must part, and own that we cannot understand each other: Only in that case we should not be angry at one another, for what neither of us could help.
>
> (Hutcheson 7: 8–9)

Reason must be self-justifying, Burnet maintains, for otherwise there can be no common understanding, only incomprehensible difference. The logic of the self-evident, which is the logic of the quixotic, must be accepted as the ultimate foundation of moral truth.

Burnet's rationalism, capable of supporting itself only by "an Appeal to some self-evident Principle or other," strikes Hutcheson as far too arbitrary a foundation upon which to establish something so important as moral truth. For reason itself is arbitrary, Hutcheson contends, its definition fixed only in relation to previously determined, desired ends. On these variable grounds, even Mandevillean egoism could be found wholly reasonable:

> IF any one should ask concerning *Publick* and *Private* Good, Which of the two is most *Reasonable?* The Answer would be various, according to the Dispositions of the Persons who are passing Judgment upon these *Ends*. A Being entirely *Selfish*, and without a *Moral Sense*, will judge that its own Pursuit of its greatest private Pleasure is most *Reasonable*.
>
> (Hutcheson 7: 30)

Hutcheson distrusts rationalism, convinced that its self-evident logic leads only to intractable rational diversity, not to universal truth. Reason does not tell us what to desire, for reason is a consequence of desire. Selfish beings and public-spirited ones will not agree on what is "most *Reasonable*," because they come to the question already desiring different moral ends; their goals not being the same, they do not regard the same principles as self-evident. Rationalism is weak and rudderless, facilely assuming as "self-evident" the very principles of morality that it should prove. "In this Circle we must run, until we acknowledge the first Original of our Moral Ideas to be from a *Sense*," Hutcheson stresses, striving to ground moral truth in sensation, the immutable authority of nature (Hutcheson 7: 40–1). Without a sentimental foundation, reason is literally a senseless fiction. As Hutcheson boldly asserts:

> If there be any other Meaning of this Word *Reasonable*, when apply'd to Actions, I should be glad to hear it well explained; and to know for what *Reason*, besides a *Moral Sense* and *Publick Affections*, any Man approves the Study of Publick Good in others, or pursues it himself, antecedently to Motives of his own private Interest.
>
> (Hutcheson 7: 32–3)

Hutcheson thus has the same objections to Burnet's "*Reason*" as Burnet has to Hutcheson's "*Moral Sense*": the weakness of the other's foundation. Hutcheson fears that Burnet's "*Reason*" serves any and all masters equally well; Burnet fears that Hutcheson's "*Moral Sense*," once vitiated, will do the same. Burnet worries the sense will betray the universality of morals, because sensation cannot be trusted to lead to consensus. Hutcheson worries that rationalism could be used to justify false universals, such as Mandeville's universal selfishness.

The rhetorical ingenuity of Hutcheson's moral sense theory emerges at this impasse. Drawing on the authority of nature, Hutcheson turns the corruptibility of the moral sense into evidence of its besieged rectitude.

Precisely because he admits to the frequent impairment of the moral sense, Hutcheson is able to celebrate minority opinion as the true (and natural) universal. He walks the thin quixotic line between benighted self-indulgence and the isolating heroism of unrewarded persistence. Fellow-feeling and social love are the *"Bonds of Nature"* that make "each particular Agent . . . subservient to the *good of the whole,"* Hutcheson states, flatly rejecting Mandevillean egoism as unnatural: "Mankind are thus link'd together, and make one great *System*, by an invisible Union" (Hutcheson 2: 178). The natural moral sense, when functioning properly, will perceive this "invisible Union" as self-evident, Hutcheson asserts. Mandevillean egoism, therefore, can only have credit with those whose moral sense has been vitiated by unnatural custom:

> IF any should look upon some Things in this *Inquiry into the Passions*, as too subtile for the common Apprehension, and consequently not necessary for the Instruction of Men in *Morals*, which are the common business of Mankind: Let them consider, that the Difficulty on these Subjects arises chiefly from some *previous Notions*, equally difficult at least, which have been already receiv'd, to the great Detriment of many a *Natural Temper*; since many have been discourag'd from all Attempts of cultivating *kind generous Affections* in themselves, by a previous Notion that there are no such Affections in Nature, and that all Pretence to them was only *Dissimulation, Affectation*, or at best some *unnatural Enthusiasm*. And farther, that to discover Truth on these Subjects, nothing more is necessary than a little *Attention to what passes in our own Hearts*, and consequently every Man may come to Certainty in these Points, without much Art or Knowledge of other Matters.
>
> (Hutcheson 2: v–vi)

The *"previous Notions"* of Mandevillean selfishness are foreign to the *"Natural Temper"* of humankind, though not always perceived as such by minds accustomed to thinking otherwise. Seeing the invisible union of social love is no harder than discerning universal selfishness; they are "equally difficult at least," but for the ease bred by familiarity. Convinced by wicked philosophers that there are no unselfish affections in nature, and that all evidence to the contrary should be dismissed as *"Dissimulation, Affectation*, or at best some *unnatural Enthusiasm,"* people grow to accept these philosophical fictions as natural truths.

Like Don Quixote's romances, Mandeville's theory of self-love, according to Hutcheson, powerfully subverts vulnerable minds. And like Don Quixote himself, these egoistic converts come to embody the very fictions they read, transforming themselves into empirical evidence of what should not exist, making the unnatural appear natural. There should be no knights-errant crusading across seventeenth-century Spain; there should be no moral agents

106

devoid of public affections. Yet within the fiction of *Don Quixote*, at least one old gentleman loses his wits and becomes proof that knight-errantry does exist. Likewise, Mandevillean converts, "discourag'd from all Attempts of cultivating *kind generous Affections* in themselves," may allow their moral sense to atrophy, thereby becoming the selfish creatures that nature never knew. Hutcheson's resourceful conjectural history enables him to circumvent the findings of his own empiricism by denying the validity of what he finds. Thoroughly selfish beings who walk among us cannot disprove Hutcheson's theory of human nature; they can only prove that this nature is corruptible. Mandevillean egoists are thus discredited as *already* quixotic, formed not by nature, but by "the *accidental Effect* of Custom, Habit, or Association of Ideas, or other preternatural Causes" (Hutcheson 2: 201). But with their quixotism being so prevalent that it goes unnoticed, egoists give true nature the *appearance* of quixotism: "The raising universally the *publick Affections*, the Desires of *Virtue* and *Honour*, would make the *Hero of Cervantes*, pining with *Hunger* and *Poverty*, no rare Character," Hutcheson avers, rehabilitating the once-criminal Don Quixote into a paragon of public virtue (Hutcheson 2: 201). Here Don Quixote represents the promptings of true nature, not the antics of art. Like a sentimental novel with multiple protagonists, the world would be full of benevolent quixotes in distress, if only it could be returned to its natural state. Hutcheson's proof for so sweeping a claim, however, is unassailably private: "nothing more is necessary than a little *Attention to what passes in our own Hearts*," he instructs, inviting each reader to witness the invisible rules lodged in his or her own breast.

Hutcheson's theory of the (vitiated) moral sense thus enables him to make an empirical argument for a universal nature that is normative rather than actual. His rhetoric turns controversial opinion into universal truth by identifying, discounting and expelling his opposition from the community of credible personages. Calling only for introspection, "a little *Attention*" to the secrets lodged in the human breast, Hutcheson does not prove his theory of the natural moral sense and public affections. Rather, by rejecting innate selfishness as a silly fiction, he strategically challenges egoists to demonstrate the validity of their own assumptions first: a proof which, if they choose to attempt it, can begin and end only with a public confession of their own selfishness. What passes in the breast is secret, after all; their confessions would describe only their own individual hearts, not humankind's. Meanwhile, Hutcheson can maintain, on the evidence of his own heart (visible to no one else), that the *"previous Notions"* of egoism are a perversion of nature, the quixotic product of minds accustomed to an unnaturally narrow range of social possibilities. He can confidently confront what Gilbert Burnet most fears—"a Man of so different a Make of Understanding from mine, that what was self-evident to me was not so to him"—because his sentimentalism, unlike Burnet's rationalism, thrives on encounters with differing makes of understanding. The sentimental mind conveniently turns these quixotic encounters into evidence of its own superior sensibility and (misunderstood) universality. It urges moral uniformity most firmly at exactly those moments in which moral diversity appears to be the rule. Even the power of ridicule, which alarmed Temple, terrified Sprat and existed everywhere, is neutralized by Hutcheson's theory, which maintains that "a *Sense* of the ridiculous . . . implanted in Human Nature" will always prompt people of just discernment to make proper distinctions between what is "really *great*" and what is "really *mean*" (Hutcheson 7: 126–8).[54] "THIS Engine of Ridicule, no doubt, may be abused, and have a bad Effect upon a weak Mind; but with Men of any Reflection, there is little fear that it will ever be very pernicious," Hutcheson opines, for "that which is truly valuable in any Character, Institution, or Office" will always be known to those whose senses are in proper order (Hutcheson 7: 128). The "*Sense* of the ridiculous" makes quixotic difference pathological, not political.[55] With dissenting opinion seen as the sign of a "weak Mind," rational disagreement becomes impossible. In the circularity of sentimental representation, quixotism meets its rhetorical match.

There is little structural difference between Mandeville's and Hutcheson's arguments. If Mandeville's is anti-quixotic, then Hutcheson's is anti-anti-quixotic. In its tautological certainty, Hutcheson's system reproduces the very aspect of Mandeville's argument that Hutcheson finds most aggravating. Hutcheson is willing to concede that some people may be as his opponent describes. He objects, however, to Mandeville's insistence that all people are inherently selfish, and that those who believe otherwise are simply deluded. Hutcheson is enraged by Mandeville's refusal to allow for the possibility of rational dissent. What could possibly be ridiculous about proposing a moral sense, he asks, when there are a number of "*Appearances* in human Nature" that are "the direct and necessary Consequences of this Supposition"? "And yet," Hutcheson fumes, "this penetrating *Swaggerer, who surpasses all Writers of Ethicks*, makes those very Appearances proofs against the Hypothesis" (Hutcheson 7: 168). By Mandeville's logic, Hutcheson's unremitting belief in natural virtue proves only the strength of his delusion, and reaffirms the truth of egoism, for egoism predicts that vain and self-interested people will be unwilling to give up their imaginary rewards, and will react just as Hutcheson does. In these terms, Hutcheson's meanings can always be subordinated to Mandeville's system, for his protests register as self-implication. Hutcheson is forced to play the wooden dummy to Mandeville's ventriloquist. Unable to talk to his opponent on equal terms, Hutcheson opts to talk over him, declaring the *Fable* to be "absolutely *Unanswerable*," like the "nonsense" defined in Addison's "fourth *Whig Examiner*" (Hutcheson 7: 156). "Nonsense," Addison had there complained:

> is that which is neither true nor false. These two great properties of nonsense, which are always essential to it, give it such a peculiar advantage over all other writings, that it is incapable of being either

answered or contradicted. It stands upon its own basis like a rock of adamant, secured by its natural situation against all conquests or attacks.[56]

Defined as perfect self-sufficiency, "nonsense" could be Gilbert Burnet's "self-evident Principle." "[S]ecured by its natural situation," "nonsense" could be Hutcheson's "moral sense." Hutcheson, however, chooses to regard "nonsense" as Mandeville's tyrannically insane attempt to twist all evidence of the moral sense into "proofs" of egoism. To Hutcheson's way of thinking, the *Fable* is nonsense because it represents human selfishness as universal truth, turning even contrary appearances into supporting evidence. Against this kind of despotic universalism, there is, of course, a familiar retort, which Hutcheson cannot resist. "HE has probably been struck with some old *Fanatick* Sermon upon *Self-Denial* in his Youth, and can never get it out of his head since," the sentimental philosopher sneers at his egoistic opponent (Hutcheson 7: 169). Don Quixote rides again.

The knowledge of benevolence: sentimental quixotism and Sarah Fielding's *David Simple*

Like many sentimental novels, Sarah Fielding's *The Adventures of David Simple* (1744) has been read in sharply divergent ways.[57] Some critics regard the novel as a cagey narrative that disguises Fielding's "real meanings," while others argue exactly the opposite: "Occasionally one might suspect that the simple tender David is being treated ironically but it would be an improper suspicion. Tenderness must always be reverenced."[58] In addition, Fielding has been famously praised for her insight into human interiority. "What a knowledge of the human heart!" Samuel Richardson gushes in a letter to the author:

> Well might a critical judge of writing say, as he did to me, that your late brother's knowledge of it was not (fine writer as he was) comparable to your's. His was but as the knowledge of the outside of a clock-work machine, while your's was that of all the fine springs and movements inside.[59]

More recently, however, her work has drawn criticism for the poverty of its psychological characterizations. "[H]er characters are a combination of personality traits rather than whole persons," one critic complains, while another marvels: "Her hero, David Simple, scarcely succeeds in being a person at all."[60] Yet what everyone might be able to agree on is that *David Simple* is a sentimental quixotic novel, a classification which goes far toward explaining the diversity of critical opinion surrounding the book. If sentimentalism is the empirical study of invisible things, then it is no wonder that Fielding's insight into the human heart should meet with skepticism, and that her means of making visible the invisible (her sincere—or are they ironic?—descriptions) should invite conflicting interpretations. Like Hutcheson's response to Mandeville, Fielding's story of *David Simple* appeals to the epistemology of experience in order to defend a universal, absolute standard of human virtue and personal merit. The novel appears sentimental (in the pejorative sense) because there is a plausible alternative in competition with this absolute standard. This alternative is the economics of self-interest, a system whose fluctuating social valuations Fielding equates with immorality. In *David Simple* Fielding acknowledges the moral diversity represented by egoistic philosophy, but does so only in order to discount it.

The Adventures of David Simple, Containing an Account of His Travels Through the Cities of London and Westminster in the Search of a Real Friend relates the history of a sentimental quixote whose goal is to create a perfect little community, entirely free of selfish interest. The novel begins with a happy ending. David's father was a prosperous merchant who made a love match with a beautiful woman of no fortune. The couple "lived many Years together, a very honest and industrious life," and were blessed with two exemplary sons,

> *David* and *Daniel*, who, as soon as capable of learning, were sent to publick School, and kept there in a manner which put them on a level with Boys of a superior Degree . . . they were respected equally with those Born in the highest Station. This indeed their Behaviour demanded; for there never appeared any thing mean in their Actions, and Nature had given them Parts enough to converse with the most ingenious of their School-fellows. The strict Friendship they kept up was remarked by the whole School; whoever affronted the one, made an Enemy of the other; and while there was any Money in either of their Pockets, the other was sure never to want it: the Notion of whose Property it was, being the last thing that ever entered into their Heads.[61]

Were this indeed the end of the story, the moral would be clear. True merit will always shine through: honest folks, even of middling to lower sort, who work hard and marry for love, should be able to hold their heads up among the best families in England. David's and Daniel's remarkable friendship, demonstrating their unselfish concern for one another, proves their social worth. The Simple brothers form a perfect little community of sentiment.

The boys' father suddenly takes ill and dies, however, abruptly ending David's "State of Happiness"—not because David's sorrow is inconsolable or the family fortune ruined—but because the death leads to "the Discovery of something in *Daniel*'s Mind" (*DS* 11). That something, hitherto hidden, is selfish interest:

IT will perhaps surprize the Reader as much as it did poor *David*, to find that *Daniel*, notwithstanding the Appearance of Friendship he had all along kept up with his Brother, was in reality one of those Wretches, whose only Happiness centers in themselves; and that his Conversation with his Companions had never any other View, but in some shape or other to promote his own Interest.

(DS 11)

Far from being the benevolent agent whom Hutcheson celebrates, Daniel is the selfish, interested, manipulative knave described by Mandeville; Daniel "had persuaded himself that there was no such thing as any one Virtue in the World" (*DS* 179).[62] His remarkable devotion to David had been motivated only by personal gain:

> While he found it for his Benefit to pretend to the same delicate Way of Thinking, and sincere Love which *David* had for him, he did not want Art enough to affect it; but as soon as he thought it his Interest to break with his Brother, he threw off the Mask, and took no pains to conceal the Baseness of his Heart.

(DS 11)

Significantly, Daniel's baseness motivates him to forge his father's will, disinheriting David in favor of himself. Emphasizing the difficulty of accurately knowing another person's will, Daniel's act of forgery represents the greatest threat possible to a sentimental community. True sentiments are invisible, hidden in the breast. They must be interpreted and inferred, for they cannot be directly known. Having "Art enough" to counterfeit his sentiments, Daniel proves the language of true feeling to be untrustworthy, as his dishonest affectation easily mimics genuine affection. David, in his simplicity, is helpless before such deceit, for he lacks the interpretive ability—the cunning—to recognize self-interested designs. When he hears the terms of the forged will, David's only concern is an uneasy feeling that somehow he must have displeased his father. He reads and values the will only as an expression of his father's sentiments and affections—as the language of feeling—fully trusting that he and Daniel will continue to live together as always, for "his honest Heart never doubted but that his Brother's Mind was like his own" (*DS* 14). Daniel's mind, however, is not like David's. Reading and valuing his father's will not as a statement of affection, but as an instrument of ownership, Daniel regards the document as a means toward establishing an interest distinct from his brother's. Sentimental community in *David Simple* cannot withstand such differences in interpretation and interpretive systems; it cannot bear such ambiguity in the meaning of human will. When David finally realizes how different Daniel's mind is from his own, his perfect little community is shattered, and he flees his brother's house.

David's disappointments and distresses are predominantly moral in nature, for his economic sufferings do not last for long. An accomplice of Daniel's soon reveals the crime, and David is promptly restored. Yet David's unhappiness persists, for he remains destitute of that perfect friendship he so dearly loves. Differences of mind, not financial misfortunes, have destroyed his world. So, once more in possession of a comfortable fortune, he resolves to begin an unusual quest:

> The only Use he had for Money, was to serve his Friends; but when he reflected how difficult it was to meet with a Person who deserved that Name, and how hard it would be for him ever to believe anyone sincere, having been so much deceived, he thought nothing in Life could be any great Good to him again. He spent whole Days in thinking on this Subject, wishing he could meet with a human Creature capable of Friendship; by which Word he meant so perfect a Union of Minds, that each should consider himself but as a Part of one entire Being; a little community, as it were of two, to the Happiness of which all the Actions of both should tend with an absolute disregard of any selfish or separate Interest.
>
> This was the Fantom, the Idol of his Soul's Admiration. In the Worship of which he at length grew such an Enthusiast, that he was in this Point only as mad as *Quixotte* himself could be with Knight Errantry; and after much amusing himself with the deepest Ruminations on this Subject, in which a fertile Imagination raised a thousand pleasing Images to itself, he at length took the oddest, most unaccountable Resolution that ever was heard of, *viz*. To travel through the whole World, rather than not meet with a real Friend.[63]
>
> (*DS* 26–7)

With the "Discovery of something in *Daniel*'s Mind" having occasioned all David's distress, David determines to travel the world over to find a mind really like his own: "to find out the Sentiments of others . . . was all he wanted to know" (*DS* 27). The "Idol of his Soul's Admiration" is a fantasy of empathy, the dream of "a Union of Minds" so perfect that no "selfish or separate Interest" will intervene. Paradoxically, David becomes "as mad as *Quixotte* himself" in order to put an end to quixotism, to escape the differences of mind and separate interests that cause social conflict. His method mimics that of the new philosophy: he will "travel through the whole World" in a systematic search for real friendship, despite the fact that the object of his study—as the example of Daniel suggests—may not be empirically knowable. Daniel, after all, had managed to fool David for years. Moreover, the friendship that David seeks may have no real existence, just as Daniel's presumed goodness proved to be imaginary. Using empirical methods to verify the empirically unverifiable reality of virtuous friendship, David is a sentimental quixote. Establishing a contrast between David's good nature and Daniel's selfish artifice, the novel implicitly compares David to the new philosophers, whose own search for "*Real Knowledge*" found an obstacle in the human "*Arts*." Like the linguistic schemes of the early empiricists, David's sentimentalism attempts to eliminate interpretive differences by fashioning a natural language.

David's natural language is the language of feeling, the sovereign authority of unmediated experience, a "faith of seeing" that discounts all interpretations contrary to his own. With Daniel's artfulness directly opposed to David's simplicity, the action of the novel depicts the triumph of David's way of understanding the world. Daniel and David embody the hermeneutic conflict that Joel Weinsheimer calls "the dichotomy of knaves and fools." According to Weinsheimer, two incommensurate interpretations of interpretation divide the field of eighteenth-century hermeneutics: that of fools, who credulously see only surfaces, "taking things to be what they seem and words to mean what they say"; and that of knaves, who suspiciously distrust the obvious, "ferreting out the real beyond the apparent, the meaning behind the word." "The fool understands everything as plain, the knave as dark and deep," Weinsheimer argues: "One continually underreads; the other overreads."[64] David is a fool, for he sentimentally reads only surfaces in a credulous, literal manner that is the very hallmark of quixotism. Daniel is a knave, manipulating appearances in order to pursue his hidden interests. The incommensurability of these two interpretive systems keeps them always in quixotic conflict, forever vying with one another for supremacy—for the power to circumscribe one another's meanings in the way that Hutcheson and Mandeville do. These interpretive systems cannot coexist as equals, because the rational standards of each define the other as wrong-headed.

The sentimentalism of *David Simple* is tactical and aggressive, participating in this competitive game of rhetorical trumps by first creating, then frustrating, the expectation for a *bildungsroman*. For seventeen years, David has incorrectly thought Daniel's mind to be just like his own. David's adventures, it would seem, should teach him how to detect real character and to avoid imposition. Yet throughout the novel, David learns nothing that he does not already know. He cannot develop, because he is already perfect: "his own Mind was a Proof to him, that Generosity, Good-nature, and a Capacity for real Friendship were to be found in the World" (*DS* 46). Having nothing to learn, David interacts with others by trusting them initially, then avoiding them once they fail to live up to his expectations. His standards are firmly fixed, though at odds with those of society—he is quixotic. While ostensibly on a voyage of discovery, looking for security in a world with no common standards and few trustworthy guides, David Simple is himself the measure of goodness. Throughout his journey, he imposes his sentiments onto others, trumping their systems of interpretation and evaluation even as they attempt to do the same to his.

For example, early in his journey, David befriends one Mr Spatter, who guides David through the scenes of "*High Life*." Spatter, as his name suggests, often indulges in ridicule, a fault David observes but interprets kindly: "he concluded that he must be good at the Bottom, and that perhaps it was only his *Love of Mankind*, which made him have such a Hatred and Detestation of their Vices, as caused him to be eager in reproaching them" (*DS* 82). David breaks with Spatter, however, as soon as this interpretation is no longer tenable—as soon as he cannot reconcile Spatter's sentiments to his own way of thinking. It is Spatter's endorsement of vengeance that fills David with "Horror for his Principles," causing David to realize that Spatter's railing against everyone does not arise from humanitarian love. His next guide, Mr Varnish, has a temperament the opposite of Spatter's. Varnish sees faults, but always puts the happiest construction upon them. Eternally serene because he lacks the strong "Sensations which arise from Good-nature" (*DS* 124), Varnish never feels the indignation and moral outrage that frequently visit David. Fielding draws this contrast early in their association, when Varnish reveals "[t]hat Spatter had represented [David] in several publick Places as a Madman, who had pursued a Scheme which was never capable of entering the Brain of one in his Senses; namely, of hunting after a real Friend" (*DS* 96). The good-natured David cannot varnish these remarks, and instantly grows angry.

> However difficult is was to raise *David*'s Resentments, yet he found an Indignation within him at having his favourite Scheme made a jest of: for his Man of Goodness and Virtue was, to him, what *Dulcinea* was to Don *Quixote*; and to hear it was thought impossible for any such thing to be found, had an equal Effect on him as what *Sancho* had on the Knight, when he told him, "His great Princess was winnowing of Wheat, and sifting Corn." He cry'd out, "Is there a Man on Earth who finds so much Badness in his own Bosom, as to convince him, for from thence he must be convinced, that there is no such thing in the World as Goodness? But I should wonder at nothing in a Man, who professes himself a Lover of Revenge, and of an inexorable Temper."
>
> (*DS* 96–7)

What distinguishes Spatter, Varnish and David Simple is their style of representation and interpretation. Spatter goes too far to abuse, Varnish too far to excuse, while David simply tells the truth. The three men read the world differently, subscribing to incompatible systems of representation. Spatter always sees the ill in humanity (including his own vengeful temper), and therefore ridicules the idealistic David as a madman who is out of his senses. David, however, who knows that the ideal friend does exist (at least in himself), quickly and warmly dismisses Spatter for solipsistically limiting all humanity to the "Badness in his own Bosom." "I should wonder at nothing in a Man" like Spatter, David indignantly concludes. The passage makes explicit that the conflict between David and his guides is quixotic, for each man maintains the supremacy of his own interpretive system by circumscribing his rivals into subordinate positions within it. Only each man's assumption of his own rightness guarantees the ridiculousness of his opponent's position. Thus David becomes a "Madman" (no longer credible), Spatter becomes a sink of "Badness" (no longer credible), while Varnish is exposed as insensible (no longer credible). David's sentimentalism, Spatter's raillery and Varnish's "eternal Chearfulness" seek to trump one another.

The point of David's journey, then, is not so much to discover a "real Friend," as to stage a competition between differing interpretive communities, a competition that David's natural language will win. Fielding achieves this effect by making self-expression a reward of true friendship. All of the real friends David finds—Cynthia, Camilla and Valentine—have suffered as victims of rhetorical competition. Unable to make themselves understood in their previous communities, they were misrepresented and devalued. Their joining with David to form a new community signals their discursive triumph; speaking David's language, they can finally speak for themselves. For example, forced into dependency upon an imperious patroness, Cynthia loses all ability to represent herself, and is "*suddenly transformed from a Wit into a Toad-eater, without any visible Change, in either her Person or Behaviour.*" As she explains,

> by that time I had remained with her two or three Months, she began to treat me as a *Creature* born to be her *Slave*: whenever I spoke, I was sure to offend her; if I was *silent*, I was *out of humour*; if I said any thing in the softest Terms, to complain of the Alteration in her Affection, I was *whimsical* and *ungrateful*.
>
> (*DS* 115)

Denied the ability to articulate her own meanings, Cynthia views herself as a "*Slave*," as one whose subjectivity has been entirely erased and written over. Her silence is declared ill-humor. Her "softest Terms" are decreed capricious ingratitude. Her interiority belongs to another: "I was to have no *Passions*, no *Inclinations* of my own," she recalls, "but was to be turned into a piece of Clockwork, which her Ladyship was to wind up or let down, as she pleased" (*DS* 116).

The distresses of Camilla and Valentine likewise stem from the misrepresentations perpetrated by their stepmother, Livia, who turned their father against them because "she thought her Interest incompatible" with theirs (*DS* 142). "She never abused us; but found means to work on our Tempers in such a manner, as in my Father's sight always to make us appear in the wrong," Camilla explains. Using "such mean Arts," Livia could make the innocent look guilty and the guilty look innocent, Camilla recounts: "I was astonished at her giving things that Turn, and she triumphed in finding how easily she could make every thing go to her Wish" (*DS* 143–4). Camilla cannot even silently endure her own suffering without it being used against her:

I was so altered with the continual Uneasiness of my Mind, that no one would have known me. This, which was owing to my tender Regret for the Loss of a Parent's Love, was imputed to Rancour and Malice; thus my very Grief was turned to my disadvantage.

(DS 147)

Like Cynthia, Camilla recognizes that her distress arises from her inability to represent herself authoritatively. In her misery, she finds herself fondly wishing for a new system of representation, a means of making truth immediately visible to all, like "the Goddess of Justice's Mirror of Truth, as it is described in that beautiful Vision in the *Tatler*" (*DS* 143).

Fielding's novel is not naïve, however. Camilla's yearning for the *Tatler*'s "Mirror of Truth" conveys a desire for representational simplicity, but not without reminding readers of the interpretive complexities of sentimental truth. With their fanciful dream of a "Mirror of Truth" that would end all misrepresentations and differences of mind, the *Tatler* essays to which Camilla alludes (nos 100 and 102) are themselves mirrors of the difficulties facing David and his friends in their quest for a natural language. The "beautiful Vision" first comes to the *Tatler*'s Mr Bickerstaff one night after he has been feeling, like Cynthia and Camilla, the stings of injured merit. Having spent the day "repining at the sudden Rise of many Persons" who are his "Juniors," and more generally brooding upon "the unequal Distribution of Wealth, Honour, and all other Blessings of Life," Mr Bickerstaff is eventually drawn into "a far more agreeable Contemplation" and restored to his "usual Temper and Serenity of Soul" by the beauty of the night sky: "The Heaven above me appeared in all its Glories, and presented me with such an Hemisphere of Stars, as made the most agreeable Prospect imaginable to one who delights in the Study of Nature." Thinking it "the richest Sky" he has ever seen, he "cannot behold a Scene so wonderfully adorned and lighted up . . . without suitable Meditations on the Author of such illustrious and amazing Objects" (*Tatler* 2: 114). What causes Bickerstaff's initial gloom, "according to the Nature of Men in Years, who have made but little Progress in the Advancement of their Fortune or their Fame," is his own overlooked merit. The signs of personal worth—advancement, wealth, honor—to him appear arbitrary and fallacious. Bickerstaff's complacency returns, however, at the prospect of true representation, figured as a night sky ablaze with all the riches and adornments that have been denied to him. The exquisite beauty of the heavens sends Bickerstaff into "suitable Meditations" on its "Author," reaffirming that true merit can indeed find reliable expression, and that Bickerstaff knows how to read these expressions correctly. Contented once more, Bickerstaff reports, "I retired to my Lodgings, with the Satisfaction of having passed away a few Hours in the proper Employments of a reasonable Creature and promising my self that my Slumbers would be sweet" (*Tatler* 2: 114). The tangle of capricious human significations recedes into insignificance under the ethereal light of natural meanings. Bickerstaff's worth may never be reflected by the arbitrary signs of advancement, wealth and honor, but his rapt attention to the night sky reveals his true merit by proving him an excellent reader of nature. Bickerstaff's own endeavors, not those of his more prominent juniors, are "the proper Employments of a reasonable Creature."

Bickerstaff's slumbers are sweet, for later that evening—as a further indication of the clarity of his moral vision—he dreams of how society would appear if true merit could suddenly be made visible. In his dream, the Goddess of Justice descends from the heavens, bearing a "Mirror of Truth" that corrects all faulty signs of social worth: "A voice was heard from the Clouds, declaring the Intention of this Visit, which was, to restore and appropriate to every one living what was his Due." Then, by the power of the mirror, the external indicators of merit—titles, estates, family and riches—abandon the unworthy and cleave to the deserving. The mirror shoots forth beams of light that burn up all "Forgery and Falshood" in legal instruments, and uncover hidden documents and records (*Tatler* 2: 116). At the same time, all ill-gotten gains are stripped from their current holders and returned to their rightful owners: fortunes change hands, wardrobes are swapped and the bankers of Lombard Street all go broke. Next, all of humankind separate into their proper families, occasioning much movement as children *"repair to their True and Natural Fathers."* Finally, the Goddess of Justice commands "[t]*hat all the Posts of Dignity and Honour in the Universe should be conferred on Persons of the greatest Merit, Abilities and Perfection"* (*Tatler* 2: 117). After the bustling dies down, "[a]ll were surprised to see so many new Faces in the most eminent Dignities," Bickerstaff remarks, "and, for my own Part, I was very well pleased to see that all my Friends either kept their present Posts, or were advanced to higher." In the end, the world is restored to a condition in which individual merit is accurately reflected by the social order. The Mirror of Truth makes interpretation simple. It also affirms Bickerstaff's own excellence as a reader, the continued success of all his friends serving as a strong recommendation of his ability to read character.

But the beautiful vision of naturalized social order does not end here, for the mirror has yet to reveal to the women their proper rank in the meritocracy: "the most important Affair among Womankind was then to be settled, which every one knows to be the Point of Place," Bickerstaff recalls (*Tatler* 2: 125). Unlike the men, for whom social status becomes the measure of real merit, the women find their virtue displayed directly upon their bodies:

> It was the particular Property of this Looking-glass to banish all false Appearances, and show People what they are. The whole Woman was represented, without Regard to the usual external Features, which were made entirely conformable to their real Characters. In short, the

most accomplished (taking in the whole Circle of Female Perfections)
were the most beautiful; and the most defective, the most deformed.

(*Tatler* 2: 126)

Banishing "all false Appearances," the mirror makes "external Features"
perfectly correspond to "real Characters." The hidden secrets of the breast
become visible. Under the influence of the glass, "multitudes started at their
own Form, and would have broke the Glass if they could have reached it."
"Blooming Features wither" in some; a "Woman of Fire and Spirit" takes on
the appearance of a fury; an "interested Mistress" becomes a harpy; a "subtle
Jilt" becomes a sphinx. Meanwhile, the features of other women improve; a
gray-haired, wrinkled little old lady standing next to Bickerstaff looks so
lovely in the mirror that he considers proposing marriage to her. Yet the alter-
ations in the women's persons are not limited merely to their reflections, for
the goddess also transforms their actual bodies, decreeing that censorious
females should lose the use of speech, and that "all should immediately be
pregnant, who in any Part of their Lives had ran the Hazard of it" (*Tatler* 2:
128). In the wake of justice, female virtue (or its lack) directly manifests itself
upon the female form. External features display inner merit, making real character immediately legible.

This dream of perfect communication, however, remains only a dream, even
in Bickerstaff's dream. For seeing need not be believing, Bickerstaff slyly
suggests, even for those who stare into the Mirror of Truth. "It was a sensible
Affliction to me to see such a Multitude of Fair Ones either dumb or big-
bellied," he sadly reports, just before revealing the heartening and ingenious
method through which the "Fair Ones" are able to reinterpret the meaning of
their new bodily appearance:

> But I was something more at Ease, when I found that they agreed
> upon several Regulations to cover such Misfortunes. Among others,
> that it should be an established Maxim among all Nations, That a
> Woman's First Child might come into the World within six Months
> after her Acquaintance with her Husband; and that Grief might
> retard the Birth of her last till Fourteen Months after his Decease.
>
> (*Tatler* 2: 129)

Bickerstaff's remarks no doubt satirize the vanity and folly of women who
would continue to deny their own faults even when their guilt can be seen by
everyone. Yet the satire cuts two ways, for it reminds readers also that facts do
not speak for themselves, that virtue is not legible on the body, that the empirical study of invisible things depends on a conventional system of
interpretation. There are "faiths of seeing." The "Maxim"—if accepted as a
"self-evident Principle" of reasoning, rather than an adamantine defense of
nonsense—changes the meaning of the facts by establishing a new interpre-

tive logic, one only mildly more ludicrous than, for example, the contorted arguments to which Hutcheson must resort in order to uphold the truth of the moral sense. Reading the body may be more, or perhaps less, than reading nature; it may be reading art as though it were nature. The existence of gendered differences between the mirror's representations—that men's real characters are revealed through family, property and position, while women's real characters appear on their bodies—further emphasizes the convention-ality that underpins "real" representation.

As depicted in Steele's essay, then, sentimental representation is selfcon-sciously paradoxical, a studied simplicity. Like the Royal Society's universal language schemes, sentimentalism seeks to discover "real Characters," to make external forms correspond directly to inner states, to render the invisible visible by representing moral worth as though it were empirically accessible. It pursues a fantasy of natural communication, offering a blissful glimpse of the potential joys of true understanding, perfect justice and real community. Ironically, however, sentimental authority's ability to depict true nature relies heavily on tutored interpretive responses, on ways of reading encouraged by sentimental fiction itself. As Todd argues:

> In all forms of sentimental literature, there is an assumption that life and literature are directly linked, not through any notion of a mimetic depiction of reality but through the belief that the literary experience can intimately affect the living one. So literary conven-tions become a way of life.[65]

Winking at his audience, Steele suggests that meaning—even the meaning of those signs written directly on the body—depends heavily upon convenient, interpretive "Regulations." If so, then Bickerstaff's dream of natural commu-nication is the greatest deception of all. Amid this shell game of art and nature, bad readers will easily grow confused. Therefore, the "beautiful Vision" of the perfectly represented moral universe is limited only to those of exquisite sensibility—to the best of readers, like Mr Bickerstaff, who not only "delights in the Study of Nature," but who is also capable of "suitable Meditations" on its "Author." In a sentimental world, moral virtue and critical ability are equivalent.

Like Bickerstaff, David Simple and his real friends dream of living in the world seen through the Mirror of Truth. They yearn for a natural language. In seeking one another, they pursue this "simple" style of representation, hoping to surround themselves with like-minded individuals who will share their "Regulations" of reading truth on the body. The novel's exaggerated and repeated descriptions of physical reactions to emotional states aim to natu-ralize this desired correspondence between outward signs and inner worth. In Weinsheimer's terms, the novel selfconsciously adopts a foolish interpretive strategy, which David epitomizes. Not a sentiment passes through his mind without also registering visibly on his body. For instance, when Mr Orgueil relates to David the history of a good man's betrayal, David's extreme physical reactions correspond directly to the sympathetic workings of his mind. Mr Orgueil tells of a handsome young man, left destitute at the age of fifteen, who is taken in by a kindly neighbor. The neighbor raises the young man as his own son, eventually buying him a commission in the army. Yet instead of showing proper gratitude, the young man seduces his benefactor's daughter. Her death (by moral trauma) swiftly follows. Of the distraught "best of fathers," witnessing his daughter's decline, Mr Orgueil recounts,

> "The poor Man stifled his Groans while she could hear them, for fear of hurting her; but the Moment she was gone, he tore his hair, beat his Breast, and fell into such Agonies, as is impossible to describe. So I shall follow the Example of the Painter, who drew a Veil before *Agamemnon*'s Face, when his Daughter was sacrificed, despairing from the utmost Stretch of his Art, to paint any Countenance that could express all that Nature must feel on such a dreadful Occasion: I shall leave your own Imagination to represent what he suffered: and only tell you, it was so much, that his Life and Misery soon ended together."
>
> Here Mr. *Orgueil* stopped, seeing poor *David* could hear no more, not being able to stifle his Sighs and Tears, at the Idea of such a Scene; for he did not think it beneath a Man to cry from Tenderness, tho' he would have thought it much too effeminate to be moved to Tears by any Accident that concerned himself only.
>
> As soon as he could recover enough to speak, he cried out, "Good God! is this a World for me to look for Happiness in, when those very Men, who seem to be the Favourites of Nature; in forming whom, she has taken such particular Care to give them everything agreeable, can be guilty of such Crimes as make them a Disgrace to the Species they are born of! What could incite a Man to such monstrous Ingratitude! there was no Circumstance to alleviate his Villainy; for if his Passion was violent, he might have married her." "Yes, (answered Mr. *Orgueil*) but that was not his Scheme, he was ambitious, and thought marrying so young would have spoiled his Fortune" . . . "Well, (replied *David*) and is this Man respected in the World? Will Men converse with him? Should he not be drove from Society, and a mark set upon him, that he might be shunned and despised? He certainly is one of the agreeablest Creatures I ever saw; but I had rather spend my time with the greatest Fool in Nature, provided he was an honest Man, than with such a Wretch."

(*DS* 62–3)

With the villainous seducer appearing to be a favorite of nature, agreeable both in looks and manner, this tale of abominable ingratitude reminds David that self-interested villainy may walk through the world perfectly concealed, that there need be no correlation between real character and external features. The story merely confirms what David already learned from his experience with Daniel. Still, chasing after Bickerstaff's dream, David can hardly believe that such villainy will not shine through for all to see. "[I]s this Man respected in the World? Will Men converse with him?" he asks incredulously, immediately proposing that the man's wickedness be published for all to read and abhor: "Should he not be drove from Society, and a mark set upon him, that he might be shunned and despised?" If David is somewhat less forgiving than God of the Old Testament, who drove Cain from society but marked him for his own protection, not so that Cain could be further despised, it is because David recognizes how necessary such distinguishing marks are to his search for sentimental community. Without them, he cannot know where to "look for Happiness," for he would not know what to look for. Virtue and merit, Fielding's narrative urges on the one hand, are not plain objects of sight.

On the other hand, even as the woeful history rehearsed above teaches David (again) that real character is invisible, David's own reactions to the account gratify readers of the novel with a pleasing fiction of visible virtue. David's "Sighs and Tears" come at precisely the right moment in Orgueil's narrative, just after David has been invited to imagine the father's extreme grief. What defies description—because art cannot express "all that Nature must feel"—David can reproduce in his imagination. The episode shows David responding to Orgueil's tale, as Sarah Fielding expects her readers to respond to David Simple's story. Of David's misery upon discovering Daniel's treachery, her narrator asserts: "What he felt . . . is not to be expressed or understood, but by the few who are capable of real Tenderness" (DS 18). Fielding thus shifts the burden of making the invisible visible from author to reader, asserting that the capacity to communicate these inner states is an exclusive ability of only the most sensitive minds. Those capable of "real Tenderness" will sympathize with David, just as David's unquestionable moral sensibility compels his tearful response to Orgueil's tale. David's strong physical reactions at just the right moments—emblems of his capacity to feel—reveal the correctness of his understanding. To see David's merit, sensible readers can read his body, for in him and in people like him, the senti-mental ideal of natural communication is already real.

Fielding's frequent reliance on the trope of inexpressibility thus serves as a preemptive means by which to discredit the skeptical laughter of anti-senti-mentalists. Reading their disbelief as incapacity, Fielding circumscribes the meaning of their critical reaction, denying them the opportunity to dissent rationally. Like Steele, Fielding recognizes the importance of the self-inter-ested "Regulations" that govern interpretation, and she exploits them to further her cause. Skeptics are not allowed to criticize her sentimentalism without first admitting their own incapacity as critics, a tribute she exacts by cleverly anticipating critical reaction and incorporating it into the novel's satire. Anti-sentimentalists must see themselves in the encounter David has with a company of critics who prattle foolishly on about "the Absurdity of almost every body," complaining that most people "can't even laugh or cry in the right place" (DS 83). "Pray, did you ever hear any thing like what my Lady True-wit said the other Night," scoffs one of these self-proclaimed wits,

> "that the part of the Play [Othello] which chiefly affected her, was, that which inspired an Apprehension of what that odious Wretch must feel, when he found out that Desdemona was innocent; as if he could suffer too much, after being guilty of so barbarous an Action."
>
> (DS 82)

Since names in David Simple generally characterize their bearer appropriately (a formal salute to representational simplicity, the only notable exception being Daniel Simple), Lady True-wit's sentiments should be regarded as true critical opinion; her generous impulse to share in what Othello "must feel" contrasts sharply with the would-be wits' desire to distance and condemn. Likewise, readers learn that when Lady True-wit and her good friend, Lady Know-all, saw Dryden's Don Sebastian (1690), they sat "with great Attention, altho' . . . quite calm" while Sebastian and Dorax quarreled, "but the Moment they were reconciled, and embraced each other, they both burst into a Flood of Tears, which they seemed unable to restrain" (DS 84). The wits laugh at this ridiculous behavior of True-wit and Know-all, who respond most intensely to scenes of tenderness, remorse, reconciliation and forgiveness. "They certainly must have something very odd in their Heads," sneers one member of the company, "and the Author is very much obliged to them, for grieving most when his Hero, Don Sebastian, had most Reason to be pleased, in finding a true Friend in the Man he thought his Enemy" (DS 84). Bad critics, such as these self-appointed judges, cannot properly read the emotional signs of the body; to them, true sensibility (like David's) looks absurd. Misinterpreting the meaning of tears, they exhibit the very shortcoming that they scorn in others: "they can't even laugh or cry in the right place." Numb to the exquisite sensibility of tender readers, unfeeling critics (such as those who do not appreciate David Simple) lack both wit and knowledge. Their criticism of sentimental representation, therefore, carries no authority, for they do not understand the impulses that they mock. Equating correct reading with sensibility, Fielding's novel preemptively excludes skeptical readers from her audience, making the only readers qualified to comment upon David Simple those who are uncritical of David's natural language.

Accordingly, the people who become David's real friends all speak this natural language of bodily emotion, fluently communicating through sighs, blushes and tears. Their goodness shines through their bodies unimpeded.

When David meets Cynthia, "He had a great Curiosity to hear *Cynthia's* Story; for there was something so good-natured in her Countenance" (*DS* 100). Cynthia, in turn, "by the Innocence of *David's* Looks, and the Sincerity which was visible in his Manner of expressing himself," is "prevail'd on to relate the History of her Life" (*DS* 101). Likewise, when David first meets Valentine and Camilla, rescuing them from near fatal poverty, they communicate much through looks alone. Valentine sometimes "looked on *David* with an Air of Softness and Gratitude, in which our Hero's Sensibility read as much as in any thing he could have said," whereas Camilla, so overcome with tenderness, joy and gratitude, "was unable to speak, or to refrain any longer from bursting into a Flood of Tears, which was the only means she had left to express her Thoughts" (*DS* 129). David, of course, "longed to know their Story," as they had "the Appearance of so much Merit" (*DS* 132). His voyage of discovery finds people with whom he can form his sentimental community, people whose sentiments are readily visible on the body, not hidden in the breast. Among David's real friends, sentimental conventions exist as a natural language, making sentimental methodology valid. For David, the empirical study of invisible things works. Having found his "little Community," his "Travels [are] now at an End" (*DS* 303).

A double wedding takes place in the last chapter of the novel, with David marrying Camilla and Valentine marrying Cynthia. The narrator celebrates the exemplary society epitomized by these four real friends:

> it is impossible for the most lively Imagination to form an Idea more pleasing than what this little Society enjoyed, in the true Proofs of each other's Love: And, as strong a Picture as this is of real Happiness, it is in the power of every Community to attain it, if every Member of it would perform the part allotted to him by *Nature*, or his *Station in Life*, with a sincere Regard to the Interest and Pleasure of the whole.
>
> (*DS* 304)

Epistemological bliss reigns as everyone in David's little society, fluent in sentimentalism's natural language, enjoys "the true Proofs" of one another's love. The narrator will not describe what these "true Proofs" are, nor will she represent the society's happiness any more explicitly than to affirm it to be beyond anything that human imagination could surpass. Anti-sentimentalists will find Fielding's "Proofs" unconvincing, for she seems to write only to readers who are already sentimental, or who wish to appear so. Though David's happiness may well be real, its truth remains the purview of exclusive sensibility, not the object of universal understanding. Skeptics may persist, for the novel offers "Real Knowledge" of David's happiness only to sentimental sympathizers who already share David's faith of seeing.

An enthusiast and empiricist at the book's beginning, David remains so at the book's end. He maintains his faith of seeing against all contrary evidence.

The narrator's optimistic claim that "it is in the power of every Community to attain" such happiness as David's, if only everyone would be true to "*Nature*" and regard the "Interest and Pleasure of the whole," follows logically from the "Regulations" of reading established within the novel, regulations designed to embarrass the world's egoists, along with their cunning "Arts" and selfish regard only for their own interest. Fielding's sentimentalism presents an alternative to egoistic philosophy; it competes against egoism as a system of social valuation. Reading mute bodies and twisting other people's meanings in order to serve her own conclusions, Fielding strives for nothing less than discursive domination over her egoistic opponents. Her fiction entirely circumscribes egoism, showing it to be an irrational perversion of sentimental values; this point is made particularly clear when the calculating Daniel Simple, on his deathbed, admits that his joyless life of poverty, illness and disappointment resulted from his being "utterly abandoned to all the Sentiments of Humanity, or the true Knowledge of [his] own Interest" (*DS* 289). Thus, while seeming to speak to sentimentalists only, Fielding in fact speaks to anti-sentimentalists as well, pressuring them to conform to her views by proclaiming their incapacity as reasoners and readers if they do not. Only plotters ignorant of their true interest, and critics willing to be marked as bad readers, can deny the truth of David's sentiments. Urging people to perform the parts allotted to them by "*Nature*," Fielding's art teaches sensible readers to be sentimental quixotes. Her rhetorically crafted "natural language" promotes the authority of sentimental convention, an authority which boasts a body that sighs and weeps.

3

COMING TO A BAD END

Sentimentalism, *The Female Quixote* and the power of interest

> Quoth *Hudibras*, It is in vain
> (I see) to argue 'gainst the grain,
> Or, like the *Stars*, encline men to
> What they'r averse themselves to do.
> For when *Disputes* are wearyed out
> 'Tis *interest* still resolves the doubt;
> But since no reason can confute yee,
> I'l try to force you to your *Duty*.
> Samuel Butler, *Hudibras*,
> II, ii, 477–84

Readers of Charlotte Lennox's novel *The Female Quixote* (1752) often leave the book feeling that the heroine, Arabella, has come to a bad end—in both senses of the phrase. Up until the penultimate chapter, Arabella is a strong, independent, admirably spirited woman. The final scenes of the novel show her defeated, humiliated and subordinated by a dogmatic clergyman, forced to her duty in the name of reason and in the interests of patriarchy. What had seemed a glorious feminist spark disappointingly fizzles into an unremarkable marriage that returns woman to her proper place.[1] Even if Arabella's concession to the patriarchy is not lamented *per se*, the abruptness of her alteration is. The "ending should have been more artistically contrived," writes one critic,[2] while another speculates that the novel's sudden conclusion unhappily resulted from the pressures of Lennox's financial distress.[3] I suggest, however, that Arabella comes to a bad end not through political or artistic compromise, but because of the recalcitrance of the problem of quixotism itself. Arabella, after all, is not only female, but also a quixote, and "female" and "quixote" are not entirely synonymous. Interpretations that ignore their differences by equating quixotism with feminism, and rationality with patriarchy, have difficulty recuperating the book's jarring and seemingly anti-feminist conclusion. To make better sense of the novel's ending, we must reimagine the

125

relations between gender, rationality and the novel's ultimate sentimentalism.[4]

Addressing the significance of quixotism in Lennox's novel, this chapter will read Arabella's sudden reformation in the penultimate chapter as an attempt to salvage social coherence in the face of radical and disturbing, albeit stylized, moral and political diversity. If quixotism, as I have argued, represents differences of mind, then a plot that reconciles a quixote to society should point the way to universal understanding. The reformation of quixotism should be the restoration of reason, or at least the instauration of a sentimental community in which there is, to borrow Sarah Fielding's words, no "selfish or separate Interest," that is to say, no significant differences between people. The advantage gained by reading *The Female Quixote* through these wider associations of quixotism is the ability to account for Arabella's conversion without conceding a feminist defeat. Lennox's novel undermines the very assumption that quixotism and sentimentalism are weaknesses particular to women's reading practices. The moral, political and epistemological problems that Lennox engages in her novel are not unique to her heroine, just as a sentimental resolution is not unique to her plot. *The Female Quixote*'s conventionality, however, carries the narrative in more radical directions, for the novel's bad ending draws attention to the similar social implications of quixotic and sentimental hermeneutics, similarities that destabilize categories such as "rational" and "irrational," "masculine" and "feminine." Arabella's "cure" is no cure, for the doctor who treats her is himself quixotic. She never really has to change. Throughout the narrative, she remains as static as David Simple; she begins the story as an empiricist, and ends the story as an empiricist. The satire in *The Female Quixote* ridicules not only romantic extravagance, but also (masculine?) rational empiricism and the reading practices associated with it. Lennox's novel mocks empiricism *as* quixotism.

One factor that has encouraged readers to oversimplify the meaning of Arabella's quixotism has been the temptation to over-identify Lennox with Arabella. Arabella's "madness," as has been often observed, is her desire to hold authority, to figure prominently in history and to wield power rather than surrendering it in marriage. Romances nourish these aspirations in her, presenting her with supposedly historical examples of heroines who maintain their autonomy by deferring matrimony. Offering Arabella this alternative idea of history, romances engender in her a singular (and single) sense of self that resists marriage to Mr Glanville, thereby keeping her at the center of attention. Arabella's quixotism may thus be seen as her feminism—her desire to be a noteworthy, fully participating member of society, on a par with men. As I have argued in Chapter 1, this reading of quixotism is not anachronistic. The anonymous "Lady" who wrote *Female Rights Vindicated* (1758) makes the connection explicit:

To endeavour refuting an Opinion of so long standing as that of *the Superiority of the Men over the Women, with respect to Genius and Abilities*, must appear to many a strange and impracticable Attempt; and Numbers, even of Women, misled by Prejudice and Custom, may believe no one would be so *Quixotic* as to list herself Champion of the Sex upon this Occasion.

Substituting romances for the long-standing opinions of history, Arabella seems "to list herself Champion of the Sex." Late twentieth-century readings frequently extend this quality in Arabella to Lennox herself, in order to applaud Lennox as an author primarily interested in challenging gender hierarchies.[5] Arabella becomes a figure for Lennox as feminist pioneer, an eighteenth-century woman struggling to write her own way through life. Arabella's opposites—the "empty-headed, selfish, and ordinary" characters, such as her cousin Miss Glanville[6]—serve as foils to Arabella and Lennox, further strengthening the reading of Arabella and Lennox as heroic feminists.

Lennox's own attitude toward romance narrative and Arabella's quixotism, however, appears to have been much more complex, the aim of her self-satire much less clear. Consider the name of "Arabella." Though not uncommon in eighteenth-century fiction (Clarissa's sister is an Arabella, as is the Vicar of Wakefield's daughter-in-law and the Fool of Quality's wife),[7] Lennox's inspiration for this name may have had a specific, historical source. In a piece written for her periodical *The Lady's Museum* (1760–1) Lennox depicts Henry the Great of France considering potential brides. One of the possibilities he mentions is "the princess Arabella of England." Lennox's footnote informs readers that this Arabella was "daughter to Charles,"

Earl of Lennox, who was grandson to Margaret queen of Scotland, eldest sister to Henry VIII. Her cousin-german, James VI. king of Scotland, having in 1602 been declared lawful heir to Queen Elizabeth, the following year a conspiracy was formed in her favour, and she died in 1616, a prisoner in the tower of London.[8]

This Arabella, like the Arabella of *The Female Quixote*, appears as a noble woman who is particularly threatening to male authority. Such a passing reference would hardly seem significant, except that Lennox habitually goes out of her way to include allusions to the Stuart family in her works. For example, Lennox's chapter on *Macbeth* in her *Shakespear Illustrated* (1753–4) is constituted in large part by acknowledged, verbatim borrowings from Johnson's *Miscellaneous Observations on the Tragedy of Macbeth* (1745). Yet at one point Lennox adds an unusual and significant interpolation to Johnson's text. Having noted the prophecy that from Banquo would spring a long line of kings, Lennox offers readers a "long Account of the Posterity of *Banquo*," allegedly in order to show Shakespeare's flattery of King James. She cites

Hector Boece's *Chronicles of Scotland* (1526), which mentions the marriage of Robert, the younger son of Banquo's great-great-great grandson, to "the Daughter of *Robert* of Cruxtoun, from which Marriage the Families of *Darnley* and *Lennox* are descended."[9] Thus, while ostensibly exposing Shakespeare's flattery, she publicizes the close relation of the Stuart, Darnley and Lennox families—a clan that seems to have fascinated her, judging from her fondness for these names. Her first novel, supposedly autobiographical,[10] relates the adventures of Harriot Stuart. The central sisters of her fourth novel, *Sophia* (1762), are Harriot and Sophia Darnley.[11] (Is there a Harriot Lennox? Yes, Lennox's daughter, born in 1765.) Quite possibly Lennox's interest in these families came via her husband, Alexander Lennox, who did in fact have pretensions to nobility. In April of 1768 he appeared at a meeting of the Peers in Edinburgh, claiming to be the rightful Earl of Lennox, "the lineal heir-male of the ancient earls of Lennox, of the name of Lennox, lineally descended from a brother of Duncan, the Seventh Earl of Lennox." For the next six years, he continued his suit for this title.[12]

It is not clear how deeply invested Lennox was in her husband's grand pretensions, though certain quirks in her biography do intimate her willingness to assume a romantic identity. Obituaries and biographical dictionaries describe Lennox as the American-born daughter of a Colonel James Ramsay, Governor of New York.[13] The source for this account of Lennox's American origins was probably Lennox herself, for in 1792 she or her friends petitioned the Royal Literary Fund to assist the "daughter of Colonel Ramsay, Royalist Governor of New York in 1720," with the year 1720 also stated as that of her birth.[14] Scholars, however, have been unable to verify this account of her life. New York never had a governor named Ramsay,[15] and Lennox's father appears to have been no more than a captain of an Independent Company of Foot while in America.[16] Moreover, the alleged year of her birth seems incorrect. Richardson's description of the *The Female Quixote*'s author as "hardly twenty-four" suggests a much later birth date, possibly at the end of the 1720s,[17] a conjecture supported as well by the arrival of her first child in 1765. If Lennox was born in the late 1720s, and Captain James Ramsay was indeed her father, then Gibraltar is the likely place of her birth.[18] The biography of Charlotte Lennox given to the Royal Literary Fund may be wrong in all its particulars, but it does present Lennox in a much more romantic light; she is a heroine, a daughter born to the warrior-ruler of a faraway land, or as the Countess in *The Female Quixote* phrases it, a princess "wandering thro' the World by Land and Sea in mean Disguises" (*FQ* 326). Lennox's identification with Arabella may thus be even stronger than people generally presume, her satiric attack on romance narratives a self-conscious indictment of her own foolish desires.

Yet in reading Lennox's interests as being exclusively aligned with the character of Arabella, we overlook another character who, if recognized also as a figure for Lennox, allows us to infer more about the novelist's concerns. If names are significant—as seems to be the case in Lennox's novels—then we should not ignore the fact that Miss Glanville, Arabella's unromantic foil, bears Lennox's own given name of "Charlotte."[19] In addition, Charlotte Glanville shares with the partially autobiographical Harriot Stuart the same defining characteristic of coquetry.[20] "Miss *Charlotte*," we are told, "had a large Share of Coquetry in her Composition" (*FQ* 80), while Harriot Stuart wittily confesses "I was born a coquet, and what would have been art in others, in me was pure nature."[21] So precocious was Harriot in the ways of coquetry that at the age of eleven she had "all the coquet inclinations of fifteen; and not only knew the full value of a smile, a sigh, or a blush, but could practice them all upon occasion" (*HS* 1: 8). Lennox saw similarities between coquettish artfulness and authorial artistry; her twice-published poem, "The Art of Coquetry" (1747, 1750), makes the connection satirically explicit by having the poet derive both her poetry and her coquetry from the same source: "The queen of love herself my bosom fires,/Assists my numbers, and my thought inspires:/Me she instructed in each secret art."[22] "Art" here refers both to poetic "numbers" and to the little coquettish tricks (the "sigh," "the starting tear," the "melting languish") that the poet later recommends. Art is indispensable to both authors and coquettes. In this context, Miss Glanville's coquetry is an important detail, for it identifies her as a contriver. Like Harriot Stuart—and, we might suppose, like Lennox herself (hence the shared name of "Charlotte")—Miss Glanville recognizes her own artfulness. In doing so, she demonstrates a level of selfconsciousness that distinguishes her from the female quixote.[23] Arabella is quixotic while Miss Glanville is not, precisely because it is the inability to recognize artifice that defines the quixote. Thus, in the contrast between the artless Arabella and the artfully aware Charlotte, Lennox depicts the pronounced interpretive differences that must be reconciled in order for the novel's plot to be effectively resolved. In this light, Arabella's "cure" is no cure at all, for it fails to bring her any closer to her more self-conscious cousin. Rather, Arabella's sentimental conversion leaves intact the naïve, essentialist assumptions of her reading practice, revealing her quixotism to be but a slight variation on the "masculine" rational authority that seeks to reform her. Miss Glanville, though unattractive at times, hints at what a truly reformed Arabella would be. By further scrutinizing the relation between these two women, we can begin to surmise the nature of the ambivalence that leads to Arabella's bad end.

Arabella's quixotism expresses itself as her insistence upon interpreting all events within the narrow expectations of romance. She assumes handsome servants to be princes in disguise; treats her often puzzled serving maid, Lucy, as a confidante; and regards unknown men on horseback as knights intent upon ravishment. Empirical evidence is powerless to alter her romantic beliefs, for her romantic beliefs are empirically derived: "she had such a strange Facility in reconciling every Incident to her own fantastic Ideas, that every new Object added Strength to the fatal deception she laboured under" (*FQ* 340). Having grown up on a secluded country estate described as the

"Epitome of *Arcadia*" (*FQ* 5), Arabella's experience has taught her to accept romances as true histories: "Her Ideas, from the Manner of her Life, and the Objects around her, had taken a romantic Turn; and supposing Romances were real Pictures of Life, from them she drew all her Notions and Expectations" (*FQ* 7). With her surroundings so conformable to those represented in her books, Arabella concludes that romance depictions are accurate, and that people should behave accordingly. Her romantic beliefs may be extraordinary, but they develop under and rely upon the very ordinary intellectual method of empiricism.

For instance, one day Arabella and Miss Glanville, traveling with their family on the road to Bath, find themselves pursued by horsemen. When Arabella sees "Three or Four Men of a genteel Appearance, on Horseback," her thorough familiarity with romances allows her immediately to recognize the situation. Sticking her head out of the coach window, she cries to the riders:

> Hold, hold, valiant Men . . . do not, by a mistaken Generosity, hazard your Lives in a Combat, to which the Laws of Honour do not oblige you: We are not violently carried away, as you falsly suppose; we go willingly along with these Persons, who are our Friends and Relations.
>
> (*FQ* 258)

By the standards of empiricism, Arabella is not insane, for she is not out of her senses. Unlike Cervantes' Don Quixote, who mistook canvas for fine cloth and stale breath for Arabian perfume, Arabella's senses are in perfect working order. She "sees" what everyone else sees: a few men genteelly clothed. Since the laws of romance have determined that ladies traveling with male companions are likely the victims of ravishment, and that well-dressed men on horseback who approach such ladies are often knights intent upon delivering them, Arabella interprets her observations along the dictates of probability, concluding that the highwaymen are "Persons of Quality," for "though they came questionless, either upon a good or bad Design, yet it cannot be doubted, but that their Birth is illustrious; otherwise they would never pretend either to fight in our Defence, or to carry us away" (*FQ* 259). Relying on romance rules of conduct, Arabella is sure that the riders could not be robbers, for their illustrious births, as evidenced by their participation in the noble conduct of succoring maidens or carrying them off, are too exalted for so base an occupation.

Obviously, Arabella's reasoning is circular. Her assumptions about the men's condition serve also as her evidence. The strength of her belief alone— her unwillingness or inability to see things in any other way—supports her analysis and conclusion. Arabella has a "faith of seeing." When her companions inform her that the men had intended to "rob us of our Money," Arabella logically responds,

How! . . . Were these Cavaliers, who appeared to be in so handsome a Garb, that I took them for Persons of prime Quality, were they Robbers? I have been strangely mistaken, it seems: However, I apprehend there is no Certainty, that your Suspicions are true; and it may still be as I say, that they either came to rescue or carry us away.

(FQ 259)

In acknowledging that she may have been mistaken, Arabella also maintains that her assumptions about the operations of the world have not been proven wrong. All she concedes is that the men may have been robbers, "it seems." And with the absence of certainty, her interpretation has as strong a truth claim as everyone else's, for unless certainty can be established, all interpretations are supported only by probability, which is itself the very issue of contention here. Within the laws of romance familiar to Arabella, the probability is greatest that the riders were knights upon some good or bad design. Arabella's companions, however, believe that such men are most likely robbers. Yet for Arabella's companions to conclude that their interpretation of the riders is correct—that the riders are most likely robbers simply because men of their appearance are probably robbers—is to use their assumptions as the evidence: in other words, to reason like the quixotic Arabella. There is a method to Arabella's madness, and that method looks strikingly similar to the empiricist epistemology employed by her "rational" companions.

Though Charlotte Glanville is among those who regard Arabella as crazed, Charlotte, as an artful coquette, also understands that representations should not always be taken at face value, that facts do not always speak for themselves. Two conversations between Miss Glanville and Arabella illustrate the difference between their interpretive practices. In the first, Arabella's romantic language, unfamiliar to Miss Glanville, leads the coquette into a pained recollection of her own indiscretions. The misunderstandings hinge upon the words "adventures" and "favours." Miss Glanville can hardly believe that Arabella would accuse her of having "adventures," and she is all the more outraged by Arabella's assumption that she would grant a lover "favours." "Have you any Reason to imagine, I would grant any Favour to a Lover?" Miss Glanville demands.

I vow, Cousin, interrupted *Arabella*, you put me in mind of the fair and virtuous *Antonia*, who was so rigid and austere, that she thought all Expressions of Love were criminal; and was so far from granting any Person Permission to love her, that she thought it a mortal Offence to be adored even in private.

Miss *Glanville*, who could not imagine *Arabella* spoke this seriously, but that it was designed to sneer at her great Eagerness to make Conquests, and the Liberties she allowed herself in, which had

131

probably come to her Knowledge, was so extremely vexed at the malicious Jest, as she thought it, that, not being able to revenge herself, she burst into Tears.

(*FQ* 89)

What is courtesy for Arabella—a polite and romantically precedented interest in her visiting cousin's "adventures"—is cruelty to Charlotte. Aware of her own shortcomings given current custom, Miss Glanville incriminates herself by presuming that Arabella assumes the worst. Too cognizant that the opinions of others may easily overrule her own hoped-for self-image, Charlotte cannot take Arabella's words literally. Rather, she infers that by "virtuous" and "austere," Arabella must ironically intend a "sneer at her great Eagerness to make Conquests." Miss Glanville, unlike the female quixote, is attuned to the conflicting presence of other people's narratives. Her understanding of the relation between lived experience and its representation as history or reputation is thus somewhat subtler than Arabella's. As her interpretation of her cousin's remarks shows, Charlotte accepts that representation is not always plain, that literal meanings cannot always be trusted. Within the hermeneutical dichotomy discussed by Joel Weinsheimer, Charlotte plays the knave to Arabella's fool: Charlotte tends to overread, inferring intentional slights and willful competition from Arabella's romantic folly and artless beauty; while Arabella underreads, accepting romance narratives as self-evident histories.[24]

This hermeneutical distinction between Arabella and Miss Glanville animates their interactions. Though Arabella retains a morally superior air throughout the novel, Charlotte recognizes the shortcomings of Arabella's credulous empiricism well enough to hold her own against it in another conversation. Upon hearing the history of Miss Groves, a young woman who ran away with her writing-master, Arabella presumes that the writing-master must have been a nobleman in disguise. "[Y]ou may as well persuade me, the Moon is made of a Cream Cheese, as that any Nobleman turned himself into a Writing-master, to obtain Miss *Groves*," an amused Charlotte replies. Arabella, however, affronted by this accusation that she "would argue upon such a ridiculous System; and compare the Second glorious Luminary of the Heavens to so unworthy a Resemblance," immediately expresses her resentment, only to draw Charlotte's laughing rejoinder:

Really I think, you have not Reason to be angry, if I supposed you might make a Comparison between the Moon and a Cream Cheese; since you say, that same Moon, which don't appear broader than your Gardener's Face, is not much less than the whole World: Why, certainly, I have more Reason to trust my own Eyes, than such whimsical Notions as these.

(*FQ* 143)

The moon looks more like a cream cheese than another world, so comparing it to a cream cheese is quite reasonable, Charlotte points out. Seeing is believing, for truth is plain. Now, clearly Miss Glanville does not believe the moon to be made of cream cheese, as she initially invokes the comparison in order to express her *disbelief* at Arabella's remarks. Yet having been chastised by Arabella for arguing upon such a "ridiculous System," Charlotte satirically reinterprets and defends her comparison within the underreader's hermeneutics characteristic of Arabella. She mimics Arabella's literal understanding in order to rally her cousin's quixotic folly. No other character manages to parry with Arabella so acutely. Arabella looks thoroughly out-maneuvered when, "unwilling to expose her Cousin's Ignorance, by a longer Dispute upon this Subject," she politely begs her "to let it drop for the present." Charlotte's remarks show her awareness of the instability of interpretive systems, particularly the quixotic inadequacy of empirical method when confronted by truly divergent perspectives. (Without space flight, how could a world-believing empiricist ever convince a cheese-believing empiricist that the moon is not a cream cheese?) The artless, underreading Arabella remains oblivious to these hermeneutical complexities.

Arabella and Charlotte, fool and knave, embody two different approaches to interpretation: one assured, absolutist, essentialist; the other self-critical, tactical, contingent. Charlotte's coquettish, manipulative approach holds little appeal, appearing "empty-headed, selfish, and ordinary." Indeed, much of Charlotte's energy goes towards her jealous, ineffective attempts to orchestrate situations in which she might outshine her cousin. Yet Arabella's quixotic confidence, when placed within the context of early eighteenth-century quixotism, is hardly more attractive. Quixotism, as I have argued above, was not the benign idealism—the dreaming of the impossible dream— that it has since become. Early eighteenth-century quixotes were loathed as tyrants, enthusiasts and cultural innovators; they were reviled as instigators of undesirable political upheaval. Arabella is an agitator of this sort. She adheres to the laws of romance because quixotism serves her interests. Like her mother, who brought romances onto the secluded estate "to soften a Solitude she found very disagreeable" (*FQ* 7), Arabella persists in the romantic way of thinking because, as many readers have stressed, it does ameliorate her own confinement as a (politically irrelevant) woman. Romance gives her power over men, authorizing her to disobey her father and to reject her suitors. When, for instance, her father urges her to marry Glanville, she considers his request in light of her reading, and concludes that his advice is unreasonable.

> The impropriety of receiving a Lover of a Father's recommending appeared in its strongest Light. What Lady in Romance ever married the Man that was chose for her? In those Cases the Remonstrances of a Parent are called Persecutions; obstinate Resistance, Constancy and Courage; and an Aptitude to dislike the Person proposed them, a

noble Freedom of Mind, which disdains to love or hate by the Caprice of others.

(FQ 27)

Turning "Remonstrances" into "Persecutions," "Resistance" into "Constancy and Courage" and "Aptitude to dislike" into "noble Freedom of Mind," romances allow Arabella to justify her conduct by changing the names of virtues and vices. So, "strengthening her own Resolutions by those Examples of heroic Disobedience," Arabella defies her father's authority, nobly assuring him that she will "always obey him in all just and reasonable Things" (FQ 27). History, as she understands it, exhorts her to put her own desires before those of her father, and invests her with the authority to determine what is "just and reasonable." In the social world created by her version of history, Arabella rules. And her authority, when exerted over the supplications of her suitors, is supreme.

When, for instance, she mistakenly detects that an acquaintance, Mr Selvin, is guilty of the crime of loving her, she sternly sentences him to banishment. Later, in a softer moment, she realizes what fatal distresses he must be suffering, and decides to preserve his life by commanding him to live. It never occurs to her that Mr Selvin could find her decrees ridiculous and disregard them, even though Glanville, catching her as she is about to dispatch the merciful missive, explains to her that her commands hold no sway: "in order to spare you the Trouble of sending to Mr. Selvin, I may venture to assure you that he is in no danger of dying," Glanville relates.

> 'Tis impossible, Sir, reply'd *Arabella*, according to the Nature of Things, 'tis impossible but he must already be very near Death—You know the Rigour of my Sentence, you know—
>
> I know, Madam, said Mr. *Glanville*, that Mr. *Selvin* does not think himself under a Necessity of obeying your Sentence; and has the Impudence to question your Authority for banishing him from his native Country.
>
> My Authority, Sir, said *Arabella* strangely surpriz'd, is founded upon the absolute Power he has given me over him.
>
> He denies that, Madam, said *Glanville*, and says that he neither can give, nor you exercise an absolute Power over him; since you are both accountable to the King, whose Subjects you are, and both restrain'd by the Laws under whose Sanction you live.
>
> *Arabella*'s apparent Confusion at these Words giving Mr. *Glanville* Hopes that he had fallen upon a proper method to cure her of some of her strange Notions, he was going to pursue his Arguments, when *Arabella* looking a little sternly upon him,

134

> The Empire of Love, said she, like the Empire of Honour, is govern'd by Laws of its own, which have no Dependence upon, or Relation to any other.
>
> (*FQ* 320)

Arabella's "histories" teach her to rule with arbitrary power. Like male "Honour," the "virtue" that Mandeville identifies as a lofty "Name" for violent and self-interested quixotism, Arabella's autonomous rules of "Love" jeopardize civil order by encouraging her to play the self-sufficient tyrant. Claiming the right to act in a manner having "no Dependence upon, or Relation to" the laws of the land, Arabella entirely ignores the texts that ratify reasonable conduct for Glanville, Selvin and the King's other subjects. Convinced of the complete separation between her empire and the King's, Arabella unabashedly exercises the supreme authority she believes Selvin to have given her. Locke would have been appalled: Selvin could never have given her such power, "[f]or a Man, not having the Power of his own Life, *cannot*, by Compact, or his own Consent, *enslave himself* to any one, nor put himself under the Absolute, Arbitrary Power of another, to take away his Life, when he pleases" (*TT* 284). Yet Locke's reasoning, anchored in the law of nature, presents a case no more authoritative than Arabella's own, for Arabella's argument also proceeds, as she herself notes, "according to the Nature of Things." As Glanville discovers from her stern reply, the ways of philosophers do not elude Arabella; she too knows how to establish her reasoning upon self-evident axioms. Content to live by her own understanding of natural authority, the female quixote maintains an alternative system of ethics, morality and law. Arabella's quixotism is rational madness: an allegiance to an alternative political ideal and a willingness to promote that cause. Like Mandeville, Lennox invokes the quixotic figure as a focal point for contemplating the elusive distinctions between gross immorality and legitimate political difference.

Arabella's confrontation with the good doctor, a Johnsonian clergyman who "cures" Arabella at the novel's end,[25] establishes that Arabella's misbehavior is a threat to political stability. If we are to believe the doctor, her offense is that most quixotic one of agitating internecine conflict and bringing on civil war. Romances, he admonishes her, are criminal because "they teach Women to expect not only Worship,"

> but the dreadful Worship of human Sacrifices. Every Page of these Volumes is filled with such extravagance of Praise, and expressions of Obedience as one human Being ought not to hear from another; or with Accounts of Battles, in which thousands are slaughtered for no other Purpose than to gain a Smile from the haughty Beauty, who sits a calm Spectatress of the Ruin and Desolation, Bloodshed and Misery, incited by herself.
>
> (*FQ* 380–1)

Despite all the other (numerous) arguments that Arabella has withstood throughout the novel, this one finally compels her consent. Chastised for indulging in tales that erode the "Sense of our Alliance with all human nature," a sense that keeps us "awake to Tenderness and Sympathy," Arabella can resist no longer. "[M]y heart yields to the Force of Truth," she concedes, "and now I wonder how the Blaze of Enthusiastic Bravery, could hinder me from remarking with Abhorrence the Crime of deliberate unnecessary Bloodshed" (*FQ* 381). With her quixotism described as a blazing enthusiasm—that unreasonable fanaticism so often associated with the quixotic—Arabella's sudden and complete transformation represents a sentimental fantasy of social, political and epistemological coherence. A "Sense of our Alliance with all human nature" restores moral uniformity, reasserting that everyone unhindered by enthusiasm really does feel the same way about moral questions, such as "Crime." The apparently insurmountable differences between Arabella and the other characters finally yield to the compelling "Truth" of this "Sense." Where reason was helpless, sentimental authority prevails, thereby resolving the novel's plot.

In bringing the plot to this resolution, however, Lennox does not decisively put to rest the issues raised by the plot's development. Why is Arabella, formerly so resistant to the arguments of her quotidian companions, suddenly swayed by a sentimental sermon? Why is there a clergyman at all? Why was the Countess unable to effect Arabella's cure? These questions, which lie behind much of the dissatisfaction with the novel's ending, can be addressed by recognizing that quixotism and sentimentalism are not opposites in the way that Arabella's and Miss Glanville's interpretative strategies are. Hutcheson's sentimentalism was not anti-quixotism, but anti-anti-quixotism; the unsentimental Mandeville was the anti-quixote.[26] David Simple could be at once both a quixote and a sentimentalist, for his desire to find a perfect "Union of Minds," free of all "selfish or separate Interest," distinguishes him less from quixotes than from selfish Mandevilleans like his brother Daniel. Read in this context,[27] Arabella's sudden transformation from singular quixote into empathic sentimentalist—"united . . . in every Virtue and laudable Affection of Mind" to her new husband Glanville (*FQ* 383)—is unsurprising. For the opposite of Arabella's quixotism is not sentimental union, but the unsentimental alliance of Miss Glanville and the scheming Sir George, who are "only married in the common Acceptation of the Word; that is, they were privileged to join Fortunes, Equipages, Titles, and Expence" (*FQ* 383). The true union of minds fittingly eludes Miss Charlotte, whose relation to representation—shared by her fortune-hunting husband and by Mandevillean politicians—has been suspicious, strategic and self-interested throughout the novel. Her skeptical, all-too-artful approach to the world leads her to a merely nominal marriage, while Arabella's naïve, literal-minded, essentialist habits of reading prime her for a complete union of minds. A sentimental resolution suits Arabella, as her quixotic ability to mistake convention for reality does not fundamentally differ from the philosophically realist assumptions driving sentimentalism. Within the imaginative world of sentimental philosophy and the sentimental quixotic novel, the greatest threat comes not from essentializing quixotes, but from rational nominalists like Miss Glanville, Daniel Simple, Mandeville—and Lennox herself, who also understands that representation and reality can often be two quite different things.

Recognizing that *The Female Quixote* shifts culpability from quixotes to nominalists explains why the Countess, a reformed reader of romances who seems at first to promise Arabella's cure, cannot bring about the heroine's "conversion." In contrast to the essentialist Arabella, who can confidently proclaim that her unyielding expectations run "according to the Nature of Things" (*FQ* 320), the Countess accepts historical contingency: "the strange Alteration of Things" that has rendered romance narratives "so improbable . . . at present" (*FQ* 326). When Arabella tries to defend her own behavior by alluding to "the Customs of antient Times," the Countess firmly assures her that such precedents cannot always be trusted.

> Custom, said the Countess smiling, changes the very Nature of Things, and what was honourable a Thousand Years ago, may probably be look'd upon as infamous now.
>
> The same Actions which made a Man a Hero in those Times, would constitute him a Murderer in These—And the same Steps which led him to a Throne Then, would infallibly conduct him to a Scaffold Now.
>
> (*FQ* 328)

Arabella, however, understands that the Countess' sentiments concede too much to historical contingency. The Countess' ethical flexibility, though seemingly reconciliatory, actually points the way to a kind of moral relativism that would be helpless to resist "the Political Offspring which Flattery begot upon Pride." Her advice carries echoes of Mandeville's complaint about Shaftesbury: "he looks upon Virtue and Vice as permanent Realities that must ever be the same in all Countries and all Ages," a notion "inconsistent with our daily Experience" (Mandeville 1: 323–4). The Countess may smile and speak of change, but she can offer no criteria by which to distinguish between real and nominal virtue. As Arabella objects:

> But Custom, Madam, said *Arabella*, cannot possibly change the Nature of Virtue or Vice: And since Virtue is the chief Characteristick of a Hero, a Hero in the last Age will be a Hero in this—Tho' the Natures of Virtue and Vice cannot be changed, replied the Countess,

yet they may be mistaken; and different Principles, Customs, and
Education, may probably change their Names, if not their Natures.

(*FQ* 328)

Focusing on the obstacles to a proper understanding of real virtue—its
mistaken nature and its changing names—the Countess counsels Arabella to
think skeptically about the relation between reality and representation. Her
advice requires too much. Despite the narrator's earlier hint that the female
quixote delights in romances *because* they change the names of filial virtues and
vices, Arabella herself will not recognize contingency in moral virtue.
Thoroughly quixotic, she makes a poor skeptic, for she does not easily distinguish between a thing and its name. Thus, when the Countess concludes,
" 'Tis certain, therefore . . . that what was Virtue in those Days, is Vice in
ours," Arabella is "surpriz'd, embarrass'd, perplex'd, but not convinced," for
she cannot "separate her Ideas of Glory, Virtue, Courage, Generosity, and
Honour, from the false Representations of them in the Actions of . . . imaginary Heroes" (*FQ* 329). The Countess' nominalist, unsentimental arguments
cannot sway the essentialist, absolutist Arabella. Abruptly, the Countess
disappears from the narrative, and the task of curing Arabella falls to the sentimental, Johnsonian clergyman.

In making the clergyman's sentimentalism serve as Arabella's cure,
however, the novel does not resolve the hermeneutical conflict driving its plot,
for this conflict does not exist between Arabella and the good doctor; rather, it
persists in the differences between Arabella and the two other main female
characters, the Countess and Miss Glanville. The clergyman reforms Arabella,
but not greatly. She begins as a naïve quixotic reader; he convinces her to
become a naïve sentimental one. That the Johnsonian clergyman's masculine
rationality—his "Scholastick Ruggedness" (*FQ* 371)—should effect so minor
a transformation is to be expected, for within the novel's dichotomy of essentialist and nominalist readers, the doctor's way of thinking clearly belongs to
the essentialist side. Unlike the Countess, who would allow the truth of
Arabella's romances but deny their current applicability to life, the clergyman
rejects romances wholesale as "senseless Fictions" (*FQ* 374). The Countess' fine
distinctions and moral flexibility are useless to a man who, like Arabella,
believes in immutable truths conveyed through venerable texts. How should
Arabella have recognized her romances to be false? "[C]ompare these Books to
antient Histories," the doctor advises, confident that the discrepancies
between his books and her books will be sufficient to convince Arabella that
hers (not his) are in error (*FQ* 378). Arabella and the good doctor reason much
alike, only she is called quixotic while he is called rational. Their virtues are
similar, yet have different names. The novel's dedication, believed to have
been written by Samuel Johnson,[28] lingers over this similarity. "MY LORD,"
it begins,

SUCH is the Power of Interest over almost every Mind that no one is long without arguments to prove any Position which is ardently wished to be true, or to justify any Measures which are dictated by Inclination.

By this subtil Sophistry of Desire, I have been persuaded to hope, that this Book may, without Impropriety, be inscribed to Your Lordship; but am not certain, that my Reasons will have the same Force upon other Understandings.

The Dread which a Writer feels of the public Censure; the still greater Dread of Neglect; and the eager Wish for Support and Protection, which is impressed by the consciousness of Imbecillity; are unknown to those who have never adventured into the World; and I am afraid, my Lord, equally unknown to those, who have always found the World ready to applaud them.

Though in the guise of timid supplication and self-effacement, this dedication firmly reminds the great of their own limitations. "Interest" often passes for reason, it warns, for the "subtil Sophistry of Desire," like romance, shows things as one would wish them to be. The "Power of Interest," able to prove any position "ardently wished to be true," is the power of self-delusion masquerading as rationality. The dedication thus presents the author as someone worried about his or her (the gender is never specified) own possible quixotism, worried whether his or her "Reasons will have the same Force upon other Understandings." Given that the addressee is a lord,[29] however, "Interest" takes on a second meaning, for lords and other great men can exert their interest—with Parliament, the Court, or with the public—to secure favors for their beneficiaries. In this light, the dedication's humble discussion of the self-deluding "Power of Interest" may be read as a sly recognition of the disingenuousness of most dedications: such is the power of this sort of interest, that those who wield it (for instance, noble lords) may be fed, throughout their entire lives, gross flatteries and outright lies (such as may be found in this very dedication, perhaps). The minds of the powerful, not just those of the weak and wishful, are formed on the fictions fashioned by interest, for who would dare to tell a great man the truth? A comprehensive understanding of the many walks of life, "unknown to those" who like Arabella have "never adventured into the World," is "equally unknown to those, who," like noble lords, "have always found the World ready to applaud them." The dedication collapses the distinctions between great men and female quixotes.[30]

Such a move is not uncharacteristic of Johnson, whose alignment of rationality and masculinity has been overstated in recent years. Patricia Meyer Spacks, for example, has used Johnson's *Rambler* essays to argue that Johnson's male "anxiety about fiction" stems from a fear that "fiction . . . dressed by desire, arouses feeling and threatens rationality."[31] As she elaborates, however, taking the *Rambler* no. 4 as her text, it becomes clear that Johnson imagines the human mind not as masculine in nature, but as feminine. Spacks cites Johnson:

> if the power of example is so great as to take possession of the memory by a kind of violence, and produce effects almost without intervention of the will, care ought to be taken that, when the choice is unrestrained, the best examples only should be exhibited; and that which is likely to operate so strongly, should not be mischievous or uncertain in its effects.

From this passage, Spacks interprets Johnson's meaning to be that "[f]iction can *take possession* of its readers, as a seducer might,"[32] an image that lends itself to the assumption that the mind is masculine while its distractions are feminine. An earlier version of Spacks' argument made the gendering more explicit: "Fiction has the power to take possession of its readers, as a seductive woman might."[33] The passage makes greater sense, however, if we suppose that Johnson imagines the mind as feminine. More so than seducers, ravishers "take possession . . . by a kind of violence," producing effects "almost without intervention of the will." Johnson describes the dangers of fiction not as the gentle blandishments of an artful woman, but as the forcible depredations of an aggressive man; fiction seizes the mind by "violence," the very term Arabella uses when she speaks of male sexual aggression: "I shall suffer the same Violence that many illustrious Ladies have done before me; and be carried away by Force from my own Home, as they were" (*FQ* 99).

Johnson's description of the power of fiction makes fiction masculine and the mind feminine. And though often pointed to as a prime example of masculine rational authority, Johnson did not disassociate himself from romances. Boswell says of the lexicographer: "when a boy he was immoderately fond of reading romances of chivalry, and he retained his fondness for them through life. . . . Yet I have heard him attribute to these extravagant fictions that unsettled turn of mind which prevented his ever fixing in any profession" (Boswell 36). Regarding himself as a reader whose head has been turned by "extravagant fictions," Johnson draws parallels between his own adult life and the errant adventures of restless, quixotic misfits. Quixotism is not specific to women, nor is it rare. Early in his *Rambler* series, Johnson moralizes:

> When the knight of La Mancha gravely recounts to his companion the adventures by which he is to signalize himself in such a manner that he shall be summoned to the support of empires, solicited to accept the heiress of the crown which he has preserved, have honours and riches to scatter about him, and an island to bestow on his worthy squire, very few readers, amidst their mirth or pity, can deny that they have admitted visions of the same kind; though they have not,

140

perhaps expected events equally as strange, or by means equally inadequate. When we pity him, we reflect on our own disappointments; and when we laugh, our hearts inform us that he is not more ridiculous than ourselves, except that he tells what we have only thought.

(Johnson 3: 11)

To Johnson's way of thinking, men can be just as quixotic as women, especially men like himself, who "aspire to the name of authors" (Johnson 3:12). Johnson's persona, Mr Rambler, admits to being "lightly touched" by this "writer's malady," "a disease, for which, when it has attained its height, perhaps no remedy will be found in the gardens of philosophy" (Johnson 3: 12). Johnson would have recognized himself in Arabella.

The Female Quixote does not gender rationality as masculine and quixotism as feminine in any straightforward way. Instead, it conflates reason and quixotism, making their gendered associations suspect. The doctor's rationality and Arabella's quixotism describe identical patterns of thought. *The Female Quixote* comes to a bad end not because Arabella is defeated—in a sense, her way of thinking, as opposed to the Countess' or Miss Glanville's, does prevail—but because in countering quixotism with sentimentalism, the novel fails to resolve the energetic tension that it so hilariously and successfully sets up between skeptical and credulous reading practices. For readers skeptical enough to doubt the existence of a universal moral sense, Lennox's novel—like the Countess—offers no criteria by which to distinguish between the nature and names of virtue. Alas, the path to universal understanding, if it is to be found in books at all, must be sought in another one.

4

SEEING THE GENERAL VIEW

Henry Fielding and quixotic authorship

> *Don Quixote* is the first modern work of literature, because in it we see the cruel reason of identities and differences make endless sport of signs and similitudes; because in it language breaks off its old kinship with things, and enters into the lonely sovereignty from which it will reappear, in its separated state, only as literature.
>
> Foucault, *The Order of Things*

Henry Fielding's fiction, "Written in Imitation of The *Manner* of Cervantes, Author of *Don Quixote*," has long been identified with the quixotic tradition, loosely defined. His novels are compared to Cervantes' because of their "facetious chapter headings and the chapter endings that entice the reader on," or their "absurd and ridiculous episodes, many of them full of rough horseplay." His characters are said to resemble the Spaniard's because they travel in pairs, confront the vanities of the world, or exude quixotic innocence.[1] Yet these comparisons, though doubtless sound, miss the deeper epistemological relation between Fielding and the English quixotic tradition. Fielding's fascination with quixotism goes beyond direct allusion to, and overt imitation of, Cervantes' book. Like many of his contemporaries, Fielding associates the quixotic with specific political and intellectual conflicts—women's equality, empiricism, moral diversity, Jacobitism—and he responds to these conflicts by embracing sentimentalism. In this respect, Fielding's work thoroughly embodies the English quixotic tradition. Like Samuel Johnson, however, he complicates quixotism by explicitly imagining it not just as a malady of readers, but as an affliction of authors as well. In the figure of the quixotic author, Fielding sees both what he is, and what he most desires not to be. He sees authority reduced to its feminine, irrational and impotent opposite.

142

Rational men and quixotic women

Fielding's authorial quixotism begins with his sentimental desire to turn art into the universal language of nature. "It is a trite but true observation, that examples work more forcibly on the mind than precepts," he writes in *Joseph Andrews* (1742): "A good man therefore is a standing lesson to all his acquaintance, and of far greater use in that narrow circle than a good book."[2] Though he values living examples above bookish representations, Fielding realizes that these examples rarely escape their "narrow circle" of influence. They may speak the language of nature, but their influence is by no means universal. This limitation sends Fielding quickly back to books, which he praises, along with their authors, for their ability to reach larger audiences:

> But as it often happens that the best men are but little known, and consequently cannot extend the usefulness of their examples a great way; the writer may be called in aid to spread their history farther, and to present the amiable pictures to those who have not the happiness of knowing the originals; and so, by communicating such valuable patterns to the world, he may perhaps do a more extensive service to mankind than the person whose life originally afforded the pattern.
>
> *(JA* 13)

What had begun as a hierarchy valuing living examples above representations, quickly inverts; "the writer" becomes better than "the best men" because his "service to mankind" is more "extensive." Because the author's "amiable pictures" are not confined only to a narrow circle, they may be more useful than even "the person whose life originally afforded the pattern." The writer's "history" offers vicarious experience that can be reproduced endlessly, spreading the "valuable patterns" to those who would otherwise never know the originals. Through their more extensive influence, the lessons of "history" surpass those of life.

What gives writers their value, then, is the remoteness of the "originals" they describe—the very circumstance that makes quixotism possible. Writers best serve mankind by making obscure examples widely known, asking readers to accept on authority what the readers have not actually experienced themselves. Fielding, like Foucault in the epigraph above, recognizes that the value of literature is its ability to separate from things. Yet deeply committed to an empirical understanding of the world, Fielding also distrusts all such literary claims to truth. His obsessive attention to the differences between his new form of "history" and "foolish Novels, and monstrous Romances" shows his sensitivity to this problem *(TJ* 487). The "Composition of Novels and Romances," he argues, requires nothing more than "Paper, Pens, and Ink, with the manual Capacity of using them" *(TJ* 489). They are easily concocted, existing as trivial forms with no real substance. Characteristically, Fielding expresses his distrust of these genres by reducing them to their external and material components: paper, pens, ink and the "manual"—not mental—capacity to write. Novels and romances are empty forms. "Hence," Fielding reasons,

> we are to derive that universal Contempt, which the World, who always denominate the Whole from the Majority, have cast on all historical Writers, who do not draw their Materials from Records. And it is the Apprehension of this Contempt, that hath made us so cautiously avoid the Term Romance, a Name with which we might otherwise have been well enough contented. Though as we have good Authority for all our Characters no less indeed than the vast authentic Doomsday-Book of Nature, as is elsewhere hinted, our Labours have sufficient Title to the Name of History.
>
> (*TJ* 489)

Fielding would be willing to call his writings "Romance," but for the stigma attached to the majority of romances.[3] Fearful that his own work might be dismissed on its genre alone—on its form—Fielding opts to designate his work a history, one guaranteed to contain substance, because drawn from "Records." These records are not particular living examples, but the general, "vast authentic Doomsday-Book of Nature." Trained in the law, Fielding here imagines "Nature" as the Doomsday Book, the survey of land holdings ordered by William the Conqueror, and still used in eighteenth-century courts as the final authority in disputes involving ancient demesne. As there was no more authentic record in law than the Doomsday Book, so in Fielding's histories there is no more authentic record than that of "Nature." This metaphor encapsulates the problematic relation between art-as-form and nature-as-substance that chronically troubles Fielding's literary endeavor. Though Fielding maintains that in his kind of writing, substance gives meaning to form and nature validates art, his chosen metaphor in fact argues the opposite, validating nature by comparing it to the final authority of a book. As is often the case in Fielding's work, the absolute authority of nature can barely be distinguished from the mediations of art. Writing fictions that he believes to be histories, Fielding appears to be a quixotic author.

Fielding, however, always remains supremely self-conscious of his apparent quixotism. His abiding admiration for Cervantes testifies to this awareness. *Don Quixote*, according to Fielding, is "the history of the whole world in general, at least that part which is polished by laws, arts, and sciences" (*JA* 159). In its comic misunderstandings and misinterpretations, *Don Quixote* records the condition of everyone who must negotiate through a world "polished" by human art. Everyone who lives in polite society must already be quixotic. This train of thought suggests that there is no self-evident nature in Fielding's part of the world, a proposition Fielding cannot bring himself to accept. He proposes, therefore, to teach his readers how to be better readers; to show them how to recognize the nature that hides behind polished surfaces and artful fictions; to instruct them, in other words, in how to distinguish between "History" and "Romance." Modeling his fiction after "The *Manner* of Cervantes," Fielding acknowledges the paradox he shares with the Spanish novelist: both authors write books that teach readers to be skeptical of what they learn from books. Fielding's famously ironic and parodic narrative style emerges from the contradictions of trying to teach readers both to believe and to doubt at the same time. While claiming to provide his readers with "no other than Human Nature" (*TJ* 32), Fielding cannot forget the literary status of what he actually provides. He recognizes the already absurd potential of didactic fiction in a world of universal quixotism. Oscillating between faith in the universal authority of reason, and suspicions about universal quixotism, Fielding writes to preserve the authority of authorship itself. But of course, the two poles of universal reason and universal quixotism are not really in opposition; rather, in an empirical age, the belief in the former brings on the latter, a logic illustrated in Fielding's most celebrated work, *Tom Jones* (1749).

Regarded as Fielding's best work, *Tom Jones* with its "perfect plot" has been praised as a masterpiece of masculine control.[4] As Martin C. Battestin explains, "Fielding saw life as he saw art, not merely as energy, but as order. What he admired in men and in the natural world was a sort of benign exuberance rationally controlled and directed toward the attainment of a desirable end."[5] Active control over experience, rather than passive reaction to it, characterizes Fielding's masculine art. The terms are clearly gendered, as Battestin affirms:

> the English novel came all at once into being as an art form, its two main directions—inward, toward the individual personality, and outward, toward the panorama of society—arising from the conflicting temperaments and literary motives of two very different men, Samuel Richardson and Henry Fielding ... from the ... conjunction of Richardson's feminine sensibilities and Fielding's robust masculinity, the modern novel was born.[6]

Battestin suggests that Fielding's "robust masculinity" is his vast comprehensiveness, his refusal to move "inward" toward the "feminine" and peculiar, his escape from that vortex of "individual personality." Instead, Fielding's energies move "outward, toward the panorama of society," as if to comprehend universal experience. Fielding's robust masculinity is, above all, an intellectual posture—a confidence in his mind's ability to comprehend the vastness and complexity of the world. "[F]eminine sensibilities" do not attempt this larger understanding, instead confining themselves to the realm of private experience familiar to those who, like the female quixote, "have never adventured into the World." With the partial knowledge of limited experience dismissed as feminine weakness, universal authority must be masculine.

Fielding himself sometimes encourages this gendered rationalization, suggesting that quixotism belongs more properly to women than to men. His warm review of Lennox's *The Female Quixote* praises the work for its greater plausibility, proudly observing that "our Countrywoman hath excelled the Spanish Writer." For,

> as we are to grant in both Performances, that the Head of a very sensible Person is entirely subverted by reading Romances, this Concession seems to me more easy to be granted in the Case of a young Lady than an old Gentleman. Nor can I help observing with what perfect Judgment and Art this Subversion of Brain in Arabella is accounted for by her peculiar Circumstances, and Education. To say Truth, I make no Doubt but that most young Women of the same Vivacity, and of the same innocent good Disposition, in the same Situation, and with the same Studies, would be able to make a large Progress in the same Follies.[7]

Fielding finds the idea of a young, female quixote more credible than that of an old, male one. Far from regarding Arabella's case as odd or unusual, he discusses it as though it were normal, easily "accounted for by her peculiar Circumstances, and Education." Arabella is typical. Most young women of the "same Vivacity," "same . . . Disposition," in the "same Situation" and with the "same Studies," would make great advances in the "same Follies." Women who have little experience of the world, who must turn inward rather than outward, can be expected to develop into quixotes.

Though Fielding's review does not always give the preference to Lennox, it does remain consistent in the gendered reasoning of its judgments. *Don Quixote* is the better book, Fielding suggests, because of "that Advantage, which the Actions of Men give to the Writer beyond those of Women." "Don Quixote is ridiculous in performing Feats of Absurdity himself," Fielding explains:

> Arabella can only become so, in provoking and admiring the Absurdities in others. In the former Case, the Ridicule hath all the Force of a Representation; it is in a Manner subjected to the Eyes; in the latter it is conveyed, as it were, through our Ears, and partakes of the Coldness of History or Narration.
>
> (*CGJ* 1: 280)

As a female protagonist, Arabella must be passive, only "provoking" or "admiring" absurdities in others, not "performing" them herself. Fielding imagines *Don Quixote* as direct experience, and *The Female Quixote* as a second-hand account. The ridicule in the former is "in a Manner subjected to the Eyes," as if the reader had actually been there, while that of the latter exists only as hearsay, "conveyed, as it were, through our Ears," like a cold "History or Narration." Male experience is real experience; female experience resembles a book. Under such conditions, women who speak from their own experience against male universalisms must by definition be quixotic.

Tom Jones makes precisely this case in the contrast between the ideal woman, Sophia, who embodies wisdom,[8] and her foolishly quixotic female relatives, Aunt Western and Mrs Fitzpatrick. Allworthy's praise of Sophia describes the perfect woman: "she always shewed the highest Deference to the Understandings of Men; a Quality, absolutely essential to the making a good Wife" (*TJ* 883). A larger understanding of the ways of the world—the prudence that Tom Jones, as Every Man, must acquire—is unnecessary and inappropriate for women. Fielding ridicules Aunt Western, precisely because she has confidence in her own experience: "She had lived about the Court, and had seen the World. Hence she acquired all that Knowledge which the said World usually communicates" (*TJ* 272). Too ready to generalize from her limited experience, Mrs Western meddles beyond her proper sphere, showing no deference to the understandings of men. "Indeed, Brother, you are not qualified for these Negotiations," she peremptorily informs Squire Western: "All your whole Scheme of Politics is wrong" (*TJ* 847).

As we might expect, Mrs Western's quixotic folly has its roots in her reading, which consists substantially of what Fielding regards to be unworthy compositions: "modern Plays, Operas, Oratorios, Poems and Romances . . . *Rapin's* History of *England*, *Eachard's Roman History*, and many *French Memoires pour servir a l'Histoire*," as well as "most of the political Pamphlets and Journals, published within the last twenty Years" (*TJ* 272–3).[9] Several of these "political Pamphlets" were apparently essays like Judith Drake's, Mary Astell's and the pseudonymous Sophia's, which assert women's equality and argue their right to participate in politics. "*English* Women, Brother, I thank Heaven, are not Slaves," Mrs Western declaims, parroting the rational feminist arguments that seemed so quixotic to many: "We have as good a Right to Liberty as yourselves. We are to be convinced by Reason and Persuasion only, and not governed by Force" (*TJ* 320). At other times she is heard to be muttering "something with an Air of Disdain, concerning Women and the Management of the Nation" (*TJ* 322) and later, after Squire Western imprisons Sophia for disobedience, Mrs Western, once again sounding like a feminist pamphleteer, officiously reminds him that "Women in a free Country are not to be treated with such arbitrary Power" (*TJ* 846). Mistaking her reading for reality, and her experience of the Court for knowledge of the world, Mrs Western fails to notice that women in Fielding's cosmos do not belong in public life, speaking their minds and pursuing their own interests. Their role instead is to marry men who can be relied upon to speak for them.

The lesson is all the more explicit in the history of Mrs Fitzpatrick, whose first mistake was marrying her husband for no better reason than that she saw him "so universally well received by the Women"—women who included Aunt Western (*TJ* 586). Without a masculine understanding to guide her, Mrs Fitzpatrick finds herself trapped in an unhappy marriage, which she can escape only by accepting the questionable attentions of an Irish peer. Fielding satirizes her predicament and the peer's compromising solicitude, using the language of quixotism:

> To say Truth, it was by his Assistance, that she had been enabled to escape from her Husband; for this Nobleman had the same gallant Disposition with those renowned Knights, of whom we read in heroic Story, and had delivered many an imprisoned Nymph from Durance. He was indeed as bitter an Enemy to the savage Authority too often exercised by Husbands and Fathers, over the young and lovely of the other Sex, as ever Knight Errant was to the barbarous Power of Enchanters: nay, to say Truth, I have often suspected that those very Enchanters with which Romance every where abounds, were in reality no other than the Husbands of those Days; and Matrimony itself was perhaps the enchanted Castle in which the Nymphs were said to be confined.
>
> (*TJ* 607)

Fielding has little sympathy for Mrs Fitzpatrick who, having made her own decision in marriage, suffers the consequences. Mock-commending the Irish peer for assisting Mrs Fitzpatrick, Fielding insinuates that any "gallant Disposition" toward opposing "savage Authority" is actually a cover for more self-interested designs: namely, the project of helping oneself to other men's wives. In Fielding's mind, quixotic idealism has not yet fully separated from criminality. He associates the monstrous "Romance" with immoral behavior, ridiculing the "heroic Story" of Mrs Fitzpatrick and the Irish peer as a tawdry glorification of libertinism. Women's complaints about the authority of "Husbands and Fathers," and other men's willingness to believe these tales, Fielding suggests, are quixotic. Women turn to the authority of "Romance" because "Romance" abets their headstrong desire to resent even proper constraints on their liberty. In the days of romance, Fielding archly conjectures, "Matrimony itself was perhaps the enchanted Castle in which the Nymphs were said to be confined." He thus hints that women's unhappiness in marriage has less to do with real "Durance" and more to do with women's perverse refusal to see any difference between "savage Authority" and "Matrimony itself." By identifying barbarous "Enchanters" as "the Husbands of those Days," Fielding rudely rides over any sympathy that might be stirring on behalf of female suffering. Women who complain about male authority, he implies, are unreasonable or immoral, for they are unwilling to show proper deference to the understandings of men. Men, like the peer, who champion such women, are just as bad, if not worse; the peer may be foolishly duped by romantic stories, but more probably he knavishly manipulates them. In Fielding's novelistic world, virtuous women do not claim Judith Drake's role of "*Don Quixot* of the Quill" in defense of the female sex. The exemplary Sophia's outrage at Jones—"To have my Name traduced in Public!" (*TJ* 732)—models reasonable female behavior in two ways, expressing both Sophia's desire to remain modestly in the private realm, and her legitimate concern that Jones, as a potential husband, be able to represent her properly. In Fielding's fiction, rational men control representations, while women and quixotes are controlled by representations.

Rational men and quixotic authorship

There are relatively few rational men in Fielding's fiction, an absence that can be traced back to the author's empiricism. For under empiricism, men too can be accounted for by their "peculiar Circumstances, and Education," madly limited by their experience. Fielding's didacticism strives to overcome these very limitations, by equating reading comprehension with comprehensive understanding. The exuberant narrator of *Tom Jones* intrudes everywhere because he knows no bounds. Teasing and exhorting men to become better readers—to learn to see the larger view by exercising their rational faculties of penetration, sagacity and foresight—the narrator epitomizes the "prudence" central to the book's theme.[10] His masterful, capacious view mocks the reader's puny view to establish the novel's rational standard as omniscience. "This Work may, indeed, be considered as a great Creation of our own," he boasts, "and for a little Reptile of a Critic to presume to find Fault with any of its Parts, without knowing the Manner in which the Whole is connected, and before he comes to the final Catastrophe, is a most presumptuous Absurdity" (*TJ* 524–5). Reasonable criticism requires that one know "the Manner in which the Whole is connected," for to exert one's authority without this Olympian view is "presumptuous Absurdity," like "a little Reptile" rebuking the Creator.

Yet Fielding's humorous efforts to teach men to be better readers simultaneously erode the distinctions he strives to maintain between quixotic presumption and the rational, masculine authority of experience. For as much as Fielding touts his "great Creation" as true nature, he cannot escape the realization that it is in fact art, and that art always comes with distinct generic limitations. As Ian Watt observes,

> it is surely very damaging for a novel to be in any sense an imitation
> of another literary work: and the reason for this seems to be that since
> the novelist's primary task is to convey the impression of fidelity to

human experience, attention to any pre-established formal conventions can only endanger his success.[11]

In Fielding's words: "when the Writer himself takes his Lines not from Nature, but from Books! Such Characters are only the faint Copy of a Copy, and can have neither the Justness nor Spirit of an Original" (*TJ* 493–4). Striving to represent unmediated "Nature," Fielding promotes universalism, but cannot really believe in universals, for he regards all representation as generalization, and all generalization as potentially inauthentic genre. Fielding cannot sustain his gendered understanding of quixotism, because ultimately he, like the female quixote, cannot distinguish between nature and art, between true experience and "the faint Copy of a Copy." Literary didacticism, Fielding's remedy for quixotism, looks strikingly like the ailment itself.

The contrast between Fielding's stated intentions in the dedication of *Tom Jones*, and the contrary lesson he later assigns to his protagonist, clearly illustrates the author's didactic difficulties and their roots in empiricism. In the dedication, Fielding announces his intention to teach his readers how to discern real character and true merit, to enable them to see the world as Isaac Bickerstaff saw it reflected in the Mirror of Truth. He will make the invisible visible. "I declare, that to recommend Goodness and Innocence hath been my sincere Endeavour in this History," Fielding asserts:

> And to say the Truth, it is likeliest to be attained in Books of this Kind; for an Example is a Kind of Picture, in which Virtue becomes an Object of Sight, and strikes us with an Idea of that Loveliness, which *Plato* asserts there is in her naked Charms.
>
> (*TJ* 7)

So revealing will Fielding's history be, that virtue will not only be visible, she will also be quite naked. Fielding imagines encounters with truth as a kind of unveiling, a glimpse of the reality beneath decorated surfaces. By "displaying that Beauty of Virtue," Fielding hopes to convince "Men, that their true Interest directs them to a Pursuit of her." "For this Purpose," he assures his readers, "I have shewn, that no Acquisitions of Guilt can compensate the Loss of that Solid inward Comfort of Mind, which is the sure Companion of Innocence and Virtue" (*TJ* 7). Hidden behind the appearance of "Interest," here depicted as material wealth ("Acquisitions"), is "true Interest," represented as feeling ("that Solid inward Comfort of Mind").

Fielding's dedication tells men that though moral truth is not easily accessible to empirical method, moral truth and its operations are still visible to the well-trained eye. His goal in writing *Tom Jones* is to disclose the hidden law of "true Interest" by heuristically incorporating it into the novel's plot. Accordingly, *Tom Jones*' plot, as R. S. Crane observes, is not a single storyline, but "the dynamic system of actions, extending throughout the novel, by which the divergent intents and beliefs of a large number of persons of different characters and states of knowledge . . . are made to cooperate" in bringing about the events of the novel.[12] Fielding requires discerning readers to recognize these intents, beliefs, characters and states of knowledge as they form a dynamic system of moral truth and its consequences. "In reality," the narrator of *Tom Jones* explains,

> there are many little Circumstances too often omitted by injudicious Historians, from which Events of the utmost Importance arise. The World may indeed be considered as a vast Machine, in which the great Wheels are originally set in Motion by those which are very minute, and almost imperceptible to any but the strongest Eyes.
>
> (*TJ* 225)

In keeping with the sentimental tradition, Fielding imagines moral truth as a scientific law: universal, but mostly invisible. It cannot be counted or assessed like material wealth, for it more closely resembles *feeling* or *interest*—an interior, hidden but inexorable force—the equivalent of gravity in a Newtonian moral universe. In *Tom Jones*, as Ian Watt argues, "all human particles are subject to an ultimate invisible force which exists in the universe whether they are there to show it or not."[13] To acquire real knowledge of human nature, one must look past appearances, beneath surfaces and beyond art, to see "almost imperceptible" forces—a project that Fielding optimistically believes will always meet with success. "[H]owever cunning the Disguise be which a Masquerader wears," he writes in his "Essay on the Knowledge of the Characters of Men" (1743), "however foreign to his Age, Degree, or Circumstance, yet if closely attended to, he very rarely escapes the Discovery of an accurate Observer; for Nature, which unwillingly submits to the Imposture, is ever endeavouring to peep forth and shew herself."[14] In this model of moral knowledge, men will be rewarded for careful empirical study.[15]

Fielding's lessons for the reader through Tom's story, however, also offer a different view of moral knowledge, one that stresses instead the inadequacy of nature to make herself known. Even Tom, as naturally expressive as he is, still requires the aid of art. The narrator extrapolates this lesson to everyone. "It is not enough that your Designs, nay that your Actions are intrinsically good," he warns:

> you must take Care they shall appear so. If your Inside be never so beautiful, you must preserve a fair Outside also. This must be constantly looked to, or Malice and Envy will take Care to blacken it so, that the Sagacity and Goodness of an *Allworthy* will not be able to see through it, and to discern the Beauties within. Let this, my young Readers, be your constant Maxim, That no Man can be good enough

to enable him to neglect the Rules of Prudence; nor will Virtue herself look beautiful, unless she be bedecked with the outward Ornaments of Decency and Decorum. And this Precept, my worthy Disciples, if you read with due Attention, you will, I hope, find sufficiently enforced by Examples in the following Pages.

(*TJ* 141)

Goodness and innocence notwithstanding, here it is appearance that matters, for the truth of nature cannot always be depended upon to peep forth and show herself. One must "preserve a fair Outside" since "the Beauties within" are hidden, unfortunately, "within." The "Inside," home to that "solid Inward Comfort of Mind" known as "true Interest," may remain forever unseen, perpetually concealed by the opaque "Outside." In direct contrast to his claims in the novel's dedication, Fielding here suggests that not even "Virtue herself" can rely on the loveliness of her naked charms. Even she must "be bedecked with the outward Ornaments of Decency and Decorum" before she will appear beautiful. Making virtue an "Object of Sight" requires authorial artistry—the "Cookery of the Author," as the narrator describes his craft in the novel's opening "Bill of Fare": "Where then lies the Difference between the Food of the Nobleman and the Porter, if both are at Dinner on the same Ox or Calf, but in the seasoning, the dressing, the garnishing and the setting forth?" Answering his own rhetorical question, the narrator concludes: "In like manner, the Excellence of the mental Entertainment consists less in the Subject, than in the Author's Skill in well dressing it up" (*TJ* 33). With the author's special skill being that of dressing up nature, Fielding should be well qualified to advise his readers in the arts of prudence. *Tom Jones* reverses Fielding's earlier opposition between nature and art by presenting the author's art as the best expression of nature. Fielding asks his readers to read his own art as nature.

Fielding's contradictory attitude toward virtue's naked beauty points to the paradox at the heart of his authorial contribution to the empirical study of invisible things. He desires his own art to be the truest expression of nature, even as he suspects that all art inevitably leads to deception. The mediation of artistic forms—the very thing that makes virtue visible—also makes hypocrisy and quixotism possible. Without the right "outward Ornaments," even virtue herself lacks beauty, yet the beauty of these ornaments cannot guarantee the presence of virtue. Readers who place too much confidence in "outward Ornaments" are bad readers, like the modern "Critics" who "have been emboldened to assume a Dictatorial Power" over authors: "these Critics being Men of shallow Capacities, very easily mistook mere Form for Substance. They acted as a Judge would, who should adhere to the lifeless Letter of the Law, and reject the Spirit" (*TJ* 210–11). They read too literally. Quixotism, as "the history of the whole world in general," presents Fielding with an empirical crisis, for it reminds him of the abiding inscrutability of inward qualities. His optimistic intent in the "Essay on the Knowledge of the Characters of Men," which "endeavoured to shew the several methods by which we can propose to get any Insight into the Characters of those with whom we converse, and by which we may frustrate all the Cunning and Designs of Hypocrisy," appears to be an impossible dream in *Tom Jones*. For the "several methods" Fielding identifies in the "Essay" are all empirical, focusing on external signs of internal qualities in men, "*viz.* by the Marks which Nature hath imprinted on the Countenance, by their Behaviour to ourselves, and by their Behaviour to others" (*Miscellanies* 178).[16] Fielding cannot decode these pregnant "Marks" for his honest readers without risking instructing his artful ones in how better to practice their deceptions. Vexatiously, the author's skill of "Cookery" is the hypocrite's specialty as well—"the dressing, the garnishing, and the setting forth" of character. Both author and hypocrite offer a cooked version of nature.

From the outside, then, Fielding's arts and those of his adversaries look the same, the salient difference between them being only motive—whether the art intends to illuminate or to deceive—a moral difference that is invisible. Fielding's empirical means continuously undermine his ethical ends, as his corrective for false art is more art. "I believe, it is much easier to make good Men wise, than to make bad Men good," he writes in the dedication, justifying the motive and method of his fiction. To which Samuel Johnson, in the famous *Rambler* no. 4, replies:

> It is . . . not a sufficient vindication of a character, that it is drawn as it appears, for many characters ought never to be drawn; nor of a narrative, that the train of events is agreeable to observation and experience, for that observation which is called knowledge of the world, will be found much more frequently to make men cunning than good.[17]

Fielding's fiction, Johnson suspects, will not defend virtue and innocence; rather, it will encourage deceit, teaching "the young, the ignorant, and the idle" to be artful. Unlike "the romances formerly written," Johnson fears, Fielding's new genre does not mark itself with sufficiently obvious generic signs—"a hermit and a wood, a battle and a shipwreck"—for "[i]ts province is to bring about natural events by easy means, and to keep up curiosity without the help of wonder" (Johnson 3: 19–20). Johnson worries that writers of Fielding's genre will be unable to control the meanings of their works, because the power of their examples "is so great, as to take possession of the memory by a kind of violence, and produce effects almost without the intervention of the will" (Johnson 3: 22). As I have argued in the previous chapter, Johnson regards quixotism as the norm; he does not dismiss it lightly as mere female troubles. Fielding, by contrast, believes he can overcome quixotism by teaching men to exercise rational, masculine control.

Of course, Fielding does not need Johnson to remind him of the unstable relation between meaning and genre. As much as any author of his satiric age, Fielding feels the ever-present, ossifying tendencies of genre, which obscure or falsify meaning by formalizing expression. Generic conventions, he knows, are mere "outsides," visible surfaces easily imitated or feigned by the artful or unthinking. Wary of how easily and how imperceptibly true representation can give way to conventional form, Fielding keeps readers on alert by testing them with frequent, unannounced parodies. The satiric obituaries in his journalism illustrate his technique:[18]

> *Dead* . . . Mr. Arthur Wight, *a Town-Clerk*. Mr. William Chettle, *ditto* . . . Mr. George North; *he was joint Clerk with his Father to the Merchant Taylors Company; by his Death therefore Half that Place is vacant* . . . Mr. Tillbury, *an eminent Scarlet Dyer*. Mr. Bick, *an eminent Wax Chandler*. The Rev. Mr. Strange, much esteemed by all that knew him. Mr. Samuel Russell, *an eminent Linen-Draper* . . . Thomas Tonkin of Polgar in Cornwal, Esq., universally lamented by his Acquaintance. Upwards of 40 Cows belonging to one at Tottenham Court, *universally lamented by all their Acquaintance.*[19]

Fielding's italics emphasize the generic aspects of the obituary's form. Meant to single out individuals for commemoration, the obituary in Fielding's irreverent hands conveys instead how little there is to distinguish most people from one another at the end of their lives. Mr Wight was a town clerk, *"ditto"* for Mr Chettle. Though Mr North may have been prominent, he can easily be replaced by the enterprising readers who make wise use of Fielding's tip: *"by his Death therefore Half that Place is vacant."*

Obituaries also report the respectful sentiments of the survivors. The obituary-as-genre, Fielding mischievously hints, must often falsify these feelings, for they are remarkably uniform: the deceased were always "much esteemed" or "universally lamented." Fielding's description of Mr Tillbury, the scarlet-dyer, and Mr Bick, the wax-chandler, each distinguished by the conventional form of "an eminent _____," immediately calls into question the generic obituary's relation to truth. Winking at the emptiness of such forms, Fielding applies the adjective *"eminent"* to common tradesmen who probably lived obscurely throughout their lives. His description of the "Upwards of 40 Cows . . . *universally lamented by all their Acquaintance*" casts a particularly withering glare onto the disparities between generic forms and true sentiments, by giving a formulaic obituary to creatures for whom the conventional phrase, *"universally lamented by all their Acquaintance,"* is meaningless. Readers must immediately recognize the cows' obituary as ridiculous, because the generic form does not apply to cows: cows do not have acquaintances. Yet in this respect, readers very likely know more about the cows than they do about Mr Tillbury or Mr Bick. Did Mr Tillbury or Mr Bick have any acquaintances?

Did anyone really regard them as eminent? Fielding's parodic obituaries stress how easily generic conventions, in the absence of real knowledge derived from experience, can be mistaken for truthful representations. And as the motives and feelings of others cannot be directly experienced, Fielding must remain deeply skeptical of their outward expressions.

Keen to the possibilities of generic subversion, Fielding relies on irony, parody, self-mockery and the trope of inexpressible feeling to control the meanings of his own text. Amidst the diversity of interpretations possible in his empirical world of "outward Ornaments," the rational, masculine authority that Fielding champions can be found only in the exclusivity of sentimentalism. In *Tom Jones*, for example, the contrast between the description of Bridget Blifil's grief upon her husband's death, and Squire Allworthy's reaction to the same event, shows how Fielding writes a genre of authentic feeling that resists satiric attack by combining comic irony with the inexpressibility of true sentiment. Fielding forestalls criticism through sentimental satire:

> Mrs. *Bridget Blifil* . . . conducted herself through the whole Season in which Grief is to make its Appearance on the Outside of the Body, with the strictest Regard to all the Rules of Custom and Decency, suiting the Alterations of her Countenance to the several Alterations of her Habit: For as this changed from Weeds to Black, from Black to Grey, from Grey to White, so did her Countenance change from Dismal to Sorrowful, from Sorrowful to Sad, and from Sad to Serious, till the Day came in which she was allowed to return to her former Serenity.
>
> (*TJ* 117)

Ever distrustful of generic conventions, Fielding depicts Bridget Blifil's feelings as suspect by emphasizing the impeccability of her form. Observing "all the Rules of Custom and Decency," adjusting the marks on her countenance to match the symbolism of her clothing, Mrs Blifil prudently bedecks herself with all the outward ornaments of decency and decorum. Mrs Blifil's "Appearance on the Outside of the Body," by perfectly reproducing the trappings and the suits of woe, strongly hints that she lacks that within which passes show. She lacks those inward qualities that constitute true feeling.

In contrast, Fielding presents a very different picture of Mr Allworthy's sorrow, one that avoids direct description altogether:

> what Reader but knows that Mr. *Allworthy* felt at first for the Loss of his Friend, those Emotions of Grief, which on such Occasions enter into all Men whose Hearts are not composed of Flint, or their Heads of as solid Materials? Again, what Reader doth not know that Philosophy and Religion, in time, moderated, and at last extinguished this Grief? The former of these, teaching the Folly and Vanity of it,

and the latter, correcting it, as unlawful, and at the same time assuaging it by raising future Hopes and Assurances which enable a strong and religious Mind to take leave of a Friend on his Death-bed with little less Indifference than if he was preparing for a long Journey; and indeed with as little less Hope of seeing him again.

(*TJ* 116–17)

Through Squire Allworthy, Fielding offers a representation of true sorrow that can never be feigned. Abandoning his effort to make inward qualities "an Object of Sight," Fielding does not particularize the effects of grief on the squire's clothing and countenance, the "Outside" of his body. Rather, Fielding gives readers seemingly direct access to the sentiments within Allworthy's mind: Allworthy suffered "Emotions of Grief" that "Philosophy and Religion" assuaged, raising in him "future Hopes and Assurances." This depiction of Allworthy's true sentiments validates itself by ridiculing attempts such as Bridget's to create external, material representations of inward qualities. Reminders of materiality here appear only to convey *lack* of sentiment ("Hearts . . . of Flint" and "Heads of as solid Materials") and refer not to any of the novel's characters, but to the readers themselves. Only sensible readers will be able to comprehend Allworthy's feelings, for the narrator never specifies exactly what Allworthy felt. The seemingly direct access to Allworthy's mind comes filtered through the response of an imagined reader of real tenderness. By presenting his descriptions as interrogatives—"what Reader but knows?"—"what Reader doth not know?"—the narrator shifts the burden of authenticating Allworthy's feelings onto the audience.

Thus disguised as satire, this rhetoric of sentimental exclusivity helps Fielding preserve authorial control. What the narrator can do to Bridget— subvert her sentiments by displaying their generic qualities—the reader cannot do to Allworthy. For if the reader finds Allworthy's feelings to be generic and therefore not credible, it means only that the reader is inadequate. What kind of "Emotions of Grief" passed through the squire's mind? The kind that all readers who have experienced "such Occasions" know to "enter into all Men whose Hearts are not composed of Flint, or their Heads of as solid Materials." Requiring readers to supply their own picture of Allworthy's genuine grief, Fielding preemptively discredits skeptical readers as irremediably insensible: stone-hearted and stone-headed. Aided by his readers' tender imaginations, he can claim to be representing true feeling, without actually having to specify the exact form that it takes. For Henry as for Sarah, real feeling can be distinguished from counterfeit only by remaining inexpressible. Though nature may be "ever endeavouring to peep forth and shew herself," Henry Fielding will not or cannot describe what she looks like. His empiricism studies invisible things; it is sentimentalism. His "Rules of Prudence" and exhortations to "Discernment" are lessons in sentimental reading.[20]

It is true that Fielding is not usually identified as a sentimental novelist.

156

Perhaps this is so because critics recognize in his controlling themes of "Prudence" and "Discernment" the activity of criticism itself, an activity that they, like Fielding, prefer to regard as rational, universal and masculine. By identifying their perspectives with the narrator's comprehensive view, critics may conveniently ignore the limitations of their own rational authority; they may partake vicariously in the heady fiction of the narrator's supreme authority. Fielding's narrator offers the dictatorial critic his fondest wish: he may speak with the voice of reason, while all others study to emulate the universal sagacity that he embodies. "We have mentioned these two as Examples only of the Task which may be imposed on Readers of the lowest Class," the narrator announces, referring to the two descriptions of grief discussed above, then warns: "Much higher and harder Exercises in Judgment and Penetration may reasonably be expected from the upper Graduates in Criticism" (*TJ* 117). These higher and harder graduate lessons promise even greater critical insight, for they will teach men to see the future: "to be able to foretel the Actions of Men in any Circumstances from their Characters" rather than "to judge their Characters from their Actions." "The former, I own, requires the greater Penetration; but may be accomplished by true Sagacity, with not less Certainty than the latter," the narrator confidently concludes, promising that men who read carefully enough will achieve the narrator's omniscience (*TJ* 117). Criticism for Fielding, unlike for Johnson, has "attained the certainty and stability of science."[21] Human action operates by some regular principle, of which "Character" is an unseen constant. Fielding's lessons in critical reading and foresight, largely exercises in judging character, follow naturally from this Newtonian vision of the science of man. Fielding makes universal knowledge of moral actions seem attainable.

Engaged in an empirical pursuit of universal moral knowledge, Fielding's masculine, rational authority is recognizable as sentimentalism. This connection becomes especially clear in Fielding's last and self-avowedly "favourite" novel, *Amelia* (1751), whose "maudlin sentimentality" has been regarded by critics as a "problem." "Despite the message of the 'exordium' Fielding seems no longer convinced by the notion developed in *Tom Jones* that morality resides in the power of prudence and the will to govern the passions," Battestin speculates, able to make sense of *Amelia* only by discounting Fielding's own words.[22] For, in fact, an unprejudiced reading of the exordium will find that Fielding actually intensifies his commitment to his earlier theme of "Prudence" by insisting that there is no luck in life, only natural consequences that play out according to fixed rules:

> I question much, whether we may not by natural Means account for the Success of Knaves, the Calamities of Fools, with all the Miseries in which Men of Sense sometimes involve themselves by quitting the Directions of Prudence, and following the blind Guidance of a predominant Passion; in short, for all the ordinary Phenomena which

are imputed to Fortune; whom, perhaps, Men accuse with no less Absurdity in Life, than a bad Player complains of ill Luck at the Game of Chess.[23]

If we recall, however, that sentimentalism is a branch of empiricism, then we should not be puzzled to see *Amelia*'s "maudlin sentimentality" coexisting with Fielding's increasingly Newtonian vision of the universe. As Joseph Glanvill wrote in defense of the new philosophy: "Yea, the most common *Phaenomena* can be neither known, nor improved, without insight into the more *hidden* frame. For *Nature* works by an *Invisible Hand* in all things" (Glanvill 180). To identify nature's hidden structures—to watch the movements of "an *Invisible Hand*"—is the work of the empirical science of man. It is also the work of Fielding's literary criticism, which likewise searches for the "natural Means" operating behind "ordinary Phenomena":

> Life may as properly be called an Art as any other; and the great Incidents in it are no more to be considered as mere Accidents, than the several Members of a fine Statue, or a noble Poem. The Critics in all these are not content with seeing any Thing to be great, without knowing why and how it came to be so. By examining carefully the several Gradations which conduce to bring every Model to Perfection, we learn truly to know that Science in which the Model is formed: As Histories of this Kind, therefore, may properly be called Models of HUMAN LIFE; so by observing minutely the several Incidents which tend to the Catastrophe or Completion of the whole, and the minute Causes whence those Incidents are produced, we shall best be instructed in this most useful of all Arts, which I call the ART OF LIFE.
>
> (*Amelia* 17)

Fielding's "Models of HUMAN LIFE" raise reading to a science. Claiming that his plots correspond perfectly to probability,[24] Fielding urges his readers to form their expectations on his "Histories." He invites them to read quixotically, as though literature were life. He encourages them to read sentimentally, as though generic convention were a natural language. He instructs them to read rationally and critically, to see "why and how" things come to be so. The power of prudence need not be opposed to sentimentalism, the empirical study of invisible things.

What sentimentalism must be opposed to, however, is experiential diversity. Fielding's rationalizing, sentimental empiricism can arrive at "universal" truth only by discrediting those whose experience has led them to contrary conclusions about human nature and its probabilities. Nowhere does Fielding indicate this more strenuously than in his discussion of the "Passion of Love" in *Tom Jones*. The passion of love is essential to Fielding's plot, for it is the "natural Means" through which Tom comes to recognize his mistakes and to amend his conduct. The credibility of the plot, therefore, depends upon the reader's understanding of this passion. Yet how does an author make love "an Object of Sight" without descending into descriptions too gross or too hackneyed to capture a sentiment so refined, so elevated, so true? This task is especially challenging for Fielding, who sees so acutely the disparity between true feeling and representational forms, that he often uses the presence of the latter to mark the absence of the former. For example, in his depiction of Jenny Waters' "Love" for Jones, Fielding conveys the inauthenticity of Jenny's "Love" (it is really lust) by making generic form itself the most noticeable aspect of the description. The mock-epic formula looms larger than any of Jenny's feelings: "First, from two lovely blue Eyes, whose bright Orbs flashed Lightning at their Discharge, flew forth two pointed Ogles. But happily for our Heroe, hit only a vast Piece of Beef which he was then conveying into his Plate, and harmless spent their Force" (*TJ* 512). The "Passion of Love" is difficult to turn into "an Object of Sight," for once turned into an object, "Love" becomes capable of alternative interpretations that bear little resemblance to the true sentiment Fielding would like his readers to imagine. "Love" embodied might merely be sex; desire embodied might merely be appetite. Reduced to "two pointed Ogles," the essence of Jenny's "Love" collides ridiculously with the materiality of "a vast Piece of Beef," re-enacting in miniature the general awkwardness with which substance meets form in Fielding's fiction. If readers do not already recognize the "Passion of Love" to exist in a manner untainted by materiality, then Fielding only undermines his own case by trying to turn "Love" into "an Object of Sight."

Therefore, rather than make the "Passion of Love" visible to those who cannot see it, Fielding peremptorily dismisses them because they have not seen it. He cannot abide readers who, because they experience love differently, doubt his representations of it. He discredits such skeptics as unanswerable, because they are, in fact, unanswerable. Specifically, Fielding has in mind those self-interested Mandevillean "Philosophers" who "pretend to have found out, that there is no such Passion in the human Breast," and who "very much alarmed the World, by shewing that there were no such things as Virtue and Goodness really existing in Human Nature, and who deduced our best Actions from Pride" (*TJ* 268). Unable to refute their loveless experience—for how could he?—Fielding summarily dismisses it as a distasteful limitation of "A BAD MIND" (*TJ* 269):

Examine your heart, my good Reader, and resolve whether you do believe these Matters with me. If you do, you may now proceed to their Exemplification in the following Pages; if you do not, you have, I assure you, already read more than you have understood; and it would be wiser to pursue your Business, or your Pleasures (such as they are) than to throw away any more of your Time in reading what you can neither taste nor comprehend. To treat of the Effects of Love

159

to you, must be as absurd as to discourse on Colours to a Man born blind; since possibly your Idea of Love may be as absurd as that which we are told such a blind Man once entertained of the Colour of Scarlet: that Color seemed to him to be much like the Sound of a Trumpet; and Love probably may, in your Opinion, very greatly resemble a Dish of Soup, or a Sir-loin of Roast-beef.

(*TJ* 271–2)

When it comes to the passions hidden in the breast, the reader must already "believe these Matters" with Fielding, or their "Exemplification" in his book will be unedifying. Examples may work more forcibly on the mind than precepts, but only for minds that already think alike. Following his sister's lead in *David Simple*, Fielding purposefully embraces a sentimental understanding of the human heart expressly to deny the universalizing claims of Mandevillean interest. His central pair of brothers in *Tom Jones* reproduce the main epistemological conflict between Daniel and David Simple. Like Daniel, Blifil is "strongly attached to the Interest only of one single Person" (*TJ* 165) and can interpret the generosity and selflessness of his brother only as simple-mindedness: "He fancied he knew *Jones* to the Bottom, and had in reality a great Contempt for his Understanding, for not being more attached to his own Interest" (*TJ* 295). Blifil and Jones are of two different minds—knave and fool, or "BAD" and "good"—and therefore experience the world in vastly different ways. Blifil's inability to feel or to imagine love is genuine; he does not feign his indifference: "For as to that entire and absolute Possession of the Heart of his Mistress, which romantic Lovers require, the very Idea of it never entered his Head" (*TJ* 294–5). Fielding satirizes Blifil and those who think like Blifil, not for hypocrisy, but for drawing general conclusions about human nature based solely on their own cramped, dark and nasty minds.

Like Hutcheson, Fielding overrules the testimony of readers who would deny the visibility of moral feeling. To justify their dismissal from his court of public opinion, Fielding impugns the reliability of their senses. "To deny the Existence of a Passion of which we often see manifest Instances, seems to be very strange and absurd," the narrator of *Tom Jones* insists, expressing some surprise at the fact that his own perceptions are not universally embraced (*TJ* 271). Fielding equates skepticism with the absence of (moral) sensation; his own inability to make real feeling self-evident thereby becomes the Mandevilleans' inability to perceive self-evident, real feeling. Anti-sentimental philosophers cannot "comprehend" Fielding's novel because they cannot "taste" it. To talk to them is "absurd" because only actual sensation can convey the idea of sensation. The blind man cannot understand color, because color and sound, being distinct simple ideas, bear no necessary relation to one another. Fielding borrows this comparison of the color scarlet and trumpet music from Locke's *Essay Concerning Human Understanding* (III, iv, 11), where Locke explains why "*Words*" can never properly substitute for the direct sensation of simple ideas:

For to hope to produce an *Idea* of Light, or Colour, by a Sound, however formed, is to expect that Sounds should be visible, or Colours audible; and to make the Ears do the Office of all the other Senses. Which is all one as to say, that we might Taste, Smell, and See by the Ears: a sort of Philosophy worthy only of *Sanco Panca*, who had the Faculty to see Dulcinea by Hearsay.

(*Essay* 425)

A good moral empiricist, Fielding argues that only direct experience of love can convey the idea of love, for the feeling of love is a simple idea, inexpressible and forever unknown to those who have no experience of it. To hope to produce the idea of love, through novels, is to expect that books should be felt, and to make the reading eye do the office of all the other (moral) senses. It would be asking readers to feel by the eyes, to "see" the invisible by hearsay, to practice a philosophy worthy only of Sancho Panza. Of course, this is exactly what Fielding asks his own readers to do.

Contrary to what Fielding implies, Lockean empiricism cannot authorize moral empiricism. Fielding may mock the comparison between love and roast beef, on the grounds that these two entities, being real and distinct, must produce very different sensations in properly sensible people. But in a strange way, his mirth serves to undercut the reality of love by emphasizing the empirically greater reality of beef. At least beef can, quite literally, be tasted—written sentiment cannot. Ultimately, Fielding's moral empiricism is betrayed by the "Cookery of the Author," which attempts to make virtue visible (and tasty) through the art of narration. For to make virtue "an Object of Sight" (and taste) through words, is to compare across incomparable senses, to substitute the figures of representation for the reality of direct experience, to imagine "Love" as "a Dish of Soup, or a Sir-loin of Roast-beef." Laughing most heartily at the absurdity of such comparisons, substitutions and similes, Fielding ridicules the very authority he claims for himself as an author.

Quixotism and Jacobitism

Most discussions of the Jacobite subplot in *Tom Jones* treat it as a "historical" or "political" aspect of the novel, distinct from the book's epistemological theme and Cervantine genealogy.[25] Yet the Jacobite presence in the novel may also be read as a reminder of the work's debt to the quixotic tradition. As I have argued in Chapter 1, Jacobitism was frequently identified as quixotic during the first half of the eighteenth century. Fielding continues this association in the character of Partridge, a declared Jacobite and "*one of the pleasantest Barbers that was ever recorded in History, the Barber of* Bagdad, *or he in* Don Quixotte *not excepted*" (*TJ* 413). Partridge embodies quixotic instability, threatening to turn the narrator's authority into jest even as the narrator defines his authority against Partridge's ridiculousness. The "Limits . . . of Probability" should mark the boundaries of rational belief, according to the narrator, who establishes his own credibility by carefully staying within the same probable expectations that he instructs his readers to embrace (*TJ* 402). Partridge challenges this rationality by placing different limits on probability. His superstitious belief in ghosts pushes even the limits of poetic license. As the narrator explains:

> The only supernatural Agents which can in any Manner be allowed to us Moderns are Ghosts; but of these I would advise an Author to be extremely sparing. These are indeed like Arsenic, and other dangerous Drugs in Physic, to be used with the utmost Caution; nor would I advise the Introduction of them at all in those Works, or by those Authors to which, or to whom a Horse-Laugh in the Reader, would be any great Prejudice or Mortification.
>
> (*TJ* 399)

With the appearance of ghosts in literature expected to cause "a Horse-Laugh in the Reader," Partridge's superstition marks the end of Fielding's probability and the beginning of the ridiculous.

Partridge's poor sense of probability does make him a bad reader of the world. Adopting the methods of probable reasoning, Partridge often doubts when he should believe, and believes when he should doubt. When, for example, he first hears Jones' story, he remains skeptical, for "he could not reconcile to himself, that Mr. Allworthy should turn his son (for so he firmly believed him to be) out of Doors, for any Reason which he had heard assigned. He concluded therefore, that the whole was a Fiction" (*TJ* 427). He reaches more gullible conclusions on other occasions, but still he remains within the forms of probable reasoning. His incredible anecdote of Frank's fight with the ghost, for instance, comes bolstered with all the support of material evidence weighed against rational expectation:

> Ay, you may laugh, Sir, and so did some others, particularly a Squire, who is thought to be no better than an Atheist; who forsooth, because there was a Calf with a white Face found dead in the same Lane the next Morning, would fain have it, that the Battle was between *Frank* and that, as if a Calf would set upon a Man.
>
> (*TJ* 469)

Scoffing at the even farther-fetched notion that a calf would attack a man, Partridge remains firmly convinced that Frank's assailant must have been a ghost. If the limits of Fielding's probability certify his art as true to nature, then the alternative limits of Partridge's probability confirm his opinions as quixotism. Accordingly, Partridge's poor sense of the probable is accompanied by an inability to distinguish between nature and art, as evidenced by his behavior at the play, which is—significantly—a performance of *Hamlet* (*TJ* 852–7). Partridge cannot tell fine acting from real emotion; he mistakes trappings and suits for that within which passes show. As laughable as he is made to appear, however, his quixotic beliefs challenge Fielding's system of moral empiricism, for they remind readers that experience cannot be expected to yield universal interpretations of invisible things with any degree of "Certainty." Partridge's Jacobitism, set against troop movements during the Jacobite Uprising of '45, reminds readers that the boundaries between the probable and the ridiculous are not solidly tied to "nature," that reason is vulnerable to revolution.

Fielding's problems before the quixotic challenge of Partridge go back to the author's sentimental assumptions about rational empiricism. Because his universalist political epistemology cannot admit the existence of experiential diversity, Fielding must discount, in some way, the experience of anyone who reaches conclusions different from his own. "I have heard of a Man who believed there was no real Existence in the World but himself; and whatever he saw without him was mere Phantom and Illusion," Fielding writes in the *True Patriot* (1–8 April 1746), beginning this anti-Jacobite essay on a theme reminiscent of *Don Quixote in England*. In this essay, as in his earlier play, Fielding complains about the fragmenting effects of occupational diversity:

> if we were to derive the Principles of Mankind from their Practice, we should be almost persuaded that somewhat like this Madness had possessed not only particular Men, but their several orders and Professions. For tho' they do not absolutely deny all Existence to other Persons and Things, yet it is certain they hold them of no Consequence, and little worth their Consideration, unless they *trench* somewhat towards their own Order or Calling.[26]

Committed to the ideal of universal reason, Fielding is vexed to confront "particular Men," "orders" and "Professions" whose way of thinking departs from, and therefore trivializes, his own. The specter before Fielding is a vision of himself as specter. He recognizes that these men hold his opinions to be "of no Consequence, and little worth their Consideration," that they deny his "real Existence in the World," that they turn him into "mere Phantom and Illusion." If these men were allowed to set the standard of reason, then Fielding himself might meet the same ridiculed fate as Partridge's ghosts. There is dangerous potential, Fielding realizes, in men who are too quick and too confident in their ability to identify and dismiss the ridiculous. As this critique could be applied to himself, however, Fielding must find means to exempt himself from his own censure.

To reconcile universal reason and the appearance of rational diversity, Fielding invokes the contrast between particular and general understanding. Diversity of opinion—the "Madness" of solipsism—results when particular knowledge is credited with too much authority. Reasonable men, Fielding maintains, will not view the world through their own partial interests. They will enlarge their perspectives so as to comprehend humankind more generally. David Hume's philosophy articulates the case succinctly. "[E]very particular man has a peculiar position with regard to others," Hume observes,

> and 'tis impossible we cou'd ever converse together on any reasonable terms, were each of us to consider characters and persons, only as they appear from his peculiar point of view. In order, therefore, to prevent those continual *contradictions*, and arrive at a more *stable* judgment of things, we fix on some *steady* and *general* points of view; and always, in our thoughts, place ourselves in them, whatever may be our present situation.[27]

Like Hume, Fielding believes that reasonable thought proceeds not from a "peculiar point of view," but from "*steady* and *general* points of view." Moreover, he imagines the writer to be the privileged purveyor of these general points of view. It is the writer's job to teach readers to transcend their peculiar positions, to converse on reasonable terms, to arrive at a stable judgment of things. "[W]e warn thee not too hastily to condemn any of the Incidents in this our History, as impertinent and foreign to our main Design, because thou dost not immediately conceive in what Manner such Incident may conduce to that Design," advises the narrator of *Tom Jones*, pointedly reminding readers that he sees the general view while they do not (*TJ* 524). This confident and comprehensive claim to the general view, epitomized by Fielding's narrator, constitutes Fielding's famed "robust masculinity." The larger the view, the more reasonable the view: readers should defer to Fielding because his is bigger.

"I have heard somewhere of a Geographer," Fielding's *True Patriot* essay continues,

> who received no other Pleasure from the *AEneid* of *Virgil*, than by tracing out the Voyage of *AEneas* in the Map. To which I may add a certain Coach-maker, who having sufficient Latin to read the Story of *Phaeton* in the *Metamorphosis*, shook his Head that so fine a Genius for making Chariots as *Ovid* had, was thrown away on making Poems.
>
> (*True Patriot* 258)

As these examples illustrate, the "Madness" of these men consists in their unwillingness or inability to recognize their own littleness, and the littleness of their orders and professions, when compared to the writer. For Fielding, madness reigns supreme when the *Aeneid* is reduced to a mapping exercise, when Ovid goes lamented as an unfulfilled coach-maker, when the writer's general view is lost amidst the clamor of particular views. "To say the truth," Fielding concludes,

> this Partiality to ourselves, our own Opinions, and our own Party, hath introduced many dangerous Evils into Commonwealths. It is this Humour which keeps up the Name of *Jacobitism* in this Kingdom; and it is this Humour only, from which his present Majesty or his Administration can derive a single Enemy within it.
>
> (*True Patriot* 260)

Fielding uses the concept of the general view to distinguish his rational political views from the ridiculous "Partiality" of Jacobitism, and to establish his authority as a writer over the competing judgments of the other orders and professions. Fielding exempts himself from his own critique of "Partiality" on the supposition that his understanding is more capacious. His is bigger.

Crucial to the logic supporting Fielding's attack on Jacobitism is the real size of his own comprehension—whether he in fact sees the general view, or whether he only thinks he does. Is Partridge's quixotism just the mirror image of Fielding's rationality, or is Fielding's rationality the authoritative measure of Partridge's ridiculousness? In the problem of Jacobitism, Fielding confronts the incommensurability of experience, the impossibility of knowing whether one's own understanding really is greater, not just different (or even, perhaps, smaller) than another's. The Jacobite subplot in *Tom Jones* dramatizes this ambivalence. Beginning with easy ridicule of Partridge—"With what Stuff and Nonsense hast thou filled thy Head?" Jones incredulously demands of his Jacobite companion (*TJ* 440)—the subplot comes to a close only after shading into the irresolvable disagreement that arises between Jones and the misanthropic Man of the Hill. The indeterminate status of Jacobitism (threatening or laughable?) is the thread that links Jones' ridicule of Partridge to the Man of the Hill's eventual dismissal of Jones. Sixty years earlier, the Man of the Hill had been just like Jones, marching off to support constitution and country, at that time against James II, under the banner of the Duke of Monmouth. Their apparently similar experience, however, does not bring about a meeting of the minds. Upon hearing the old man's story, Jones exclaims:

> "What you say . . . is very true; and it has often struck me, as the most wonderful thing I ever read of in History, that so soon after this convincing Experience, which brought our whole Nation to join so unanimously in expelling King *James*, for the Preservation of our Religion and Liberties, there should be a Party among us mad enough to desire the placing his Family again on the Throne." "You are not in Earnest!" answered the old Man; "there can be no such Party. As bad an Opinion as I have of Mankind, I cannot believe them infatuated to such a Degree! . . . I cannot believe it; no, no, young Man,

unacquainted as I am with what has past in the World for these last thirty Years, I cannot be so imposed upon as to credit so foolish a Tale."

(*TJ* 477–8)

Contrary to Jones' expectations, the "convincing Experience" of Stuart tyranny does not lead to national unanimity, a prospect entirely unimaginable to the secluded Man of the Hill. Isolated for decades, the old man can only judge current events by past experience. By this measure, the recent history that Jones tells sounds as "foolish" to the old man as Partridge's "Nonsense" sounds to Tom. Jones might never be guilty of Partridge's supernatural beliefs, but to the old man, Jones' conversation registers as equally ridiculous and improbable.

Yet even as the Man of the Hill rejects Jones' report of the Jacobite party as "so foolish a Tale," Partridge sits quietly in the room, living proof of the Jacobite cause that the old man finds unthinkable. The old man does not see what is literally right in front of him, because the Jacobitism in Partridge's heart is invisible. Heightening the irony of the old man's disbelief is his status as a devotee of the new science. "My design when I went abroad," the Man of the Hill recounts to Jones, "was to divert myself by seeing the wondrous Variety of Prospects, Beasts, Birds, Fishes, Insects, and Vegetables, with which God hath been pleased to enrich the several Parts of this Globe" (*TJ* 481). His cabin still remains filled with "a great Number of Nick-nacks, and Curiosities, which might have engaged the Attention of a Virtuoso" (*TJ* 445–6). Committed to empirical study, the old man is one of those pedantic virtuosi often ridiculed for their inattention to morals and manners. He now lives in isolation on the hill because his empirical study of invisible things has taught him that all men are dishonest, cruel, ungrateful and treacherous. The good-natured Jones, of course, wishes to correct this conclusion, but in doing so soon discovers the limitations of empirical authority: namely, that experience may lead to fragmented understandings and intractable differences, not to universal truth.

After hearing the Man of the Hill's history, Jones offers his contradictory opinion. "I believe, as well as hope," Jones affirms,

> "that the Abhorrence which you express for Mankind, in the Conclusion, is much too general. Indeed you here fall into an Error, which, in my little Experience, I have observed to be a very common one, by taking the Character of Mankind from the worst and basest among them; whereas indeed, as an excellent Writer observes, nothing should be esteemed as characteristical of a Species, but what is to be found among the best and most perfect Individuals of that Species. This Error, I believe, is generally committed by those who, from Want of proper Caution in the Choice of their Friends and

Acquaintance, have suffered Injuries from bad and worthless Men; two or three Instances of which are very unjustly charged on all Human Nature."

(TJ 485)

Jones admonishes the old man for not recognizing the limitations of his experience and understanding. According to Jones, the Man of the Hill does not see the general view, and therefore errs by claiming the authority of universal truth based only on his own particular misfortunes in love and friendship: "two or three Instances" of "bad and worthless Men . . . are very unjustly charged on all Human Nature." Sounding much like the later Fielding, whose all-seeing "Prudence" in *Amelia* eliminates fortune entirely, Jones insists that the old man should have placed his disappointing experiences of betrayal in a larger context: "'But you will pardon me,' cries *Jones*, 'if I desire you to reflect who that Mistress, and who that Friend were.'" The general view of the situation—which Jones derives from his own "little Experience," guided by the privileged perspective of "an excellent Writer"[28]—supports far different conclusions, Jones earnestly protests. Jones presumes that his own understanding is the bigger one. He does not doubt the old man's observations, but he does deny their status as knowledge of mankind. He accepts the old man's experience, but not its authority. "I have lived but a short Time in the World," Jones testifies, offering to enlarge the old man's understanding, "and yet have known Men worthy of the highest Friendship, and Women of the highest Love" (*TJ* 485). Like Fielding, Jones has faith in the power of moral empiricism to reach comprehensive, benevolent conclusions about mankind. Upholding universal rational authority—Fielding's "robust masculinity"—Jones leans toward sentimentalism.

The Man of the Hill's reply, however, easily turns Jones' argument back on itself, by pointing to the limitations of Jones' own view. "Alas! young Man," the old man sighs, "you have lived, you confess, but a very short Time in the World; I was somewhat older than you when I was of the same Opinion" (*TJ* 485). The old man assumes his own understanding is the bigger one. Able to remember when he thought just as Jones does, the Man of the Hill dismisses Tom's opinion as the delusion of youthful inexperience, reminding Jones that he has not yet seen enough to know what the general view is. The old man does not doubt Jones' experience, but he does deny its status as knowledge of mankind. With neither man willing to accept the authority of the other, their discussion reaches an epistemological stand-off. Through moral empiricism, they arrive not at universal truth, but at conflicting versions of universal truth.

Their disagreement completes a progression of disbelief that grows increasingly ominous in tone: Jones' dismissal of Partridge's Jacobite credulity, followed by the Man of the Hill's dismissal of the Jacobite party, concludes with Jones' and the Man of the Hill's dismissal of one another. Read against the backdrop of the Jacobite rebellion in the north, this escalating strife resonates with the dangers of moral diversity. The continuing discussion between Jones and the old man adds to the tension, for it reveals their differences to be passionately felt and rationally irreconcilable. Stung by the old man's patronizing disavowal of Jones' good-natured opinion, our hero spiritedly retorts:

> "You might have remained [of this opinion] still . . . if you had not been unfortunate, I will venture to say incautious in the placing your Affections. If there was indeed much more Wickedness in the World than there is, it would not prove such general Assertions against Human Nature, since much of this arrives by mere Accident, and many a Man who commits Evil, is not totally bad and corrupt in his Heart. In Truth, none seem to have any Title to assert Human Nature to be necessarily and universally evil, but those whose own Minds afford them one Instance of this natural Depravity; which is not, I am convinced, your Case."
>
> "And such," said the Stranger, "will be always the most backward to assert any such thing. Knaves will no more endeavour to persuade us of the Baseness of Mankind, than a Highwayman will inform you that there are Thieves on the Road. This would indeed be a Method to put you on your Guard, and to defeat their own Purposes. For which Reason tho' Knaves, as I remember, are very apt to abuse particular Persons; yet they never cast any Reflection on Human Nature in general." The old Gentleman spoke this so warmly, that as *Jones* despaired of making a Convert, and was unwilling to offend, he returned no Answer.
>
> (*TJ* 485–6)

With each man urging his own view as the general view, Tom and the Man of the Hill engage in the quixotic conflict of fools and knaves. Though explicitly denying it, Jones insinuates that the old man's opinions arise not from experience, but from "natural Depravity." Only knaves regard human nature as "universally evil," Jones argues, for they project onto everyone else the dark suspicions that pollute their own minds. In Jones' good-natured world, the existence of one such depraved mind seems far more probable than that of many, so Jones concludes that suspicious knaves must be the true (rare) examples of what they universally discover in others. Jones inserts his disclaimer—"which is not, I am convinced, your Case"—perhaps because it has occurred to him the old man could be such a knave.

In the Man of the Hill's malevolent world, however, probabilities are different. True knaves abound, but will never draw attention to themselves, for fear of "defeat[ing] their own Purposes" by alerting others to their presence. As the Man of the Hill explains, knaves "are very apt to abuse particular Persons; yet they never cast any Reflection on Human Nature in general." Significantly, he makes this argument just after Jones has defended human nature in general by accusing particular individuals of natural depravity. The old man's speech insinuates that between the two of them, Jones is more likely to be the knave. With the Man of the Hill speaking his words "warmly," Jones recognizes that their differences cannot be resolved. Both men appeal to the authority of experience, yet their experience, and perhaps more importantly, their way of interpreting that experience, differs, leaving them on the brink of a harsh exchange. Moral empiricism yields particular ideas, not universal truth. Jones can return no answer. Having shown the limits of sentimental reconciliation, Jones' encounter with the Man of the Hill brings the Jacobite subplot to a close.[29]

Sentimentalism and Sophia's body

Shortly after leaving the Man of the Hill, Jones begins to pursue Sophia to London. Whereas reconciliation between Jones and the old man appears impossible, an eventual accord between Jones and Sophia is necessary to end the romance plot. To bring this resolution about, Jones must show Sophia the sincerity of his love for her. He must convince her that his inward feelings have always been true, even though his outward forms have looked so bad. (The task before Tom might be seen as a variation on his troubles with the Man of the Hill, who also distrusted Tom's expressions of sentiment.) The problem of redeeming Tom thus poses a particularly challenging authorial difficulty for Fielding, whose goal in the novel has been to raise readers' skepticism toward all outward forms. To bring Jones and Sophia together, Fielding must restore his readers' confidence in the outward appearances necessary to moral empiricism. Sophia lays down the challenge to Jones: "After what past at *Upton*, so soon to engage in a new Amour with another Woman, while I fancied, and you pretended, your Heart was bleeding for me!—Indeed, you have acted strangely. Can I believe the Passion you have profest to me to be sincere?" (*TJ* 972). How can Jones make Sophia understand that his past actions were "Indiscretions" only, not statements of his heart? Before the plot can happily conclude, Jones must prove that he has learned how to represent himself accurately, that he now knows how to maintain "a fair Outside." And Fielding, finally and emphatically, must show his readers how to recognize true sentiment despite the distorting influences of representational forms.

The usual sentimental methods of reading the body are not available to Jones, for his body has already spoken all too eloquently—with Molly Seagrim, Jenny Waters and Lady Bellaston. Jones' body cannot be the guarantor of natural truth and constancy. On the contrary, he entreats Sophia to read his body's past actions as belonging to the untrustworthy realm of outward forms, and to rely on her own body for the empirical proofs of his sincere repentance:

> He replied, "Don't believe me upon my Word; I have a better Security, a Pledge for my Constancy, which it is impossible to see and

to doubt." "What is that?" said *Sophia*, a little surprised. "I will show
you, my charming Angel," cried *Jones*, seizing her Hand, and carrying
her to the Glass. "There, behold it there, in that lovely Figure, in that
Face, that Shape, those Eyes, that Mind which shines through those
Eyes: Can the Man who shall be in Possession of these be inconstant?
Impossible! my *Sophia*."

(*TJ* 973)

Whereas Jones is just a man, Sophia is the perfect sentimental being. Her
outward form perfectly matches her inner beauty: "it is impossible to see and
to doubt." As the sentimental ideal, her qualities are generically anti-generic,
expressed but inexpressible. The narrator indicates this by initially introducing her in mock-epic style: epic, because the genre describes her; mock,
because Fielding will not reduce her to genre.

Do thou, sweet *Zephyrus*, rising from thy fragrant Bed, mount the
western Sky, and lead on those delicious Gales, the Charms of which
call forth the lovely *Flora* from her Chamber, perfumed with pearly
Dews, when on the first of *June*, her Birth-day, the blooming Maid, in
loose Attire, gently trips it over the verdant Mead, where every flower
rises to do her Homage, till the whole Field becomes enamelled, and
Colours contend with Sweets which shall ravish her most,

the narrator sings of Sophia (*TJ* 154). His subsequent detailed description of
the beauty of her body, "the Outside of *Sophia*," followed by his assurances that
"[h]er Mind was every way equal to her Person," confirms her as the complete
sentimental being, capable of that perfect sentimental self-representation
which was lacking in Jones. Further proof of Sophia's ideal sentimentality
comes when Aunt Western catches her reading a book generally supposed to
be Sarah Fielding's *David Simple*; its author is described by Sophia as "a young
Lady of Fashion," and dismissed by Aunt Western as being "of a very good
Family, but . . . not much among People one knows" (*TJ* 286). Sophia praises
the work's "true Tenderness and Delicacy," and weeps over it copiously: "it
hath cost me many a Tear," she confesses. More importantly, she embodies its
lessons, as her own feelings appear plainly on her body. "You blush, my dear
Sophia," Aunt Western exclaims: "Ah! Child, you should read Books, which
would teach you a little Hypocrisy, which would instruct you how to hide
your Thoughts a little better" (*TJ* 287). Aunt Western's words describe
exactly the kind of book that *David Simple* is not, and precisely those lessons
which Sophia will never learn. With body and mind in perfect correspondence, Sophia becomes Jones' mirror of truth. Thus he may argue that the
"Possession" of her "Figure," her "Face," her "Shape" and her "Eyes"—through
which her mind shines directly—will correct his deficiencies, guaranteeing
his good conduct for the future. "You could not doubt it, if you could see with

any Eyes but your own," Jones urges, claiming to have a general view unavailable to Sophia (*TJ* 973).

Still, Sophia persists in holding Jones accountable for his history: "'If I am to judge,' said she, 'of the future by the past, my Image will no more remain in your Heart, when I am out of your Sight, than it will in this Glass when I am out of the Room'" (*TJ* 973). Like a good reader of Fielding, she is determined to judge the future by the past, to avoid misfortune by correctly reading history. Jones counters, however, that she misinterprets—she cannot help it—because her gender prevents her from attaining the general view. Men and women are different, and their differences limit her understanding (though apparently not his): "By Heaven, by all that is sacred," Jones fervently replies, "it never was out of my Heart. The Delicacy of your Sex cannot conceive the Grossness of ours, nor how little one Sort of Amour has to do with the Heart" (*TJ* 973). Due to her "Delicacy," Sophia misreads Jones. To know Jones' true sentiments, she must understand that the hermeneutics of the body is relative to gender; men and women perceive, and therefore must be perceived, differently. Yet to a perfect sentimental being, moral behavior never is relative. Sophia insists that Jones abide by her standards: "'I will never marry a Man,' replied *Sophia*, very gravely, 'who shall not learn Refinement enough to be as incapable as I am myself of making such a Distinction'" (*TJ* 973).

For his own part, Jones vows that he has already learned the "Refinement" necessary to banish all inconstancy from his thoughts: "I have already learnt it. The first Moment of Hope that my *Sophia* might be my Wife taught it me at once; and all the rest of her Sex from that Moment became as little the Objects of Desire to my Sense, as of Passion to my Heart" (*TJ* 973). He assures Sophia that he has the general view, for he now comprehends both his own former "Grossness" as well as her "Delicacy." Rhapsodizing about the uniqueness of Sophia's body, Jones perversely argues that *her* inimitable outward form faithfully conveys the recent alteration in *his* "Mind," because her riveting qualities so outshine those of all other women. She is so superior that he can now desire no one else. Jones achieves discretion and happiness through the power of Sophia's sentimental body. The narrator confirms this point by concluding the history not with a marriage, but with a consummation. Lingering with his readers through the wedding night, the narrator reports:

> the Squire sat in to his cups, in which he was, by Degrees, deserted by all the Company, except the Uncle of young *Nightingale*, who loved his Bottle as well as *Western* himself. These two therefore sat stoutly to it, during the whole Evening, and long after that happy Hour which had surrendered the charming *Sophia* to the eager Arms of her enraptured *Jones*.
>
> Thus, Reader, we have at length brought our History to a Conclusion, in which, to our great Pleasure, tho' contrary perhaps to thy Expectation, Mr. *Jones* appears to be the happiest of all human

Kind: For what Happiness this World affords equal to the Possession of such a Woman as *Sophia*, I sincerely own I have never yet discovered.

(*TJ* 979)

Only after Sophia has "surrendered . . . to the eager Arms of her enraptured *Jones*" does the narrator feel it appropriate to announce the conclusion of the history. It appears that the narrator, in order to vindicate Jones' promise that "Possession" of Sophia's "Figure," "Face," "Shape," "Eyes" and "Mind" will guarantee constancy, has deliberately tarried until the moment of this "Possession." Now the narrator may confirm that Jones' assurances to Sophia were indeed sincere. Our hero did represent himself truly; he will remain constant, "For what Happiness this World affords equal to the Possession of such a Woman as *Sophia*, I sincerely own I have never yet discovered." With Jones and the narrator (two men of experience) each attesting to Sophia's extraordinary ability to make men happily constant (and they should know), her idealized body assures the truth of Jones' penitential self-representations. He will never stray because there is nothing better to stray to.

The perfect plot of *Tom Jones*, then, winds up neatly due to the anomaly of Sophia's sentimental body. Tom Jones may represent Every Man, but Sophia does not represent Every Woman. It is the superlative status of her body as beauty and truth that keeps Tom from continuing his profligate ways with (just about) Every Other Woman. But in a novel of cause and effect, of actions and consequences, of "great Wheels . . . set in Motion by those which are very minute," how is such a creature as Sophia formed? Raised and educated by Squire Western and Aunt Western, Sophia's existence is difficult to explain as the product of education and example. She is a miracle of nature, or a perfectly fantastic production of Fielding's art. An intervention such as hers in Jones' history, therefore, can hardly be expected to occur in Every Other Man's life, a probability that undermines the didactic function of Fielding's novel. What is the value of an example that cannot be reproduced? In the end, despite all his protests to the contrary, Fielding remains dedicated to a quixotic model of reading, for he encourages people to aspire to the condition of literary forms that can be imitated only imperfectly. He wants life to strive toward a literary ideal, for promoting this "ART OF LIFE" is the writer's service to mankind.

DE GUSTIBUS NON EST DISPUTANDUM

Tristram Shandy and "the production of a rational Being"

It is the variety of tastes obvious in mankind, that renders it necessary to enquire concerning the standard of taste. But the variety is so great as to render it difficult to fix a standard; and even doubtful, in the opinion of some, whether any standard can be fixed. Either we must allow that all these different and opposite tastes are equally good, or we must acknowledge that some of them deserve the preference, and that there are means of determining, which these are. The former supposition seems to have been so generally admitted, as to have passed into a proverb, That tastes are not to be disputed: yet it is too wild to be seriously admitted by any, in its full latitude. It would imply that every man is to himself an infallible judge of beauty and deformity, of excellence and defect; it would imply that the same objects, and the same qualities of objects, may merit at once approbation and disgust; it would imply that our natural principles of taste, unlike to all the rest both of our mental faculties, and our bodily powers, are incapable of being either improved or perverted; it would infer that it is absurd to censure any relish, however singularly gross; it would put all critical discussions precisely on a level with Don Quixote's dissertations on giants and enchantments.

Alexander Gerard, *An Essay on Taste* (1759)[1]

"Nothing odd will do long. *Tristram Shandy* did not last," Samuel Johnson declared in 1776.[2] Of course, this famous statement has been proven substantially wrong in that *Tristram Shandy* still persists and shows few signs of imminent obscurity. Yet Johnson's apparent error may come from his assumptions, for *Tristram Shandy* is not really so odd. Though Tristram frequently claims that he and his family are singular, whimsical and out of "the ordinary way" (*TS* 53), the fragmented perspectives and limited understandings that

173

collide to form his absurd world typify sentimental quixotism. Read within this tradition, *Tristram Shandy*'s oddity appears generic: the book contemplates the usual themes of moral empiricism, the gendered nature of intellect, religious difference, conflicting rational systems and enthusiasms of all kinds. What is different about *Tristram Shandy* is its madcap embrace of quixotic diversity, both in content and in form. Whereas Fielding recognizes quixotism as a problem to be corrected, and recommends a comprehensive, scientific, orderly, Newtonian general view of human behavior, Sterne celebrates quixotic idiosyncrasy as an unavoidable feature of humanity. As Stuart Tave has shown, other writers of the period were fond of the quixotic.[3] Few of them, however, match Sterne's appreciation of quixotism as a sign of inevitable particularity and diversity. Sterne's quixotic sentimentalism does not attempt to justify a general view.[4] It does not transform Don Quixote, as Hazlitt does, into a character of "the most perfect disinterestedness,"[5] nor does it romantically reimagine quixotism as manful, transcendent heroism. Instead, *Tristram Shandy* revels in the feminized, limited and arbitrary sallies of the early eighteenth-century quixote, tweaking all efforts—be they rational or sentimental—to establish fixed standards and general principles. Sterne's novel is "odd" because it delights in the prospect of a world full of "rational" men who think like female quixotes.

Certain standards of taste: Hume and Gerard

Sterne began work on *Tristram Shandy* in 1759, the same year that saw the publication of Alexander Gerard's prize-winning *Essay on Taste*. Though there is no evidence that Sterne's novel responds to Gerard specifically, *Tristram Shandy*'s delight in quixotic particularity certainly satirizes those who would agree with Gerard. Awarded the Select Society of Edinburgh's gold medal for "the best essay on Taste,"[6] Gerard's treatise asserts the existence of a universal standard of taste, a stance he takes in opposition to a more famous member of the Select Society, David Hume. Hume's "Of the Standard of Taste" had appeared a couple of years earlier,[7] ostensibly arguing in favor of "a Standard of Taste; a rule by which the various sentiments of men may be reconciled."[8] This "Standard," however, becomes increasingly elusive as Hume's essay progresses. Though admitting that sentiments vary so greatly that the "proverb has justly determined it to be fruitless to dispute concerning tastes," Hume nonetheless begins his essay by declaring the existence of a true standard. Noting the widespread and timeless reputation of Homer, Hume concludes that behind the diversity of taste so apparent in the world, there must be natural, general principles:

> It appears then, that, amidst all the variety and caprice of taste, there are certain general principles of approbation or blame, whose influence a careful eye may trace in all operations of the mind. Some particular forms or qualities, from the original structure of the

internal fabric, are calculated to please, and others to displease; and if they fail of their effect in any particular instance, it is from some apparent defect or imperfection in the organ. . . . In each creature, there is a sound and a defective state; and the former alone can be supposed to afford us a true standard of taste and sentiment.

(Hume, *Essays* 233–4)

The "general principles" that constitute "a true standard of taste and sentiment" are to be found in the "uniformity of sentiment" shared by men "in the sound state of the organ," Hume asserts. Yet he undercuts these pronouncements upon the "common sense" of taste immediately and deliberately by the illustrative example he proposes. "And not to draw our philosophy from too profound a source," Hume instructs, "we shall have recourse to a noted story in Don Quixote" (Hume, *Essays* 234).

Astonishingly, Sancho Panza's wine-tasting abilities serve as Hume's model of the true standard of taste (*DQ* II, xiii). As Hume recounts the adventure, Sancho explains that his good taste in wine is "hereditary," as revealed by an incident that befell two of his kinsmen. These two were asked to judge of a wine "supposed to be excellent, being old and of good vintage." The first kinsman pronounced "the wine to be good, were it not for a small taste of leather, which he perceived in it." The other likewise praises the wine, only regretting "a taste of iron, which he could easily distinguish." "You cannot imagine how much they were both ridiculed for their judgment," Hume recalls of Sancho's anecdote: "But who laughed in the end? On emptying the hogshead, there was found at the bottom, an old key with a leathern thong tied to it" (Hume, *Essays* 234–5). Pointing to the "great resemblance between mental and bodily taste," Hume then argues by analogy that the organs of mental taste, like those of bodily taste, may be more refined in some people than in others, resulting in the appearance of diverse and irreconcilable mental tastes. In reality, however, not all of these tastes are equally correct. As Hume's example shows, Sancho's kinsmen at first suffer unimaginable ridicule for their aberrant taste, but eventually get the last laugh when they are vindicated by the discovery of the old key and leather thong. In the end, their taste proves to be correct and indisputable.

The sustained ridicule suffered by Sancho's kinsmen and its sudden reversal are apparently an embellishment added to Sancho's story by Hume, for they receive no mention in *Don Quixote*. The addition of this period of ridicule serves Hume's purpose by allowing him to emphasize that the "general principles" of true taste might differ sharply from the commonly held principles of taste, at any given time. Hume's general rules should not be confused with majority rule, for they need not be obvious or even widely agreed upon. Rather than blazing forth like nature's truth, the general rules may hide like nature's secrets. "To produce these general rules or avowed patterns of composition," Hume explains, is like finding the key with the leathern thong; which justified the verdict of Sancho's kinsmen, and confounded those pretended judges who had condemned them. Though the hogshead had never been emptied, the taste of the one was still equally delicate, and that of the other equally dull and languid: But it would have been more difficult to have proved the superiority of the former, to the conviction of every by-stander. In like manner, though the beauties of writing had never been methodized, or reduced to general principles; though no excellent models had ever been acknowledged; the different degrees of taste would still have subsisted, and the judgment of one man been preferable to that of another; but it would not have been so easy to silence the bad critic, who might always insist upon his particular sentiment, and refuse to submit to his antagonist.

(Hume, *Essays* 235–6)

The period of ridicule suffered by Sancho's kinsmen corresponds to the apparent diversity of taste described by the proverb. It depicts a period in which taste cannot be disputed, or worse, one in which poor taste can parade over delicate taste. The true standard of taste never alters, Hume contends; it is just harder to detect in some instances. Draining the hogshead and finding the key at its bottom may not change anyone's taste, but it does offer empirical support for the superiority of some tastes over others. Hume's "general principles" seek their justification in natural sensibility and empirical demonstration.

Hume's essay thus does an odd thing. It asserts the certainty and stability of a natural standard of taste, while simultaneously suggesting that this standard could look like quixotism. It "leaves us with a very peculiar sort of norm," Barbara Herrnstein Smith observes, though she does not consider that Hume may have been aware of the peculiarity of his norm, that is to say, conscious of his quixotism.[9] Surely Hume knew that his decision to showcase Sancho Panza as the example of true and natural taste would invite at least some skepticism toward his principles, no matter how axiomatically he laid down the rest of the argument. (In fact, paradoxically, the more axiomatic one believes Hume to be in this essay, the more one must suspect him of sly skepticism instead, for why would anyone choose the indiscriminately proverb-quoting Sancho Panza to illustrate axiomatic truth?) If qualities beyond wine-tasting are also hereditary in the Panza family, then perhaps Sancho resembles his kinsmen in his quixotism as well, an interpretation Hume encourages by inventing the detail about the Panzas' suffering through universal ridicule. What distinguishes true and natural standards of taste from quixotic delusions?

Though Hume affirms the "general principles" of taste, he offers little means by which to identify them. Individual opinion cannot be trusted, for Hume's true standard of taste requires that all personal considerations be laid aside: "I must . . . considering myself as a man in general, forget, if possible, my individual being and my peculiar circumstances," Hume maintains (Hume, *Essays* 239). Yet generally held standards—such as the widespread opinion that universally ridiculed Sancho's kinsmen—may be no more reliable. In Hume's example, after all, the peculiar view ridiculed as quixotic (the Panza family belief that the wine tasted of impurities) turned out to be the true standard of taste, while the socially sanctioned, generally held view turned out to be wrong.

Hume's standard of taste, therefore, is a very peculiar sort of norm, for it appears to be a self-consciously impotent norm, a norm with no power to normalize anything. Initially ringing with confident authority, Hume's essay soon retreats from articulating the true standard of taste, to claim instead that it is "sufficient for our present purposes" merely "to acknowledge a true and decisive standard to exist somewhere, to wit, real existence and matter of fact" (*Essays* 242). But upon asserting the "real existence" of a true standard, Hume uses this "matter of fact" not to prescribe taste, but to encourage tolerance toward diverse standards. In light of a true but unknown standard, Hume reasons, men who wish to dispute taste "must produce the best arguments, that their invention suggests to them," but they must also "have indulgence to such as differ from them in their appeals to this standard" (*Essays* 242). Hume's claims about taste are supple and elusive. We must agree that a standard exists, but we need not agree on what it is. We must admit general principles, but not their particular forms. A real standard exists somewhere, but disputes about taste, which always concern particulars, will be endless.

Hume stresses this endless disputation by concluding his essay with a discussion of the "two sources of variation" that often confound attempts "to fix a standard of taste." These two confounding variations are the manifestations of particularity: "The one is the different humours of particular men; the other, the particular manners and opinions of our age and country." Owing to the power of individual difference ("humours") and cultural variation ("manners and opinions of our age and country"), it may not be possible, Hume concedes, for everyone to reconstitute himself (or herself?) as "a man in general." Therefore the true standard may remain forever hidden:

> where there is such a diversity in the internal frame or external situation as is entirely blameless on both sides, and leaves not room to give one the preference above the other; in that case a certain degree of diversity in judgment is unavoidable, and we seek in vain for a standard, by which we can reconcile the contrary sentiments.
>
> (*Essays* 243–4)

Tastes may be disputed, but such disputes may never be resolved. Hume urges, in theory, a natural philosophy of universal taste governed by general rules, but he recognizes, in practice, a political philosophy of individual tastes governed by personal and social particularities.

It is this latter, subjective understanding of taste to which Alexander Gerard opposes himself in the above epigraph. Eager to prevent all "critical discussions" from falling to the level of "Don Quixote's dissertations on giants and enchantments," Gerard denies the proverbial wisdom that declares "different and opposite tastes" to be "equally good." Instead, he endeavors to show that "principles of science form the most accurate standard of excellence in the fine arts" (Gerard 273), rejecting Hume's quixotic "diversity in judgment" as too tentative.

> One eye is more piercing, one ear more quick, one palate, one smell, one touch, more delicate than another; and there are, in most cases, infallible means of determining, to which the superiority belongs: and why should we hesitate to own, that one taste is superior to another?

demands Gerard, converting perceptual differences into an argument for infallible perceptual hierarchy (Gerard 213). "A standard of taste is not something by which all tastes may be reconciled and brought to coincide," he asserts: "it is only something by which it may be determined, which is the best among tastes various, contending, and incapable of coinciding perfectly" (Gerard 216). Unwilling to accept diversity of sentiment as an argument against universal standards, Gerard maintains that tastes can and must be disputed and settled. "[P]hilosophical enquiries" into taste "are not the amusements of the idle, or the entertainments of the speculative," Gerard pronounces: "They rest not in gratifying curiosity, by unvailing the inward springs of our sensations. They are of real and extensive utility. . . . The principle established by means of them, admit as indubitable certainty, and as great precision, as those of any science" (Gerard 274). Though tastes may never be reconciled, they can at least—following scientific principles—be declared superior or inferior, right or wrong.

Against such attempts as Gerard's to establish a scientific standard of taste—to elevate critical discussion above the level of Don Quixote—*Tristram Shandy* shines as a constant and exuberant reminder that rational standards are quixotism. "*De gustibus non est disputandum*;—that is, there is no disputing against Hobby-Horses," declares Tristram happily at the outset of his story, establishing as a recurrent theme the very proverb that Hume questions and Gerard denies (*TS* 12). The "infallible," scientific, rational method that Gerard proposes as the proper mediator of dispute becomes, in Sterne's hands, the wacky and arbitrary career of Tristram's erratic history. John Traugott contends that the "undermining skeptical arguments of Hume (which recommend his doctrine of sympathy) find almost a descriptive statement in *Tristram*."[10] I would add, however, that Sterne's satire on science includes, rather than recommends, Humean sympathy. Eighteenth-century sentimentalism had scientific aspirations, as I have argued, and these feed *Tristram Shandy*'s learned wit.[11] Science and sentimentalism each present systems of fixed standards and general rules that cannot defend themselves against Tristram's stubborn particularity.

Disputing against hobby-horses: Shandean rationality

Rational systems do not fare well in *Tristram Shandy*. "I wish either my father or my mother, or indeed both of them, as they were in duty both equally bound to it, had minded what they were about when they begot me," Tristram laments, a victim of systematic failure:

> had they duly consider'd how much depended upon what they were then doing;—that not only the production of a rational Being was concern'd in it, but that possibly the happy formation and temperature of his body, perhaps his genius and the very cast of his mind;—and, for aught they knew to the contrary, even the fortunes of his whole house might take their turn from the humours and dispositions which were then uppermost:—Had they duly weighed and considered all this, and proceeded accordingly,—I am verily persuaded I should have made a quite different figure in the world, from that, in which the reader is likely to see me.
>
> (*TS* 5)

In his opening words, Tristram introduces his narrative as an effort to explain the causal relations leading up to "the production of a rational Being," namely, himself. If only his parents had "minded what they were about," "duly weighed and considered" the consequences of their actions upon their offspring's "body," "genius," "cast of his mind" and "fortunes," then Tristram would have cut "a quite different figure in the world"—or so he believes. If only Walter and Elizabeth Shandy had proceeded more rationally, with greater sagacity and penetration (especially Walter); if only they could have foreseen all the turnings and twistings of those trains of events that Fielding teaches his readers to see; then might Tristram now appear in his full masculine glory, complete with nose, name and other parts intact, in active control of his own course through life, and not "the continual sport of what the world calls Fortune," forever pelted "with a set of as pitiful misadventures and cross accidents as ever small HERO sustained" (*TS* 10). Yet even as Tristram wishes that his parents had behaved more like prudent Fieldingesque protagonists, Sterne undercuts the idea of rational masculine control. In Sterne's fiction, efforts such as Fielding's and Gerard's to reduce humankind to a science are portrayed as sallies into the empirical study of invisible things. Their outcomes are anything but infallible. In *Tristram Shandy*, what appears irrational is rational explanation itself. Significantly, all the Shandy men share a zeal for rational explanation.

The person in Shandy Hall most desirous of promoting and maintaining rational masculine control is that incorrigibly systematic thinker, Walter Shandy. He was "systematical, and, like all systematick reasoners, he would move both heaven and earth, and twist and torture every thing in nature to support his hypothesis," Tristram writes of his father (*TS* 45), comparing him to "the Hero of *Cervantes*" (*TS* 43). Like a perceptive reader trained by Fielding, Walter quixotically attempts to explain the workings of the world as a "regular succession of ideas . . . which follow each other in train" (*TS* 151). Foreseeing great consequences in small details (such as names and noses), Walter is determined to act prudently. Sterne satirizes such efforts at rational masculine control by depicting them as rational, masculine, but futile—a combination of qualities that has led readers to disagree sharply over whether *Tristram Shandy* should be seen as piggishly chauvinistic or presciently feminist.[12] The matter may be better understood by recognizing that *Tristram Shandy* is quixotic: it idealizes masculine reason, but presents it as unattainable. A romantic reading of quixotism, therefore, would make the book appear sexist, for it would idealize the pursuit of masculine reason as noble and heroic. An unromantic, early eighteenth-century reading of quixotism, however, might make the book appear feminist, for it would ridicule masculine reason as crack-brainedness. As it would seem more plausible, from a historical perspective, to place Sterne within a tradition that preceded him, rather than within one which post-dated him, I will read *Tristram Shandy* against the unromantic quixotic tradition.

Walter's reason is impotent in Tristram Shandy's world, a failure made conspicuous by his disgusted attempts to distinguish his active intellect from the inscrutable docility of his wife, Elizabeth Shandy. "Cursed luck!" Walter would cry,

> "—for a man to be master of one of the finest chains of reasoning in nature,—and have a wife at the same time with such a head-piece, that he cannot hang up a single inference within side of it, to save his soul from destruction."
>
> (*TS* 117)

Walter had not always regarded his wife as so unthinking. Prior to his marriage, Walter had been convinced by brother Toby that his bride-to-be might have the active intelligence of a Mandevillean knave. Though willing to allow her to lie-in at London, Walter worried that she might dishonestly impose upon his good nature in order to visit town more frequently. To prevent such deceptions, Walter had included in their marriage articles a clause forbidding her from using pregnancy as a pretext for visiting London; should she put Mr Shandy through the trouble of a trip to town with "false cries and tokens," then she should forfeit her right to lie-in at London during the next pregnancy (*TS* 35). "This, by the way, was no more than what was reasonable," Tristram explains, "and yet, as reasonable as it was, I have ever thought it hard that the whole weight of the article should have fallen entirely, as it did, upon myself" (*TS* 35–6). Trying to foresee and pre-empt the consequences of self-interested behavior on the part of Elizabeth, Walter Shandy unleashes a series of more troubling consequences. His efforts to ward these off as well, in defense of ratiocination and his son's masculinity, form his principal project throughout the novel.

Mrs Shandy, of course, did experience a false alarm, causing an agitated Walter to invoke the terms of the contract. Tristram must be born in the country. Still, Walter foresees some difficulties in this design, for he adheres to Fielding's advice well enough to want to preserve a fair outside. Like Fielding's historian, who can see how "the great Wheels are originally set in Motion by those which are very minute," Walter too has "extensive views of things." "He knew the world judged by events," and that should anything happen to Mrs Shandy or the child, he would be vilified for not allowing his wife to seek better care in London (*TS* 39). As the pregnancy advances, the sagacious Walter can already hear voices back-forming a history out of potential events not yet come to pass:

> "Alas o'day!—had Mrs. Shandy, poor gentlewoman! had but her wish in going up to town just to lye-in and come down again;—which, they say, she begg'd and pray'd for upon her bare knees,—and which, in my opinion, considering the fortune which Mr. Shandy got with her,—was not such mighty matter to have complied with, the lady and her babe might both of 'em have been alive at this hour."
>
> This exclamation, my father knew was unanswerable.
>
> (*TS* 39)

Reasoning extensively, Walter concludes that the resulting gender politics of such an unanswerable charge would be unacceptable and deeply injurious to "the publick good," for it would "infallibly throw a balance of power, too great already, into the weaker vessels" by generating sympathy for his wife and blame for himself (*TS* 39–41). A follower of Sir Robert Filmer, Walter fears that such an undermining of "paternal power" will "prove fatal to the monarchical system of domestick government established in the first creation of things by God" (*TS* 41). His logic roots itself in nature and necessity, identifying itself "infallibly" with science, origins and absolutes, "the first creation of things by God." Forewarned by these extensive views, he urgently desires that "a scientifick operator," a "man-midwife," be chosen to assist with Mrs Shandy's lying-in, so as to minimize the possibility of complications at birth and the subsequent destruction of paternal power. He pleads with his wife to "suffer him to choose for her," as the concern is now no longer a private affair, but a matter of "the publick good." But unlike an amiable Fielding wife, who defers to her husband's political opinions, Mrs Shandy insists "upon her privilege in this matter, to choose for herself," and resolves to hire a woman instead. Thus begins the first of many incidents that leave Walter "baffled and overthrown in all his little systems and wishes," helplessly watching "a train of events perpetually falling out against him, and in so critical and cruel a way, as if they had purposedly been plann'd and pointed against him, merely to insult his speculations" (*TS* 47). Walter has learned Fielding's lessons on discernment and penetration very well; he too associates his "extensive" understanding with manly rationality and its obligation to make decisions for women. But in the disjointed plot of *Tristram Shandy*, so different from the architectonic "perfect plot" of *Tom Jones*, Walter's general view does not improve his success in the world. It only brings him cruel bafflement, allowing him to see far enough into the future to discern his own powerlessness and ineffectuality.

Perhaps nothing mocks Walter's Fieldingesque cultivation of the "ART OF LIFE" more than the ever-belated Tristra-paedia. Meant to be a "system of education" for Tristram, the Tristra-paedia is Walter's "last stake" in perpetuating a masculine presence in the world. "[H]e had already lost my brother Bobby entirely," Tristram explains, "he had lost, by his own computation, full three fourths of me—that is, he had been unfortunate in his three first great casts for me—my geniture, nose, and name,—and there was but this one left; accordingly my father gave himself up to it" (*TS* 298). In writing the Tristra-paedia, Walter hopes to write Tristram out of his passive, feminized position by inculcating rational masculine understanding:

> Prejudice of education, he would say, *is the devil*,—and the multitudes of them which we suck in with our mother's milk—*are the devil and all*.—We are haunted with them, brother *Toby*, in all our lucubrations and researches; and was a man fool enough to submit tamely to what they obtruded upon him,—what would his book be? Nothing,—he would add, throwing his pen away with a vengeance,—nothing but a farrago of the clack of nurses, and of the nonsense of old women (of both sexes) throughout the kingdom.
>
> (*TS* 300)

Like John Locke and others,[13] Walter regards with consternation the passivity of human understanding, the ease with which absurd and ridiculous doctrines—"that have been derived from no better original, than the Superstition of a Nurse, or the Authority of an old Woman," as Locke had disapprovingly noted (*Essay* 81)—flow effortlessly from mother to helpless (male) child. As Walter distastefully acknowledges, "we suck [them] in with our mother's milk." For Walter, "Prejudice of education" is a feminine legacy, the bane of masculine reason. The spurious authority of "nurses" and "old women" stands as the exemplar of irrationality, the enemy of "lucubrations," "researches" and manly efforts to write books. What would a man's book be if not distinguished from absurd, feminized ideas? "Nothing." To "submit tamely" to these distaff obtrusions, Walter proclaims, would be to abandon manly reason for womanish "nonsense." It would be to admit that men do not control representations, but that they are controlled by them. Like Fielding, Walter believes himself to be defending men against the incursions of quixotic, feminine irrationality—hence his recognition that there are "old women (of both sexes) throughout the kingdom."

Yet if men control representations, while women and quixotes are controlled by representations, there can be little doubt as which group Walter, or any of the Shandean men, belongs to. The failure of language and communication in *Tristram Shandy* has long been recognized: no one in Shandy Hall controls representations well.[14] Walter's Tristra-paedia fails to achieve its goal, for he cannot write it faster than Tristram lives: "he was three years and something more, indefatigably at work," Tristram recalls, "and at last, had scarce completed, by his own reckoning, one half of his undertaking: the misfortune was, that I was all that time totally neglected and abandoned to my mother" (*TS* 300), where presumably Tristram imbibes all those prejudices of education Walter had hoped to shield him from. Walter's quixotic obsession with the devilish difficulty of producing a rational being seems to turn him into one of those nonsensical "old women" of the male sex.

Toby fares no better. His masculinity is likewise suspect, not only because his modesty "arose to such a height in him, as almost to equal, if such a thing could be, even the modesty of a woman" (*TS* 54), but because of the mystery surrounding the wound to his groin. The wound hints at a physical emasculation (the truth of which the novel never reveals) while effecting an intellectual emasculation. Like Walter, Toby's hobby-horse is born of a frustrated effort to explain historical causes and consequences. "The history of a soldier's wounds beguiles the pain of it," Toby's friends believe, so as he convalesces, they frequently ask him to describe the events leading up to his injury (*TS* 65). He soon discovers that he is unable to represent his circumstances accurately:

> the many perplexities that he was in, arose out of the almost insurmountable difficulties he found in telling his story intelligibly, and giving such clear ideas of the differences and distinctions between the scarp and counterscarp,—the glacis and covered way,—the half-moon and ravelin,—as to make his company fully comprehend where and what he was about.
>
> Writers themselves are too apt to confound these terms;—so that you will the less wonder, if in his endeavours to explain them, and in opposition to many misconceptions, that my uncle *Toby* did oft times puzzle his visiters; and sometimes himself too.
>
> (*TS* 67)

Amidst these unintelligibilities, incomprehensions and puzzlements—as he languishes with his wound—it occurs to Toby that a map of the battlegrounds "might be a means of giving him ease," for he could then better explain himself by pointing to "the identical spot of ground where he was standing in when the stone struck him" (*TS* 68–9). Suddenly Toby's intellectual emasculation begins to abate; this superior means of representation rapidly frees him "from a world of sad explanations," simultaneously healing the injury to his groin. In the end, Toby's abandonment of words in favor of things—his retreat from verbal explanations, to the clear lines of maps, and eventually to reconstructed military fortifications and re-enacted military sieges—becomes his "HOBBY-HORSE" (*TS* 69). Toby's peculiarity grows out of his attempts to explain things rationally. His military science turns into a quixotic obsession that causes him to collect as many "books of military architecture, as Don *Quixote* was found to have of chivalry, when the curate and barber invaded his library" (*TS* 73).

The differences between Walter and Toby are, therefore, more apparent than real, like the differences between reason and sentimentalism. Walter is distinguished by his rational systems and famed facility with language: "Persuasion hung upon his lips, and the elements of Logick and Rhetorick were so blended up in him . . . that NATURE might have stood up and said,— 'This man is eloquent'" (*TS* 44). Toby, meanwhile, is beloved for his sentimental reticence: "he was so unhappy as to have very little choice" in his words, and "could not philosophize . . . 'twas enough he felt it was so" (*TS* 54, 68). Still, Toby's sentimental body speaks volumes:

> There was a frankness in my uncle Toby,—not the *effect* of famil-
> iarity,—but the *cause* of it,—which let you at once into his soul, and
> shewed you the goodness of his nature; to this, there was something
> in his looks, and voice, and manner, superadded, which eternally
> beckoned to the unfortunate to come and take shelter under him.
>
> (*TS* 342)

One brother represents reason, while the other represents sentiment. Both, however, are sentimental, for Sterne acknowledges that rationality and sentimentality are not opposites. As Traugott points out, "Tristram says twice that not Toby but Walter is preeminently the man of sensibility [2, 12, 114; 9, 1, 599]."[15] And Tristram further confirms his father's credentials as a sentimental quixote by revealing Walter's dedication to the empirical study of invisible things. "THO' my father was a good natural philosopher,—yet he was something of a moral philosopher too," Tristram writes (*TS* 82). Subjectivity is impenetrable in Sterne's fiction, as Iser has observed,[16] but Walter purports to penetrate it nonetheless. "There are a thousand unnoticed openings, which let a penetrating eye at once into a man's soul," Walter announces, sounding much like Henry Fielding (*TS* 333). As a result, Walter goes through life "a

184

great MOTIVE-MONGER, and consequently a very dangerous person for a man to sit by, either laughing or crying,—for he generally knew your motive for doing both, much better than you knew it yourself" (*TS* 367). Like a sentimental critic, Walter imposes meanings on the opaque bodies before him.

I argue, therefore, against Traugott's suggestion that the "core of Sterne's sentimentalism lies in his insistence that by certain public signs—conduct, reaction, and attitude—we can come to understand individuality,"[17] for to regard this sentimentalism as Sterne's is to confuse the author's views with Walter's. Tristram acknowledges the flaws in his father's thinking, deliberately contrasting the secret nature of human motives with the illuminating fiction of "*Momus*'s glass, in the breast":

> had the said glass been there set up, nothing more would have been wanting, in order to have taken a man's character, but to have taken a chair and gone softly, as you would to a dioptrical bee-hive, and look'd in,—view'd the soul stark naked—observ'd all her motions,— her machinations;—traced all her maggots from their first engendering to their crawling forth;—watched her loose in her frisks, her gambols, her capricios; and after some notice of her more solemn deportment, consequent upon such frisks, *&c.*—then taken your pen and ink and set down nothing but what you had seen, and could have sworn to:—But this is an advantage not to be had by the biographer in this planet . . . our minds shine not through the body, but are wrapt up here in a dark covering of uncrystalized flesh and blood; so that if we would come to the specifick characters of them, we must go some other way to work.
>
> (*TS* 59–60)

Here Tristram imagines, but rejects, the sentimental dream of representational simplicity, the fantasy of a window through which to espy the otherwise invisible secrets of the breast: "nothing more would have been wanting, in order to have taken a man's character, but to have . . . look'd in . . . then taken your pen and ink and set down nothing but what you had seen." Unmediated by the misleading meanings of particular forms, the essential soul would be "stark naked," like the beauty of virtue Fielding had initially extolled in the dedication of *Tom Jones*. Like Fielding, however, Tristram abandons the idea of a directly visible soul, for "our minds shine not through the body." The empirical study of invisible things requires more subtle methods; to assess character, "we must go some other way to work." Tristram then proposes a series of alternatives, eventually dismissing them each in favor of drawing a man's character "from his HOBBY-HORSE" (*TS* 61).

As a solution to the problem of opaque souls, Tristram offers a paradox. The hobby-horse, Iser observes, has a "dual significance": "its substitutional aspect signalises the inaccessibility, and its schematic aspect the conceivability of

185

subjectivity."[18] Unable to penetrate the dark coverings of uncrystallized flesh that hide the soul, Tristram instead offers a predictable reduction of human motivation akin to the ruling passion:

> A man and his HOBBY-HORSE, tho' I cannot say they act and re-act exactly after the same manner in which the soul and body do upon each other: Yet doubtless there is a communication between them of some kind, and my opinion rather is, that there is something in it more of the manner of electrified bodies,—and that by means of the heated parts of the rider, which come immediately into contact with the back of the HOBBY-HORSE.—By long journies and much friction, it so happens that the body of the rider is at length fill'd as full of HOBBY-HORSICAL matter as it can hold;—so that if you are able to give but a clear description of the nature of the one, you may form a pretty exact notion of the genius and character of the other.
>
> (*TS* 61)

Tristram knows that the soul's relation to the body cannot be exactly specified, that the body cannot be read directly as signs of the soul within. Yet he has enough of Walter in him not to give up on the project entirely, proposing scientific-sounding speculations about "electrified bodies" in order to establish the hobby-horse as an accurate indicator of "genius and character." For Tristram, the hobby-horse makes others comprehensible by turning their particularities into predictable generalities: "*De gustibus non est disputandum*;—that is, there is no disputing against HOBBY-HORSES," suggests not only that individuals are so particular that it is pointless to try to argue against their hobby-horsical eccentricity, but also that the presence of the hobby-horse itself is so universal that it is pointless to dispute its effects: "Sir, have not the wisest of men in all ages, not excepting *Solomon* himself,—have they not had their HOBBY-HORSES" (*TS* 12)? Representing singularity in a universal form, the hobby-horse is the product of Tristram's own quixotic obsession with rational explanation. The concept of the hobby-horse reveals Tristram's own hobby-horse, his unrelenting desire to explain every aspect of himself and his family in rational, general terms, yet to do so in a way that affirms their particularity. To remain firmly seated upon his pad, Tristram exploits the paradox of rational empirical authority: his own experience may be unique, but for that very reason it cannot be refuted. By emphasizing his singularity, Tristram denies the world its authority to judge generically by events.

Tristram is proudly and compulsively preoccupied with the sovereignty of his own particularity throughout the entire narrative. Shortly after the story begins, he reports his father's sad foreboding, "That I should neither think nor act like any other man's child" (*TS* 7). Tristram then spends the rest of the narrative valiantly attempting to validate this prediction, urging his own peculiarity at every opportunity: "I should beg Mr. *Horace*'s pardon;—for in writing what I have set about, I shall confine myself neither to his rules, nor to any man's rules that ever lived" (*TS* 8). Unwilling to write an account that looks like any other man's, Tristram compulsively thwarts expectations, leading to the story's numerous generic oddities: digressive narrative lines; dedications and prefaces that occur well into the work rather than in their usual places at the beginning; black pages, marbled pages, blank pages; blank chapters that allow the eighteenth and nineteenth chapters to be written between the twenty-fifth and the twenty-sixth chapters. "All I wish is, that I may be a lesson to the world, *'to let people tell their stories their own way,'*" Tristram insists (*TS* 524), defending his effort to be the singular author of his own life. If Tristram has his way, no reader should ever be able to predict the course of his narrative:

> 'tis impossible for you to guess;—if you could,—I should blush; not as a relation,—not as a man,—nor as a woman,—but I should blush as an author; inasmuch as I set no small store by myself upon this very account, that my reader has never yet been able to guess at any thing. And in this, Sir, I am of so nice and singular a humour, that if I thought you was able to form the least judgment or probable conjecture to yourself, of what was to come in the next page,—I would tear it out of my book.
>
> (*TS* 63)

With valid "probable conjecture" cause for the ripping-out of pages, Tristram aspires to write anti-didactic didactic fiction, to teach people not to draw conclusions; to keep his readers in a state of perpetual guessing; to subordinate the general view to his own particularity; to control representation and interpretation more effectively than his cruelly baffled father.

Sentimentalism, therefore, does not quite serve Tristram's purpose, for it encourages motive-mongering, and treats biography-writing as the easy exercise of tracing the outlines seen through Momus' glass. Determined to "do all things out of rule" (*TS* 225), Tristram can never achieve the fiction of unmediated truth created by the unselfconscious acceptance of sentimental convention. His tender descriptions often redirect attention back to their own formality, through exaggeration or the addition of odd details. For instance, bodily gestures, so legible in the sentimental tradition, assume a comic opacity in *Tristram Shandy*, as when Toby expresses the depths of exasperated feeling, "throwing himself back in his arm-chair, and lifting up his hands, his eyes, and one leg" (*TS* 56). The sudden collapse, the lifting of hands and eyes as if to implore heaven—these conventional gestures directly convey Toby's heartfelt sentiments, until his leg pops up as well. What could be the meaning of this leg's imploring of heaven? The detail of Toby's leg, because so unexpected, appears not as a sign of inward sentiment, but literally as itself—as a leg sticking up in the air—thereby drawing attention back to Toby's other gestures, which might have passed for sentimental immediacy, but which now must be recognized as formal convention, the difference between a hand raised to heaven and a leg raised to heaven being only that readers generally interpret the meaning of the former as self-evident.

Likewise, when Walter is stricken with the news of Tristram's crushed nose, he collapses on his bed,

> in the most lamentable attitude of a man borne down with sorrows, that ever the eye of pity dropp'd a tear for.—The palm of his right hand, as he fell upon the bed, receiving his forehead, and covering the greatest part of both his eyes gently sunk down with his head (his elbow giving way backwards) till his nose touch'd the quilt;—his left arm hung insensible over the side of the bed, his knuckles reclining upon the handle of the chamber pot, which peep'd out beyond the valance,—his right leg (his left being drawn up towards his body) hung half over the side of the bed, the edge of it pressing upon his shin-bone.—He felt it not. A fix'd, inflexible sorrow took possession of every line of his face.—He sigh'd once,—heaved his breast often,—but utter'd not a word.
>
> (*TS* 171)

Tristram here describes his father in sentimental tones, making his readers see Walter, through sentimental eyes, as a man more lamentable than "ever the eye of pity dropp'd a tear for." Yet Tristram's careful attention to physical detail—those sentimental empirical signs of true feeling—is excessive, threatening to overwhelm the description itself. He conveys his father's sorrow by relating the exact placement of Walter's right hand, forehead, eyes, elbow, nose, left arm, knuckles, right leg and shin. The oddly illegible detail of Toby's leg finds a parallel in "the handle of the chamber pot" upon which Walter's knuckles gently rest. Disturbing the smooth flow of conventional representation, this unexpected chamber pot serves to heighten the reader's awareness of Tristram's description as a description. Walter's overpowering feeling may make him insensible to the material means through which his feeling finds representation—the edge of the bed pressing into his shin-bone goes unfelt—but Tristram makes his readers notice each breath and every movement: "He sigh'd once,—heaved his breast often,—but utter'd not a word." Of course Walter cannot speak, for we know that sentimental convention would not allow it. Paradoxically, Sterne prevents readers from reading sentimentally by pointing out that they *are* reading sentimentally. Readers must read as though they are watching themselves read.

Even the much-celebrated sentimental set-piece, the story of Le Fever, engages in this sentimental self-consciousness. Gently parodying the sentimental fiction of unmediated representation, the climactic conclusion of the story of Le Fever exaggerates the correspondence between Tristram's text and

Le Fever's body. Words and things, form and substance, fuse into a seamless unity as the end of Tristram's chapter perfectly coincides with the end of Le Fever's life:

> The blood and spirits of Le Fever, which were waxing cold and slow within him, and were retreating to their last citadel, the heart,— rallied back,—the film forsook his eyes for a moment,—he looked up wishfully in my uncle Toby's face,—then cast a look upon his boy,— and that *ligament*, fine as it was,—was never broken.—
>
> Nature instantly ebb'd again,—the film returned to its place,— the pulse fluttered—stopp'd—went on—throb'd—stopp'd again—moved—stopp'd—shall I go on?—No.
>
> (TS 343)

Sterne seems to make good on Thomas Sprat's promise that "by long studying of the *Spirits*, of the *Bloud*," and of other qualities "which belong to *humane bodies*"—all of which fall within the "Province" of the new philosophy— "there, without question, be very neer ghesses made, even at the more *exalted*, and *immediate* actions of the *Soul*" (Sprat 82–3). Meticulously detailing the "blood and spirits of Le Fever," Sterne comically reveals the workings of the soul as though they were immediately legible upon the body. In a literary fantasy of natural language and immediate representation, Sterne's text fuses with Le Fever's body, his words coinciding perfectly with the dying man's heartbeat: "the pulse fluttered—stopp'd—went on—throb'd—stopp'd again—moved—stopp'd—shall I go on?—No." It is impossible to determine whether that final question—"shall I go on?"—issues from Le Fever's fluttering heart or from Tristram the narrator. The point, however, is that it does not matter, for the two have become one and the same. Sterne's sentimental fiction of unmediated representation thus mocks the perfect union of minds it purports to convey, adding self-conscious laughter where there should be only sympathetic tears. It not only encourages contrary responses from among the novel's many readers, but also prompts individual readers to be of two minds about the same scene. Like Walter's impotent rational systems, Tristram's sentimentalism is a failure, incapable of establishing uniform opinion.

Tristram's ironic sentimentalism is thus a form of anti-sentimentalism, just as Fielding's ironic anti-sentimentalism is in fact a form of sentimentalism. As Fielding's definition *"Of Love"* turns into an appeal for an exclusive sentimental community of readers, so Tristram's refusal to define love becomes a rejection of any such community:

> 'TWILL come out of itself by and bye.—All I contend for is, that I am not obliged to set out with a definition of what love is; and so long as I can go on with my story intelligibly, with the help of the word itself, without any other idea to it, than what I have in common with

the rest of the world, why should I differ from it a moment before the time?—When I can get on no further,—and find myself entangled on all sides of this mystick labyrinth,—my Opinion will then come in, in course,—and lead me out.

(TS 375)

Less anxious than Fielding to regulate the interpretive community, Tristram carelessly trusts to the "common" definition, relying on the spontaneous and singular ingenuity of his own "Opinion" to extract him from whatever difficulties he may subsequently encounter. "Let love therefore be what it will," Tristram breezily concludes, "—my uncle *Toby* fell into it" (*TS* 375). Not presuming to prescribe the opinions of others, Tristram invites each (male) reader to imagine the "temptation" of the Widow Wadman for himself:

> To conceive this right,—call for pen and ink—here's paper ready to your hand.—Sit down, Sir, paint her to your own mind—as like your mistress as you can—as unlike your wife as your conscience will let you—'tis all one to me—please but your own fancy in it.

(TS 376)

Whereas Fielding's humorous description of love disciplines readers by classifying them into good minds and bad minds, then ridiculing those who do not identify with the former, Sterne refuses to standardize opinion. While Fielding describes his most beloved heroine, Sophia, in mock-epic form, relying on irony to recuperate a feeling of particularity from this generic representation, Sterne dispenses with genre and generalities, offering his readers only a blank page upon which to "paint" as particular an image of the Widow Wadman as they please.

The general rules of beauty become the particular views invited by the blank page, which affords each reader the liberty to imagine their peculiar tastes as universal. "—Was ever any thing in Nature so sweet!—so exquisite!" Tristram can then exclaim, free to pursue his plot line as an inevitability:

> – Then, dear Sir, how could my uncle *Toby* resist it?
> Thrice happy book! thou wilt have one page, at least, within thy covers, which MALICE will not blacken, and which IGNORANCE cannot misrepresent.

(TS 378)

The issues that so required Fielding's rational masculine control—probable conjecture and misrepresentation—ironically disappear here because Tristram abandons all forms of rational masculine control. Agreement appears possible only because Tristram does not require it, instead allowing each reader to believe quixotically in the authority of his own suppositions. Sterne's general view paradoxically asserts the non-existence of a general view: the blank page is limited to no particular view, because it contains no view at all. In Tristram's world, the community of perfect understanding remains unoccupied. Sentimentalism is a blank, *carte blanche* for quixotes to find their own Dulcinea.

The "already written" law of "God and reason"

Far from representing a scientific, moral, or emotional norm by which particular experience leads inevitably to general principles and fixed standards, Tristram's life and opinions argue the reverse: that general principles always scatter before particular experience. One final illustration of this process, particularly telling for how it depicts moral knowledge, may be found in Yorick's sermon. Yorick, closely identified with Sterne himself ever since the publication of Sterne's own sermons as *The Sermons of Mr. Yorick* (1760), exhibits all the quixotic qualities characteristic of the Shandean universe. Compared to "the peerless knight of *La Mancha*," Yorick more than anyone allows himself to be controlled by representations. Rational masculinity entirely eludes him: "he was utterly unpractised in the world; and, at the age of twenty-six, knew just about as well how to steer his course in it, as a romping, unsuspicious girl of thirteen" (*TS* 19, 22). Sentimental immediacy governs his conduct: "Yorick had no impression but one, and that was what arose from the nature of the deed spoken of; which impression he would usually translate into plain *English* without any periphrasis . . . he seldom shun'd occasions of saying what came uppermost, and without much ceremony" (*TS* 23–4). As befits this sentimental quixotic parson and the Humean themes of Sterne's satiric novel, Yorick's sermon on conscience proclaims the fixed and immutable standards of moral law, while simultaneously illustrating the ironies, uncertainties and difficulties of recognizing these standards.

Discovered in Uncle Toby's *Stevinus* and performed by Trim before Toby, Walter, and Dr Slop, Yorick's sermon takes its text from Hebrews 13:18, "*For we* trust *we have a good conscience*," and instructs its audience to place the shared truth of "God and reason" above individual conscience. In the context of *Tristram Shandy*, the sermon's ironies are thick. Hebrews itself paradoxically argues that change is really no change, asserting that Jesus Christ is "the same yesterday, and to day, and for ever" (Hebrews 13:8), even as it reaffirms historical difference by exhorting the Hebrews not to revert to the Old Covenant. As the contradiction between historical change and eternal moral truth conjures images of quixotic behavior, the subject of Yorick's sermon weaves gracefully into Sterne's quixotic theme. In Hebrews, faith—"the substance of things hoped for, the evidence of things not seen" (Hebrews 11:1)—is the means through which to reconcile the old with the new. Of course, "the substance of things hoped for, and the evidence of things not seen" could be quixotic delusion instead. Yorick's sermon is both a disquisition upon and an example of quixotic understanding.

The sermon strives to reconcile the vagaries of individual conscience with the demands of eternal moral law. Beginning with the supposition that conscience is the most reliable truth, Yorick steadily undermines this certainty. "TRUST! trust we have a good conscience! Surely if there is any thing in this life which a man may depend upon, and to the knowledge of which he is capable of arriving upon the most indisputable evidence, it must be this very thing,—whether he has a good conscience or no" (*TS* 99–100). Despite what little he may know of anything else, a man should at least know himself, Yorick postulates. "If a man thinks at all . . . he must be privy to his own thoughts and desires;—he must remember his past pursuits, and know certainly the true springs and motives which, in general, have governed the actions of his life," Yorick reasons:

> In other matters we may be deceived by false appearances. . . . But here the mind has all the evidence and facts within herself;—is conscious of the web she has wove;—knows its texture and fineness, and the exact share which every passion has had in working upon the several designs which virtue or vice has plann'd before her.
>
> (*TS* 100)

Knowledge of other people and the physical world may be deceptive, hidden behind "false appearances," but surely the mind at least has immediate knowledge—"all the evidence and facts"—of itself?

Not so. Like the larger narrative pattern of *Tristram Shandy*, which endlessly complicates the seemingly straightforward task of depicting Tristram's thoughts, desires, past pursuits and true motives, Yorick's sermon soon turns the self-evident into the doubtful. Conscience, the very source of certainty, may be corrupt, Yorick warns, fearing as Hutcheson did that the moral sense can be vitiated:

> the conscience of man, by long habits of sin, might (as the scripture assures it may) insensibly become hard;—and, like some tender parts of his body, by much stress and continual hard usage, lose, by degrees, that nice sense and perception with which God and nature endow'd it.
>
> (*TS* 101)

The power of "Interest" figures prominently among these corrupting influences (*TS* 101), which cause the estrangement between a man and his own conscience. Why is conscience not more watchful? Because it soon grows autonomous and unconcerned:

Alas! CONSCIENCE had something else to do, all this time, than break in upon him; as *Elijah* reproached the God *Baal*,—this domestick God *was either talking, or pursuing, or was in a journey, or peradventure he slept and could not be awoke.*

Perhaps HE was gone out in company with HONOUR to fight a duel;—to pay off some debt at play;—or dirty annuity, the bargain of his lust: Perhaps CONSCIENCE all this time was engaged at home, talking loud against petty larceny, and executing vengeance upon some such puny crimes as his fortune and rank in life secured him against all temptation of committing; so that he lives as merrily . . . sleeps as soundly in his bed;—and at last meets death as unconcernedly;—perhaps much more so than a much better man.

(*TS* 102)

Like a false god, a corrupted conscience rationalizes self-delusion by instilling false confidence. Yorick imagines this errant conscience as a separate and distinct individual, complete with his own busy schedule of appointments and engagements, bustling about like a man of affairs. By personifying conscience, Yorick emphasizes the human fallibility of this "domestick God."

As *The Female Quixote* had warned of the "subtil Sophistry of Desire," so does Yorick's sermon warn of the mind's false lights. For Yorick, the rationalizing, self-indulgent and unruly human mind resembles a little society whose differing interests and diverse activities remain conflicted, dispersed and not fully known. The mind is not privy to its own thoughts, nor conscious of the web it has woven, Yorick argues:

Thus conscience, this once able monitor,—placed on high as a judge within us, and intended by our maker as a just and equitable one too,—by an unhappy train of causes and impediments, takes often such imperfect cognizance of what passes,—does its office so negligently,—sometimes so corruptly,—that it is not to be trusted alone; and therefore we find there is a necessity, an absolute necessity of joining another principle with it to aid, if not govern, its determinations.

(*TS* 105)

An autonomous conscience offends "the eternal measures of right and wrong," Yorick cautions (*TS* 107). Imperfectly cognizant, negligent and occasionally corrupt, conscience should not rely on its own lights. The discipline of "religion and morality" are necessary to "aid, if not govern, its determinations." "What is written in the law of God?" Yorick demands: "—How readest thou?—Consult calm reason and the unchangeable obligations of justice and truth;—what say they?" (*TS* 105). Only the written law of God, read rightly and joined to calm reason and unchangeable moral truth, makes conscience reliable, Yorick preaches, for the power of interest is otherwise too great, leaving conscience with no firm foundation. Morality without religion rests fickly on "interest," "pride," "ease, or some such little and changeable passion" (*TS* 108), while religion without morality produces the wild, "misguided saint-errant" (*TS* 109). Yorick, therefore, honors the eternal laws of religion and morality more than the arbitrary dictates of autonomous conscience. "[Y]our conscience is not a law," he concludes resoundingly:

> —No, God and reason made the law, and have placed conscience within you to determine;—not like an *Asiatick* Cadi, according to the ebbs and flows of his own passions,—but like a *British* judge in this land of liberty and good sense, who makes no new law, but faithfully declares the law he knows already written.
>
> (*TS* 112)

Beginning with apparent confidence in individual conscience, Yorick's sermon ends in deference to the "already written" law of "God and reason."

Invoking the rational authority of "already written" law to chasten the overweening conscience of the "saint-errant," Yorick's sermon reiterates the Lockean argument against quixotism: reason, law and (natural) obligation should oppose arbitrary power and the perversions of interest. Yet in making this claim, the sermon does not escape the quixotic uncertainty against which it preaches. For like the careful *"British* judge" who "makes no new law," quixotes also faithfully declare only that which they know to be already written. Meticulously wedded to precedent, quixotes defy historical change by championing eternal standards; they conflate delusion and anachronism. This reading of quixotism was increasingly prevalent in Sterne's time, as chivalric romances ceased to be regarded as ridiculous fictions, and were instead accorded the status of authentic histories. "Chivalry was no absurd and freakish institution, but the natural and even sober effect of the feudal policy," Bishop Hurd wrote in 1762, while the Reverend John Bowle asserted in 1777 that "Romances" contain

> faithful and exact descriptions of the manners and customs of the times in which they were wrote: Though the facts related were in themselves as fabulous as the heroes of whom they were told, yet similar events frequently occurred: In this respect, they deserve some esteem as histories, because these latter enumerate several facts similar to those they particularly mention.[19]

If chivalric romance may be esteemed as history, then perhaps Don Quixote might qualify for a British judgeship. Delusion and anachronism are near allied: faithful obedience to laws "already written" does not preclude quixotic errancy, for (as Arabella was shocked to learn from the Countess) times do change. What seems "absurd and freakish" now may have been "natural and even sober" then.

Thus, in Yorick's sermon, the eternal measures of right and wrong remain forever circumscribed within the quixotic conflict between innovation and anachronism. The sermon's appeal to the unshakable authority of "already written" law becomes more comic in light of the Shandean auditors who receive it. As Trim reads the sermon aloud, a divergent and contentious commentary among Slop, Toby, Walter and Trim frequently interrupts the performance. Despite the sermon's being already written, none of these men understand it in quite the same way. Dr Slop focuses on its anti-Catholicism; Trim bemoans it as a description of his brother's sufferings under the Inquisition in Portugal; Walter evaluates it as a formal piece of rhetoric; Toby perks up at its metaphorical mention of military fortifications. Each hearer's comments reveal how differently the sermon may be interpreted. "What is written in the law of God?" the sermon had asked: "—How readest thou?" The questions seem straightforward enough—as the task of writing one's life and opinions would appear to be straightforward enough—but the men in Shandy Hall cannot even agree upon how to read the sermon itself, much less the written law of God. This hermeneutic problem is pervasive: "in Shandy Hall every mode of experience down to the simplest sense perception . . . offers a problem of interpretation," James Swearingen observes.[20] Yorick's argument against particular conscience and in support of universal rules (which are not really universal, as an Asiatic Cadi might attest) represents itself as simple and already rational, but its coherence depends upon myriad individuals coming to the same conclusions as to what is the "already written" means—a process undermined by *Tristram Shandy* itself. Tristram shows only contempt for already written rules: "The duce of any other rule have I to govern myself by in this affair," he exclaims,

> —and if I had one—as I do all things out of rule—I would twist it and tear it to pieces, and throw it into the fire when I had done—Am I warm? I am, and the cause demands it—a pretty story! is a man to follow rules—or rules to follow him?
>
> (*TS* 225)

As Tristram explains his own principles of writing, they begin to sound like arbitrary power. If other writers have thought in similar ways, Sterne implies, then perhaps the supposedly general view contained in the "already written" is in fact merely a particular view – like Tristram's, only older.

Most readers of *Tristram Shandy* recognize Sterne's satire on universal rationality and laugh along with it. Yet this response is often superficial. Apparently deeply embarrassed by Sterne's critique of reason, many of his admirers ultimately ignore the satire, attempting to retrieve the general view and masculine rationality that are forever deferred within *Tristram Shandy*. They acknowledge Sterne's odd emphasis on particularity, only to dismiss it with abrupt declarations to the contrary. Traugott, for instance, commends Sterne for having "nothing to do with self-indulgence, nothing to do with a fatuous, uncritical benevolism, nothing to do with irresponsibility"; Sterne's sympathetic process, Traugott asserts, "admits no particularity or limits. It is perfectly general."[21] Swearingen, though an astute and impassioned critic of intellectual self-importance and scientific hubris, still universalizes Sterne himself, calling the author "a thinker of unusual insight into the general nature of consciousness."[22] J. Paul Hunter maintains that the "odd and unsettled particularity of *Tristram Shandy* justly represents general nature, too."[23] More recently, Michael Rosenblum: "for all of Tristram's insistence upon the particulars of his account, his narrative is inescapably general in its thrust."[24] That such generality should be described as a "thrust" metaphorically recalls the gendered nature of universal reason within the eighteenth-century quixotic tradition. If *Tristram Shandy* is general in nature, then masculine rationality is safe.

"It is possible to argue that Tristram sees the crisis of European life primarily as a male phenomenon," Swearingen reluctantly concedes, on his way to denying this very possibility. (Women, Swearingen eventually concludes, are no exception to the general rule: Mrs Shandy "is implicated in the general sterility, both physical and spiritual, that afflicts life at Shandy Hall."[25]) Significantly, in defending the generality of the Shandean critique, Swearingen believes himself to be championing the power of reason:

> it is evident that Walter conceives of reason and passion as rival forces of equal status, thereby ignoring the ancient structure whereby reason as active agent was understood to give form to passion. The rivalry that Walter describes implicitly exalts passion, degrades reason, and prepares the way for the position of Hume that reason is and ought to be the slave of the passions, a view that Walter unwittingly exemplifies in that his rationalistic theories are really instruments in the service of his desires, the desire especially to annihilate rhetorical opposition.[26]

Swearingen's analysis attempts to recover masculine reason by interpreting Walter as a peculiar perversion of the rational norm. Walter is ridiculous because he "degrades reasons," yields to the subtle sophistry of desire, and exemplifies the position of Hume (the philosopher to whom Battestin attributes Fielding's increasing sentimentalism).[27] To sustain this position, however, Swearingen must repress the obvious: namely, that not only Walter, but all men in *Tristram Shandy*, are quixotic. To single out Walter as the lone, unwitting adherent of rationalistic theories that are really in the service of desire is to misread the book. In Sterne's novel, there is no manly rational transcendence against which Walter falls short. Rather, *Tristram Shandy* describes a world of universal quixotism, where endless peculiarity, insuperable limitations and diversity in judgment converge to mortify masculine intellect and to ridicule rational standards. In light of these impediments to common understanding, the critical attempt to recuperate reason by reaffirming the general nature of Sterne's narrative becomes as paradoxical as Hume's discussion of the "general principles" of "a true standard of taste and sentiment." One may choose to read the quixotic figure as ultimately transcendent, and therefore to discover "general nature" amidst Sterne's peculiarity. After all, the quixotism of Sancho's kinsmen proved in the end the existence of a true standard of taste, so perhaps too the quixotism of *Tristram Shandy* might support the existence of a true standard of reason. But reading the quixotic figure in this way can be accomplished only at the cost of accepting the quixotic figure, at least for the time being, *as* the true standard. In other words, the quest for universal reason puts all critical discussions precisely on a level with Don Quixote's dissertations on giants and enchantments.

6

LAYING DOWN THE GENERAL RULE

Adam Smith, impartial spectators and the philosopher's trade

Adam Smith (1723–1790) is a man for our time—or ought to be.

Robert J. Samuelson[1]

Adam Smith owes much of his fame to the anachronistic quality of his thought: he is a man for our time, or ought to be, as the above epigraph asserted in 1996. Smith, it appears, is eternal: economists still defer to his "timeless counsel" in what can only be described as reverential tones.[2] Milton Friedman honors Smith's thought as profoundly current even after two centuries,[3] while George J. Stigler writes assuredly of Smith: "if on first hearing a passage of his you are inclined to disagree, you are reacting inefficiently; the correct response is to say to yourself: I wonder where I went amiss?"[4] But perhaps Paul A. Samuelson best captures the worshipful attitude shown by "the grandsons of Adam Smith" toward their mythic progenitor. "The first human was Adam," Samuelson explains: "The first economist (if one can make the distinction) was Adam Smith."[5]

Yet if the eighteenth century was an age of quixotism, there can be little doubt that Adam Smith—a man for our time, a man for all time—was also a man of his time. The same problems of rational explanation and moral empiricism that provoke so much comedy in *Tristram Shandy* pervade Smith's writings as well. Like Sterne, Smith takes as his theme the relation of individuals to the social whole, seeking to explain how a general truth can be imagined when everyone is known to be quixotically self-interested. Smith, in other words, attempts to resolve the problem of quixotism, to reconcile particular differences to general rules. His good standing as the father of rational self-interest suggests that his efforts succeeded. In this chapter, however, I argue that Smith's moral philosophy does not describe an alternative to quixotism, for the foundational ideas of his arguments prove to be oddly insubstantial. The figure of the "impartial spectator," through which Smith mediates the disparity between particular feeling and general moral principles in *The Theory of Moral Sentiments* (1759), begins as a human spectator afflicted

198

with human limitations, but mysteriously metamorphoses into an infallible, godlike, ideal spectator. Likewise, in *The Wealth of Nations* (1776) Smith seeks to describe the general principles of an economy too vast and specialized to be comprehended by any particular individual, except for "the philosopher," whose "trade" inexplicably transcends the self-interested, peculiar perspectives experienced by everyone else. In both *The Theory of Moral Sentiments* and *The Wealth of Nations* Smith establishes a rational standard indistinguishable from a quixotic one.

Imagined philosophy, Newtonian method and the laughing artisan

Although the majority of Adam Smith's unpublished manuscripts were burnt at his own request just before his death, Smith did direct that a few works be spared.[6] In particular, he showed concern over the fate of a brief essay entitled, "The principles which lead and direct philosophical enquiries; illustrated by the history of astronomy," probably composed between 1746 and 1748. As early as 1773, while putting his earthly affairs in order, Smith had recommended to Hume's attention "a fragment of a great work, which contains a history of the astronomical systems that were successively in fashion down to the time of Des Cartes."[7] This "great work," Vernard Foley speculates, may have been "a sort of universal intellectual history,"[8] an ambitious attempt to comprehend the historical limits of comprehension itself. Smith's unfinished *magnum opus* seeks to place previously held, though now exploded, philosophical systems in historical perspective, in order to explain why once authoritative systems can now properly be regarded as ridiculous. Systems of rational thought vary over time, Smith recognizes. His projected "great work" would have rationalized this historical relativism by establishing the superiority of modern truths over past beliefs. A teleological understanding of intellectual history can read historical difference as progressive, rather than quixotic.

Quixotism persists as the shadow of Smith's argument. Indeed, in the "History of astronomy," the quixotic logic of narrative expectation parallels Smith's scientific method. The mind naturally attempts to "methodise" all its ideas, always seeking "to connect" what it currently observes with what it already knows to be "the ordinary train of things," Smith argues.[9] A world well understood is one that closely conforms to predictable plots:

> When two objects, however unlike, have often been observed to follow each other, and have constantly presented themselves to the senses in that order, they come to be so connected together in the fancy, that the idea of the one seems, of its own accord, to call up and introduce that of the other. If the objects are still observed to succeed each other as before, this connection, or, as it has been called, this

association of their ideas, becomes stricter and stricter, and the habit of the imagination to pass from the conception of the one to that of the other, grows more and more rivetted and confirmed.

("Astronomy" 40–1)

The specter of the quixotic haunts Smith's explanation, as he seriously posits the epistemological mechanisms so much satirized in *The Female Quixote* and *Tristram Shandy*. "Fancy" and "imagination" forge associations of ideas that grow "more and more rivetted and confirmed" over time. When unexpected events occur, however, the mind's habitual connections are disturbed: the "imagination no longer feels that usual facility of passing from the event which goes before to that which comes after" ("Astronomy" 41). A "gap" or "interval" in the understanding results, which prompts "the imagination" to supply a bridge:

The supposition of a chain of intermediate, though invisible events, which succeed each other in a train similar to that in which the imagination has been accustomed to move, and which link together those two disjointed appearances, is the only means by which the imagination can fill up this interval, is the only bridge which, if one may say so, can smooth its passage from one object to the other.

("Astronomy" 42)

Scientific knowledge, for Smith, is "a chain . . . of invisible events" that proceed along lines already familiar to the "imagination." Such knowledge would, of course, be specific to experience, cumulative in nature and resistant to change. The habits of the imagination, once established, are not easily corrected.

"It is thus that too severe an application to study sometimes brings on lunacy and frenzy," Smith elaborates, "in those especially who are somewhat advanced in life, but whose imaginations, from being too late in applying, have not got those habits which dispose them to follow easily the reasonings in the abstract sciences" ("Astronomy" 43). Smith's "abstract sciences," which may lead older students to become "confused, then giddy, and at last distracted," recall nothing so much as Don Quixote's romances, a connection easily made in light of the quixotic reputation of the new philosophy. Don Quixote, after all, began his studies at the age of fifty or so, with such "Application" that he soon abandoned all other activities. The "intricate Expressions" contained in his romances "strangely puzzled the poor Gentleman's understanding," and

[i]n fine, he gave himself up so wholly to the reading of Romances, that a-Nights he would pore on 'till 'twas Day, and a-Days he would read on 'till 'twas Night; and thus by sleeping little and reading

much, the Moisture of his Brain was exhausted to that Degree, that at last he lost the Use of his Reason.

(*DQ* 2–3)

Smith envisions a similar quixotic fate for anyone whose imagination must too suddenly adjust to new ways of thinking so late in life. To clarify this point, he presents the extreme example of a perfectly reasonable person who, accustomed to the natural laws of earth, is suddenly "transported alive to some other planet, where nature [is] governed by laws quite different from those which take place here." By ceaselessly attempting to reconcile this entirely new world to his stubborn old logic, this hapless space traveler, Smith concludes, will naturally feel "confusion and giddiness," and "at last end in . . . lunacy and distraction" ("Astronomy" 43).

Yet Smith is well aware that one need not land on a new planet in order to feel as though one has, for the experiential diversity ordinarily found among different groups of people, even within the same society, already offered formidable challenges to the smooth movement of a mature imagination. "The same orders of succession, which to one set of men seem quite according to the natural course of things, and such as require no intermediate events to join them, shall to another appear altogether incoherent and disjointed, unless some such events be supposed," Smith maintains, "and this for no other reason, but because such orders of succession are familiar to the one, and strange to the other" ("Astronomy" 44). What appears "natural" and thus in no need of explanation to some, looks "incoherent and disjointed" to others. Reason arises from habit, Smith argues, sounding much like his friend David Hume. "According to my system," Hume had written in his *Treatise of Human Nature*, which Smith, while a student at Oxford, was reprimanded for reading, "all reasonings are nothing but the effects of custom."[10] In a move often made within the eighteenth-century quixotic tradition, Smith illustrates the problem of rational diversity and experiential uniqueness by pointing to occupational diversity:

When we enter the work-houses of the most common artizans; such as dyers, brewers, distillers; we observe a number of appearances, which present themselves in an order that seems to us very strange and wonderful. Our thought cannot easily follow it, we feel an interval betwixt every two of them, and require some chain of intermediate events, to fill it up, and link them together. But the artizan himself, who has been for many years familiar with the consequences of all the operations of his art, feels no such interval. They fall in with what custom has made the natural movement of his imagination: they no longer excite his Wonder, and if he is not a genius superior to his profession, so as to be capable of making the very easy reflection, that those things, though familiar to him, may be strange to us, he

will be disposed rather to laugh at, than sympathize with our
Wonder. . . . It is their nature, he tells us, to follow one another in
this order, and that accordingly they always do so.

("Astronomy" 44)

Reasoned understanding proceeds from particular experience, especially the
particular experience generated by economic diversification. "We"—who are
presumably philosophers, not artisans—find their work-houses strange and
wonderful, because "we" lack the experience of an artisan. Accustomed to the
processes of his trade, however, the artisan needs no philosophy to explain
what he regards as self-evident. He will be more inclined to laugh at "our"
ridiculous ignorance than to sympathize with it. Only philosophers, wide-
eyed with wonder before the simple operations of industrial art, feel
compelled to offer strange and elaborate explanations for what is self-evident
to everyone else there. "Philosophers, indeed," Smith dryly acknowledges,
imagining how philosophers would appear to artisans, " . . . often look for a
chain of invisible objects to join together events that occur in an order familiar
to all the world" ("Astronomy" 45). The artisan laughs because philosophical
quixotism is funny.

An odd, mutual condescension emerges between philosopher and artisan as
Smith simultaneously defends and criticizes the potential for unified understanding. The laughing artisan has knowledge that "we" do not. But in not
recognizing the insularity of his own perspective, the artisan demonstrates his
intellectual weakness, reinforcing Smith's presumptions about the stupidity
of artisans in general; an artisan who laughs at the philosopher's ignorance,
Smith observes, is "not a genius superior to his profession." Smith thus makes
two contradictory assumptions: on the one hand, he assumes that all
tradesmen, by virtue of their specialization, will have limited understandings
(an expectation fulfilled whenever artisans laugh at, rather than "sympathize"
with, philosophers); on the other hand, Smith insists on how "very easy" it
would be for the artisan to escape his limitations by simply observing that
"those things, though familiar to him, may be strange to us." Ultimately,
Smith does not take rational difference seriously, discounting the artisan's
understanding because the artisan cannot even make the "very easy reflection"
that his limited view is not the general view. Smith seems unconcerned that
the artisan himself might discount the philosopher for the very same reason.
After all, the artisan does not need the philosopher's explanations, theories and
"intermediate events." These philosophical chains of invisible objects have no
apparent relevance to the artisan's life. From the artisan's perspective, the
philosopher's general view must look mighty peculiar.

Smith's division of labor, therefore, divides more than occupations. It
divides experience, which divides knowledge, which divides the imaginative
"chains" that link that knowledge together. It displaces the philosophical
general view into the realm of the imagination, for a vast and diverse world

can never actually be experienced by one person, and so must be imagined. "Philosophy," Smith announces, " . . . may be regarded as one of those arts which address themselves to the imagination" ("Astronomy" 46). Like Cervantes' Don Quixote, who having "lost the Use of his Reason," faced "a world of disorderly Notions" that "crouded into his Imagination" (*DQ* 3), Adam Smith's philosopher, when placed in a common workhouse, perceives "an order that seems . . . very strange," and which strains "the natural movement of his imagination." Don Quixote's odd madness strongly resembles Adam Smith's philosophical norm. In Smith's essay, the problem of philosophical inquiry is the problem of quixotism: the incomprehension that occurs when people, unable to agree on basic premises, find themselves debating the finer distinctions between the self-evident and the nonsensical.

Smith does not fully approve the results of this imaginative philosophy, devoting the rest of the essay to a history of astronomy that functions as a counter-example to the theories he has just proposed. Rather than investigating philosophical quixotism, Smith's history of astronomy depicts the progressive triumph of "real" knowledge over the imagination. The contrast he articulates between the earliest and latest astronomical systems suggests gradual intellectual improvement. In "the first ages of society," Smith explains, the "savage" way of life did not encourage contemplation, instead prompting in mankind the "most pusillanimous superstition" and "impotence of mind." To a "savage," "every object of nature . . . whose operations are not perfectly regular, is supposed to act by the direction of some invisible and designing power" ("Astronomy" 49). All those aspects of natural order, which primitive people observe but cannot explain, are superstitiously attributed to "the invisible hand of Jupiter," Smith remarks ("Astronomy" 49). This dependence on an "invisible hand"—"some invisible and designing power"—indicates that the civilized, rational and manful intellect has not yet come into its powers. As an explanatory device, the "invisible hand" points to a failure of reason.[11] Savages and primitives ascribe "all the irregular events of nature to the favour or displeasure of intelligent, though invisible beings, to gods, daemons, witches, genii, fairies," Smith notes with casual condescension, secure in the superiority of modern rational systems.

The history Smith tells supports his Olympian regard. His review of the astronomical systems that followed upon these rude beginnings—the astronomy of the Greeks, the Romans, the Schoolmen, Copernicus, Tycho Brahe, Galileo, Kepler, Descartes—resoundingly concludes that the Newtonian principles current in Smith's own day offer by far the best philosophy. So powerful are Newton's theories that they seem to defy their own status as theories. "And even we," Smith writes,

> while we have been endeavouring to represent all philosophical systems as mere inventions of the imagination, to connect together the otherwise disjointed and discordant phaenomena of nature, have

insensibly been drawn in, to make use of language expressing the connecting principles of this one, as if they were the real chains which Nature makes use of to bind together her several operations. Can we wonder then, that it should have gained the general and complete approbation of mankind, and that it should now be considered, not as an attempt to connect in the imagination the phaenomena of the Heavens, but as the greatest discovery that ever was made by man, the discovery of an immense chain of the most important and sublime truths, all closely connected together, by one capital fact, of the reality of which we have daily experience.

("Astronomy" 105)

With the advent of Newton, philosophy seems no longer to exist "as mere inventions of the imagination" invoked to connect disjointed phenomena. Instead, Smith finds himself talking about them as though they were "real chains" in nature. Noting this slippage in his own "language," Smith can hardly fault the rest of humankind, who regard Newton's system not as a set of imaginary connections, but as the "greatest discovery" of an "immense chain"—now apparently real, not imagined—"of the most important and sublime truths," connected "by one capital fact." This fact is gravity, the "reality" of which is confirmed by "daily experience." Thus, though Smith begins his essay by discussing imaginary connections and chains of invisible events that differ between people of differing experience, he concludes his discourse in praise of the "real chains" of sublime truth universally experienced by everyone each day. The philosopher's general view is right. His difficulties with the daily operations of the artisan recede before this triumph of universal truth.

Smith's "History of astronomy," therefore, hints at the universality of quixotism, while emphasizing a progressive remedy. Smith acknowledges the presence of conflicting rational systems, raised by imagination and varying across historical periods and occupational classes, only to suggest that they will eventually give way to "real" knowledge, to a philosophical system that deserves and receives "the general and complete approbation of mankind." These general principles, however, crucially depend on the particular example Smith adopts as his illustration. In the history of astronomy, capped by the halo of Newton, Smith found the very strongest eighteenth-century case for steady advancement toward "general and complete approbation" in the natural sciences. Pope's famous couplet succinctly sums up the universal admiration enjoyed by Newton: "Nature, and Nature's Laws lay hid in Night./God said, *Let Newton be!* and All was *Light*."[12] In these lines, Newton himself becomes the "intermediate event" connecting *fiat* and *lux*. As an illustration of philosophical principles, the extraordinary success of Newton within the history of astronomy is atypical, and therefore perhaps not the most appropriate example from which to generalize.

Smith's illustration overstates his case in one other important way as well. Smith does not distinguish between natural and moral philosophy. The history of astronomy describes developments in natural philosophy, which Smith extends to moral subjects. Like his teacher Francis Hutcheson and the novelist Henry Fielding, Smith assumes that Newtonian methods of natural science can and should be applied to humanistic study. "[I]n the manner of Sir Isaac Newton," Smith instructed his students in a class lecture,

> we may lay down certain principles known or proved in the beginning, from whence we account for the severall Phenomena, connecting all together by the same Chain.—This . . . Newtonian method is undoubtedly the most Philosophical . . . in every scien<c>e w<h>ether of Moralls or Nat<urall> phi<losophy>.[13]

Yet for moral empiricists, laying down these "certain principles known or proved in the beginning" is frequently the problem, not the solution. Quixotic conflict, such as the mutual condescension that obtains between the laughing artisan and the amazed philosopher of the self-evident, marks those moments in which initial principles, rather than being "known or proved in the beginning," themselves prove to be controversial.

The success of Newton may offer philosophy its strongest case against quixotic rational diversity in the natural sciences, but Adam Smith's most influential works both pursue the science of humankind. And in this science, as I have argued, Newtonianism (in the form of moral empiricism) offers one of the weakest defenses against quixotic difference. Smith's "Newtonian method" in "Moralls," though much celebrated even into modern times, practices the empirical study of invisible things. Both *The Theory of Moral Sentiments* and *The Wealth of Nations* exemplify the uneasy fit between Smith's Newtonian method and his moral subject matter, for their "certain principles known or proved in the beginning" prove in the end to be unstable and controversial.[14] In *The Theory of Moral Sentiments*, sympathy and the role of the "impartial spectator" form the uncertain premises of Smith's argument, while in *The Wealth of Nations*, self-interest and the role of the "philosopher" do the same. In the end, both figures prove to be more slippery than solid.

Impartial spectators and the man within

Published the same year as the first two volumes of *Tristram Shandy*, Smith's *Theory of Moral Sentiments* takes up similar themes—psychological experience, manly virtue, self-deception, conscience, sympathy and the misunderstandings that attend moral empiricism. Like Sterne's novel, *The Theory of Moral Sentiments* addresses the difficulties of imagining collective truth and the individual's proper authority within it, when all individuals are perceived to be quixotically self-interested and all too eager to tell their stories in their own way. Smith's Newtonian method offers to bring order to this unruly phenomena by laying down certain principles known or proved in the beginning, from whence to connect and to account for all. The project is more easily imagined than executed, however, for like the "already written" rules of Yorick's sermon, Smith's "certain principles," once laid down, do not stay down. Rather than methodically erecting a Newtonian system of morals upon solid principles, Smith builds his system of ethics on principles that gradually and silently transform over the course of his argument. The shifting nature of the "impartial spectator" offers a case in point.

In *The Theory of Moral Sentiments*, Smith is concerned with the epistemology of ethics. In addition to querying "wherein does virtue consist?" Smith also discusses "by what power or faculty in the mind is it, that this character [of virtue], whatever it be, is recommended to us?" Smith sees four possible answers to this latter question: the "virtuous character" may be "recommended to us by self love"; "or by reason"; "or by a peculiar power of perception, called a moral sense"; "or last of all, by some other principle in human nature, such as a modification of sympathy" (*TMS* 265–6). Smith establishes his own theory of morals on this last alternative, attempting to show that a person's natural desire for sympathy with his fellows gives rise to the standard of virtue. For Smith, "sympathy" is the certain principle in human nature that makes the Newtonian method in morals possible. "His Theory of Moral Sentiments founded on Sympathy," one of Smith's students later recalled, was "a very ingenious attempt to account for the principal phaenomena in the moral world from this one general principle, like that of Gravity in the natural World."[15] As the motion of the planets may be explained with respect to gravity, so moral sentiments may be explained with respect to sympathy.

Smith, however, is "a good empiricist."[16] By "sympathy," he does not mean an impossibly sentimental, direct communication between souls. Smith's sympathy takes an unmistakably empirical form, occurring when a "spectator" observes someone else and intuits what this other person feels. Scrupulously, Smith reminds readers of the limitations of this approach. "As we have no immediate experience of what other men feel," he explains,

> we can form no idea of the manner in which they are affected, but by conceiving what we ourselves should feel in a like situation. Though our brother is upon the rack, as long as we ourselves are at our ease, our senses will never inform us of what he suffers. They never did, and never can, carry us beyond our own person, and it is by imagination only that we can form any conception of what are his sensations.
>
> (*TMS* 9)

Sympathy, like philosophy, is an art that addresses itself to the imagination. It is an aid to understanding, rather than the literal truth, inspiring fellow-feeling, but falling short of the sympathetic identification later celebrated by Romantic authors.[17] In Smith's empiricist and atomistic universe, empathy does not occur. Even in imagination, sympathetic spectators never leave their own persons.

Smithean spectators, in other words, always remain spectators, closed off from direct knowledge of other minds, unable to transcend the peculiarity of their own circumstances. The act of imagination does not bring about a true meeting of minds. Our response to madmen, Smith argues, shows that we remain fixed in our own point of view:

> Of all the calamities to which the condition of mortality exposes mankind, the loss of reason appears, to those who have the least spark of humanity, by far the most dreadful, and they behold that last stage of human wretchedness with deeper commiseration than any other. But the poor wretch, who is in it, laughs and sings perhaps, and is altogether insensible of his own misery. The anguish which humanity feels, therefore, at the sight of such an object, cannot be the reflection of any sentiment of the sufferer. The compassion of the spectator must arise altogether from the consideration of what he himself would feel if he was reduced to the same unhappy situation, and, what perhaps is impossible, was at the same time able to regard it with his present reason and judgment.
>
> (*TMS* 12)

Smith's sympathetic spectator does not actually feel what others feel. When confronted by a madman, the spectator imagines not the madman's experiences, but the despair he himself would feel were he able to witness himself reduced to the madman's position. Bound to his own point of view, Smith's spectator does not imagine the madman's perspective. Like the philosopher confronted by the laughing artisan, the spectator cannot comprehend the laughing madman. He can only attempt to rationalize the differences between them, measuring everything against the standard of his own experience, reason and judgment. "I judge of your sight by my sight, of your ear by my ear, of your reason by my reason, of your resentment by my resentment, of your love by my love," Smith insists: "I neither have, nor can have, any other way of judging about them" (*TMS* 19). As he did in the "History of astronomy," Smith here begins his inquiry by emphasizing the barriers to common understanding in an empirical world.

It is the function of sympathy to attenuate these incomprehensible differences. According to Smith, sympathy proceeds from humanity's natural aversion to diverse understandings. "[N]othing pleases us more than to observe in other men a fellow-feeling with all the emotions of our own breast; nor are we ever so much shocked as by the appearance of the contrary," Smith asserts (*TMS* 13). Through the natural workings of sympathy, we actively seek to make our feelings correspond with those of others, striving to achieve uniformity of sentiment by correcting for personal bias. For instance, in cases of personal misfortune, in which our own "peculiar relation" to the situation interests us much more deeply than it would an unconcerned spectator, sympathy operates to create a common level of feeling between us and the spectator. The spectator will try to imagine what must be our suffering, but the intensity of his feelings will naturally always fall short of those pangs felt by "the person principally concerned." The person principally concerned will recognize this disparity, however, and in pursuit of "a more complete sympathy," will lower "his passion to that pitch, in which the spectators are capable of going along with him" (TMS 21–2). Through this process of simultaneous imagination and moderation, the sufferer and the spectators will reach a common level of emotional response, "as is sufficient for the harmony of society. Though they will never be unisons, they may be concords, and this is all that is wanted or required" (TMS 22).

Smith's theory of sympathy thus may be recognized as an attempt to explain how overly indulgent particular feeling comes to be modulated into socially appropriate general feeling, and subsequently, into moral rules. Virtue, for Smith, consists in calibrating one's feelings to the social register, judging one's own actions through the eyes of the "impartial spectator" so as to experience the approbation of one's fellows: "complete sympathy" is "that perfect harmony and correspondence of sentiments that constitutes approbation" (TMS 44). "And hence it is," Smith asserts,

> that to feel much for others and little for ourselves, that to restrain our selfish, and to indulge our benevolent affections, constitutes the perfection of human nature; and can alone produce among mankind that harmony of sentiments and passions in which consists their whole grace and propriety. As to love our neighbour as we love ourselves is the great law of Christianity, so it is the great precept of nature to love ourselves only as we love our neighbour, or what comes to the same thing, as our neighbour is capable of loving us.
>
> (TMS 24–5)

Smith's *Theory* seeks to formulate an objective view of proper emotional response, and to deduce the standard of virtue from this objective perspective. The "impartial spectator," free of the individual bias of the person principally concerned, represents the socially appropriate norm, "what every indifferent person" would feel.

An advantage of Smith's *Theory of Moral Sentiments*, as Smith himself explained to a critical Gilbert Elliot, is that it confirms the doctrine "that our judgements concerning our own conduct have always a reference to the sentiments of some other being."[18] By fixing moral sentiments in relation to the sentiments of others, Smith's system can refute moral self-sufficiency while retaining the ability to explain cultural difference. The standard of virtue may vary across time and circumstance, but this variation does not justify individual whim. To illustrate the point, Smith turns once again to the example of economic diversity. "The object with which men in the different professions and states of life are conversant, being very different, and habituating them to very different passions, naturally form in them very different characters and manners," he writes: "We expect in each rank and profession, a degree of those manners, which, experience has taught us, belong to it." These sorts of differences are acceptable, for they are the effects of socialization, not self-indulgence. "A man, we say, should look like his trade and profession," Smith allows, though not without misgivings: "yet the pedantry of every profession is disagreeable," he adds (*TMS* 201).

Smith explains cultural variation in the same way:

> The different situations of different ages and countries are apt, in the same manner, to give different characters to the generality of those who live in them, and their sentiments concerning the particular degree of each quality, that is either blamable or praise-worthy, vary, according to that degree which is usual in their own country, and in their own times.
>
> (*TMS* 204)

Virtue, Smith's empirical analysis seems to intimate, is as fickle as the crowd: "Every age and country look upon that degree of each quality, which is commonly to be met with in those who are esteemed among themselves, as the golden mean of that particular talent or virtue" (*TMS* 204). It was apparently this perceptible instability of the virtuous standard that drew Elliot's criticism, for Smith sent Elliot revisions of *The Theory of Moral Sentiments*, expressly assuring him that "real magnanimity and conscious virtue can support itselfe under the disapprobation of all mankind." Elliot's criticisms of Smith do not survive, but Smith's response suggests that Elliot may have compared Smith's flexible standards in *The Theory of Moral Sentiments* to Mandeville's scandalously nominalist concept of fictive moral virtue. In addition to the revisions he sent, Smith urged Elliot "to read what I say upon Mandevilles system and then consider whether upon the whole I do not make Virtue sufficiently independent of popular opinion."[19]

The revisions Smith sent Elliot, incorporated into the second edition of *The Theory of Moral Sentiments*, drastically alter the nature of the impartial spectator. Rather than being the quotidian reality of "any indifferent person," someone whose particular circumstances differ from those of the person principally concerned, the impartial spectator becomes—mysteriously—"a man in general," like Hume's judge of true taste. Unlike Hume's "man in general," however, Smith's "man in general" is divinely inspired: the "impartial spectator" is an "inmate of the breast," an "abstract man," "the representative of mankind and the Substitute of the Deity, whom nature has appointed the Supreme arbiter of all their actions."[20] This wording did not survive into the sixth edition of *The Theory of Moral Sentiments*, the last to be issued during Smith's lifetime, but language equally strong indicates in this final edition that Smith had not changed his opinion about the divine qualities of the impartial spectator.

In the sixth edition, Smith attributes the doctrine of sympathy to the "all-wise Author of Nature," who created man "after his own image, and appointed him his vicegerent upon earth, to superintend the behaviour of his brethren." In seeking the approval of his fellows, man seeks the approval of God. The divine rectitude of the impartial spectator persists, Smith assures his readers, even in the event of widespread moral corruption; that is, even if the vicegerents err:

> But though man has, in this manner, been rendered the immediate judge of mankind, he has been rendered so only in the first instance; and an appeal lies from his sentence to a much higher tribunal, to the tribunal of their own consciences, to that of the supposed impartial and well-informed spectator, to that of the man within the breast, the great judge and arbiter of their conduct.
>
> (*TMS* 130)

Here, sympathetic concord is no longer the founding principle of the standard of virtue, for conscience now functions independently of sympathy, existing as "a much higher tribunal," capable of identifying and correcting misplaced sympathies. The "supposed impartial" spectator—"supposed" because now in no way to be regarded as an actual spectator—has become conscience itself, "the man within the breast, the great judge and arbiter" of conduct, distinct from the (corrupted) opinions of other men. This supposed impartial spectator, no longer the product of other men's opinions, can now resist the censure of "real spectators":

> We scarce dare to absolve ourselves, when all our brethren appear loudly to condemn us. The supposed impartial spectator of our conduct seems to give his opinion in our favour with fear and hesitation; when that of all the real spectators, when that of all those with whose eyes and from whose station he endeavours to consider it, is unanimously and violently against us. In such cases, this demigod within the breast appears, like the demigods of the poets, though partly of immortal, yet partly too of mortal extraction. When his judgments are steadily and firmly directed by the sense of praise-worthiness and blame-worthiness, he seems to act suitably to his divine extraction: But when he suffers himself to be astonished and confounded by the judgments of ignorant and weak man, he discovers

his connexion with mortality, and appears to act suitably, rather to the human, than to the divine.

(*TMS* 131)

Whereas the opinions of the impartial spectator were earlier defined to be approximations of what real spectators would actually be thinking, Smith now imagines the impartial spectator as one who may occasionally brave disapprobation by rejecting the (errant) opinions of "all our brethren." The impartial spectator has risen to the level of a "demigod," merely "demi" because at times he will be unable to resist the pull of his desire for sympathy. As long as he functions "steadily and firmly," the "man within the breast" is in fact a god, acting "suitably to his divine extraction." He errs into humanity only when he capitulates to fellow-feeling, going along with the "judgments of ignorant and weak man," allowing the vulnerabilities of his nature to overcome him.

The "man within the breast" is clearly gendered as a man. He represents active spirit, generality, rectitude and self-command, in sharp contrast to the feminine associations of passive body, particularity, impropriety and self-indulgence. "Humanity is the virtue of a woman, generosity that of a man," Smith declares:

Humanity consists merely in the exquisite fellow-feeling which the spectator entertains with the sentiments of the persons principally concerned, so as to grieve for their sufferings, to resent their injuries, and to rejoice at their good fortune. The most humane actions require no self-denial, no self-command, no great exertion of the sense of propriety. They consist only in doing what this exquisite sympathy would of its own accord prompt us to do. But it is otherwise with generosity. We never are generous except when in some respect we prefer some other person to ourselves, and sacrifice some great and important interest of our own to an equal interest of a friend or of a superior.

(*TMS* 191)

This gendered distinction is vexed by an unannounced shift in perspective. When discussing the virtue of woman, Smith describes women as the spectators, remarking how much more readily they enter into the sentiments of the person principally concerned. When discussing the virtue of man, Smith depicts men as the persons principally concerned, praising the self-command they exercise to "accommodate themselves to the sentiments of the spectator" (*TMS* 191). Feminine virtues are passive, doing only what "exquisite sympathy would of its own accord prompt us to do," while masculine virtues are active, requiring us to subdue nature by sacrificing "some great and important interest of our own." When men feel for others, they exhibit a superior form of merit: "Our sensibility to the feelings of others, so far from being inconsistent with the manhood of self-command, is the very principle upon which that manhood is founded" (*TMS* 152). When women feel for others, they "merely" submit to their natural tendencies as women, succumbing to the peculiarities of their gender.

Exercising the masculine virtue of self-command, men can occupy a level of generality and impartiality uncharacteristic of women, Smith reasons. Real men have the general view. The "man of real constancy and firmness" does not "merely affect the sentiments of the impartial spectator," Smith intones: "He really adopts them. He almost identifies himself with, he almost becomes himself that impartial spectator, and scarce even feels but as that great arbiter of his conduct directs him to feel" (*TMS* 146–7). Thus, although Smith's moral empiricism begins with the limitations of personal experience ("I judge of your sight by my sight, of your ear by my ear, of your reason by my reason"), it soon soars into a lofty fantasy of moral objectivity upheld and authorized by "the judgement of the ideal man within the breast" (*TMS* 148). "When our passive feelings are almost always so sordid and selfish, how comes it that our active principles should often be so generous and so noble?" Smith asks. He finds the answer in the masculine impartial spectator, not the feminine power of sympathy:

> It is not the soft power of humanity, it is not that feeble spark of benevolence which Nature has lighted up in the human heart, that is thus capable of counteracting the strongest impulses of self-love. It is a stronger power, a more forcible motive. . . . It is reason, principle, conscience, the inhabitant of the breast, the man within, the great judge and arbiter of our conduct.
>
> (*TMS* 137)

The "soft" and "feeble spark" of fellow-feeling is insufficient to counteract the "impulses of self-love." Something "stronger" and "more forcible" is required, such as "reason," "principle," "conscience." Smith celebrates impartiality as masculinity.

In short, Smith reaches the very conclusion that Sterne will not allow. In Yorick's sermon on conscience, Sterne emphasizes the ubiquity and subtlety of self-deception. The language of Yorick's sermon rings with the same metaphors as Smith's *Theory of Moral Sentiments*: "conscience" is a "god," "placed on high as a judge within us, and intended by our maker as a just and equitable one too" (*TS* 102–5). For Sterne, however, conscience imagined as such may be a false god, a fallibility that Sterne conveys by personifying conscience as a separate man who lodges within the breast, but who is frequently abroad: "Perhaps HE was gone out . . . to fight a duel;—to pay off some debt at play;—or dirty annuity, the bargain of his lust" (*TS* 102). Acknowledging the mind's subtle sophistry of desire, its "imperfect cognizance of what passes," Sterne cannot, as I suggest in the previous chapter, go along with Smith's ideas about the manly coherence of moral empiricism. Sterne contemplates the infinity of interconnections, sympathies, antipathies, accidents and self-deceptions that go into the production of a rational being, while Smith focuses on sympathetic concord primarily to extol the manly virtues of individual autonomy. Sterne's attention to subjective incoherence and peculiarity emphasizes human diversity, while Smith's attention to subjective coherence and general human principles emphasizes human sameness. Although Smith ostensibly develops the figure of the impartial spectator to invalidate the position of radical subjectivism, he in fact seems largely unconcerned with the prospect of creeping moral relativism. *The Theory of Moral Sentiments* rarely treats moral differences in a sustained or serious manner.

Smith's casual assessment of the "difference" between the "virtue of a woman" and "that of a man" offers a case in point. Smith's theory of sympathy presumes that spectators will have difficulties matching their feelings to those of the person principally concerned, and hence it requires the person principally concerned to moderate his feelings to match those of the spectator. This moderation constitutes masculine self-command. Yet this articulation of the theory presumes that all members of society are men, for women, being naturally sympathetic, do not have any difficulty raising their sentiments to the same pitch as those of the person principally concerned. Thus, if all spectators were women and all persons principally concerned were men—a circumstance Smith seems to imagine in his discussion of "humanity" and "generosity," for there he discusses women only as spectators and men only as persons principally concerned—then very little self-command would be necessary for men to retain the sympathy of the spectators. In other words, the masculine autonomy that Smith celebrates as the impartial spectator's triumph turns out to be the very quality that makes the impartial spectator so necessary in the first place: it is masculine autonomy itself, which makes men *as spectators* unable to sympathize fully with the person principally concerned, which in turn necessitates the presence of the impartial spectator. Presuming that the universal human is male, *The Theory of Moral Sentiments* describes the moral development of men among men. Smith's observation that women are different would seem to complicate, perhaps even undo, his argument, yet these complexities of diversity do not detain Smith.

Gender is not the only difference that Smith's assumption of human sameness must suppress. Smith's *Theory* has no way to account for differences in character. For instance, Smith cannot explain why some people strive to be praiseworthy, while others seek only to be praised. To be praiseworthy, Smith asserts,

> we must become the impartial spectators of our own character and conduct. We must endeavour to view them with the eyes of other people, or as other people are likely to view them. When seen in this light, if they appear to us as we wish, we are happy and contented.

But it greatly confirms this happiness and contentment when we find that other people, viewing them with those very eyes with which we, in imagination only, were endeavouring to view them, see them precisely in the same light in which we ourselves had seen them. Their approbation necessarily confirms our own self-approbation.

(*TMS* 114)

The world judges by events, as Walter Shandy knew. Smith, like Henry Fielding, advises us to imagine what the world sees, and to regulate our character and conduct accordingly. Unlike the hermeneutically vexed world of *Tristram Shandy*, in which no two people can be expected to reason alike, the world of Adam Smith, like that of *David Simple*, is populated by already like-minded individuals. We may expect other people to see with "those very eyes" with which we see; we may expect them to see us "precisely in the same light" in which we see ourselves. Self-approbation occurs when minds meet in this way.

Still, Smith knows that some people do not think as he does. They desire not to be praiseworthy, only to be praised. "A woman who paints," a "foolish liar," an "important coxcomb"—these serve as Smith's examples of people who seek "groundless applause." But in recognizing that such people exist, Smith cannot bring himself to acknowledge that their difference from him may be fundamental and sincere. Rather, he concludes that they must know of their error, at some level:

> their vanity arises from so gross an illusion of the imagination, that it is difficult to conceive how any rational creature should be imposed upon by it. When they place themselves in the situation of those whom they fancy they have deceived, they are struck with the highest admiration for their own persons. They look upon themselves, not in the light in which, they know, they ought to appear to their companions, but in that in which they believe their companions actually look upon them. Their superficial weakness and trivial folly hinder them from ever turning their eyes inwards, or from seeing themselves in that despicable point of view in which their own consciences must tell them that they would appear to every body, if the real truth should ever come to be known.

(*TMS* 115)

Confronted by minds of so different a make from his own, Smith cannot comprehend their difference. He therefore throws their rationality into doubt, responding as he had earlier attested any spectator would when viewing a happy madman. Smith does not imagine the sentiments of the mere praise-seekers themselves, only his own feelings were he ever to witness himself reduced to their condition. Accordingly, he presumes that "they know" how they ought to appear to their companions, even though they believe that they appear differently. He maintains that they cannot see what "their own consciences must tell them" the "real truth" is. In Smith's analysis, mere praise-seekers both know and do not know how they really appear to others. Knowing one thing but believing another, they are self-deceived.

Mere praise-seekers, then, occupy a quixotic role in Smith's moral system. They are incomprehensible to Smith, because they refuse to yield to the authority of Smith's impartial spectator, and follow their own authority instead. They are happy madmen. Smith dismisses their beliefs as "fancy," and faults them for irrationally succumbing to a "gross . . . illusion of the imagination." Yet because his own philosophical system presumes imagination to be a founding principle of moral sentiments, Smith finds himself in the quixotic position of judging their imaginations by the measure of his own, of superimposing his own beliefs onto them. He cannot accommodate their difference. He can only trivialize it by presuming that they must agree with him: "they know" (that is, *he* knows) how they ought to appear to their companions, for "their own consciences must tell them" (that is, *his* conscience tells him) how they would appear were the "real truth" (that is, *his* understanding of the situation) to be known. The doctrine of sympathetic imagination can explain in general why moral sentiments vary collectively across time and nations, but it cannot easily distinguish between cultural difference and self-deception on an individual basis.

The problem of self-deception is sufficiently acute to warrant its own chapter in *The Theory of Moral Sentiments*. Unlike Hutcheson, Smith does not believe in the concept of the moral sense, for had we such a faculty, then judging ourselves would be easier than judging others. As our "passions would be more immediately exposed to the view of this faculty, it would judge with more accuracy concerning them, than concerning those of other men, of which it had only a more distant prospect," Smith reasons (*TMS* 158). The distorting influences of self-love would pose no problem were there a moral sense, and Smith sees clearly that self-love is a problem. "This self-deceit, this fatal weakness of mankind, is the source of half the disorders of human life," he ·remarks. Yet he remains hopeful:

> Nature, however, has not left this weakness, which is of so much importance, altogether without a remedy; nor has she abandoned us entirely to the delusions of self-love. Our continual observations upon the conduct of others, insensibly lead us to form to ourselves certain general rules concerning what is fit and proper either to be done or to be avoided. Some of their actions shock all our natural sentiments. We hear every body about us express the like detestation against them. This still further confirms, and even exasperates our natural sense of their deformity. It satisfies us that we view them in the proper light, when we see other people view them in the same light.

We resolve never to be guilty of the like, nor ever, upon any account, to render ourselves in this manner the objects of universal disapprobation. We thus naturally lay down to ourselves a general rule, that all such actions are to be avoided, as tending to render us odious, contemptible, or punishable, the objects of all those sentiments for which we have the greatest dread and aversion. Other actions, on the contrary, call forth our approbation, and we hear every body around us express the same favourable opinion concerning them. They excite all those sentiments for which we have by nature the strongest desire; the love, the gratitude, the admiration of mankind. We become ambitious of performing the like; and thus naturally lay down to ourselves a rule of another kind, that every opportunity of acting in this manner is carefully to be sought after.

It is thus that the general rules of morality are formed.

(*TMS* 159)

These general rules of morality, Smith confidently declares, "when they have been fixed in our mind by habitual reflection, are of great use in correcting the misrepresentations of self-love concerning what is fit and proper to be done in our particular situation" (*TMS* 160). He describes a process in which the "natural sentiments" of individuals are strengthened by the universal confirmation of humankind into the authority of moral law. Once more, Smith's analysis allows no room for significant rational differences among people. Our "natural sentiments" are shocked or pleased, everyone agrees with us, and so we lay down a general rule.

Smith, however, does not mean that each individual repeats this process in the course of his own moral development. Rather, Smith appears to imagine this sequence of events as a conjectural history of moral origins, a process mysteriously enacted long ago to create the general rules. These general rules, passed down through the ages, take on added importance to Smith, because in fact he doubts the ability of each individual to derive these rules independently. Most men must take these rules on authority, for the natural sentiment from which the rules arise can be felt only by an exceptional few. For most men, "duty," not feeling, is the principle of moral action:

The regard to those general rules of conduct, is what is properly called a sense of duty, a principle of the greatest consequence in human life, and the only principle by which the bulk of mankind are capable of directing their actions. Many men behave very decently, and through the whole of their lives avoid any considerable degree of blame, who yet, perhaps, never felt the sentiment upon the propriety of which we found our approbation of their conduct, but acted merely from a regard to what they saw were the established rules of behaviour.

(*TMS* 162)

216

What had appeared to be rooted in natural sentiment, and upheld by the correspondent feelings of all mankind, has now paled into a set of "established rules" that "the bulk of mankind" follow because that is all they are "capable" of doing.[21] They have "never felt the sentiment" that gave rise to the general rules, so they do not act in accordance with what Smith had earlier extolled as "reason, principle, conscience, the inhabitant of the breast." Instead, they passively defer to the laws they know to be already written. Though Parson Yorick might approve, Sterne would smile at this moral quixotism. In typical sentimental style, Smith's argument begins with the universal authority of nature, only to retreat to the exclusive authority of exquisite feeling. The result is an argument utterly ungrounded. Natural sentiment, never felt by "the bulk of mankind," cannot be universal, while exclusive sentiment, by definition, would never acquire the universal confirmation of mankind.

Like Mandeville, Smith is a moral empiricist without a moral sense. As such, he is left with no secure foundation for moral virtue. Though he insists that general rules are founded "upon experience of what, in particular instances, our moral faculties, our natural sense of propriety, approve, or disapprove of" (*TMS* 159), he can present no one who ever felt this way. He distrusts the sentiments of "the bulk of mankind," but depreciates "exquisite fellow-feeling" as "merely" a womanish virtue. Eventually, Smith suggests that moral feeling is not to be found in individual sentiments at all, but in the conformity of individuals to general rules. "Without this sacred regard to general rules," Smith declares,

> there is no man whose conduct can be much depended upon. It is this which constitutes the most essential difference between a man of principle and honour and a worthless fellow. The one adheres, on all occasions, steadily and resolutely to his maxims, and preserves through the whole of his life one even tenour of conduct. The other, acts variously and accidentally, as humour, inclination, or interest chance to be uppermost.
>
> (*TMS* 163)

Because "no man" can be trusted to make his own rules, each man must submit to the authority of the already written rules, adhering "steadily and resolutely to his maxims." The image is one of quixotic persistence; after all, the perpetually proverb-quoting Sancho Panza stuck steadily and resolutely to his maxims. Smith requires the "man of principle and honour" to persevere in dogged submission to the sacred authority of the past, even though Smith can offer no coherent account of how these general rules solidified out of the mists of time. Haunting Smith's discussion is Mandeville's loathed definition of "Honour," "a Chimera without Truth or Being, an Invention of Moralists and Politicians," that signifies a certain Principle of Virtue not related to Religion, found in some Men that keeps 'em close to their Duty and Engagements whatever they be, as for Example a Man of Honour enters into a Conspiracy with others to Murder a King; he is obliged to go thorough Stitch with it; and if overcome by Remorse or Good-nature he startles at the Enormity of his Purpose, discovers the Plot, and turns a Witness against his Accomplices, he then forfeits his Honour, at least among the Party he belonged to.

(Mandeville 1: 198)

Like Smith's man of honor, Mandeville's quixotic man of honor—"*Don Quixote*" was the last great practitioner of "ancient Honour" (Mandeville 1: 199)—can only be depended upon insofar as he holds steadily and resolutely to his maxims, going "thorough Stitch" with his sense of "Duty." Though Smith does try to distinguish his man of honor from Mandeville's, by rooting the principles of virtue in religion, his effort is undermined by the history of moral sentiments that he himself tells. The "*general Rules of Morality*" are "*justly regarded as the Laws of the Deity,*" Smith proclaims, for they are "first impressed by nature, and afterwards confirmed by reasoning and philosophy" to be "the commands and laws of the Deity" (*TMS* 163). In other words, the process whereby general rules come to be recognized as divine law merely mimics that which establishes the general rules in the first place; in the former as in the latter, natural sentiment prompts, then the approval of mankind confirms. Divine law justifies the general rules of morality, because the general rules of morality have been determined to be divine law.

The circularity of Smith's arguments was not lost on his contemporaries. Thomas Reid, Smith's successor at the University of Glasgow, complains of Smith's *Theory*:

it is obvious that according to [Smith's] System there is no fixed Standard of Virtue at all[;] it depends not upon our own Actions but upon the Tone of our Passions[,] which in different men is different from Constitution. . . . It is evident that the ultimate Measure and Standard of Right and Wrong in human Conduct according to this System of Sympathy, is not any fixed Judgment grounded upon Truth or upon the dictates of a well informed Conscience but the variable opinions and passions of Men. . . . Its lesson amounts to this—we are to despise the trustworthy voice of our own conscience, and to run after the fallible imaginations of other men.[22]

For Reid, as apparently for Gilbert Elliot, Smith's virtue is not sufficiently independent of popular opinion. Smith's "System of Sympathy" allows nature to be overcome by custom, and "Truth" to be supplanted by the fictitious and "fallible imaginations of other men."

Likewise, Adam Ferguson, in a fictional dialogue between Robert Clerk, David Hume and Adam Smith, criticizes *The Theory of Moral Sentiments* for its equivocations. "Your Book is to me a Heap of absolute Nonsense," Clerk declares to a "stunned" Adam Smith in this dialogue. "How can I believe that Person is in the right because I sympathise with him?" Clerk presses:

> May not I myself be in the wrong? Does the presence of any sympathy ascertain a good action, or the want, a bad one?
>
> SMITH: No! I have cleared up that point. Parties concerned in any transaction may be willing each to flatter himself or both Mutually to flatter one another, But to the monitor may not fail to present himself. The well informed and impartial observer will bring to view what the Ignorant or prejudiced would overlook.
>
> CLERK: That is convenient, to be able to bring Virtue itself to aid when actual Sympathy fails. You began with calling Sympathy to explain Moral Sentiment. You now call up moral sentiment to explain itself: what is a well informed & impartial observer, but a Virtuous Person whose Sympathy may be relied on as a Test of Virtue?[23]

To Ferguson's Clerk, the possibility of self-deception ("May not I myself be in the wrong?") undoes Smith's moral system. The impartial spectator cannot be both the product of sympathy and the corrective to sympathy, "when actual Sympathy fails." Moral sentiment must exist independently of sympathy, and therefore Smith's concept of "sympathy" explains nothing at all. Even Smith's comments on Mandeville's system, though they do indicate that Smith does not regard himself as a follower of Mandeville, do not put to rest the suspicion that Smith's "praiseworthiness" might be another name for Mandeville's "flattery begot upon pride." Smith refutes Mandeville by merely assuming that moral virtue is real, the very premise that Mandeville's system denies. "There is an affinity between vanity and the love of true glory, as both these passions aim at acquiring esteem and approbation," Smith concedes: "But they are different in this, that the one is a just, reasonable, and equitable passion, while the other is unjust, absurd, and ridiculous" (*TMS* 310). Of course, reason is rational, and absurdity is ridiculous. Smith presents Mandeville's error as self-evident.

Founded upon variable "Passion" rather than rational "Action," endlessly supple in its reasonings, and repeatedly reduced to womanish particularity even as it strives for manly generality, Smith's system, by eighteenth-century standards, is quixotic. In keeping with the sentimental mode, it represents moral diversity only to deny the validity of these differences. Smith's moral theory cannot fathom rational political difference; his impartial spectator cannot reconcile partisan opinions to the general view. Faced with the "animosity of hostile factions," the impartial spectator vanishes. "It is needless to observe, I presume," Smith comments dryly, acknowledging the irrationality of popular opinion,

> that both rebels and heretics are those unlucky persons, who, when things have come to a certain degree of violence, have the misfortune to be of the weaker party. In a nation distracted by faction, there are, no doubt, always a few, though commonly but a very few, who preserve their judgment untainted by the general contagion. They seldom amount to more than, here and there, a solitary individual, without any influence, excluded, by his own candour, from the confidence of either party, and who, though he may be one of the wisest, is necessarily, upon that very account, one of the most insignificant men in the society. . . . The real, revered, and impartial spectator, therefore, is, upon no occasion, at a greater distance than amidst the violence and rage of contending parties. To them, it may be said, that such a spectator scarce exists any where in the universe.
>
> (*TMS* 155–6)

In times of factionalism, Smith's impartial spectator is helpless to resist the arbitrary law of the stronger. Here, sympathy does not mean a mere concord of sentiments, for that would make moral sentiment vulnerable to popular opinion. Smith's *Theory of Moral Sentiments*, like sentimentalism itself, acknowledges moral diversity only to deny it. Smith refuses to recognize political difference as rational difference, as an intellectual problem to be reckoned with. Instead, he represents factionalism as a simple inversion of the normal moral order, a special case in which the contagion of tainted judgment has become too "general," while the wisdom of virtue has become too particular, "a solitary individual, without any influence." Smith's analysis always focuses on the general—on general rules of conduct or on the general contagion of misconduct—for the impartial spectator, "the great judge and arbiter of our conduct" (*TMS* 137), functions only at the most general of levels. He can never judge or arbitrate particular disputes, and therefore "scarce exists" amid "the violence and rage of contending parties." By focusing only on generality and sameness—what everyone has in common—Smith describes a universal moral system that coheres only when everyone already agrees. His system of morals works only when it is least needed.

The philosopher's trade

Adam Smith's *Theory of Moral Sentiments* would probably be little read today had he not gone on to write the more famous and influential *Inquiry into the Nature and Causes of the Wealth of Nations*. As the founding text of the modern science of economics, *The Wealth of Nations* speaks with an authority often presumed to transcend the particular circumstances of history and culture. *The*

Wealth of Nations appears to be universal and eternal. "More than ever before, Adam Smith must be reckoned the most influential political thinker of the modern world," wrote one reviewer in 1996.[24] In that same year, an economist could introduce a discussion of Smith's masterpiece by pointing to its increasing centrality at the end of the Cold War:

> At a time when several Eastern European countries are seeking to establish the market system, at least some of their intellectuals may have a desire to scrutinize the origins of Western support for it. To most people, the classic work *The Wealth of Nations* would seem to be the first place to begin.[25]

If not the guiding light of public policy from the time of its inception, *The Wealth of Nations* has since risen to that influential position, and seems to be accruing ever more credibility.[26] Within the context of eighteenth-century British literature, however, this deference to the authority of *The Wealth of Nations* might best be described as quixotic, for it uncritically attributes universal understanding to one particular perspective. In *The Wealth of Nations* the general view belongs only to the philosopher, who, like the impartial spectator of *The Theory of Moral Sentiments*, must be simultaneously *of* and *above* the system he regards. At issue in *The Wealth of Nations* is the authority of the philosopher and his modern descendant, the economist, as coherent and rational observers.

The problematic relation between particular experiences and general truth concerns Smith from the very outset of *The Wealth of Nations*. Beginning his work, Smith seeks to establish, as a general truth, that division of labor vastly increases productivity. Economic historians have lamented that Smith chose to illustrate so important a truth with the example of a "silly little pin factory," rather than that of a more extensive manufacture, such as the Carron iron-works, which maintained a warehouse in Smith's own hometown of Kirkcaldy.[27] Smith, I suggest, selected the pin factory as his example precisely because it is little. He chose it for the benefit of skeptical empiricists. As Smith explains, the efficacy of division of labor can best be confirmed in small manufactures, where "those employed in every different branch of the work can often be collected into the same workhouse, and placed at once under the view of the spectator."[28] Pin factories, unlike ironworks, allow for easy empirical verification. Moreover, pin factories, unlike ironworks, were clichés by the later eighteenth century. In England, the example of the pin factory was used to illustrate the effects of division of labor as early as 1730, and by 1759, was so well known that Oliver Goldsmith could cryptically allude to it while satirizing the mechanical production of literary magazines.[29] In presenting the "silly little pin factory" as his example, Smith could hardly have been more uncontroversial.

Smith, as I have argued above, habitually prefers to overstate points of agreement, while understating points of difference. Using the pin factory to emphasize what everyone would agree to, Smith deflects attention away from the more contentious points raised by his analysis. The easy assurance with which he depicts the workings of the divided economy in this opening section of *The Wealth of Nations* ignores the problem of knowledge and reason that undermines his system. John Barrell has argued that much imaginative literature of the eighteenth century sought to comprehend social diversity, to find "proportion and unity" in an economy recognized to be increasingly differentiated and complex.[30] But because to have an occupation meant to be interested, it was difficult to locate anyone capable of disinterestedness. "Professional men, tradesmen, merchants, and (when they were considered) artisans and labourers did not have that potential," Barrell explains, "for the practitioners of any particular occupation were assumed to be concerned solely or largely with the immediate ends of that occupation."[31] Like Fielding's Dr Drench and Mr Brief, working men are too quixotic to have rational opinions, too concerned with the immediate ends of their own (pre)occupations.

By carving society into increasingly distinct divisions, occupational specialization precludes general knowledge by requiring workers to concentrate on ever more minute forms of particular knowledge. "[I]n consequence of the division of labour," Smith writes, "the whole of every man's attention comes naturally to be directed towards some one very simple object" (*WN* 1: 20). With this sharpening of focus, technical advancements and refinements in mechanical skills flourish. Broader intellectual skill, however, disappears from the general population and comes to be designated as a distinct trade. Smith defines "philosophers or men of speculation" as those

> whose trade it is, not to do anything, but to observe every thing; and who, upon that account, are often capable of combining together the powers of the most distant and dissimilar objects. In the progress of society, philosophy or speculation becomes, like every other employment, the principal or sole trade and occupation of a particular class of citizens.
>
> (*WN* 1: 21)

Here, the general becomes the particular, as "philosophy or speculation," which combines together the "distant and dissimilar," becomes the province of a "particular class of citizens." Oxymoronically, philosophers specialize in general knowledge. According to Barrell, the "economic philosopher" thus emerges as a "transcendent subject" who sees "transcendent truth."[32] Such a conclusion, I suggest, oversimplifies Smith's relation to his own occupational knowledge, in the same way that the metaphor of the "invisible hand," for which his work has become so famous, evades the most pressing question introduced by his theory. In an empirical world, why should we trust an invisible hand? In a specialized world, how do we recognize transcendent truth?

The metaphor of the "invisible hand" appears only once in *The Wealth of Nations*, where Smith uses it to argue that transcendent understanding of the economy is unnecessary. For Smith, albeit in a manner more reminiscent of Mandeville than of Pope, self-interest and social are the same: by pursuing one's own interests, one unwittingly pursues the public good as well.

> As every individual, therefore, endeavours as much as he can both to employ his capital in the support of domestick industry, and so to direct that industry that its produce may be of the greatest value; every individual necessarily labours to render the annual revenue of the society as great as he can. He generally, indeed, neither intends to promote the publick interest, nor knows how much he is promoting it. By preferring the support of domestick to that of foreign industry, he intends only his own security; and by directing that industry in such a manner as its produce may be of the greatest value, he intends only his own gain, and he is in this, as in many other cases, led by an invisible hand to promote an end which was no part of his intention. Nor is it always the worse for the society that it was no part of it. By pursuing his own interest he frequently promotes that of the society more effectually than when he really intends to promote it.
>
> (*WN* 1: 456)

Smith also uses this metaphor of the "invisible hand" similarly in *The Theory of Moral Sentiments* (*TMS* 184). In both instances, the metaphor praises the efficiency of a system devoid of general understanding. Under the guiding invisible hand, the limitations of mind—those selfish concerns with one's own peculiar circumstances—will do more to promote social good than will intentional efforts on behalf of "the publick interest." Ordinary people need not comprehend the workings of the invisible hand in order to benefit from it. Philosophers, however, are a separate class of citizens. "[C]apable of combining together the powers of the most distant and dissimilar objects," Smith's "philosophers" are those whose mental efforts should most readily follow the workings of the invisible hand itself. As tradesmen, they deal in universal knowledge of the public good, producing ways of comprehending social diversity, and creating a unified understanding of society's various and competing interests. In other words, philosophers produce rational authority.

The rational authority Smith imagines as the product of the philosophical trade, however, is tenuous at best. In the "History of astronomy," Smith's ambivalence toward philosophical authority had appeared in his discussion of the laughing artisan, who found the philosopher's ruminations upon self-evident nature to be ridiculous. If philosophy is really a trade in which the philosopher produces "a chain of invisible objects to join together events that occur in an order familiar to all the world," then why should "the world" trade anything for what the philosopher has to offer ("Astronomy" 45)? Philosophers appear to offer explanations for problems that no one else has.

Philosophical dignity suffers further humiliations at Smith's hands in *The Wealth of Nations*. Discussing the factors that determine wage rates across various employments, Smith notes that the "liberal and honourable professions," though "evidently under-recompenced," still draw numerous novitiates: "all the most generous and liberal spirits are eager to crowd into them," because such persons readily overestimate their chance of success in these fields (*WN* 1: 123). "Put your son apprentice to a shoemaker," Smith explains, "there is little doubt of his learning to make a pair of shoes: But send him to study law, it is at least twenty to one if ever he makes such proficiency as will enable him to live by the business" (*WN* 1: 122). In the learned trades, even the successful do not enjoy their proper rewards, Smith warns:

> In a perfectly fair lottery, those who draw the prizes ought to gain all that is lost by those who draw the blanks. In a profession where twenty fail for one that succeeds, that one ought to gain all that should have been gained by the unsuccessful twenty. . . . How extravagant soever the fees of counsellors at law may sometimes appear, their real retribution is never equal to this.
>
> (*WN* 1: 122–3)

Even as a "lottery," the practice of law "as well as that of many other liberal and honourable professions" is a losing proposition. Thus, Smith concludes, it is "romantick hopes," not rational economic expectation, that motivate those who choose to enter the "liberal professions" such as "physick," "law" and especially "poetry and philosophy" (*WN* 1: 123, 126). Through the selection of their trade, all philosophers have already proven themselves to be very capable of poor judgment.

As a final irony, the "invisible hand" itself is a strange metaphor for Smith to employ, seemingly inapt in at least two ways. First, Smith had written of an invisible hand once before, but to a much different effect: in the "History of astronomy," the "invisible hand of Jove" had been the frightened invention of "pusillanimous superstition" and "impotence of mind," a sign that the rational and manful intellect was yet in its infancy. And second, as Smith was well aware, "invisible" things can hardly be expected to command universal assent. In a discussion of social rank reminiscent of Mandeville's satiric account of "Honour" as an "invisible Ornament," Smith reminds his readers of the ceaseless controversies that surround "invisible qualities":

> The qualifications of the body, unless supported by those of the mind, can give little authority in any period of society. He is a very strong man who, by mere strength of body, can force two weak ones to obey him. The qualifications of the mind can alone give very great

authority. They are, however, invisible qualities; always disputable, and generally disputed. No society, whether barbarous or civilized, has ever found it convenient to settle the rules of precedency, of rank and subordination, according to those invisible qualities; but according to something that is more plain and palpable.

(WN 2: 711)

"[A]lways disputable, and generally disputed," the "invisible qualities" of mind are paradoxically both the only source of "very great authority," and an authority that compels very little assent. "No society" settles questions of merit by these invisible qualities, for it is more convenient to determine rank by qualities "more plain and palpable." (Gender might be one of these less rational but more palpable marks of distinction, as Smith's contrast between "mere strength of body" and "qualifications of the mind" suggests, perhaps unintentionally.) What authority can the philosopher have, if philosophical understanding is unnecessary to daily life, and "invisible qualities" of mind are generally disputed? At the core of Smith's economic analysis is the problem of quixotic reason. The philosopher embodies a rational authority that few people respect. He makes the artisan laugh.

It is thus a matter of some convenience that the empirical science of economics now chooses to find its justification in the metaphor of the invisible hand—not a great and wise mind, but an invisible hand. Quixotic reason is a problem that the "invisible hand" hides in plain sight. A hand does not think, after all. By imagining economic order as the work of an invisible hand rather than the product of numerous and varied thinking minds, the philosopher (or economist) need not risk his already fragile authority before the laughter of common artisans. He evades acknowledging the limitations of his own under-standing by refusing to imagine the potential diversity of all those other minds. The philosopher's trade is a paradoxical activity, producing universal authority that looks silly to most. Like the impartial spectator of *The Theory of Moral Sentiments*, the philosopher is both of the system (a tradesman within the economy) and above the system (independent of the professional biases that beset everyone else). He is both particular and general at the same time.

The philosopher's situation is complicated by a further requirement, for it is not enough that he have the general view. He must also be recognized (by all those other minds) to have the general view, or else his philosophical confla-tion of particular and general will become indistinguishable from a quixotic conflation of particular and general. In division of labor, Smith sees a real threat to the rationality of intellectual, moral and political life. "In the progress of the division of labour," Smith writes in a passage now famous,

the employment of the far greater part of those who live by labour, that is, of the great body of the people, comes to be confined to a very few simple operations; frequently one or two. But the understandings

225

of the greater part of men are necessarily formed by their ordinary employments. The man whose whole life is spent in performing a few simple operations, of which the effects too are, perhaps always the same, or very nearly the same, has no occasion to exert his understanding, or to exercise his invention in finding out expedients for removing difficulties which never occur. He naturally loses, therefore, the habit of such exertion, and generally becomes as stupid and ignorant as it is possible for a human creature to become. The torpor of his mind renders him, not only incapable of relishing or bearing a part in any rational conversation, but of conceiving any generous, noble, or tender sentiment, and consequently of forming any just judgment concerning many even of the ordinary duties of private life. Of the great and extensive interests of his country, he is altogether incapable of judging; and unless very particular pains have been taken to render him otherwise, he is equally incapable of defending his country in war.

(WN 2: 781–2)

Division of labor makes men "stupid," for it confines the vast majority of them to a life of regularity, repetition and utter predictability. Smith regrets that such a system thwarts laborers from contemplating "difficulties which never occur," for lacking this exercise, they lose their imaginative, and hence their philosophical, capacities. They become "not only incapable of relishing or bearing a part in any rational conversation," but perhaps more importantly, incapable also of feeling "any generous, noble, or tender sentiment." Blinkered by their particular circumstances and so unable to see the general view, their sympathetic, and hence their moral, abilities desert them. They can no longer be trusted to form "any just judgment concerning many even of the ordinary duties of private life." Public life is out of the question, for such cramped understandings could never comprehend the "great and extensive interests" of a nation, and would be "equally incapable of defending [the] country in war."

In short, lost to the drudgery of economic specialization is masculine virtue. A stupid man can no longer exercise generosity, putting others' interests before his own. The regularity of his life "corrupts the courage of his mind," making him fear the "adventurous life of the soldier," and corrupts "the activity of his body," sapping his "vigour and perseverance" in all employments but the one to which he has grown accustomed. "His dexterity at his own particular trade seems, in this manner, to be acquired at the expence of his intellectual, social, and martial virtues," Smith concludes (WN 2: 783). Division of labor may accelerate productivity and increase wealth, but it also increases social diversity and undermines patriotism. The title of The Wealth of Nations itself describes the paradox: what is good for wealth may not be good for nations.[33] Like Benedict Anderson, Smith seems to regard nations as

226

"imagined communities."[34] Specialization threatens nationalist sentiment by atrophying the imaginative capacities of "the great body of the people."

It is therefore in the government's own interest to subsidize education for the working poor, Smith contends, lest the "mental mutilation" of the masses render them incapable of recognizing and respecting rational authority. "The state . . . derives no inconsiderable advantage from their instruction," Smith reasons:

> The more they are instructed, the less liable they are to the delusions of enthusiasm and superstition, which, among ignorant nations, frequently occasion the most dreadful disorders. An instructed and intelligent people . . . feel themselves, each individually, more respectable, and more likely to obtain the respect of their lawful superiors, and they are therefore more disposed to respect those superiors. They are more disposed to examine, and more capable of seeing through, the interested complaints of faction and sedition, and they are, upon that account, less apt to be misled into any wanton or unnecessary opposition to the measures of government.
>
> (WN 2: 788)

Uncorrected by a sound general education, a nation of specialists would be a nation of quixotes. Their "delusions of enthusiasm" would "occasion the most dreadful disorders," for they would respect no authority but their own, while being incapable of disinterested examination. Widespread "faction," "sedition" and reckless "opposition to the measures of government" would prevail. For the sake of peace and stability, Smith argues, education cannot be left to the dispensations of an invisible hand that does not think.

In attending to the relation between education and the free market, Smith finally confronts directly the problem of rational thought in a diversified economy.[35] How is rational thought to be defined and produced? The instability of the philosopher's trade, its vacillation between the ideal of philosophical disinterestedness and the reality of professional interestedness, frustrates Smith's analysis. "A private teacher could never find his account in teaching, either an exploded and antiquated system of a science acknowledged to be useful, or a science universally believed to be a mere useless and pedantick heap of sophistry and nonsense," Smith asserts, advocating the salutary effects of competition among educators (WN 2: 780–1). Private teachers, being unaffiliated with academic institutions, must teach only the best and most useful information to stay in business. Were they to teach "antiquated systems" and "nonsense," they would soon lose all their students. Competition among philosophers for students improves education because philosophers, being self-interested like everyone else, naturally do as little as possible to get by. To support this claim, Smith points to the abuses of "publick teachers," whose affiliation with academic institutions shields them from competition.

"In modern times, the diligence of publick teachers is more or less corrupted by the circumstances, which render them more or less independent of their success and reputation in their particular professions," Smith observes (*WN* 2: 780). As a result of this insulation from market forces, scholastic institutions such as Smith's own Balliol College, Oxford, can continue to teach "useless," "antiquated" and "exploded" systems.[36] "Were there no publick institutions," Smith avers,

> a gentleman, after going through, with application and abilities, the most complete course of education, which the circumstances of the times were supposed to afford, could not come into the world completely ignorant of every thing which is the common subject of conversation among gentlemen and men of the world.
>
> (*WN* 2: 781)

In Smith's opinion, the usefulness of education has been sacrificed to the sloth of those public teachers who have the power to confer or deny credentials. Public teachers are protected from competition by their colleges' near monopolistic powers of graduation; a private teacher may confer an education, but only a college can confer a degree. It might seem as though Smith would support a free market in education.

A free market in education is not Smith's ideal, however, as his discussion of the laboring poor shows. When Smith imagines a world without fixed rational standards, he does not like the "enthusiasm" and "superstition" that he foresees. He therefore proposes a two-pronged preventative: that the "publick" encourage "the children of the common people" to acquire the "most essential parts of education by giving them small premiums," while at the same time, imposing

> upon almost the whole body of the people the necessity of acquiring those most essential parts of education, by obliging every man to undergo an examination or probation in them before he can obtain the freedom in any corporation, or be allowed to set up any trade either in a village or a town corporate.
>
> (*WN* 2: 786)

Smith advises that the government grant or withhold the credentials necessary to a tradesman's livelihood, based on the tradesman's performance on a required examination into his command of the "most essential parts of education." A man "can obtain the freedom" to work, only by passing the test. In effect, Smith's remedy would establish an *actual* monopoly in educational credentials, not just a *monopolistic* school system. He makes no mention of who will write or grade the exam.

Nor does Smith choose to limit this proposal only to the laboring and presumably stupefied bulk of humanity. Even higher ranks of men are prone to enthusiasm, Smith observes. To curtail this "dangerous" and "troublesome" zeal, he recommends "the study of science and philosophy, which the state might render almost universal among all the people of middling or more than middling rank" (*WN* 2: 796). This scientific and philosophical education would be maintained not by subsidizing teachers,

> but by instituting some sort of probation, even in the higher and more difficult sciences, to be undergone by every person before he was permitted to exercise any liberal profession, or before he could be received as a candidate for any honourable office of trust or profit.
>
> (*WN* 2: 796)

Smith's educational plan, even for those practitioners of a "liberal profession" such as the philosopher's trade, is to deny a livelihood to anyone unable to meet the academic requirements of a government monopoly on educational credentials. Forced here to consider the potential diversity of all those other minds—for educational differences create intellectual differences—Smith retreats into a fuzzy universalism, prudently supporting the "essential parts of education" without specifying what they are. Faced with the question of where rational standards come from in a diversified world, Smith simply defers to the authority of an unspecified government bureaucrat who will administer exams and evaluate probationers.

The problem of rational thought amidst diversity, I suggest, is precisely the difficulty that Adam Smith, at the outset of *The Wealth of Nations*, sought to avoid by discussing "a silly little pin factory" instead of a larger, more extensive manufacture. The problem is that of generalization: how to infer general theory from particular examples, in order to ensure that the public sphere justly transcends the private realm. Smith seeks to protect the (public) general view against usurpation by (particular) private interests. He thus urges government intervention in education, but only in those instances in which he perceives the public good to be endangered without it, for example, when the state is weakened by stupid workmen unable to sympathize with the "great and extensive interests" of their country, or when enthusiasts of any rank stir up faction and sedition. In contrast, private education for the private sphere, Smith happily leaves to the free market. "There are no publick institutions for the education of women," he writes:

> and there is accordingly nothing useless, absurd, or fantastical in the common course of their education. They are taught what their parents or guardians judge it necessary or useful for them to learn; and they are taught nothing else. Every part of their education tends evidently to some useful purpose; either to improve the natural attractions of their person, or to form their mind to reserve, modesty, to chastity, and to oeconomy: to render them both likely to

become the mistresses of a family, and to behave properly when they have become such. In every part of her life a woman feels some conveniency or advantage from every part of her education. It seldom happens that a man, in any part of his life, derives any conveniency or advantage from some of the most laborious and troublesome parts of his education.

(*WN* 2: 781)

Women's education is entirely practical—there is "nothing useless, absurd, or fantastical" in it—for women are not expected to have any general knowledge. Women have only one occupation to understand: mistress of a family. Their curriculum, therefore, may be safely limited to whatever their parents or guardians judge necessary in that regard. Neither Adam Smith nor the state has any further interest in the education of women, because women are not educated for public life. Women do not need the general view. Female virtues are all retiring, confining, limiting: "reserve," "modesty," "chastity," "oeconomy" (*not* political economy). Hence, according to Smith, women always feel "conveniency or advantage" from their educations, whereas men do not. Women can be taught useful particulars and "nothing else"; they do not have to learn general theories. Smith places women in the role of the laughing artisan: fitted to their station, taught nothing absurd and not expected to contemplate "difficulties which never occur." Women are like silly little pin factories, isolated models of how the system could work if only it were smaller and more easily contextualized. Smith's men, however, must be more extensive, more imaginative, more philosophical, more willing to puzzle their brains over "events that occur in an order familiar to all the world." Smith's men, in other words, must be a touch quixotic, for that is the nature of theorists who work amidst almost infinite variety.

EPILOGUE

"The grandsons of Adam Smith": of rational limits and quixotic excess

> But the age of chivalry is gone. That of sophisters, economists; and calculators has succeeded; and the glory of Europe is extinguished forever.
>
> Edmund Burke, *Reflections on the Revolution in France* (1790)[1]

The "grandsons of Adam Smith" is the phrase used by Donald McCloskey to describe the familial relation between modern economists and the famous Scottish philosopher.[2] Like many families, this one likes to keep a few things about itself hidden. "I will tell you a secret," writes Paul A. Samuelson, the Nobel Prize-winning economist, in a conspiratorial gesture:

> Economists are supposed to be dry as dust, dismal fellows. This is quite wrong, the reverse of the truth. Scratch a hard-boiled economist of the libertarian persuasion and you find a Don Quixote underneath. No lovesick maiden ever pined for the days of medieval chivalry with such sentimental impracticality as some economists long for the return to a Victorian marketplace that is completely free. Completely free? Well, almost so. There must, of course, be the constable to ensure that voluntary contracts are enforced and to protect the property rights of each molecule which is an island unto itself.[3]

But under what conditions is Samuelson's "secret" a secret? It is an inversion of ideas now long familiar to us, though once lamented dramatically by Burke as the end of chivalry. We all know that economists are supposed to be "hard-boiled": rational, practical, individualist, law-abiding, public-minded, scientific, masculine and committed to daring capitalist freedom. The revelation of "a Don Quixote underneath" undoes all these assumptions, turning economists into their supposed (secret) opposite—"a lovesick maiden": sentimental, impractical, dependent, errant, self-indulgent, preferring ideal reveries to scientific realities, and yearning for the security of gendered, feudal bondage (a knight in shining armor). Samuelson's secret is the truth of the

231

philosopher's trade, when seen in the context of the forgotten relations between eighteenth-century quixotism, sentimentalism and political economy. His secret points to the insight that the pursuit of universal rationality is quixotism.

Within the cultural history I have traced out in the foregoing chapters, economists are of course Don Quixotes underneath. This conclusion is practically self-evident, as economics—the self-proclaimed "Queen of the Social Sciences"[4]—grounds its practice upon the assumption of universal rationality,[5] models its method upon the empiricism of Newtonian science,[6] and ambitiously extends its scope to annex literary study, the social sciences, ethics and historical interpretation, as sub-fields.[7] By eighteenth-century standards, the pretensions of modern economics could hardly be more quixotic. Yet, in modern times, economics has managed to lay claim to the authority of "science" in a way that other humanistic disciplines have not, and has used its newfound scientific authority to belittle the interests, methods and conclusions of these other fields. George J. Stigler, for example, reportedly maintains that "it is folly to become concerned with methodology before the age of sixty-five" (so much for philosophy and theory).[8] At any rate, he certainly advises that "the word 'past'" is irrelevant to the reading of "scientific works," for "the correct way to read Adam Smith is the correct way to read the forthcoming issues of a professional journal" (so much for philology, literary theory and historicisms of all kinds).[9] That Stigler's strictures speak to disciplinary hierarchy, not merely to disciplinary difference, can be inferred from his observation that "the young economist will increasingly share the view of the more advanced formal sciences that the history of the discipline is best left to those underendowed for fully professional work at the modern level."[10] In other words, those who can—do; those who can't—study the humanities. In Stigler's master narrative of "science," humanistic inquiries are the intellectual scraps that fall to "underendowed" and out-dated amateurs.

This tyrannical rhetoric of economics strains against the discipline's assumptions of universal rationality in much the same way as the eighteenth-century quixotic held reason and arbitrary power in a taut and uneasy relation.[11] (If rationality is universal, then what need is there for hierarchy?) Moreover, like quixotism, economics has close ties to the sentimental mode of understanding. As Sheldon Wolin has argued, Lockean liberal theory accounts only for the "outside" of mankind, not for "interior life": "All that men could know for certain was the consequences of an individual's actions, never his reasons for doing them."[12] Empirical method, as many eighteenth-century authors knew, offers only an awkward approach to the study of humanity. A similar point was made, at the beginning of this century, by the prominent economist Frank Knight, whose insistence on the importance of "*communication between consciousnesses*" left his colleagues only a choice between imposing meaning from the outside (quixotism) or presuming immediate sympathetic understanding (sentimentalism). "[W]e have . . . reasons for accepting consciousness as real and potent in the fact of *communication*," Knight writes:

> The conclusive reason for believing that an action is conscious is that the subject can *tell us so*, and tell us about the motives. Logically, the behaviourist is right; we do not perceive consciousness, in any other person at least; we cannot prove or verify it; we only infer it from behaviour. But in spite of logic we all recognize that as a matter of fact we know consciousness more surely and positively than we know the behaviour from which theoretically we infer it. We cannot scientifically explain, except most superficially, how we communicate feelings or read expression in the looks and acts and words of others. Yet if anything in human life is clear it is that our whole intellectual life is built upon the fact of communication. Without it we could never develop the idea of objectivity, the foundation of scientific reasoning . . . the test of reality is the possibility of verification, which depends on communication with the consciousness of others.[13]

For Knight, the science of economics (and any science) must always be bounded by the limits of interpretation and communication. The "outside" approach ("we do not perceive consciousness . . . only infer it from behaviour") foregrounds the study of interpretation, placing the authority of science upon the uncertain, irrational ("in spite of logic") foundation of the self-evident (what we all "surely and positively" know). Acknowledging the logic of inferring others' consciousness from their behavior, Knight nonetheless chooses to subordinate this empirical way of knowing to our supposedly intuitive knowledge of others' consciousness. He is perfectly willing to concede that "man is at heart a sentimentalist, as far, in general, as he can be and live, or at little farther,"[14] a conclusion that leads Knight to value "unscientific" approaches to humanistic study. Rejecting the rigor of utilitarian ethical standards as "in essence merely the ethics of power,"[15] Knight proposes that the field of economics be enlarged and divided into three distinct approaches: "a scientific view," "culture history" and "a Criticism of Values," which would be akin to "literary and artistic criticism," and which would operate "through sympathetic interpretation rather than intellectual cognition."[16]

Some perspective on the affinity between literary studies and economics may be gained by observing that literary theory since the New Criticism has been trying to exculpate itself from this sort of sentimental intuitionism by proposing ever more "scientific"—or scientific-sounding—explanations of "how we communicate feelings or read expression in the looks and acts and words of others." Economists, however, have gone even further toward inverting Knight's methodological hierarchy, by trusting interiority inferred from behavior ("revealed preferences") exclusively over that which might be learned from the telling of motives. Thus, in expanding their discipline to account for all human desire and motivation—reaching into areas of human interiority that were formerly the province of literature, ethics and the other social sciences—economists now aspire to an expertise apparently at odds with their exterior methodology. Economic methodology proceeds as though our minds do indeed shine through the body; it is an empirical study of invisible things, guided fittingly enough by an "invisible hand."

Gary Becker has done as much as anyone toward imposing the methodology of economics onto broader aspects of social life. Demonstrating "The economic way of looking at life," Becker discovers rational, welfare-maximizing motivations behind the observable behavior (not the words) of bigots, criminals, guilt-inducing parents and selfish children.[17] Certainly all kinds of behaviors could be described as rational, for rationality is a matter of definition. But in discussing these "rational" behaviors, Becker never questions his own definition of rationality, and therefore never has to defend it, never has to think about it, never has to limit its scope. Instead, he confidently presents rational choice theory as the essential explanation for a range of phenomena— such as racism, crime and family structure—traditionally studied by other disciplines. The result is a reductive homogenization of ideas and human possibilities: not interdisciplinarity, but disciplinary colonialism. "The rational choice model," he maintains, favoring intellectual unification, "provides the most promising basis presently available for a unified approach to the analysis of the social world by scholars of all different social sciences."[18]

A taste of this "unified approach to the analysis of the social world"—"the science of Man"?—may be gotten from the famous essay, "De gustibus non est disputandum," co-authored by Stigler and Becker. In this essay the authors interpret the old motto of their title in a way that would make *Tristram Shandy* seem necessary to be written, had it not been written already. Observing that the proverb is usually taken "as advice to terminate a dispute when it has been resolved into a difference of tastes," the authors surprisingly contend:

> Our title seems to us to be capable of another and preferable interpretation: that tastes neither change capriciously nor differ importantly between people. On this interpretation one does not argue over tastes for the same reason that one does not argue over the Rocky Mountains—both are there, will be there next year, too, and are the same to all men.[19]

For Stigler and Becker, culture and history are irrelevant, for they lead to no significant differences in individual preferences; human tastes "are stable over time and similar among people." The *appearance* of differences in taste, the authors argue, is the effect of real changes in prices and incomes, which alter people's consumption patterns. In other words, the common humanity that everyone shares is a culturally neutral, universal, rational economic mind. "Our hypothesis is trivial," the authors maintain with what can only be described as the profoundly humble arrogance of a Don Quixote, "for it merely asserts that we should apply standard economic logic as extensively as possible."[20] Pleased with the "generality and power" of their approach—in fact, equating generality with power—the authors pursue their Newtonian quest, never questioning whether the Newtonian method is fully compatible with social phenomena. They do not imagine Smith's laughing artisan.

Stigler, therefore, may be thought to act out of self-interest when he denies the value of methodological inquiry, for in refusing to contemplate method, he saves himself the endless labor of having to imagine the potential diversity of other minds. Universal rationality is for him an unassailable methodological assumption, for anyone who becomes "concerned with methodology" must be either foolish, or metaphorically, if not literally, out-to-pasture (past "the age of sixty-five"). F. A. Hayek, however, has already asked the question that Stigler works to evade: "How can the combination of fragments of knowledge existing in different minds bring about results which, if they were to be brought about deliberately, would require a knowledge on the part of the directing mind which no single person can possess?"[21] How, in other words, can the invisible hand be trusted, when, unlike the workers in a little pin factory, its effects cannot be "placed at once under the view of the spectator" (WN 1: 14)?

Hayek's answers to this question return economics to the epistemological paradoxes from which it emerged. Unified knowledge in the form of "conscious control," Hayek argues, is unnecessary and even detrimental to the smooth functioning of an economy.[22] The free market works despite the fragmentation of knowledge. Yet with no known mechanism guaranteeing the superiority of a "division of labor" that "did not have to be consciously created," Hayek would seem simply to be advocating faith in the wise dispensations of providence. (Jacob Viner has argued that for Adam Smith, the invisible hand was indeed a providential one, very much attached to God.[23]) Unwilling to commit himself to this magnitude of faith, Hayek soon reasserts the need for conscious control and unified understanding in a free society. "Least of all shall we preserve democracy or foster its growth," he warns, wary of big government, "if all the power and most of the important decisions rest with an organization far too big for the common man to survey or comprehend."[24] In politics, unified knowledge and conscious control of the system is necessary, while in economics it is not—an important distinction to be stressed whenever the concept of the free market and that of a free society are too quickly elided.[25] Hayek attempts to reconcile free-market unconsciousness with political rational agency by advocating what he calls "the Rule of Law," a mechanism that seems similar to Smith's "established rules of behaviour." Like so many before him, Hayek seeks to explain why seemingly arbitrary outcomes can be regarded as rational after all.

According to Hayek, observing the Rule of Law

means that government in all its actions is bound by rules fixed and announced beforehand—rules which make it possible to foresee with fair certainty how the authority will use its coercive powers in given circumstances and to plan one's individual affairs on the basis of this knowledge.[26]

These *"formal rules,"* he insists, would be the opposite of "arbitrary government." In their formality and their stability, they could be regarded as neutral, for they would not "aim at the wants and needs of particular people." On the contrary, "they are, or ought to be, intended for such long periods that it is impossible to know whether they will assist particular people more than others."[27] Yet at the same time, the purpose of the Rule of Law is also to make the actions of the state "predictable." Hayek elaborates: "It means, not that everything is regulated by law, but . . . that the coercive power of the state can be used only in cases defined in advance by the law and in such a way that it can be foreseen how it will be used."[28] Hayek's Rule of Law is thus a paradox: it must be predictable (so that people can make plans), yet unpredictable (to preserve its neutrality); its effects must be both foreseen and unforeseen; it must endure for so long that its path will be "impossible to know," while at the same time regulating state power "in advance . . . and in such a way that it can be foreseen how it will be used." By urging that government be bound by the Rule of Law, Hayek in effect displaces the political and economic problem of knowledge onto the problem of constitutional interpretation. Frank Knight's emphasis on the importance of communication appears ever more relevant: "the test of reality is the possibility of verification, which depends on communication with the consciousness of others." Hayek, to extricate himself from the problem of imperfect knowledge, stumbles into the problem of authorial intention. Does it matter what the framers of the constitutional text intended? Can interpretive authority be trusted in the visible hands of (potentially quixotic) readers? The limits of economic science are the limits of reading in an empirical age, the challenges of trying to understand other minds that can be perceived only through the mediations of language, convention and art.

NOTES

INTRODUCTION

1 Trans. Tobias Smollett, New York: Farrar, Straus and Giroux, 1986, 501. In subsequent citations of *Don Quixote*, I will refer to the Motteux translation, as it seems to have been more widely read by many of the authors I will be discussing. I cite from Smollett's translation here simply because his compression of this scene works better as an epigraph.

2 Alexander Welsh, *Reflections on the Hero as Quixote*, Princeton NJ: Princeton University Press, 1981; Eric J. Ziolkowski, *The Sanctification of Don Quixote: From Hidalgo to Priest*, University Park PA: Pennsylvania State University Press, 1991.

3 I have chosen to end my argument in the 1770s because through this decade, the primary political context for reading *Don Quixote* was the Puritan Revolution, followed by the Glorious Revolution and its aftermath. After the 1770s the political context for reading *Don Quixote* changes to that of the French Revolution, a shift that is too large for me to discuss here. On the French Revolution and the meanings of romance, see David Duff, *Romance and Revolution: Shelley and the Politics of a Genre*, Cambridge: Cambridge University Press, 1994, 8–53.

4 Published in 1605 in Spain, *Don Quixote* was first translated into English in 1612 by Thomas Shelton. The second part of *Don Quixote* (1615) could be read in English by 1620. Shelton's translation was reissued in 1652 and 1675. John Phillips, a nephew of Milton, wrote a new translation in 1687. John Stephen's revision of the Shelton translation (1700–5) appeared contemporaneously with Motteux's translation (1700–3); Motteux was revised and reissued by Ozell in 1719. The turn of the century also saw *Don Quixote* squeezed into chapbook form—at least four versions. In 1711 Edward Ward translated *Don Quixote* into Hudibrastic verse. Two serial editions of *Don Quixote* were begun in the early eighteenth century (1725 and 1726), though neither was ever completed. In 1742 Charles Jarvis' translation appeared; Smollett's following in 1755; George Kelly's in 1769; Charles Henry Wilmot's in 1774. The Rev. John Bowle's edition was published in 1781. See William A. Jackson, "The Carl T. Keller Collection of *Don Quixote*," *Harvard Library Bulletin*, 1, 1947: 306–10; and Edwin B. Knowles' two essays, "Cervantes and English literature," in *Cervantes Across the Centuries*, eds Angel Flores and M. J. Benardete, New York: The Dryden Press, 1947, 267–93; and "*Don Quixote* abridged," *The Papers of the Bibliographical Society of America*, 49, 1955: 19–36.

5 *The Much esteemed History of The Ever-Famous Knight Don Quixote de la Mancha: Containing his many wonderful Adventures and Atchievements, Very Pleasant and Diverting. With the Comical Humours of Sancho Pancha, his Remarkable 'Squire, &c. In Two Parts*, London, 1716.

6 On the prevalence of eighteenth-century fears about arbitrary power, see James T. Boulton, *Arbitrary Power: An Eighteenth-Century Obsession*, Nottingham: University of Nottingham, 1967. For an interesting critique of Hobbes' conception of power, see Sheldon Wolin, *Politics and Vision: Continuity and Innovation in Western Political Thought*, Boston MA: Little, Brown, 1960, 285.

7 John Locke, *Two Treatises of Government*, ed. Peter Laslett, student edn, Cambridge: Cambridge University Press, 1988, 267–8.

8 *An Essay Concerning Human Understanding*, ed. Peter H. Nidditch, Oxford: Clarendon Press, 1975, 668.

9 Matthew Prior, *The Literary Works of Matthew Prior*, eds H. Bunker Wright and Monroe K. Spears, 2 vols, Oxford: Clarendon Press, 1959, 1: 598–9.

10 The eighteenth century responded in all these ways, with early interpretations of Don Quixote burlesquing his lunacy, mid-century interpretations accepting him as an amiable humorist, and late-century readings elevating him to the status of romantic hero. See Stuart Tave, *The Amiable Humorist*, Chicago IL: University of Chicago Press, 1960, 151–63; Edwin B. Knowles, "Cervantes and English literature"; and Ziolkowski, *The Sanctification of Don Quixote*, 37–61.

11 Miguel de Cervantes, *The Ingenious Gentleman Don Quixote de La Mancha*, trans. Peter Motteux, revised by Ozell, New York: Modern Library, 1950, 3. Subsequent quotations of this work will refer to this edition unless otherwise specified.

12 Michael V. De Porte, *Nightmares and Hobbyhorses: Swift, Sterne, and Augustan Ideas of Madness*, San Marino CA: The Huntington Library, 1974, 28.

13 Tobias Smollett's quixotic character, Sir Launcelot Greaves, even takes a stand on the issue, proclaiming:

> I am neither an affected imitator of Don Quixote, nor, as I trust heaven, visited by that spirit of lunacy so admirably displayed in the fictitious character exhibited by the inimitable Cervantes. I have not yet encountered a windmill for a giant; nor mistaken this public house for a magnificent castle; neither do I believe this gentleman to be a constable; nor that worthy practitioner to be master Elizabat, the surgeon recorded in Amadis de Gaul, nor you to be the enchanter Alquife, nor any other sage of history or romance.—I see and distinguish objects as they are discerned and described by other men.
>
> *The Life and Adventures of Sir Launcelot Greaves*, ed. Peter Wagner, Harmondsworth: Penguin, 1988, 50.

14 Charlotte Lennox, *The Female Quixote*, ed. Margaret Dalziel, Oxford: Oxford University Press, 1973, 257–9. Subsequent citations will appear parenthetically within the text.

15 Laurence Sterne, *The Life and Opinions of Tristram Shandy*, ed. Ian Campbell Ross, Oxford: Oxford University Press, 1983, 43ff., 175ff.

16 See *The Minutes of a Court-Martial . . . Enquiring into the Conduct of the Commanders of the* Hampton-Court *and the* Dread-nought, *for not engaging the* Fleuron *and* Neptune, *two French Men of War* (London, 1745); William Laird Clowes, *The Royal Navy: A History from the Earliest Times to the Present*, 5 vols (London, 1898) 3: 276–7; and John Charnock, *Biographia Navalis: Or, Impartial Memoirs of the Lives and Characters of Officers of the Navy of Great Britain*, 4 vols (London, 1796) 4: 225–7.

17 Public Record Office, ADM 1/2100, 28 Jan. 1744.

18 As a rear-admiral in 1756, Mostyn was regarded by his men as "a strict disci-
plinarian," the "extreme of tyranny and despotism." See N. A. M. Rodger, *The
Wooden World: An Anatomy of the Georgian Navy*, London: Collins, 1986, 72.

19 Public Record Office, ADM 1/2100, 28 Jan. 1745.

20 Public Record Office, ADM 1/5284.

21 *An Enquiry into the Conduct of Capt. M—n. Being Remarks on the Minutes of the Court-
Martial, and other incidental Matters. Humbly addressed to the Honourable House of
Commons. By a SEA-OFFICER* (London, 1745) 4–5.

22 On the separation of naval justice and civil justice, see Rodger, *The Wooden World*,
225–6.

23 See Kathleen Wilson, "Empire, trade and popular politics in mid-Hanoverian
Britain: the case of Admiral Vernon," *Past and Present*, 121, 1988, 74–109.

24 *A Vindication of the Conduct of Capt. M—N and of the Court-Martial. By a SEA-
OFFICER* (London, 1745) 7.

25 Philonauticus Antiquixotus, *The Rule of Two to One: Or, the Difference betwixt
Courage and Quixotism* (London, 1745).

26 The rules of eighteenth-century football were much less standardized than those
of modern versions of football. So by comparing Mostyn's case to football,
Antiquixotus perhaps acknowledges that different games may require different
strategies, while yet emphasizing that some principles—such as the disadvantage
of being outmanned—absolutely make sense, no matter what the rules of engagement. On eighteenth-century football, see Robert W. Malcolmson, *Popular
Recreations in English Society 1700–1850*, Cambridge: Cambridge University Press,
1973, 34–40. My thanks to Thomas Hothem who, via C18-L@psuvm.psu.edu,
brought this source to my attention.

27 See Joseph Priestley's *Lectures on History and General Policy*, ed. J. T. Rutt, London:
1826, 31–2.

28 Bolingbroke, Henry St John Viscount, *Letters on the Study and Use of History*,
London: 1752, 64.

29 *Dictionary of National Biography*, 13: 1089; Clowes, *The Royal Navy*, 3: 278;
Charnock, *Biographia Navalis*, 4: 430; Rodger, *The Wooden World*, 249; *Naval
Administration 1715–50*, ed. Daniel A. Baugh, London: Naval Records Society,
1977, 198; H. W. Richmond, *The Navy in the War of 1739–48*, 3 vols, Cambridge:
Cambridge University Press, 1920, 2: 114–16.

30 *The Works of Henry Fielding, Esq.*, ed. Leslie Stephen, 10 vols, London: 1882, 3:
118–19.

31 "Of Good Nature," *Miscellanies by Henry Fielding, Esq.*, ed. Henry Knight Miller,
2 vols, Oxford: Wesleyan University Press, 1972, 1: 31.

32 Adam Smith, *The Theory of Moral Sentiments*, eds D. D. Raphael and A. L. Macfie,
1976, Indianapolis IN: Liberty Classics, 1982, 10.

33 On the relation between "good-nature" and political controversies of the seven-
teenth century, see R. S. Crane, "Suggestions toward a genealogy of the 'Man of
Feeling,'" *ELH*, 1, 1934: 205–30. Crane's essay has been challenged by Donald
Greene, "Latitudinarianism and sensibility: the genealogy of the 'Man of Feeling'
reconsidered," *Modern Philology*, 75, 1977: 159–83, and defended by Elizabeth
Duthie, "The genuine man of feeling," *Modern Philology*, 78, 1981: 279–85.

34 See Bernhard Baumrin, introduction, *British Moralists: Being Selections from Writers
Principally of the Eighteenth Century*, ed. L. A. Selby-Bigge, 2 vols, Indianapolis IN:
Bobbs-Merrill, 1964, who explains that

all of the major ethical theorists fall into one of two schools of thought
and consciously oppose their views to those of the members of the other

school: each is either a rationalist or a sentimentalist. That is to say that on the fundamental epistemological problem of ethics, i.e., from whence spring our notions of vice and virtue, moral good and moral right, justice and injustice and the like, a writer either believes that these notions spring from human thought in the same way as scientific knowledge springs from human thought or mathematical knowledge springs from human thought, or he believes, just as profoundly, that it springs from ordinary sensation in one way or another.

(xiv)

35 R. F. Brissenden, *Virtue in Distress: Studies in the Novel of Sentiment from Richardson to Sade*, London: Macmillan, 1974, 22, 24. On the relation between sentimentalism and empiricism, see also Ann Jessie Van Sant, *Eighteenth-Century Sensibility and the Novel: The Senses in Social Context*, Cambridge: Cambridge University Press, 1993.

36 David Hume, *A Treatise of Human Nature*, ed. L. A. Selby-Bigge, 2nd edn revised by P. H. Nidditch, Oxford: Clarendon Press, 1978, xiii.

37 Brissenden, *Virtue in Distress*, 24.

38 On the relation between general knowledge and particular feeling in Hume's philosophy, see John Mullan, *Sentiment and Sociability: The Language of Feeling in the Eighteenth Century*, Oxford: Clarendon Press, 1988, 1–56.

39 On the scientific ideology of consensus, see Richard W. F. Kroll, *The Material Word: Literate Culture in the Restoration and Early Eighteenth Century*, Baltimore MD: Johns Hopkins University Press, 1991.

40 Martin Price, introduction, *Eighteenth-Century Studies*, 4, 1970: 1–5, cit. 4.

41 Janet Todd discusses this tendency to read sentimentalism as self-parody. See her *Sensibility: An Introduction*, London: Methuen, 1986, 109.

42 According to Kenneth MacLean, Locke maintained that morality could be demonstrated in the same way as mathematics because moral terms, like mathematical ones, are purely definitional, "wholly an invention of the human mind," and hence can become "as certain a part of human knowledge as that of a perfect square." See *John Locke and English Literature of the Eighteenth Century*, New Haven CT: Yale University Press, 1936, 162–4. Burnet's uneasiness with such an account may have owed something to Hobbes' earlier observation that definitions are not always easily arrived at:

> For I doubt not, but if it had been a thing contrary to any mans right of domination, or to the interest of men that have dominion, *That the three Angles of a Triangle should be equall to two Angles of a Square*: that doctrine should have been, if not disputed, yet by the burning of all books of Geometry, suppressed, as farre as he whom it concerned was able.
> *Leviathan*, ed. C. B. Macpherson, Harmondsworth: Penguin Books, 1968, 166

43 Thomas Burnet, *Remarks on John Locke, with Locke's Replies*, ed. George Watson, Doncaster: Brynmill, 1989, 24. Subsequent citations to this work will appear parenthetically within the text.

44 On Burnet's ideas as the "seed of moral-sense theory," see Watson's introduction and Ernest Lee Tuveson, *The Imagination as a Means of Grace: Locke and the Aesthetics of Romanticism*, Berkeley CA: University of California Press, 1960, 46–9.

45 This dialogue, along with three others, was probably written around 1721, though all four remained unpublished until 1907. Despite their lack of publication, the *Dialogues* had some eighteenth-century readers, including the poet

240

Alexander Pope. See Fredrick M. Keener, *English Dialogues of the Dead*, New York: Columbia University Press, 1973, 54, 124–5.

46 For an account of Smith's life, see John Rae, *Life of Adam Smith*, introduction by Jacob Viner, New York: Augustus M. Kelley, 1965; and Ian Simpson Ross, *The Life of Adam Smith*, Oxford: Clarendon Press, 1995.

47 See Stephen Copley, "Introduction: Reading the *Wealth of Nations*," *Adam Smith's Wealth of Nations: New Interdisciplinary Essays*, eds Stephen Copley and Kathryn Sutherland, Manchester: Manchester University Press, 1995, 1–22.

48 Donald Winch, *Adam Smith's Politics: An Essay on Historiographic Revision*, Cambridge: Cambridge University Press, 1978; Patricia H. Werhane, *Adam Smith and His Legacy for Modern Capitalism*, New York: Oxford University Press, 1991; Vivienne Brown, *Adam Smith's Discourse: Canonicity, Commerce, and Conscience*, London: Routledge, 1994.

49 Winch, *Adam Smith's Politics*, 27.

50 Jonas Barish, *The Antitheatrical Prejudice*, Berkeley CA: University of California Press, 1981, 243–55; David Marshall, *The Figure of Theater: Shaftesbury, Defoe, Adam Smith, and George Eliot*, New York: Columbia University Press, 1986, 165–92; and Jean-Christophe Agnew, *Worlds Apart: The Market and the Theater in Anglo-American Thought, 1550–1750*, Cambridge: Cambridge University Press, 1986, 177–94.

51 See for example Claudia L. Johnson's discussion of the ways in which sentimentalism constrained female subjectivity in the late eighteenth century, *Equivocal Beings: Politics, Gender, and Sentimentality in the 1790s*, Chicago IL: University of Chicago Press, 1995.

1 TURNING AUTHORITY INTO JEST

1 Peter Anthony Motteux, "The Translator's Preface," *The History of the Renown'd Don Quixote De la Mancha* (London, 1700) sig. A5.

2 On Don Quixote's transformation from madman to romantic hero, see Stuart Tave, *The Amiable Humorist*, Chicago IL: University of Chicago Press, 1960, 151–63; Edwin B. Knowles, "Cervantes and English literature," *Cervantes Across the Centuries*, eds Angel Flores and M. J. Benardete, New York: The Dryden Press, 1947, 267–93; Eric J. Ziolkowski, *The Sanctification of Don Quixote: From Hidalgo to Priest*, University Park PA: Pennsylvania State University Press, 1991, 37–61.

3 Shaftesbury, Anthony Ashley Cooper, Third Earl, *Characteristics of Men, Manners, Opinions, Times*, ed. John M. Robertson, 2 vols, Gloucester MA: Peter Smith, 1963, 1: 14–15.

4 William Temple, *Essays on Ancient and Modern Learning and Poetry*, ed. J. E. Spingarn, Oxford: Clarendon Press, 1909, 41–2.

5 On Temple's role in the "Battle of the Books," the controversy between the ancients and the moderns, see Joseph M. Levine, *The Battle of the Books: History and Literature in the Augustan Age*, Ithaca NY: Cornell University Press, 1991, 13–46; and Irvin Ehrenpreis, *Swift: The Man, His Works, and the Age*, 3 vols, Cambridge MA: Harvard University Press, 1962, 1: 226–37.

6 Jonathan Swift, *The Prose Works of Jonathan Swift*, ed. Herbert Davis, 14 vols, Oxford: Oxford University Press, 1939–68, 1: 105.

7 In order to appease the gods, and thereby to preserve the Roman Republic, Marcus Curtius cast himself into a chasm that had appeared in the middle of the Forum (Livy, VII, vi). The philosopher, poet and mystagogue Empedocles, by one account, threw himself into the crater of Mount Etna in order to confirm the report that he had become a god; apparently, he had not (Diogenes Laertius, VIII).

8 On the transmission of Revolution Principles, see Richard Ashcraft and M. M. Goldsmith, "Locke, Revolution Principles and the formation of Whig ideology," *Historical Journal*, 26, 1983: 773–800.

9 On the ideological distinctions between Whigs, Tories and Jacobites see F. J. McLynn, "The ideology of Jacobitism on the eve of the rising of 1745: Part I," *History of European Ideas*, 6, 1985: 1–18.

10 For a history of the concept of "interest," see J. A. W. Gunn, " 'Interest will not lie': a seventeenth-century political maxim," *Journal of the History of Ideas*, 29, 1968: 551–64.

11 See also the note on page 201 of Peter Laslett's edition of the *Two Treatises* by John Locke, student edition, Cambridge: Cambridge University Press, 1988; Locke apparently liked *Don Quixote*, for he owned four different editions of it. He praises it for having "*Nature* at the bottom," and recommends it "for the improvement of the Understanding." See *Some Thoughts Concerning Education*, eds John W. Yolton and Jean S. Yolton, Oxford: Clarendon Press, 1989, 325–6.

12 Andrew Marvell, "An Horatian ode upon Cromwell's return from Ireland," *The Complete Poems of Andrew Marvell*, ed. Elizabeth Story Donno, Harmondsworth: Penguin, 1985, 55–8, ll. 119–20.

13 Michel Foucault, *The Order of Things: An Archaeology of the Human Sciences*, New York: Vintage, 1973, xv–xxiv.

14 Jack Catch, *A Hue and Cry After the Pretender* (London, 1716).

15 Daniel Defoe, *Captain Tom's Remembrance to His Old Friends the Mobb of London, Westminster, Southwark, and Wapping* (London, 1711).

16 Catch, *Hue and Cry*, 1.

17 Richard Newyear, *Gibraltar, or the Pretender, &c.* (London, 1727) 7–13.

18 *The Chevalier's Declaration* (1745?).

19 Fielding, *The Works of Henry Fielding*, ed. Leslie Stephen, 10 vols (London, 1882) 6: 182–8.

20 George Berkeley, *The Works of George Berkeley Bishop of Cloyne*, eds A. A. Luce and T. E. Jessop, 9 vols, London: Nelson, 1953, 6: 18–19.

21 For a detailed account of the Sacheverell affair, see Geoffrey Holmes, *The Trial of Doctor Sacheverell*, London: Eyre Methuen, 1973.

22 Henry Sacheverell, *The Perils of False Brethren, both in Church and State* (London, 1709) 12.

23 On the intricacies of Godolphin's relation to the Whig party, see Holmes, *Trial*, 70.

24 Holmes, *Trial*, 41–2.

25 The proceedings against Sacheverell are attributed to Godolphin's ire by Roy A. Sundstrom, *Sidney Godolphin: Servant of the State*, Newark DE: University of Delaware Press, 1992, 243. William Calvin Dickinson, however, disagrees in his *Sidney Godolphin, Lord Treasurer 1702–1710*, Studies in British History, vol. 18, Lewiston NY: Edwin Mellen Press, 1990, 211.

26 Sundstrom, 242–3. See also Holmes, *Trial*, 75. Holmes, in "the most narrowly conservative estimate," claims that the sermon would have been read "by at least a quarter of a million men and women, in other words by a number equal to the whole electorate of England and Wales."

27 The trial was a major attraction. Westminster Hall was too small to accommodate all the would-be spectators, despite the additional seating hurriedly constructed by Sir Christopher Wren and a team of fifty workmen. Tickets to the trial had to be issued. See Holmes, *Trial*, 112–29.

28 Holmes, *Trial*, 111–13.

29 "Said to be dropt in the House of C[ommon]s," in *Whig and Tory: Or, Wit on both Sides* (London, 1712) part 1, 3–4.

30 For a discussion of political legitimacy during this period, see Gerald M. Straka, "1688 as the Year One: eighteenth-century attitudes towards the Glorious Revolution," *Studies in Eighteenth-Century Culture*, ed. Louis T. Milic, vol. 1, Cleveland OH: Case Western Reserve University Press, 1971, 143–67.

31 "Said to be found upon a Great Lady's Toylet," in *Whig and Tory*, part 1, 3.

32 "The Age of Wonders," in *Whig and Tory*, part 4, 8. For a discussion of Dryden's *Annus Mirabilis* as a response to political instability, see Michael McKeon's *Politics and Poetry in Restoration England*, Cambridge MA: Harvard University Press, 1975.

33 "Fair Warning," in *Whig and Tory*, part 3, 22.

34 "An Answer to the Fair Warning. By N. F. G.," in *Whig and Tory*, part 3, 23.

35 "Good Advice, if rightly taken," in *Whig and Tory*, part 2, 22.

36 See Holmes, *Trial*, 156–78. Holmes describes the social composition of the rioters in "The Sacheverell Riots," *Past and Present*, 72, 1976: 55–85.

37 "The History of the Imp[eachme]nt: OR, The Nation's gone mad. A new ballad," in *Whig and Tory*, part 1, 9.

38 Holmes, *Trial*, 176.

39 John Dunton, *The Bull-Baiting: Or, Sach{evere}ll Dress'd up in Fire-Works* (London, 1710).

40 Jack Touchwood, *Quixote Redivivus: Or, The Spiritual Knight Errant, in a Letter to Isaac Bickerstaff, Esq.* (London, 1710) 12. Touchwood's letter is dated 20 January 1710. Another edition, signed "John Distaff," and dated 16 March 1710, bears the title *A character of Don Sacheverellio, knight of the firebrand; in a letter to Isaac Bickerstaff, Esq* (Dublin, 1710). Another edition, bearing the same title as the John Distaff imprint, adds "Dublin: printed and re-printed at Edinburgh in the year 1710." See F. F. Madan, *A Critical Bibliography of Dr Henry Sacheverell*, ed. W. A. Speck, Library Series, 49, Lawrence KS: University of Kansas Libraries, 1978, 44–5.

41 Dunton, 6.

42 "Don Higginisco" refers to the Reverend Francis Higgins, another high-flying cleric. The full title of Defoe's pamphlet leaves little for the body of the text to add: *Instructions From Rome, In Favour of the Pretender, Inscrib'd to the most Elevated Don Sacheverellio, And his Brother Don Higginisco. And which All Perkinites, Non Jurors, High-flyers, Popist Desirers, Wooden Shoe Admirers, and absolute Non Resistance Drivers, are obliged to pursue and maintain (under pain of his Unholinesses Damnation) in order to carry on their intended Subversion of a Government, fix'd upon Revolution Principles* (London, 1710).

43 Holmes, *Trial*, 218.

44 Touchwood, 5.

45 Touchwood, 6.

46 *Whig and Tory*, part 1, 11.

47 *Whig and Tory*, part 2, 36.

48 Cited in Paul Kléber Monod, *Jacobitism and the English People 1688–1788*, Cambridge: Cambridge University Press, 1989, 19.

49 *The Examiner*, 23–6 April 1714. The "*Martial Lunacy*" the *Examiner* describes here might also be read as a satire on the Whigs' pro-war policy.

50 Holmes, *Trial*, 207.

51 Holmes, *Trial*, 233–55.

52 Locke's epistemology cannot be fully reconciled with his political theory. Both eighteenth-century and recent critics have noticed logical inconsistencies in

Locke's discussion of the "natural law" as it appears in the *Essay* and in the *Two Treatises*. See Laslett, introduction, 66, 80–3, where he suggests that Locke's recognition of the inconsistency between the two works was one of the reasons why Locke refused to admit his authorship of both books. See also Richard Ashcraft, "Faith and knowledge in Locke's philosophy," *John Locke: Problems and Perspectives*, ed. John W. Yolton, Cambridge: Cambridge University Press, 1969, 194–223.

53 If Don Gregorio Mayáns y Siscár's life of Cervantes is to be believed, some people suggested that Charles V was the model for Don Quixote. Mayáns, however, dismisses this rumor summarily:

> they are very much mistaken who take *Don Quixote de la Mancha* to be a Representation of *Charles* the Vth. without any other Foundation than their fancying it to be so, or their desiring it should be so. *Cervantes* revered, as he ought, the Memory of a Prince of so many and such Heroick Virtues; and he oftentimes mentions him with the greatest Respect.
>
> *The Life of Michael de Cervantes Saavedra*, trans. Mr Ozell, in *The Life and Exploits of the ingenious Gentleman Don Quixote De La Mancha*, trans. Charles Jarvis, 4 vols (Dublin, 1747) 1: 112

54 The similarities between Don Quixote and Swift's Hack have been discussed by Ronald Paulson in *Theme and Structure in Swift's Tale of a Tub*, 1960; Hamden CT: Archon, 1972, 83–6.

55 See H. Bunker Wright and Monroe K. Spears, *The Literary Works of Matthew Prior*, 2 vols, Oxford: Clarendon Press, 1959, 2: 920; Dickinson, 213–14; Sundstrom, 245.

56 Alexander Pope, *Epistle to Dr. Arbuthnot*, l. 209, in *The Poems of Alexander Pope*, ed. John Butt, one-volume edition of the Twickenham text, New Haven CT: Yale University Press, 1963.

57 *The Whig-Examiner*, no. 1, 14 September 1710; and *Tatler* no. 239, 19 October 1710. See the commentary on Prior's essay by Wright and Spears, 2: 920.

58 *The Spectator*, ed. Donald F. Bond, 5 vols, Oxford: Clarendon Press, 1965, 1: 510–11 (no. 125).

59 John Barrell, *English Literature in History, 1730–80: An Equal, Wide Survey*, New York: St Martin's Press, 1983, 32.

60 Barrell, *English Literature in History*, 35.

61 *The Tatler*, ed. Donald F. Bond, 3 vols, Oxford: Clarendon Press, 1987, 2: 468. No. 178 is attributed to Steele.

62 No. 155 (6 April 1710) by Addison; no. 160 (18 April 1710) by Addison; no. 178 (30 May 1710) by Steele; and no. 232 (3 October 1710) by Steele. One *Tatler* edition (Philadelphia, 1844) identifies a certain Mr Arne, an upholsterer in Covent Garden, as the model for the *Tatler*'s upholsterer (see the note, 303). Such particulars aside, Addison, Steele and their Whig readers would probably have relished a satiric portrait of such an "unfortunate tradesman," for London tradesmen were predominantly Tory. See Nicholas Rogers, "Popular protest in early Hanoverian London," *Past and Present*, 79, 1978: 70–100.

63 The relation between Lockean liberalism and feminism has been discussed in recent years, leading to the general acknowledgment that Locke's political theory treats the question of women's political participation mainly with inconsistency or silence. See, for example, Susan Moller Okin, "Women and the making of the sentimental family," *Philosophy & Public Affairs*, 11, 1981: 65–88; and Carole

Pateman, *The Sexual Contract*, Stanford CA: Stanford University Press, 1988, 91–5. An analysis that regards Locke's ideas, despite their inconsistency, as ultimately conducive to feminism is Melissa A. Butler's "Early liberal roots of feminism: John Locke and the attack on patriarchy," *The American Political Science Review*, 72, 1978: 135–50. Agreeing with these scholars, my discussion here seeks to illustrate how proto-feminist writers exploited these inconsistencies by adopting the very language of Revolution Principles.

64 *Female Rights Vindicated; Or, the Equality of the Sexes Morally and Physically Proved* (London, 1758) preface. This essay appears to be a loose translation of François Poulain de la Barre's *Discours Physique et Moral de l'Egalité des deux Sexes* (1673), published in English translation as *The Woman As Good As The Man* (1677).

65 For surveys of proto-feminist writings in Restoration and early eighteenth-century England, see Hilda L. Smith, *Reason's Disciples: Seventeenth-Century English Feminists*, Urbana IL: University of Illinois Press, 1982; A. H. Upham, "English femmes savantes at the end of the seventeenth century," *Journal of English and Germanic Philology*, 12, 1913: 262–76; Jerome Nadelhaft, "The Englishwoman's sexual and civil war: feminist attitudes towards men, women, and marriage 1650–1740," *Journal of the History of Ideas*, 43, 1982: 555–79; and Keith Thomas, "Women and the Civil War sects," *Crisis in Europe 1560–1660: Essays from* Past and Present, ed. Trevor Aston, London: Routledge and Kegan Paul, 1965, 317–40.

66 *An Essay in Defence of the Female Sex* (London, 1696) 3–4. Subsequent references to this work will appear parenthetically within the text.

67 *Some Reflections Upon Marriage* (1730), New York: Source Book Press, 1970, 86.

68 Sophia, *Woman Not Inferior to Man: Or, A Short and Modest Vindication of the Natural Right of the Fair-Sex to a Perfect Equality of Power, Dignity, and Esteem, with the Men* (London, 1739) 51. Subsequent citations will refer to this edition, and will appear parenthetically within the text. Sophia's identity has not yet been established; according to Moira Ferguson, "Nothing is known about Sophia that is not speculation." One of these speculations has been that Sophia is Lady Mary Wortley Montagu, although Lady Mary was on the Continent for the most part of 1739–41, the years during which Sophia published. Though Sophia's identity remains a mystery, her argument has been identified as an adaptation of François Poulain de la Barre's *Discours Physique et Moral de l'Egalité des deux Sexes* (1673). See Moira Ferguson, *First Feminists: British Women Writers 1578–1799*, Bloomington IN and Old Westbury NY: Indiana University Press and Feminist Press, 1985, 266; and the reprinted edition of *Woman Not Inferior to Man* (1739), London: Brentham Press, 1975.

69 *The Ladies Defence: Or, A Dialogue Between Sir John Brute, Sir William Loveall, Melissa, and a Parson* (1701), in *The Poems and Prose of Mary, Lady Chudleigh*, ed. Margaret J. M. Ezell, New York: Oxford University Press, 1993, 8, ll. 95–8.

70 So trite is this Tory critical analysis of Revolution Principles that it earns a place in Swift's compendium of clichés, *A Tritical Essay upon the Faculties of Mind*: "SOME Men admire Republicks; because Orators flourish there most, and are the great Enemies of Tyranny: But my Opinion is, that one Tyrant is better than an Hundred." *The Prose Works of Jonathan Swift*, ed. Herbert Davis, 14 vols, Oxford: Oxford University Press, 1939–68, 1: 250.

71 Astell's own politics were staunchly Tory, perhaps even Jacobite. The apparent contradiction between her "Whiggish" arguments for women's liberty and her conservative attitudes toward monarchical government has been remarked (Smith, *Reason's Disciples*, 132). For detailed discussion on the relation between Astell's public and domestic politics, see Joan K. Kinnaird, "Mary Astell and the

conservative contribution to English feminism," *Journal of British Studies*, 19, 1979: 53–75; Ruth Perry, *The Celebrated Mary Astell: An Early English Feminist*, Chicago IL: University of Chicago Press, 1986, 163–80; and Catherine Gallagher, "Embracing the absolute: the politics of the female subject in seventeenth-century England," *Genders*, 1, 1988: 24–39.

72 *The Challenge, Sent by a Young Lady to Sir Thomas: Or, the Female War* (London, 1697) 99. I am grateful to Shawn Maurer for drawing my attention to this text.

73 Madam Godfrey here refers to Livy II, xii.

74 For a discussion of the identification made between women and the genre of romance, see Laurie Langbauer, *Women and Romance: The Consolations of Gender in the English Novel*, Ithaca NY: Cornell University Press, 1990.

75 The biography was first published in 1760 with an edition of the playwright's collected works, *The Dramatic Works of the Celebrated Mrs Centlivre*, 3 vols (1760; 1872), New York: AMS Press, 1968, 1: x–xi.

2 COMMON SENSE, MORAL SENSE AND NONSENSE

1 See Bernhard Baumrin, introduction, *British Moralists: Being Selections from Writers Principally of the Eighteenth Century*, ed. L. A. Selby-Bigge, 2 vols, Indianapolis IN: Bobbs-Merrill, 1964, xiv.

2 John Mullan, *Sentiment and Sociability: The Language of Feeling in the Eighteenth Century*, Oxford: Clarendon Press, 1988, 16. However, Michael McKeon suggests that the novel of sensibility may be regarded as a purely non-referential "aesthetic" mode of literature; see *The Origins of the English Novel, 1600–1740*, Baltimore MD: Johns Hopkins University Press, 1987, 125–6.

3 Cowley's ode was included in the prefatory material to *The History of the Royal Society* (1667), by Thomas Sprat, eds Jackson I. Cope and Harold Whitmore Jones, St Louis MO: Washington University Studies, 1958.

4 "The vanity of dogmatizing," in *The Vanity of Dogmatizing: The Three "Versions,"* Hove: Harvester Press, 1970, 152.

5 The novelty of proclaiming the visibility of Authority's body all the more strikingly appears when considered against an older political theory of authority, that of the King's Two Bodies. According to this theory, the king had two bodies: one natural, mortal and visible; and the other infallible, immortal and invisible. The authority of the king as king was largely identified with the invisible, immortal body (whereby the continuity of the king's authority was assured—the king never died). See Ernst H. Kantorowicz, *The King's Two Bodies: A Study in Mediaeval Political Theology*, Princeton NJ: Princeton University Press, 1957.

6 See P. B. Wood, "Methodology and apologetics: Thomas Sprat's *History of the Royal Society*," *The British Journal for the History of Science,* 13, 1980: 1–26. R. F. Jones calls the *History* "an official statement on the matter. It was written at the instigation and under the auspices of the Society, was closely followed by the members during its composition, and when finished was heartily approved by them." See Richard Foster Jones, *Ancients and Moderns: A Study of the Background of the Battle of the Books*, Washington University Studies, n.s. 6, St Louis MO: Washington University Press, 1936, 231–2. Wood complicates Jones' interpretation somewhat, reminding us that the *History* does not accurately reflect the full diversity of beliefs within the Society, but rather exists as an exercise in public relations.

7 Steven Shapin and Simon Schaffer, *Leviathan and the Airpump: Hobbes, Boyle, and the Experimental Life*, Princeton NJ: Princeton University Press, 1985, 341.

8 See Shapin and Schaffer, *Leviathan and the Airpump*, 110–54.

9 From his *Plus Ultra: Or the Progress and Advancement of Knowledge Since the Days of Aristotle* (London, 1668). Cited in R. F. Jones, 250.

10 Thomas Sprat, *History of the Royal Society*, eds Jackson I. Cope and Harold Whitmore Jones, St Louis MO: Washington University Studies, 1958, 53, 119.

11 Barbara J. Shapiro, *Probability and Certainty in Seventeenth-Century England*, Princeton NJ: Princeton University Press, 1983, 22.

12 On the difference between a demonstrative and probabilist philosopher during the period, see Shapin and Schaffer, *Leviathan and the Airpump*, 146–54.

13 Shapiro, *Probability and Certainty*, 24–5.

14 "Discourse concerning the original and progress of satire," *The Works of John Dryden*, 20 vols, Berkeley CA: University of California Press, 1956–89, 4: 19–20.

15 Richard Kroll remarks upon how many of the "luminaries of Restoration and early eighteenth-century culture" were born between 1630 and 1636 in *The Material Word: Literate Culture in the Restoration and Early Eighteenth Century*, Baltimore MD: Johns Hopkins University Press, 1991, 44. Dryden, born in 1631, was elected a Fellow of the Royal Society in 1662, though his participation appears to have been half-hearted and he was expelled for non-payment of dues four years later. See James Anderson Winn, *John Dryden and His World*, New Haven CT: Yale University Press, 1987, 129.

16 For an extended discussion of the relation between Restoration science and Restoration theology, see Robert Markley, *Fallen Languages: Crises of Representation in Newtonian England 1660–1740*, Ithaca NY: Cornell University Press, 1993.

17 *Absalom and Achitophel*, ll. 1030–1, *The Works of John Dryden*, 2: 36.

18 Stubbe, who wrote no fewer than seven books and pamphlets against the Royal Society, was reportedly hired to his task as the Society's detractor by one Dr Baldwin Hamey, a member of the Royal College of Physicians, who feared that the fame of the newly formed Society would eclipse that of the Royal College. See Appendix B of the Cope and Jones edition of the *History of the Royal Society*. At the time, the Royal College of Physicians was a defender of the authority of Galen, one of the ancients whom the new philosophy distrusted (R. F. Jones 222–3). James R. Jacob has more recently argued that Stubbe's attack on the Royal Society may have been motivated by his religious views as a radical dissenter; he objected to "the active and deliberate alliance growing up between the Royal Society and a certain kind of Anglican orthodoxy, namely, latitudinarianism or liberal Anglicanism." See Jacob's *Henry Stubbe, Radical Protestantism and the Early Enlightenment*, Cambridge: Cambridge University Press, 1983, 7. R. H. Syfret also discusses Stubbe's reaction to the Royal Society in "Some early critics of the Royal Society," *Notes and Records of The Royal Society of London*, 8, 1950: 20–64.

19 "Preface to the reader" in *Legends No Histories: Or, A Specimen of Some Animadversions Upon the History of the Royal Society* (London, 1670).

20 See *Legends No Histories*, "Preface to the Reader," and Stubbe's *Campanella Revived, Or an Enquiry into the History of the Royal Society, Whether the Virtuosi there do not pursue the Projects of Campanella for the reducing England unto Popery* (London, 1670) 3–4. Claiming Spain to be the rightful inheritor of the "*Universal Monarchy of the World*," Campanella had proposed, in *De Monarchia Hispanica*, some means by which the Spanish king might enlarge his dominions to include the rebellious Protestant states. Generally, Campanella recommended that the king promote the study of mathematics, philosophy and the natural sciences in lieu of theological study, "that so by this means the Younger Heads might be busied, and taken up with these kind of Speculations, rather then [*sic*] spend their time in Heretical Studies." In other words, to distract people from theological study was to distract them from challenging papal authority. For the English in particular, Campanella

advised spreading among them "the Seeds of Schisme and Divisions in the *Natural Science.*" Stubbe's margin note reads, " *'Tis much better done by the* Virtuosi *now.*"

Stubbe claims to follow the English edition of *De Monarchia Hispanica*, which would have been available to him in two editions, both translated by Edmund Chilmead. The earlier edition appeared in 1654 as *A Discourse Touching the Spanish Monarchy*. The later edition, probably more accessible to Stubbe because issued in 1660, went under the title *Thomas Campanella, An Italian Friar and Second Machiavel. His Advice to the King of Spain for attaining the Universal Monarchy of the World.*

21 Stubbe himself appears to have been the one more interested in "*Democratical* contrivances." See Jacob, *Henry Stubbe*, esp. 78–108.

22 Stubbe's criticism of the uselessness of experimental learning would have been difficult to refute, for the new philosophy's projects did not yield practical improvements to seventeenth-century life. See Richard S. Westfall, "Robert Hooke, mechanical technology, and scientific investigation," *The Uses of Science in the Age of Newton*, ed. John G. Burke, Los Angeles CA: William Andrews Clark Memorial Library, 1983, 85–110.

23 See Syfret, "Some early critics," 42–64.

24 Syfret, "Some early critics," 39; Shapiro, *Probablity and Certainty*, 24.

25 Thomas Shadwell, *The Virtuoso*, eds Marjory Hope Nicholson and David Stuart Rodes, Lincoln NE: University of Nebraska Press, 1966, 22, 72. For an extended discussion of Shadwell's satire on the Royal Society, see Claude Lloyd, "Shadwell and the virtuosi," *PMLA*, 44, 1929: 472–94.

26 *An Essay in Defence of the Female Sex*, in *The Pioneers*, eds Marie Mulvey Roberts and Tamae Mizuta, London: Routledge/Thoemmes Press, 1995, 86–7. The passage appears on pages 90–1 of the 1696 edition in a very slightly altered form, apparently a printer's error.

27 Ned Ward, *The London Spy*, ed. Paul Hyland, East Lansing MI: Colleagues Press, 1993, 54.

28 Susannah Centlivre, *A Bold Stroke for A Wife*, ed. Thalia Stathas, Lincoln NE: University of Nebraska Press, 1968, 46–7.

29 Aphra Behn, *The Rover and Other Plays*, ed. Jane Spencer, Oxford: Oxford University Press, 1995, 281.

30 Motteux, "The translator's preface," *Don Quixote* (London 1700) sig. A5.

31 John Arbuthnot *et al.*, *Memoirs of the Extraordinary Life, Works, and Discoveries of Martinus Scriblerus*, ed. Charles Kerby-Miller, New York: Oxford University Press, 1988, 93, 91.

32 *The Philosophical Quixote; Or, Memoirs of Mr. David Wilkins. In a Series of Letters*, 2 vols (London, 1782) 1: 12, 2: 55–6. The name "Wilkins" is suggestive of Dr John Wilkins, a leader in the effort to establish the Royal Society.

33 The figure looming large behind this conjunction of materialism and atheism is, as Jones points out, Hobbes (R. F. Jones 242). For a discussion of the strong seventeenth-century reaction against Hobbes' materialism, see Samuel I. Mintz, *The Hunting of Leviathan: Seventeenth-Century Reactions to the Materialism and Moral Philosophy of Thomas Hobbes*, Cambridge: Cambridge University Press, 1962.

34 Samuel Butler, "The elephant in the moon," *Hudibras Parts I and II and Selected Other Writings*, eds John Wilders and Hugh de Quehen, Oxford: Clarendon Press, 1973, ll. 459–62.

35 See Michael McKeon, *Origins of the English Novel*, 68–73, cit. 69.

36 Ian Hacking, *The Emergence of Probability: A Philosophical Study of Early Ideas about Probability, Induction, and Statistical Inference*, London: Cambridge University Press, 1975, 12.

37 McKeon, *Origins of the English Novel*, 71.

38 On the Society's interest in fusing words and things via the "plain style," real characters, and universal languages, see Jackson I. Cope and Harold Whitmore Jones, introduction, *The History of the Royal Society*, by Thomas Sprat, St Louis MO: Washington University Studies, 1958, xxv–xxx; James B. Knowlson, *Universal Language Schemes in England and France 1600–1800*, Toronto: University of Toronto Press, 1975, 72–107; Barbara J. Shapiro, *Probability and Certainty*, 232–46; and Joel Reed, "Restoration and repression: the language projects of the Royal Society," *Studies in Eighteenth-Century Culture*, 19, 1989: 399–412. Richard Kroll complicates the usual arguments made about the Society's efforts to assert the correspondence between words to things, defending Restoration thinkers against charges of linguisitic naiveté in *The Material Word*, 183–238.

39 Foucault, *The Order of Things: An Archaeology of the Human Sciences*, New York: Vintage, 1973, 48–9.

40 John K. Sheriff, *The Good-Natured Man: The Evolution of a Moral Ideal, 1660–1800*, University AL: University of Alabama Press, 1982, 39; Janet Todd, *Sensibility: An Introduction*, London: Methuen, 1986, 108.

41 Todd, *Sensibility: An Introduction*, 108.

42 On the transformation of Don Quixote, see Stuart Tave, *The Amiable Humorist*, Chicago IL: University of Chicago Press, 1960, 151–63; Edwin B. Knowles, "Cervantes and English literature," *Cervantes Across the Centuries*, eds Angel Flores and M. J. Benardete, New York: The Dryden Press, 1947, 267–93; Eric J. Ziolkowski, *The Sanctification of Don Quixote: From Hidalgo to Priest*, University Park PA: Pennsylvania State University Press, 1991, 37–61. Interestingly enough, as Don Quixote metamorphosed from burlesque fool to sentimental hero through the eighteenth century, Cervantes himself underwent a parallel transformation from gentleman satirist into good-natured man; see A. P. Burton, "Cervantes the man seen through English eyes in the seventeenth and eighteenth centuries," *Bulletin of Hispanic Studies*, 45, 1968: 1–15.

43 Richard Voitle, "The reason of the English Enlightenment," *Studies on Voltaire and the Eighteenth Century*, ed. Theodore Besterman, 27, 1963: 1735–74, 1774.

44 Mandeville's *Fable* has a complex publication history, appearing first in 1705 as a poem of modest length called *The Grumbling Hive: or Knaves Turn'd Honest*. Over the next twenty-four years, the piece swelled into the two volumes it now fills as Mandeville added hundreds of pages of prose commentary on the subject. See F. B. Kaye's introduction to *The Fable of the Bees*, by Bernard Mandeville, 1924, Indianapolis IN: Liberty Classics, 1988, xxxiii–xxxvii.

45 Kaye, introduction, cxvi.

46 Bernard Mandeville, *The Fable of the Bees or Private Vices, Publick Benefits*, commentary by F. B. Kaye, 2 vols, 1924, Indianapolis IN: Liberty Classics, 1988, 1: 51.

47 Shaftesbury, Anthony Ashley Cooper, Third Earl, *Characteristics of Men, Manners, Opinions, Times*, ed. John M. Robertson, 2 vols, Gloucester MA: Peter Smith, 1963, 258.

48 Law, *Remarks upon the Fable of the Bees*, introduction by F. D. Maurice (Cambridge, 1844) 15. Law's intellectual development eventually led him away from the epistemological position he took against Mandeville's *Fable*, turning him into something of an enthusiast by the end of his career. See John Sitter, *Literary Loneliness in Mid-Eighteenth-Century England*, Ithaca NY: Cornell University Press, 1982, 50–73.

49 The empiricist problem of negation—how to prove that something does not exist—was recognized as far back as the fourteenth century by William of Ockham (1300–49). See Etienne Gilson, *The Unity of Philosophical Experience*, New

York: Scribner's, 1956, 78–80. See also Locke, *An Essay Concerning Human Understanding*, ed. Peter H. Nidditch, Oxford: Clarendon Press, 1975, 374.

50 *The Collected Works of Francis Hutcheson*, facsimile edition prepared by Bernhard Fabian, 7 vols, Hildesheim: Georg Olms, 1971, 1: 109.

51 Philosophically, Hutcheson's argument introduces some confusion because it disrupts the Lockean division between simple and complex ideas. See T. A. Roberts, *The Concept of Benevolence: Aspects of Eighteenth-Century Moral Philosophy*, London: Macmillan, 1973, 3; and Peter Kivy, *The Seventh Sense: A Study of Francis Hutcheson's Aesthetics and its Influence in Eighteenth-Century Britain*, New York: Burt Franklin, 1976, 25.

52 *An Essay on the Nature and Conduct of the Passions and Affections* (1728), *The Collected Works of Francis Hutcheson*, 2: vi.

53 Citations from this volume will follow the pagination of the edition, not the original eighteenth-century pagination.

54 Hutcheson discusses the *"Sense* of the *Ridiculous"* in *Reflections upon Laughter, and Remarks upon The Fable of the Bees*, first published in the *Dublin Weekly Journal* from 1725 to 1726. Later they were brought out separately as *Reflections upon Laughter, and Remarks upon The Fable of the Bees* (Glasgow, 1750) and *Thoughts on Laughter, and Observations on The Fable of the Bees* (Glasgow, 1758). See Fabian, "Bibliographical note," *Collected Works of Francis Hutcheson*, xi. Interestingly, in these essays, Hutcheson identifies *"Hudibras* and *Don Quixote"* as the model for all ridicule in the "Boldness of our age" (Hutcheson 7: 115).

55 See Barbara Herrnstein Smith's discussion of the "aesthetic axiology," in *Contingencies of Value: Alternate Perspectives for Critical Theory*, Cambridge MA: Harvard University Press, 1988, 36–42.

56 *The Works of the Right Honourable Joseph Addison*, 6 vols (London, 1811) 5: 458.

57 *David Simple* was first published in 1744, then revised by Henry Fielding and reissued that same year. In 1747, Sarah Fielding published *Familiar Letters Between the Principle Characters in David Simple, and Some Others*, followed by *David Simple Volume the Last* in 1753. See Malcolm Kelsall, introduction, *The Adventures of David Simple* by Sarah Fielding, Oxford: Oxford University Press, 1973, x–xi.

58 On *David Simple* as disguised narrative, see C. Woodward, "'Feminine virtue, ladylike disguise, women of community': Sarah Fielding and the female I am at mid-century," *Transactions of the Samuel Johnson Society of the Northwest*, 15, 1984: 57–71; and Deborah Downs-Miers, "Springing the trap: subtexts and subversions," *Fetter'd or Free?: British Women Novelists, 1670–1815*, eds Mary Anne Schofield and Cecilia Macheski, Athens OH: Ohio University Press, 1986, 308–23. Janet Todd, *The Sign of Angelica: Women, Writing and Fiction, 1660–1800*, New York: Columbia University Press, 1989, 171, is quoted above, allaying "improper suspicions." Gillian Skinner, "'The Price of a Tear': economic sense and sensibility in Sarah Fielding's *David Simple*," *Literature and History*, 3rd series, 1.1, 1992: 16–28, argues that David's characteristic simplicity should be seen in its "doubleness," as commendable but also weak and silly.

59 *The Correspondence of Henry and Sarah Fielding*, eds Martin Battestin and Clive T. Probyn, Oxford: Clarendon Press, 1993, 132.

60 "Sarah Fielding, 1710–1768," *Literature Criticism from 1400–1800*, ed. Dennis Poupard, vol. 1, Detroit MI: Gale, 1984, 267–80, cit. 267; Kelsall, introduction, xii.

61 *The Adventures of David Simple*, ed. Malcolm Kelsall, Oxford: Oxford University Press, 1973, 9. Subsequent citations to the novel will be included parenthetically in the text and will refer to this edition.

62 See also Gillian Skinner's discussion of David as the "Mandevillian fool," in "'The Price of a Tear,'" 16ff.

63 Henry Fielding substantially revised this passage, inserting the comparison to Don Quixote, which some have read as an effort to place a kind of family stamp on Sarah's novel. See Kelsall's "Note on the text" in his edition of *David Simple*, xix. The comparison which Henry brings to the beginning, however, may have been inspired by Sarah's mention, in a later chapter, that David's "Man of Goodness and Virtue," the real friend whom he seeks, "was, to him, what *Dulcinea* was to Don *Quixote*" (*DS* 96).

64 Joel C. Weinsheimer, *Eighteenth-Century Hermeneutics: Philosophy of Interpretation in England from Locke to Burke*, New Haven CT: Yale University Press, 1993, 1–2.

65 Todd, *Sensibility: An Introduction*, 4.

3 COMING TO A BAD END

1 Readers disappointed by Arabella's defeat include Leland E. Warren, "Of the conversation of women: *The Female Quixote* and the dream of perfection," *Studies in Eighteenth-Century Culture*, 2, 1982: 367–80; Margaret Anne Doody, "Shakespeare's novels: Charlotte Lennox illustrated," *Studies in the Novel*, 19, 1987: 296–310; and Patricia Meyer Spacks, *Desire and Truth: Functions of Plot in Eighteenth-Century English Novels*, Chicago IL: University of Chicago Press, 1990: 12–33.

2 Margaret Dalziel, introduction, *The Female Quixote* by Charlotte Lennox, Oxford: Oxford University Press, 1973, xviii.

3 Duncan Isles, appendix, *The Female Quixote* by Charlotte Lennox, Oxford: Oxford University Press, 1973, 423–5.

4 On the sentimentalism of the novel's conclusion, see also James J. Lynch, "Romance and realism in Charlotte Lennox's *The Female Quixote*," *Essays in Literature*, 14, 1987: 51–63.

5 See Warren, "Of the conversation of women"; Doody, "Shakespeare's novels"; Laurie Langbauer, *Women and Romance: The Consolations of Gender in the English Novel*, Ithaca NY: Cornell University Press, 1990, 62–92; and Judith Dorn, "Reading women reading history: the philosophy of periodical form in Charlotte Lennox's *The Lady's Museum*," *Historical Reflections/Réflexions Historiques*, 18, 1992: 7–27.

6 Langbauer, *Women and Romance*, 89.

7 Samuel Richardson, *Clarissa* (1747–8); Oliver Goldsmith, *The Vicar of Wakefield* (1766); Henry Brooke, *The Fool of Quality* (1765–70).

8 Charlotte Lennox, "The History of the Dutchess of Beaufort," *The Lady's Museum*, 2 vols (London, 1760–1) 1: 72–3.

9 Charlotte Lennox, *Shakespear Illustrated: Or the Novels and Histories, On which the Plays of Shakespeare Are Founded, Collected and Translated from the Original Authors. With Critical Remarks*, 2 vols (London, 1753) 2: 276–8. A third volume followed in 1754.

    Hector Boece wrote in Latin. Since Lennox apparently knew no Latin (*Shakespear Illustrated*, 2: 219), she may have relied upon John Bellenden's Scots translation of *The Chronicles* (1531).

10 See Miriam Rossiter Small, *Charlotte Ramsay Lennox: An Eighteenth-Century Lady of Letters*, 1935, Archon, 1969, 118. *Harriot Stuart* was published in 1751.

11 *Sophia* was first published serially in *The Lady's Museum* as "The history of Harriot and Sophia."

12 Agnes Mary Kynaston, "The life and writings of Charlotte Lennox, 1720–1804," unpublished dissertation, University of London, 1936, 26–7.

13 Kynaston, 1.

14 Philippe Séjourné, *The Mystery of Charlotte Lennox: First Novelist of Colonial America (1727?–1804)*, Aix-en-Provence: Publications des Annales de la Faculté des Lettres, 1967, 11–12.

15 Kynaston, 2.

16 Duncan Isles, chronology of Charlotte Lennox, *The Female Quixote*, ed. Margaret Dalziel, Oxford: Oxford University Press, 1973.

17 Small, 14–15. Isles offers 1729–30 as a more accurate birth year, while Séjourné guesses 1727.

18 Isles, chronology.

19 David Marshall, in another context, also argues for identifying Lennox with Charlotte Glanville. See his "Writing masters and 'masculine exercises' in *The Female Quixote*," *Eighteenth-Century Fiction*, 5, 1993: 105–35. Marshall's essay is primarily interested in accounting for "the problem of *writing*" in *The Female Quixote*, not "the problem of *reading*" (106–7). My own essay focuses on the problem of reading.

20 Unlike the accounts of Lennox's American origins, some of the autobiographical elements in *Harriot Stuart* can be verified to a greater extent, as they do not solely depend on Lennox's own report. See Small, 4–6.

21 *The Life of Harriot Stuart. Written by Herself*, 2 vols (London, 1751) 1: 8.

22 "The Art of Coquetry," ll. 9–11. For text and commentary on this poem, see Small, 232–6.

23 Deborah Ross discusses the contrast between Charlotte's belabored artifice and Arabella's artlessness in "Mirror, mirror: the didactic dilemma of *The Female Quixote*," *SEL*, 27, 1987: 455–73, especially 466–7.

24 Joel C. Weinsheimer, *Eighteenth-Century Hermeneutics: Philosophy of Interpretation in England from Locke to Burke*, New Haven CT: Yale University Press, 1993, 1–22.

25 It has been suggested that Johnson himself actually wrote the chapter in which the good doctor appears, but there is no consensus on the matter. See John Mitford, "Dr Johnson's literary intercourse with Mrs Lennox," *The Gentleman's Magazine*, 175, 1843: 132, and his follow-up, "Chapter by Dr Johnson in *The Female Quixote*," *The Gentleman's Magazine*, 176, 1844: 41. Isles refutes the attribution, appendix, 421. Modern readers rarely bother to take sides in this old debate, though they do sometimes remark how much the doctor resembles Johnson: Spacks, *Desire and Truth*, 15–16; Ross, 459.

26 Lennox did know Hutcheson's work; his *Essay on the Nature and Conduct of the Passions and Affections* drew from her the poetic response, "On reading HUTCHISON on the PASSIONS" in Small, 155. Small also notes that this poem "was apparently Mrs Lennox's favorite of her own creation as she reprints it three times after the initial printing."

27 Sarah Fielding's novel seems a likely enough context for Lennox's. The works were similar enough to make Lady Mary Wortley Montagu suspect that Sarah Fielding was *The Female Quixote*'s author. See *The Complete Letters of Lady Mary Wortley Montagu*, ed. Robert Halsband, 3 vols, Oxford: Clarendon Press, 1967, 3: 67, 88.

28 Boswell records that Johnson wrote the dedication for Lennox's novel. *Life of Johnson*, ed. R. W. Chapman, Oxford: Oxford University Press, 1985, 260. Boswell mistakenly records the year of the dedication as 1762, however, exactly a decade after the novel was first published.

29 Charles Sackville, Earl of Middlesex (1711–69).

30 See also Spacks, who argues that a major feature of Arabella's quixotism is her desire, as a woman, "to inhabit the public sphere": Arabella, Spacks asserts, "claims male prerogatives, welcomes male responsibility—and declares both 'female.'" *Desire and Truth*, 28.

31 Spacks, *Desire and Truth*, 31.

32 Spacks, *Desire and Truth*, 22.

33 Patricia Meyer Spacks, "The subtle sophistry of desire: Dr Johnson and *The Female Quixote*," *Modern Philology*, 85, 1988: 532–42, cit. 539.

4 SEEING THE GENERAL VIEW

1 Edwin B. Knowles, "Cervantes and English literature," *Cervantes Across the Centuries*, eds Angel Flores and M. J. Benardete, New York: The Dryden Press, 1947, 267–93, cit. 283; Martin C. Battestin, introduction, *Joseph Andrews*, by Henry Fielding, Boston: Houghton Mifflin, 1961, xxix; Susan Staves, "Don Quixote in eighteenth-century England," *Comparative Literature*, 24, 1972: 193–215.

2 Henry Fielding, *Joseph Andrews*, ed. Martin C. Battestin, Boston: Houghton Mifflin, 1961, 13. Subsequent citations will appear parenthetically within the text.

3 On *Tom Jones* as a romance, see Henry Knight Miller, *Henry Fielding's Tom Jones and the Romance Tradition*, Victoria BC: University of Victoria, 1976.

4 For a summary of critical reaction to the novel's plot, see H. George Hahn, "Main lines of criticism of Fielding's *Tom Jones*, 1900–78," *British Studies Monitor*, 10.1–2, 1980: 8–35. On Fielding's famed masculinity, see Jill Campbell, *Natural Masques: Gender and Identity in Fielding's Plays and Novels*, Stanford CA: Stanford University Press, 1995, 2–5; April London, "Controlling the text: women in *Tom Jones*," *Studies in the Novel*, 19, 1987: 323–33; and Angela J. Smallwood, *Fielding and the Woman Question: The Novels of Henry Fielding and Feminist Debate, 1700–1750*, New York: Harvester Wheatsheaf and St Martin's Press, 1989.

5 Martin Battestin, introduction, *Tom Jones* by Henry Fielding, ed. Fredson Bowers, Middletown CT: Wesleyan University Press, 1975, xxx.

6 Martin C. Battestin, introduction, *Joseph Andrews*, v.

7 Henry Fielding, *The Covent-Garden Journal*, ed. Gerard Edward Jensen, 2 vols, 1915, New York: Russell and Russell, 1964, 1: 280–1. Subsequent citations will appear parenthetically within the text.

8 Martin Battestin, "Fielding's definition of wisdom: some functions of ambiguity and emblem in *Tom Jones*," *ELH*, 35, 1968: 188–217.

9 On Fielding's attitudes toward these works, see Battestin's notes in *Tom Jones*, 273.

10 On "prudence" as the controlling idea in *Tom Jones*, see Glenn W. Hatfield, *Henry Fielding and the Language of Irony*, Chicago IL: University of Chicago Press, 1968, 179–96; Battestin, "Fielding's definition of wisdom"; and Eleanor Newman Hutchens, "'Prudence': a case study," in *Irony in* Tom Jones, University AL: Alabama University Press, 1965, 101–18.

11 Ian Watt, *The Rise of the Novel*, Berkeley CA: University of California Press, 1957, 13.

12 R. S. Crane (ed.) "The concept of plot and the plot of *Tom Jones*," in *Critics and Criticism: Ancient and Modern*, Chicago IL: University of Chicago Press, 1952, 616–47, cit. 624.

13 Watt, *The Rise of the Novel*, 271.

14 "An essay on the knowledge of the characters of men," *Miscellanies*, ed. Henry Knight Miller, 2 vols, Oxford: Wesleyan University Press, 1972, 1: 155.

15 It does appear that Fielding intends to instruct specifically men, not women, in the lessons of human experience. The image of men falling in love with Virtue's nakedness suggests as much, and the "Essay on the knowledge of the characters of men" is even more specific. Fielding uses the same image of Virtue's naked charms—"It is truly said of Virtue, that, could men behold her naked, they would be all in love with her" (*Miscellanies* 173)—in this essay, while acknowledging that he confines his advice only to the characters of men. The "Essay" does not apply to "the Fair Sex," he writes, "the Knowledge of the Characters of Women being foreign to my intended Purpose; as it is in Fact a Science, to which I make not the least Pretension" (*Miscellanies* 161).

16 On Fielding's exterior approach to representation, see Thomas A. Stumpf, *"Tom Jones* from the outside," *The Classic British Novel*, eds Howard M. Harper Jr and Charles Edge, Athens GA: University of Georgia Press, 1972, 3–21; Malinda Snow, "The judgment of evidence in *Tom Jones," South Atlantic Review*, 48, 1983: 37–51; and Alexander Welsh, *Strong Representations: Narrative and Circumstantial Evidence in England*, Baltimore MD: Johns Hopkins University Press, 1992, 48–76.

17 Samuel Johnson, *The Yale Edition of the Works of Samuel Johnson*, eds W. J. Bate and Albrecht B. Strauss, 16 vols, New Haven CT: Yale University Press, 1969, 3: 22.

18 See Hatfield, 86–7.

19 *The True Patriot*, 19 November 1745.

20 See James J. Lynch, "Moral sense and the narrator of *Tom Jones," SEL*, 25, 1985: 599–614.

21 Samuel Johnson, *Rambler* no. 158, *The Yale Edition of the Works of Samuel Johnson*, 5: 76.

22 Martin C. Battestin, "The problem of *Amelia*: Hume, Barrow, and the conversion of Captain Booth," *ELH*, 41, 1974: 613–48, cit. 613, 635.

23 Henry Fielding, *Amelia*, ed. Martin C. Battestin, Middletown CT: Wesleyan University Press, 1983, 16.

24 On the relation between probability and Fielding's fiction, see Douglas Lane Patey, *Probability and Literary Form: Philosophic Theory and Literary Practice in the Augustan Age*, Cambridge: Cambridge University Press, 1984, 197–212.

25 See Campbell, *Natural Masques*, 137–200; Battestin, "Tom Jones and 'His Egyptian Majesty': Fielding's parable of government," *PMLA*, 82, 1967: 68–77; Anthony Kearney, "Tom Jones and the Forty-five," *Ariel*, 4.2, 1973: 68–78; Peter J. Carlton, *"Tom Jones* and the '45 once again," *Studies in the Novel*, 20, 1988: 361–73; and Thomas Cleary, "Jacobitism in *Tom Jones*: the basis for an hypothesis," *Philological Quarterly*, 52, 1973: 239–51.

26 Henry Fielding, *The True Patriot and Related Writings*, ed. W. B. Coley, *The Wesleyan Edition of the Works of Henry Fielding*, Middletown CT: Wesleyan University Press, 1987, 256. On Fielding's distrust of professional jargon, see Hatfield, 127–51.

27 Hume, *A Treatise of Human Nature*, ed. L. A. Selby-Bigge, 2nd edition revised by P. H. Nidditch, Oxford: Clarendon Press, 1978, 581–2. Fielding's relation to Hume is unclear, though it has drawn critical attention. See Battestin, "The problem of *Amelia*," 642–8; and Eve Tavor, *Scepticism, Society and the Eighteenth-Century Novel*, Houndmills: Macmillan, 1987, 108–66.

28 The writer is identified by Battestin as Cicero, see *Tom Jones*, 485, note 1.

29 The following day, Jones meets Jenny Waters, the adventures at the inn at Upton follow, and Jones abandons his martial ambitions to pursue Sophia to London. On the pivotal nature of this middle section of the novel, see Martin C. Battestin, "Fielding's definition of wisdom."

5 DE GUSTIBUS NON EST DISPUTANDUM

1 Alexander Gerard, *An Essay on Taste, Together with Observations Concerning the Imitative Nature of Poetry*, facsimile reproduction of the third edition (1780) by Walter J. Hipple Jr, Gainesville FL: Scholars' Facsimiles & Reprints, 1963, 207–8.

2 James Boswell, *Life of Johnson*, ed. R. W. Chapman, Oxford: Oxford University Press, 1985, 696; Laurence Sterne, *The Life and Opinions of Tristram Shandy, Gentleman*, ed. Ian Campbell Ross, Oxford: Oxford University Press, 1983. Subsequent references to *Tristram Shandy* will come from this edition.

3 See Stuart Tave, *The Amiable Humorist*, Chicago IL: University of Chicago Press, 1960, 151–63.

4 See Joan Joffe Hall, "The hobbyhorsical world of *Tristram Shandy*," *Modern Language Quarterly*, 24, 1963: 131–43; and Michael V. DePorte, *Nightmares and Hobbyhorses: Swift, Sterne, and Augustan Ideas of Madness*, San Marino CA: The Huntington Library, 1974, who each read Sterne's work as an endorsement of idiosyncrasy and relativism.

5 Cited in Tave, *The Amiable Humorist*, 163.

6 On the Select Society of Edinburgh's subcommittee, "The Edinburgh Society for encouraging arts, sciences, manufactures, and agriculture in Scotland," which awarded Gerard the prize, see John Rae, *Life of Adam Smith*, introduction by Jacob Viner, New York: Augustus M. Kelley, 1965, 112–19.

7 Hume added "Of the Standard of Taste," first published in 1757 in a work entitled *Four Dissertations*, to the 1758 edition of his *Essays and Treatises*. See Eugene F. Miller, foreword, *Essays Moral, Political, and Literary* by David Hume, ed. Eugene F. Miller, revised edition, Indianapolis IN: Liberty Classics, 1985, xiv, note 9.

8 David Hume, *Essays Moral, Political, and Literary*, ed. Eugene F. Miller, revised edition, Indianapolis IN: Liberty Classics, 1985, 229.

9 Barbara Herrnstein Smith, *Contingencies of Value: Alternate Perspectives for Critical Theory*, Cambridge MA: Harvard University Press, 1988, 37.

10 John Traugott, *Tristram Shandy's World: Sterne's Philosophical Rhetoric*, New York: Russell and Russell, 1954, 19.

11 On *Tristram Shandy* as a satire on learning, see D. W. Jefferson, "*Tristram Shandy* and the tradition of learned wit," *Essays in Criticism*, 1, 1951: 225–48.

12 See Ruth Perry, "Words for sex: the verbal-sexual continuum in *Tristram Shandy*," *Studies in the Novel*, 20, 1988: 27–42; J. Paul Hunter, "Clocks, calendars, and names: the troubles of Tristram and the aesthetics of uncertainty," *Rhetorics of Order/Ordering Rhetorics in English Neoclassical Literature*, eds J. Douglas Canfield and J. Paul Hunter, Newark DE: University of Delaware Press, 1989, 173–98; Melvyn New, "Job's wife and Sterne's other women," *Out of Bounds: Male Writers and Gender(ed) Criticism*, eds Laura Claridge and Elizabeth Langland, Amherst MA: University of Massachusetts Press, 1990, 55–74; Paula Loscocco, "Can't live without 'em: Walter Shandy and the woman within," *The Eighteenth Century*, 32, 1991: 166–79; Barbara M. Benedict, "'Dear Madam': rhetoric, cultural politics and the female reader in Sterne's *Tristram Shandy*," *Studies in Philology*, 89, 1992: 485–98.

13 Addison expresses similar sentiments in the *Spectator* no. 12, in which he disapproves of ghost stories: "we ought to arm ourselves against them by the Dictates of Reason and Religion, *to pull the old Woman out of our Hearts* (as Persius expresses it in the Motto of my Paper,) and extinguish those impertinent Notions which we imbibed at a Time that we were not able to judge of their Absurdity." *The Spectator*, ed. Donald F. Bond, 5 vols, Oxford: Clarendon Press, 1965, 1: 54. Several decades earlier, Joseph Glanvill's attack on irrational belief had proceeded

along the same lines: "The best account that many can give of their *belief*, is, that they were *bred* in it; which indeed is no better, then that which we call, the *Womans Reason.*" *The Vanity of Dogmatizing: The Three "Versions,"* Hove: Harvester Press, 1970, 127.

14 See Traugott, *Tristram Shandy's World*, 51–61; Earl R. Wasserman, *The Subtler Language: Critical Readings of Neoclassical and Romantic Poems*, Baltimore MD: Johns Hopkins University Press, 1959, 169–72; Joan Joffe Hall, "The hobbyhorsical world of *Tristram Shandy*."

15 Traugott, *Tristram Shandy's World*, 74.

16 Wolfgang Iser, *Laurence Sterne: Tristram Shandy*, trans. Henry David Wilson, Cambridge: Cambridge University Press, 1988, 17.

17 Traugott, *Tristram Shandy's World*, 75.

18 Iser, *Laurence Sterne: Tristram Shandy*, 54.

19 Bishop Richard Hurd, *Hurd's Letters on Chivalry and Romance With the Third Elizabethan Dialogue*, ed. Edith J. Morley, London: Henry Frowde, 1911, 84–5; John Bowle, *A Letter to the Reverend Dr. Percy, Concerning A New and Classical Edition of Historia Del Valeroso Cavallero Don Quixote De La Mancha* (London, 1777) 3.

20 James E. Swearingen, *Reflexivity in* Tristram Shandy*: An Essay in Phenomenological Criticism*, New Haven CT: Yale University Press, 1977, 6.

21 Traugott, *Tristram Shandy's World*, 73.

22 Swearingen, *Reflexivity in* Tristram Shandy, 36.

23 Hunter, "Clocks, calendars, and names," 196.

24 Michael Rosenblum, "Why what happens in Shandy Hall is not 'a matter for the police,'" *Eighteenth-Century Fiction*, 7, 1995: 145–64, cit. 164.

25 Swearingen, *Reflexivity in* Tristram Shandy, 220–4.

26 Swearingen, *Reflexivity in* Tristram Shandy, 218.

27 Martin C. Battestin, "The problem of *Amelia*: Hume, Barrow, and the conversion of Captain Booth," *ELH*, 41, 1974: 613–48, esp. 642–8.

6 LAYING DOWN THE GENERAL RULE

1 Robert J. Samuelson, "The spirit of Adam Smith," *Newsweek*, 2 December 1996: 63.

2 The phrase "timeless counsel" comes from Joseph Spengler, introduction, *Adam Smith's Relevance for 1976* by Milton Friedman, Los Angeles CA: International Institute for Economic Research, 1976.

3 Milton Friedman, *Adam Smith's Relevance for 1976*, Los Angeles CA: International Institute for Economic Research, 1976.

4 George J. Stigler, "The economist as preacher," *The Economist As Preacher and Other Essays*, Chicago IL: University of Chicago Press, 1982, 4.

5 The phrase "grandsons of Adam Smith" comes from Donald McCloskey, *The Rhetoric of Economics*, Madison WI: University of Wisconsin Press, 1985, 3; Paul A. Samuelson, "Modern economic realities and individualism," *The Collected Scientific Papers of Paul A. Samuelson*, ed. Joseph E. Stiglitz, 5 vols, Cambridge MA: MIT Press, 1966, 2: 1408.

6 See Ian Simpson Ross, *The Life of Adam Smith*, Oxford: Clarendon Press, 1995, 404–5.

7 Cited in Vernard Foley, *The Social Physics of Adam Smith*, West Lafayette IN: Purdue University Press, 1976, 12. The "History of astronomy" was published posthumously under the title of *Essays on Philosophical Subjects* (1795).

8 Foley, *The Social Physics of Adam Smith*, 11–18.

9 Adam Smith, "The principles which lead and direct philosophical inquiries; illus-
trated by the history of astronomy," *Essays on Philosophical Subjects*, eds W. P. D.
Wightman and J. C. Bryce, 1980, Indianapolis IN: Liberty Classics, 1982, 37–40.
Subsequent citations will appear parenthetically within the text.

10 Hume, *A Treatise of Human Nature*, ed. L. A. Selby-Bigge, 2nd edition revised by
Peter H. Nidditch, Oxford: Clarendon Press, 1978, 149. For the anecdote of
Smith's being caught reading Hume at Oxford, see Ross, *The Life of Adam Smith*,
77.

11 Oddly, the suggestion that the "invisible hand" might point to a failure of reason
seldom receives serious attention. Alec Macfie has attempted, though unconvinc-
ingly, to reconcile this "capricious" use of the "invisible hand" to Smith's later
"natural" uses of it. See "The invisible hand of Jupiter," *Journal of the History of
Ideas*, 32, 1971: 595–9. The preface to *The New Palgrave: The Invisible Hand*, eds
John Eatwell, Murray Milgate and Peter Newman, New York: W. W. Norton,
1989, simply ignores the superstitious invisible hand, claiming that Adam Smith
mentions the invisible hand "only twice." Karen Vaughn's essay on "the invisible
hand" in this same volume clarifies that these two instances occur in *The Wealth of
Nations*, IV, ii, and *The Theory of Moral Sentiments*, IV, i, 10. Her omission of this
third instance of the invisible hand appears deliberate, for her essay discusses the
metaphor in both *The Wealth of Nations* and *The Theory of Moral Sentiments*, says
nothing of its appearance in "The history of astronomy," yet uses other ideas
expressed in "The history of astronomy" in order to interpret "the invisible hand"
as it appears in *The Theory of Moral Sentiments* and *The Wealth of Nations*, Vaughn
170.

12 Alexander Pope, "Epitaph. Intended for Sir Isaac Newton, in Westminster-
Abbey," *The Poems of Alexander Pope*, ed. John Butt, one-volume edition of the
Twickenham text, New Haven CT: Yale University Press, 1963, 808. Smith
himself was described by his successors as "the 'Newton' of the history of civil
society"; see Duncan Forbes, "'Scientific' whiggism: Adam Smith and John
Millar," *Cambridge Journal*, 7, 1954: 643–70, cit. 646. On the general popularity
and dissemination of Newtonian ideas in the eighteenth century, see *The
Methodological Heritage of Newton*, eds Robert E. Butts and John W. Davis, Toronto:
University of Toronto Press, 1970; and Larry Stewart, *The Rise of Public Science:
Rhetoric, Technology, and Natural Philosophy in Newtonian Britain, 1660–1750*,
Cambridge: Cambridge University Press, 1992.

13 Adam Smith, *Lectures on Rhetoric and Belles Lettres*, ed. J. C. Bryce, 1983,
Indianapolis IN: Liberty Classics, 1985, 145–6. Cited in Ross, *Life of Adam Smith*,
56.

14 The famous "Adam Smith problem" may be seen as a legacy of Smith's own
Newtonianism, for it arises from the recognition that Smith's "certain principles"
appear to differ radically across his two major works. "Sympathy" is the "one
capital fact" connecting everything in *The Theory of Moral Sentiments*, while "self-
interest" occupies this role in *The Wealth of Nations*. Raphael and Macfie have
declared this "problem" to be a non-problem, arguing that Smith "recognizes a
variety of motives" for action, of which "self-interest" is only one in both *The
Theory of Moral Sentiments* and *The Wealth of Nations*. Jacob Viner disagrees,
stressing the diminished role of benevolence in *The Wealth of Nations* compared to
its importance in *The Theory of Moral Sentiments*, and asserting that "self-interest"
is not just one of many motives for action in *The Wealth of Nations*, but the only
motive discussed there. The "Adam Smith problem" is the problem of connecting
both of Smith's works with the same Newtonian chain. Raphael and Macfie see
no problem because they are eager to celebrate Smith himself as the "certain

principle" connecting the two books, doggedly declaring his steadiness and constancy in tones approaching shrill: "Nobody with any sense" should accept the hypothesis that Smith "did an about-turn from altruistic to egoistic theory in the WN owing to the influence of the French 'materialist' thinkers whom he met in Paris in 1766." Viner, however, looks to constant principles, not autonomous genius, to unite the works, and so continues to see an "Adam Smith problem." In either case, the Newtonian method that Smith endorsed continues to be validated. See D. D. Raphael and A. L. Macfie, introduction, *The Theory of Moral Sentiments* by Adam Smith, 1976, Indianapolis IN: Liberty Classics, 1982, 20–5, and Jacob C. Viner, "Adam Smith and Laissez Faire," *Essays on the Intellectual History of Economics*, ed. Douglas A. Irwin, Princeton NJ: Princeton University Press, 1991, 85–113, esp. 93–8.

15 Cited in Ross, *The Life of Adam Smith*, 126.

16 D. D. Raphael, "The Impartial Spectator," *Essays on Adam Smith*, eds Andrew S. Skinner and Thomas Wilson, Oxford: Clarendon Press, 1975, 83–99, cit. 98.

17 See Walter Jackson Bate, "The sympathetic imagination in eighteenth-century English criticism," *ELH*, 12, 1945: 144–64.

18 Adam Smith, *The Correspondence of Adam Smith*, eds Ernest Campbell Mossner and Ian Simpson Ross, 1977, Indianapolis IN: Liberty Classics, 1987, 49.

19 Adam Smith, *Correspondence*, 49.

20 Adam Smith, *Correspondence*, 54–5.

21 Smith's moral elitism has been attributed to the influence of Stoicism on his thinking. See Norbert Waszek, "Two concepts of morality: a distinction of Adam Smith's ethics and its stoic origin," *Journal of the History of Ideas*, 45, 1984: 591–606.

22 Cited in Ross, *The Life of Adam Smith*, 192–3.

23 The text of the dialogue is edited by Ernest Campbell Mossner and published in his "'Of the principle of moral estimation: a discourse between David Hume, Robert Clerk, and Adam Smith': an unpublished MS by Adam Ferguson," *Journal of the History of Ideas*, 21, 1960: 222–32, cit. 228–9.

24 David Frum, "Adam Smith, the sensible philosopher," *The New Criterion*, March 1996: 14–17, cit. 14.

25 Edwin G. West, "Adam Smith on the cultural effects of specialization: splenetics versus economics," *History of Political Economy*, 28, 1996: 83–105, cit. 83.

26 On the reception history of *The Wealth of Nations*, see Salim Rashid, "Adam Smith's rise to fame: a reexamination of the evidence," *The Eighteenth Century: Theory and Interpretation*, 23, 1982: 64–85; and Keith Tribe, "Natural liberty and laissez faire: how Adam Smith became a free trade ideologue," *Adam Smith's Wealth of Nations: New Interdisciplinary Essays*, eds Stephen Copley and Kathryn Sutherland, Manchester: Manchester University Press, 1995, 23–44.

27 See Phyllis Deane, *The Evolution of Economic Ideas*, Cambridge: Cambridge University Press, 1978, 11–12. Jacob Viner suggests that Smith chose the pin factory example out of personal familiarity. See Viner's "Guide to John Rae's *Life of Adam Smith*," *Life of Adam Smith* by John Rae, 105–7.

28 Adam Smith, *An Inquiry into the Nature and Causes of the Wealth of Nations*, eds R. H. Campbell, A. S. Skinner and W. B. Todd, 2 vols, 1976, Indianapolis IN: Liberty Classics, 1981, 1: 14. Subsequent citations to this work will appear parenthetically within the text.

29 See *A Brief State of the Inland or Home Trade* (1730), cited in John McVeagh, "Defoe and the romance of trade," *Durham University Journal*, n.s. 39, 1978: 141–7. Goldsmith wrote of the pin factory in *The Bee*, no. 1, 6 October 1759: "Thus a Magazine is not the result of any single man's industry; but goes through as many

hands as a new pin, before it is fit for the public." *Collected Works of Oliver Goldsmith*, ed. Arthur Friedman, 5 vols, Oxford: Clarendon Press, 1966, 1: 354. The pin factory example was used by a German writer as early as 1722–3; see Viner, "Guide to John Rae's *Life of Adam Smith*," 108.

30 John Barrell, *English Literature in History, 1730–80: An Equal, Wide Survey*, New York: St Martin's Press, 1983, 19, 31.

31 Barrell, *English Literature in History*, 33.

32 John Barrell, "Visualizing the division of labour," John Barrell, *The Birth of Pandora*, Philadelphia PA: University of Pennsylvania Press, 1992, 93–4.

33 Smith's description of the debilitating effects of capitalism has received much attention, notably because it lends authority to Marxists' arguments, and therefore had important implications within Cold War politics. See Nathan Rosenberg, "Adam Smith on the division of labour: two views or one?" *Economica*, n.s. 32, 1965: 127–39, which reads Smith's apparent reservations about capitalist production as a concern only applicable to the laboring poor, for "Smith sees the upper ranks of society as a group which is wholly insulated from the ravages of the division of labour" (138); Robert L. Heilbroner, "The paradox of progress: decline and decay in *The Wealth of Nations*," *Essays on Adam Smith*, eds Andrew S. Skinner and Thomas Wilson, Oxford: Clarendon Press, 1975, 524–39, which interprets the paradox as a sign of Smith's historically determined, class-bound consciousness; and E. G. West, "Adam Smith and alienation: wealth increases, men decay?" *Essays on Adam Smith*, eds Andrew S. Skinner and Thomas Wilson, 540–52, which energetically distinguishes Smith from Marx, arguing that Smith saw a remedy for social decline in public education subsidized by "the very capitalist production that was the source of the complaint" (540). West returns to the topic in "Adam Smith on the cultural effects of specialization: splenetics versus economics" (1996), which suggests that there are "two Adam Smiths at work," one heavily influenced by an admiration of "the early Greek republics and Roman states, with their emphasis on discipline and order," the other "more creative and pioneering," a "classical liberal Adam Smith" that "offers a glimpse of the emergence of the modern liberal state" (103–4).

34 Benedict Anderson, *Imagined Communities: Reflections on the Origin and Spread of Nationalism*, revised edition, London: Verso, 1991.

35 For other assessments of education and market forces, see Donald Winch, *Adam Smith's Politics: An Essay on Historiographic Revision*, Cambridge: Cambridge University Press, 1978, 80–7; Mark Blaug, "The economics of education in English classical political economy," *Essays on Adam Smith*, eds Andrew S. Skinner and Thomas Wilson, 568–99; and William L. Miller, "The economics of education in English classical economics," *Southern Economic Journal*, 32, 1965–6: 294–309.

36 On Smith's disenchantment with his experiences at Oxford, see Ross, *The Life of Adam Smith*, 60–80. In one memorable line about the slackness of academic life at Oxford, Ross writes that "the Fellows were reported to have so little to do that they spent their time sitting in Broad Street to watch the passage of the London mail coach" (69).

EPILOGUE

1 Edmund Burke, *Reflections on the Revolution in France*, ed. J. G. A. Pocock, Indianapolis IN: Hackett, 1987, 66.

2 Donald McCloskey, *The Rhetoric of Economics*, Madison WI: University of Wisconsin Press, 1985, 3.

3 "Modern economic realities and individualism," *The Collected Scientific Papers of Paul A. Samuelson*, ed. Joseph E. Stiglitz, 5 vols, Cambridge MA: MIT Press, 1966, 2: 1408.

4 Paul A. Samuelson, *Economics*, 11th edn, New York: McGraw-Hill, 1980, 4.

5 The assumptions about rational choice remain surprisingly strong within the discipline of economics, despite a long and powerful tradition of critique. See for example Frank H. Knight, "The limitations of scientific method in economics," *The Ethics of Competition and Other Essays*, New York: Harper, 1935, 105–47; Jacob C. Viner, "Monopoly and laissez faire," *Essays on the Intellectual History of Economics*, ed. Douglas A. Irwin, Princeton NJ: Princeton University Press, 1991, 63–77; Laurence H. Tribe, "Policy science: analysis or ideology?" *Philosophy & Public Affairs,* 2, 1972: 66–110; Amartya K. Sen, "Rational fools: a critique of the behavioral foundations of economic theory," *Philosophy & Public Affairs*, 6, 1977: 317–44; Paula England and Barbara Stanek Kilbourne, "Feminist critiques of the separative model of self: implications for rational choice theory," *Rationality and Society*, 2, 1990: 156–71; *Beyond Economic Man: Feminist Theory and Economics*, eds Marianne A. Ferber and Julie A. Nelson, Chicago IL: University of Chicago Press, 1993; Viktor Vanberg, "Rational choice, rule-following and institutions," *Rationality, Institutions and Economic Methodology*, eds Uskali Mäki, Bo Gustafsson and Christian Knudsen, London: Routledge, 1993, 171–200.

6 Economists and their forebears have been comparing their theories to Newtonian mechanics since the eighteenth century. The practice continues into this century unabated. See for example Frank H. Knight, "Economic psychology and the value problem," *The Ethics of Competition and Other Essays*, 82–3; George J. Stigler, "The successes and failures of Professor Smith," *The Economist as Preacher and Other Essays*, Chicago IL: University of Chicago Press, 1982, 158; Paul A. Samuelson, "Modern economic realities and individualism," *The Collected Scientific Papers of Paul A. Samuelson*, 2: 1408; Viktor Vanberg, "Rational choice, rule-following and institutions," *Rationality, Institutions and Economic Methodology*, 193.

7 See, for example, Gary Becker's contention that "marriages involving love are likely to be part of the equilibrium sorting because in market terms they are more productive than other marriages." *A Treatise on the Family*, enlarged edn, Cambridge MA: Harvard University Press, 1991, 124; and David M. Levy's discussion of the relation between Homeric "narrative style" and "rational choice principles" in *The Economic Ideas of Ordinary People: From Preferences to Trade*, London: Routledge, 1992, 109–34.

8 James M. Buchanan, *Economics: Between Predictive Science and Moral Philosophy*, College Station TX: Texas A&M University Press, 1987, 21.

9 George J. Stigler, "Does economics have a useful past?" *The Economist As Preacher*, 110.

10 Stigler, "Does economics have a useful past?" *The Economist As Preacher*, 107.

11 Some economists have sought to place limits on the relevance of economic theory to other fields of inquiry. See Frank H. Knight, *The Ethics of Competition and Other Essays*, 19–147; Jacob Viner, *Essays on the Intellectual History of Economics*, 77, 385–95; Donald N. McCloskey, *The Rhetoric of Economics*.

12 Sheldon Wolin, *Politics and Vision: Continuity and Innovation in Western Political Thought*, Boston MA: Little, Brown, 1960, 340–41.

13 Knight, "Economic psychology and the value problem," and "The limits of scientific method in economics," *The Ethics of Competition*, 83, 120–1.

14 Knight, "The limitations of scientific method in economics," *The Ethics of Competition*, 146.

15 Knight, "The ethics of competition," *The Ethics of Competition*, 70.

16 Knight, "Ethics and the economic interpretation," *The Ethics of Competition*, 40.

17 Gary S. Becker, *Accounting for Tastes*, Cambridge MA: Harvard University Press, 1996, 139–61. A revised version of Becker's Nobel Lecture, the essay was originally published in the *Journal of Political Economy*, 101, 1993: 385–409.

18 Becker, *Accounting for Tastes*, 156.

19 Becker, *Accounting for Tastes*, 24. The essay originally appeared in the *American Economic Review*, 67, 1977: 76–90.

20 Becker, *Accounting for Tastes*, 49.

21 Friedrich A. Hayek, "Economics and knowledge," *Individualism and Economic Order*, Chicago IL: University of Chicago Press, 1948, 54.

22 Hayek, *The Road to Serfdom*, Chicago IL: University of Chicago Press, 1944, 43–55.

23 See Viner, *Essays on the Intellectual History of Economics*, 89, 251; and his *The Role of Providence in the Social Order: An Essay in Intellectual History*, Jayne Lectures for 1966, Philadelphia PA: American Philosophical Society, 1972, 81–2.

24 Hayek, *Road to Serfdom*, 235.

25 I am thinking, for instance, of arguments such as Milton Friedman's *Capitalism and Freedom*, 1962, Chicago IL: University of Chicago Press, 1982, which conflate political and economic freedom by comparing dollars to votes: "The characteristic feature of action through political channels is that it tends to require or enforce substantial conformity. The great advantage of the market, on the other hand, is that it permits wide diversity. It is, in political terms, a system of proportional representation. Each man can vote, as it were, for the color of the tie he wants and get it; he does not have to see what color the majority wants and then, if he is in the minority, submit" (15). Friedman does not pursue the analogy long enough to consider the implications of there being disparities in the amount of people's disposable votes.

26 Hayek, *Road to Serfdom*, 72.

27 Hayek, *Road to Serfdom*, 73.

28 Hayek, *Road to Serfdom*, 83–4.

BIBLIOGRAPHY

Addison, Joseph, *The Works of the Right Honourable Joseph Addison*, 6 vols, London, 1811.

Addison, Joseph and Steele, Richard, *The Spectator*, ed. Donald F. Bond, 5 vols, Oxford: Clarendon Press, 1965.

Agnew, Jean-Christophe, *Worlds Apart: The Market and the Theater in Anglo-American Thought, 1550–1750*, Cambridge: Cambridge University Press, 1986.

Anderson, Benedict, *Imagined Communities: Reflections on the Origin and Spread of Nationalism*, rev. edn, London: Verso, 1991.

Antiquixotus, Philonauticus, *The Rule of Two to One: Or, the Difference betwixt Courage and Quixotism*, London, 1745.

Arbuthnot, John *et al.*, *Memoirs of the Extraordinary Life, Works, and Discoveries of Martinus Scriblerus*, ed. Charles Kerby-Miller, New York: Oxford University Press, 1988.

Ashcraft, Richard, "Faith and knowledge in Locke's philosophy," in John W. Yolton (ed.) *John Locke: Problems and Perspectives*, Cambridge: Cambridge University Press, 1969.

Ashcraft, Richard and Goldsmith, M. M., "Locke, Revolution Principles and the formation of Whig ideology," *Historical Journal*, 26, 1983: 773–800.

Astell, Mary, *Some Reflections Upon Marriage*, 1730, New York: Source Book Press, 1970.

Barish, Jonas, *The Antitheatrical Prejudice*, Berkeley CA: University of California Press, 1981.

Barrell, John, *English Literature in History, 1730–80: An Equal, Wide Survey*, New York: St Martin's Press, 1983.

——*The Birth of Pandora*, Philadelphia PA: University of Pennsylvania Press, 1992.

Bate, Walter Jackson, "The sympathetic imagination in eighteenth-century English criticism," *ELH*, 12, 1945: 144–64.

Battestin, Martin C., "Fielding's definition of wisdom: some functions of ambiguity and emblem in *Tom Jones*," *ELH*, 35, 1968: 188–217.

——"The problem of *Amelia*: Hume, Barrow, and the conversion of Captain Booth," *ELH*, 41, 1974: 613–48.

——"Tom Jones and 'His *Egyptian* Majesty': Fielding's parable of government," *PMLA*, 82, 1967: 68–77.

Baugh, Daniel A. (ed.) *Naval Administration 1715–50*, London: Naval Records Society, 1977.

Becker, Gary S., *Accounting for Tastes*, Cambridge MA: Harvard University Press, 1996.

——*A Treatise on the Family*, enlarged edn, Cambridge MA: Harvard University Press, 1991.

Behn, Aphra, *The Rover and Other Plays*, ed. Jane Spencer, Oxford: Oxford University Press, 1995.

Benedict, Barbara M., "'Dear Madam': rhetoric, cultural politics and the female reader in Sterne's *Tristram Shandy*," *Studies in Philology*, 89, 1992: 485–98.

Berkeley, George, *The Works of George Berkeley Bishop of Cloyne*, eds A. A. Luce and T. E. Jessop, 9 vols, London: Thomas Nelson and Sons, 1953.

Bolingbroke, Henry St John Viscount, *Letters on the Study and Use of History*, London, 1752.

Boswell, James, *Life of Johnson*, ed. R. W. Chapman, Oxford: Oxford University Press, 1985.

Boulton, James T., *Arbitrary Power: An Eighteenth-Century Obsession*, Nottingham: University of Nottingham, 1967.

Bowle, John, *A Letter to the Reverend Dr. Percy, Concerning A New and Classical Edition of Historia Del Valeroso Cavallero Don Quixote De La Mancha*, London, 1777.

Brissenden, R. F., *Virtue in Distress: Studies in the Novel of Sentiment from Richardson to Sade*, London: Macmillan, 1974.

Brown, Vivienne, *Adam Smith's Discourse: Canonicity, Commerce, and Conscience*, London: Routledge, 1994.

Buchanan, James M., *Economics: Between Predictive Science and Moral Philosophy*, College Station TX: Texas A&M University Press, 1987.

Burke, Edmund, *Reflections on the Revolution in France*, ed. J. G. A. Pocock, Indianapolis IN: Hackett, 1987.

Burnet, Thomas, *Remarks on John Locke, with Locke's Replies*, ed. George Watson, Doncaster: Brynmill, 1989.

Burton, A. P., "Cervantes the man seen through English eyes in the seventeenth and eighteenth centuries," *Bulletin of Hispanic Studies*, 45, 1968: 1–15.

Butler, Melissa A., "Early liberal roots of feminism: John Locke and the attack on patriarchy," *The American Political Science Review*, 72, 1978: 135–50.

Butler, Samuel, *Hudibras Parts I and II and Selected Other Writings*, eds John Wilders and Hugh de Quehen, Oxford: Clarendon Press, 1973.

Butts, Robert E. and Davis, John W., *The Methodological Heritage of Newton*, Toronto: University of Toronto Press, 1970.

Campbell, Jill, *Natural Masques: Gender and Identity in Fielding's Plays and Novels*, Stanford CA: Stanford University Press, 1995.

Carlton, Peter J., "*Tom Jones* and the '45 once again," *Studies in the Novel*, 20, 1988: 361–73.

Catch, Jack, *A Hue and Cry After the Pretender*, London, 1716.

Centlivre, Susannah, *A Bold Stroke for A Wife*, ed. Thalia Stathas, Lincoln NE: University of Nebraska Press, 1968.

——*The Dramatic Works of the Celebrated Mrs Centlivre*, 3 vols, 1760, 1872, New York: AMS Press, 1968.

Cervantes, Miguel de, *Don Quixote*, trans. Tobias Smollett, New York: Farrar, Straus and Giroux, 1986.

——*The Ingenious Gentleman Don Quixote de La Mancha*, trans. Peter Motteux, rev. Ozell, New York: Modern Library, 1950.

——*The Much esteemed History of The Ever-Famous Knight Don Quixote de la Mancha: Containing his many wonderful Adventures and Atchievements, Very Pleasant and Diverting. With the Comical Humours of Sancho Pancha, his Remarkable 'Squire, &c. In Two Parts*, London, 1716.

The Challenge, Sent by a Young Lady to Sir Thomas: Or, the Female War, London, 1697.

Charnock, John, *Biographia Navalis: Or, Impartial Memoirs of the Lives and Characters of Officers of the Navy of Great Britain*, 4 vols, London, 1796.

The Chevalier's Declaration (1745?).

Chudleigh, Lady Mary, *The Poems and Prose of Mary, Lady Chudleigh*, ed. Margaret J. M. Ezell, New York: Oxford University Press, 1993.

Cleary, Thomas, "Jacobitism in *Tom Jones*: the basis for an hypothesis," *Philological Quarterly*, 52, 1973: 239–51.

Clowes, William Laird, *The Royal Navy: A History from the Earliest Times to the Present*, 5 vols, London, 1898.

Copley, Stephen and Sutherland, Kathryn (eds) *Adam Smith's Wealth of Nations: New Interdisciplinary Essays*, Manchester: Manchester University Press, 1995.

Crane, R. S., "The concept of plot and the plot of *Tom Jones*," in R. S. Crane (ed.) *Critics and Criticism: Ancient and Modern*, Chicago IL: University of Chicago Press, 1952, 616–47.

——"Suggestions toward a genealogy of the 'Man of Feeling,'" *ELH*, 1, 1934: 205–30.

Deane, Phyllis, *The Evolution of Economic Ideas*, Cambridge: Cambridge University Press, 1978.

Defoe, Daniel, *Captain Tom's Remembrance to His Old Friends the Mobb of London, Westminster, Southwark, and Wapping*, London, 1711.

——*Instructions From Rome, In Favour of the Pretender, Inscrib'd to the most Elevated Don Sacheverellio, And his Brother Don Higginisco*, London, 1710.

DePorte, Michael V., *Nightmares and Hobbyhorses: Swift, Sterne, and Augustan Ideas of Madness*, San Marino CA: The Huntington Library, 1974.

Dickinson, William Calvin, *Sidney Godolphin, Lord Treasurer 1702–1710*, Studies in British History, vol. 18, Lewiston NY: Edwin Mellen Press, 1990.

Doody, Margaret Anne, "Shakespeare's novels: Charlotte Lennox illustrated," *Studies in the Novel*, 19, 1987: 296–310.

Dorn, Judith, "Reading women reading history: the philosophy of periodical form in Charlotte Lennox's *The Lady's Museum*," *Historical Reflections/Réflexions Historiques*, 18, 1992: 7–27.

Downs-Miers, Deborah, "Springing the trap: subtexts and subversions," in Mary Anne Schofield and Cecilia Macheski (eds) *Fetter'd or Free?: British Women Novelists, 1670–1815*, Athens OH: Ohio University Press, 1986, 308–23.

Drake, Judith, *An Essay in Defence of the Female Sex*, London, 1696.

——"An Essay in Defence of the Female Sex," in Marie Mulvey Roberts and Tamae Mizuta (eds) *The Pioneers*, London: Routledge/Thoemmes Press, 1995.

Dryden, John, *The Works of John Dryden*, 20 vols, Berkeley CA: University of California Press, 1956–89.

Duff, David, *Romance and Revolution: Shelley and the Politics of a Genre*, Cambridge: Cambridge University Press, 1994.

Dunton, John, *The Bull-Baiting: Or, Sach{evere}ll Dress'd up in Fire-Works*, London, 1710.

Duthie, Elizabeth, "The genuine man of feeling," *Modern Philology*, 78, 1981: 279–85.

Eatwell, John, Milgate, Murray and Newman, Peter (eds) *The New Palgrave: The Invisible Hand*, New York: W. W. Norton, 1989.

Ehrenpreis, Irvin, *Swift: The Man, His Works, and the Age*, 3 vols, Cambridge MA: Harvard University Press, 1962.

England, Paula and Stanek Kilbourne, Barbara, "Feminist critiques of the separative model of self: implications for rational choice theory," *Rationality and Society*, 2, 1990: 156–71.

An Enquiry into the Conduct of Capt. M—n. Being Remarks on the Minutes of the Court-Martial, and other incidental Matters. Humbly addressed to the Honourable House of Commons. By a SEA-OFFICER, London, 1745.

The Examiner, 23–6 April 1714.

Female Rights Vindicated; Or, the Equality of the Sexes Morally and Physically Proved, London, 1758.

Ferber, Marianne A. and Nelson, Julie A. (eds) *Beyond Economic Man: Feminist Theory and Economics*, Chicago IL: University of Chicago Press, 1993.

Ferguson, Moira, *First Feminists: British Women Writers 1578–1799*, Bloomington IN/Old Westbury NY: Indiana University Press/Feminist Press, 1985.

Fielding, Henry, *Amelia*, ed. Martin C. Battestin, Middletown CT: Wesleyan University Press, 1983.

——*The Covent-Garden Journal*, ed. Gerard Edward Jensen, 2 vols, 1915, New York: Russell and Russell, 1964.

——*Joseph Andrews*, ed. Martin C. Battestin, Boston MA: Houghton Mifflin, 1961.

——*Miscellanies by Henry Fielding, Esq*, ed. Henry Knight Miller, 2 vols, Oxford: Wesleyan University Press, 1972.

——*Tom Jones*, ed. Fredson Bowers, introduction by Martin Battestin, Middletown CT: Wesleyan University Press, 1975.

——*The True Patriot*, 19 November 1745.

——*The True Patriot and Related Writings*, ed. W. B. Coley, *The Wesleyan Edition of the Works of Henry Fielding*, Middletown CT: Wesleyan University Press, 1987.

——*The Works of Henry Fielding, Esq.*, ed. Leslie Stephen, 10 vols, London, 1882.

Fielding, Henry and Fielding, Sarah, *The Correspondence of Henry and Sarah Fielding*, eds Martin Battestin and Clive T. Probyn, Oxford: Clarendon Press, 1993.

Fielding, Sarah, *The Adventures of David Simple*, ed. Malcolm Kelsall, Oxford: Oxford University Press, 1973.

Foley, Vernard, *The Social Physics of Adam Smith*, West Lafayette IN: Purdue University Press, 1976.

Forbes, Duncan, "'Scientific' whiggism: Adam Smith and John Millar," *Cambridge Journal*, 7, 1954: 643–70.

Foucault, Michel, *The Order of Things: An Archaeology of the Human Sciences*, New York: Vintage, 1973.

Friedman, Milton, *Adam Smith's Relevance for 1976*, introduction by Joseph Spengler, Los Angeles CA: International Institute for Economic Research, 1976.

——*Capitalism and Freedom*, 1962, Chicago IL: University of Chicago Press, 1982.

Frum, David, "Adam Smith, the sensible philosopher," *The New Criterion*, March 1996: 14–17.

Gallagher, Catherine, "Embracing the absolute: the politics of the female subject in seventeenth-century England," *Genders*, 1, 1988: 24–39.

Gerard, Alexander, *An Essay on Taste, Together with Observations Concerning the Imitative Nature of Poetry*, facsimile reproduction of the 3rd edn, 1780, by Walter J. Hipple Jr, Gainesville FL: Scholars' Facsimiles & Reprints, 1963.

Gilson, Etienne, *The Unity of Philosophical Experience*, New York: Charles Scribner's Sons, 1956.

Glanvill, Joseph, "The vanity of dogmatizing," in *The Vanity of Dogmatizing: The Three "Versions,"* Hove: Harvester Press, 1970. ·

Goldsmith, Oliver, *Collected Works of Oliver Goldsmith*, ed. Arthur Friedman, 5 vols, Oxford: Clarendon Press, 1966.

Greene, Donald, "Latitudinarianism and sensibility: the genealogy of the 'Man of Feeling' reconsidered," *Modern Philology*, 75, 1977: 159–83.

Gunn, J. A. W., "'Interest will not lie': a seventeenth-century political maxim," *Journal of the History of Ideas*, 29, 1968: 551–64.

Hacking, Ian, *The Emergence of Probability: A Philosophical Study of Early Ideas about Probability, Induction, and Statistical Inference*, London: Cambridge University Press, 1975.

Hahn, H. George, "Main lines of criticism of Fielding's *Tom Jones*, 1900–78," *British Studies Monitor*, 10.1–2, 1980: 8–35.

Hall, Joan Joffe, "The hobbyhorsical world of *Tristram Shandy*," *Modern Language Quarterly*, 24, 1963: 131–43.

Hatfield, Glenn W., *Henry Fielding and the Language of Irony*, Chicago IL: University of Chicago Press, 1968.

Hayek, F. A., *Individualism and Economic Order*, Chicago IL: University of Chicago Press, 1948.

——*The Road to Serfdom*, Chicago IL: University of Chicago Press, 1944.

Hobbes, Thomas, *Leviathan*, ed. C. B. Macpherson, Harmondsworth: Penguin, 1968.

Holmes, Geoffrey, *The Trial of Doctor Sacheverell*, London: Eyre Methuen, 1973.

——"The Sacheverell Riots," *Past and Present*, 72, 1976: 55–85.

Hume, David, *Essays Moral, Political, and Literary*, ed. Eugene F. Miller, rev. edn, Indianapolis IN: Liberty Classics, 1985.

——*A Treatise of Human Nature*, ed. L. A. Selby-Bigge, 2nd edn. rev. P. H. Nidditch, Oxford: Clarendon Press, 1978.

Hunter, J. Paul, "Clocks, calendars, and names: the troubles of Tristram and the aesthetics of uncertainty," in J. Douglas Canfield and J. Paul Hunter (eds) *Rhetorics of Order/Ordering Rhetorics in English Neoclassical Literature*, Newark DE: University of Delaware Press, 1989, 173–98.

Hurd, Bishop Richard, *Hurd's Letters on Chivalry and Romance With the Third Elizabethan Dialogue*, ed. Edith J. Morley, London: Henry Frowde, 1911, 84–5.

Hutchens, Eleanor Newman, "'Prudence': a case study," in *Irony in* Tom Jones, University AL: Alabama University Press, 1965.

Hutcheson, Francis, *The Collected Works of Francis Hutcheson*, facsimile edn prepared by Bernhard Fabian, 7 vols, Hildesheim: Georg Olms, 1971.

Iser, Wolfgang, *Laurence Sterne: Tristram Shandy*, trans. Henry David Wilson, Cambridge: Cambridge University Press, 1988.

Jackson, William A., "The Carl T. Keller Collection of *Don Quixote*," *Harvard Library Bulletin*, 1, 1947: 306–10.

Jacob, James R., *Henry Stubbe, Radical Protestantism and the Early Enlightenment*, Cambridge: Cambridge University Press, 1983.

Jefferson, D. W. "*Tristram Shandy* and the tradition of learned wit," *Essays in Criticism*, 1, 1951: 225–48.

Johnson, Claudia L., *Equivocal Beings: Politics, Gender, and Sentimentality in the 1790s*, Chicago IL: University of Chicago Press, 1995.

Johnson, Samuel, *The Yale Edition of the Works of Samuel Johnson*, eds W. J. Bate and Albrecht B. Strauss, 16 vols, New Haven CT: Yale University Press, 1969.

Jones, Richard Foster, *Ancients and Moderns: A Study of the Background of the Battle of the Books*, Washington University Studies, n.s. 6, St Louis MO: Washington University Press, 1936.

Kantorowicz, Ernst H., *The King's Two Bodies: A Study in Mediaeval Political Theology*, Princeton NJ: Princeton University Press, 1957.

Kearney, Anthony, "Tom Jones and the Forty-five," *Ariel*, 4.2, 1973: 68–78.

Keener, Fredrick M., *English Dialogues of the Dead*, New York: Columbia University Press, 1973.

Kinnaird, Joan K., "Mary Astell and the conservative contribution to English feminism," *Journal of British Studies*, 19, 1979: 53–75.

Kivy, Peter, *The Seventh Sense: A Study of Francis Hutcheson's Aesthetics and its Influence in Eighteenth-Century Britain*, New York: Burt Franklin, 1976.

Knight, Frank H., *The Ethics of Competition and Other Essays*, New York: Harper, 1935.

Knowles, Edwin B., "Cervantes and English literature," in Angel Flores and M. J. Benardete (eds) *Cervantes Across the Centuries*, New York: The Dryden Press, 1947, 267–93.

——"*Don Quixote* abridged," *The Papers of the Bibliographical Society of America*, 49, 1955: 19–36.

Knowlson, James B., *Universal Language Schemes in England and France 1600–1800*, Toronto: University of Toronto Press, 1975.

Kroll, Richard W. F., *The Material Word: Literate Culture in the Restoration and Early Eighteenth Century*, Baltimore MD: Johns Hopkins University Press, 1991.

Kynaston, Agnes Mary, "The life and writings of Charlotte Lennox, 1720–1804," unpublished dissertation, University of London, 1936.

Langbauer, Laurie, *Women and Romance: The Consolations of Gender in the English Novel*, Ithaca NY: Cornell University Press, 1990.

Law, William, *Remarks upon the Fable of the Bees*, introduction by F. D. Maurice, Cambridge, 1844.

Lennox, Charlotte, *The Female Quixote; Or, The Adventures of Arabella*, ed. Margaret Dalziel, chronology by Duncan Isles, Oxford: Oxford University Press, 1973.

——*The Lady's Museum*, 2 vols, London, 1760–1.

——*The Life of Harriot Stuart. Written by Herself*, 2 vols, London, 1751.

——*Shakespear Illustrated: Or the Novels and Histories, On which the Plays of Shakespeare Are Founded, Collected and Translated from the Original Authors. With Critical Remarks*, 3 vols, London, 1753–4.

Levine, Joseph M., *The Battle of the Books: History and Literature in the Augustan Age*, Ithaca NY: Cornell University Press, 1991.

Levy, David M., *The Economic Ideas of Ordinary People: From Preferences to Trade*, London: Routledge, 1992.

Lloyd, Claude, "Shadwell and the virtuosi," *PMLA*, 44, 1929: 472–94.

Locke, John, *An Essay Concerning Human Understanding*, ed. Peter H. Nidditch, Oxford: Clarendon Press, 1975.

——*Some Thoughts Concerning Education*, eds John W. and Jean S. Yolton, Oxford: Clarendon Press, 1989.

——*Two Treatises of Government*, ed. Peter Laslett, student edn, Cambridge: Cambridge University Press, 1988.

London, April, "Controlling the text: women in *Tom Jones*," *Studies in the Novel*, 19, 1987: 323–33.

Loscocco, Paula, "Can't live without 'em: Walter Shandy and the woman within," *The Eighteenth Century*, 32, 1991: 166–79.

Lynch, James J., "Moral sense and the narrator of *Tom Jones*," *SEL*, 25, 1985: 599–614.

——"Romance and realism in Charlotte Lennox's *The Female Quixote*," *Essays in Literature*, 14, 1987: 51–63.

Macfie, Alec, "The invisible hand of Jupiter," *Journal of the History of Ideas*, 32, 1971: 595–9.

MacLean, Kenneth, *John Locke and English Literature of the Eighteenth Century*, New Haven CT: Yale University Press, 1936.

Madan, F. F., *A Critical Bibliography of Dr Henry Sacheverell*, ed. W. A. Speck, Library Series, 49, Lawrence KS: University of Kansas Libraries, 1978.

Mäki, Uskali, Gustafsson, Bo and Knudsen, Christian (eds) *Rationality, Institutions and Economic Methodology*, London: Routledge, 1993.

Malcolmson, Robert W., *Popular Recreations in English Society 1700–1850*, Cambridge: Cambridge University Press, 1973.

Mandeville, Bernard, *The Fable of the Bees or Private Vices, Publick Benefits*, ed. F. B. Kaye, 2 vols, 1924, Indianapolis IN: Liberty Classics, 1988.

Markley, Robert, *Fallen Languages: Crises of Representation in Newtonian England 1660–1740*, Ithaca NY: Cornell University Press, 1993.

Marshall, David, *The Figure of Theater: Shaftesbury, Defoe, Adam Smith, and George Eliot*, New York: Columbia University Press, 1986.

——"Writing masters and 'masculine exercises' in *The Female Quixote*," *Eighteenth-Century Fiction*, 5, 1993: 105–35.

Marvell, Andrew, *The Complete Poems of Andrew Marvell*, ed. Elizabeth Story Donno, Harmondsworth: Penguin, 1985.

Mayáns y Siscár, Don Gregorio, *The Life of Michael de Cervantes Saavedra*, trans. Ozell, in *The Life and Exploits of the ingenious Gentleman Don Quixote De La Mancha*, trans. Charles Jarvis, 4 vols, Dublin, 1747.

McCloskey, Donald, *The Rhetoric of Economics*, Madison WI: University of Wisconsin Press, 1985.

McKeon, Michael, *The Origins of the English Novel, 1600–1740*, Baltimore MD: Johns Hopkins University Press, 1987.

——*Politics and Poetry in Restoration England*, Cambridge MA: Harvard University Press, 1975.

McLynn, F. J., "The ideology of Jacobitism on the eve of the rising of 1745: Part I," *History of European Ideas*, 6, 1985: 1–18.

McVeagh, John, "Defoe and the romance of trade," *Durham University Journal*, n.s. 39, 1978: 141–7.

Miller, Henry Knight, *Henry Fielding's Tom Jones and the Romance Tradition*, Victoria BC: University of Victoria, 1976.

Miller, William L., "The economics of education in English classical economics," *Southern Economic Journal*, 32, 1965–6: 294–309.

Mintz, Samuel I., *The Hunting of Leviathan: Seventeenth-Century Reactions to the Materialism and Moral Philosophy of Thomas Hobbes*, Cambridge: Cambridge University Press, 1962.

The Minutes of a Court-Martial . . . Enquiring into the Conduct of the Commanders of the Hampton-Court *and the* Dread-nought, *for not engaging the* Fleuron *and* Neptune, *two* French *Men of War*, London, 1745.

Mitford, John, "Chapter by Dr Johnson in *The Female Quixote*," *The Gentleman's Magazine*, 176, 1844: 41.

——"Dr Johnson's literary intercourse with Mrs Lennox," *The Gentleman's Magazine*, 175, 1843: 132.

Monod, Paul Kléber, *Jacobitism and the English People 1688–1788*, Cambridge: Cambridge University Press, 1989.

Montagu, Lady Mary Wortley, *The Complete Letters of Lady Mary Wortley Montagu*, ed. Robert Halsband, 3 vols, Oxford: Clarendon Press, 1967.

Mossner, Ernest Campbell, "'Of the principle of moral estimation: a discourse between David Hume, Robert Clerk, and Adam Smith': an unpublished MS by Adam Ferguson," *Journal of the History of Ideas*, 21, 1960: 222–32.

Motteux, Peter Anthony, translator's preface, *The History of the Renown'd Don Quixote De la Mancha*, London, 1700.

Mullan, John, *Sentiment and Sociability: The Language of Feeling in the Eighteenth Century*, Oxford: Clarendon Press, 1988.

Nadelhaft, Jerome, "The Englishwoman's sexual and civil war: feminist attitudes towards men, women, and marriage 1650–1740," *Journal of the History of Ideas*, 43, 1982: 555–79.

New, Melvyn, "Job's wife and Sterne's other women," in Laura Claridge and Elizabeth Langland (eds) *Out of Bounds: Male Writers and Gender(ed) Criticism*, Amherst MA: University of Massachusetts Press, 1990, 55–74.

Newyear, Richard, *Gibraltar, or the Pretender, &c*, London, 1727.

Okin, Susan Moller, "Women and the making of the sentimental family," *Philosophy & Public Affairs*, 11, 1981: 65–88.

Pateman, Carole, *The Sexual Contract*, Stanford CA: Stanford University Press, 1988.

Patey, Douglas Lane, *Probability and Literary Form: Philosophic Theory and Literary Practice in the Augustan Age*, Cambridge: Cambridge University Press, 1984.

Paulson, Ronald, *Theme and Structure in Swift's Tale of a Tub*, 1960, Hamden CT: Archon, 1972.

Perry, Ruth, *The Celebrated Mary Astell: An Early English Feminist*, Chicago IL: University of Chicago Press, 1986, 163–80.

——"Words for sex: the verbal-sexual continuum in *Tristram Shandy*," *Studies in the Novel*, 20, 1988: 27–42.

The Philosophical Quixote; Or, Memoirs of Mr David Wilkins. In a Series of Letters, 2 vols, London, 1782.

Pope, Alexander, *The Poems of Alexander Pope*, ed. John Butt, one-volume edition of the Twickenham text, New Haven CT: Yale University Press, 1963.

Price, Martin, introduction, *Eighteenth-Century Studies*, 4, 1970: 1–5.

Priestley, Joseph, *Lectures on History and General Policy*, ed. J. T. Rutt, London, 1826.

Prior, Matthew, *The Literary Works of Matthew Prior*, eds H. Bunker Wright and Monroe K. Spears, 2 vols, Oxford: Clarendon Press, 1959.

Rae, John, *Life of Adam Smith*, introduction by Jacob Viner, New York: Augustus M. Kelley, 1965.

Rashid, Salim, "Adam Smith's rise to fame: a reexamination of the evidence," *The Eighteenth Century: Theory and Interpretation*, 23, 1982: 64–85.

Reed, Joel, "Restoration and repression: the language projects of the Royal Society," *Studies in Eighteenth-Century Culture*, 19, 1989: 399–412.

Richmond, H. W., *The Navy in the War of 1739–48*, 3 vols, Cambridge: Cambridge University Press, 1920.

Roberts, T. A., *The Concept of Benevolence: Aspects of Eighteenth-Century Moral Philosophy*, London: Macmillan, 1973.

Rodger, N. A. M., *The Wooden World: An Anatomy of the Georgian Navy*, London: Collins, 1986.

Rogers, Nicholas, "Popular protest in early Hanoverian London," *Past and Present*, 79, 1978: 70–100.

Rosenberg, Nathan, "Adam Smith on the division of labour: two views or one?" *Economica*, n.s. 32, 1965: 127–39.

Rosenblum, Michael, "Why what happens in Shandy Hall is not 'A Matter for the Police,'" *Eighteenth-Century Fiction*, 7, 1995: 145–64.

Ross, Deborah, "Mirror, mirror: the didactic dilemma of *The Female Quixote*," *SEL*, 27, 1987: 455–73.

Ross, Ian Simpson, *The Life of Adam Smith*, Oxford: Clarendon Press, 1995.

Sacheverell, Henry, *The Perils of False Brethren, both in Church and State*, London, 1709.

Samuelson, Paul A., *Economics*, 11th edn, New York: McGraw-Hill, 1980.

——"Modern economic realities and individualism," in Joseph E. Stiglitz (ed.) *The Collected Scientific Papers of Paul A. Samuelson*, 5 vols, Cambridge MA: MIT Press, 1966.

Samuelson, Robert J., "The spirit of Adam Smith," *Newsweek*, 2 December 1996: 63.

"Sarah Fielding 1710–1768," in Dennis Poupard (ed.) *Literature Criticism from 1400–1800*, vol. 1, Detroit MI: Gale, 1984, 267–80.

Séjourné, Philippe, *The Mystery of Charlotte Lennox: First Novelist of Colonial America (1727?–1804)*, Aix-en-Provence: Publications des Annales de la Faculté des Lettres, 1967.

Selby-Bigge, L. A. (ed.) *British Moralists: Being Selections from Writers Principally of the Eighteenth Century*, introduction by Bernhard Baumrin, 2 vols, Indianapolis IN: Bobbs-Merrill, 1964.

Sen, Amartya K., "Rational fools: a critique of the behavioral foundations of economic theory," *Philosophy & Public Affairs*, 6, 1977: 317–44.

Shadwell, Thomas, *The Virtuoso*, eds Marjory Hope Nicholson and David Stuart Rodes, Lincoln NE: University of Nebraska Press, 1966.

Shaftesbury, Anthony Ashley Cooper, Third Earl, *Characteristics of Men, Manners, Opinions, Times*, ed. John M. Robertson, 2 vols, Gloucester MA: Peter Smith, 1963.

Shapin, Steven and Schaffer, Simon, *Leviathan and the Airpump: Hobbes, Boyle, and the Experimental Life*, Princeton NJ: Princeton University Press, 1985.

Shapiro, Barbara J., *Probability and Certainty in Seventeenth-Century England*, Princeton NJ: Princeton University Press, 1983.

Sheriff, John K., *The Good-Natured Man: The Evolution of a Moral Ideal, 1660–1800*, University AL: University of Alabama Press, 1982.

Sitter, John, *Literary Loneliness in Mid-Eighteenth-Century England*, Ithaca NY: Cornell University Press, 1982.

Skinner, Andrew S. and Wilson, Thomas (eds) *Essays on Adam Smith*, Oxford: Clarendon Press, 1975.

Skinner, Gillian, "'The Price of a Tear': economic sense and sensibility in Sarah Fielding's *David Simple*," *Literature and History*, 3rd series, 1.1, 1992: 16–28.

Small, Miriam Rossiter, *Charlotte Ramsay Lennox: An Eighteenth-Century Lady of Letters*, 1935, n.p.: Archon, 1969.

Smallwood, Angela J., *Fielding and the Woman Question: The Novels of Henry Fielding and Feminist Debate, 1700–1750*, New York: Harvester Wheatsheaf/St Martin's Press, 1989.

Smith, Adam, *The Correspondence of Adam Smith*, eds Ernest Campbell Mossner and Ian Simpson Ross, 1977, Indianapolis IN: Liberty Classics, 1987.

——*Essays on Philosophical Subjects*, eds W. P. D. Wightman and J. C. Bryce, 1980, Indianapolis IN: Liberty Classics, 1982.

——*An Inquiry into the Nature and Causes of the Wealth of Nations*, eds R. H. Campbell, A. S. Skinner and W. B. Todd, 2 vols, 1976, Indianapolis IN: Liberty Classics, 1981.

——*Lectures on Rhetoric and Belles Lettres*, ed. J. C. Bryce, 1983, Indianapolis IN: Liberty Classics, 1985.

——*The Theory of Moral Sentiments*, eds D. D. Raphael and A. L. Macfie, 1976, Indianapolis IN: Liberty Classics, 1982.

Smith, Barbara Herrnstein, *Contingencies of Value: Alternate Perspectives for Critical Theory*, Cambridge MA: Harvard University Press, 1988.

Smith, Hilda L., *Reason's Disciples: Seventeenth-Century English Feminists*, Urbana IL: University of Illinois Press, 1982.

Smollett, Tobias, *The Life and Adventures of Sir Launcelot Greaves*, ed. Peter Wagner, Harmondsworth: Penguin, 1988.

Snow, Malinda, "The judgment of evidence in *Tom Jones*," *South Atlantic Review*, 48, 1983: 37–51.

Sophia, *Woman Not Inferior to Man*, 1739, London: Brentham Press, 1975.

——*Woman Not Inferior to Man: Or, A Short and Modest Vindication of the Natural Right of the Fair-Sex to a Perfect Equality of Power, Dignity, and Esteem, with the Men*, London, 1739.

Spacks, Patricia Meyer, *Desire and Truth: Functions of Plot in Eighteenth-Century English Novels*, Chicago IL: University of Chicago Press, 1990.

——"The subtle sophistry of desire: Dr Johnson and *The Female Quixote*," *Modern Philology*, 85, 1988: 532–42.

Sprat, Thomas, *The History of the Royal Society*, eds Jackson I. Cope and Harold Whitmore Jones, St Louis MO: Washington University Studies, 1958.

Staves, Susan, "Don Quixote in eighteenth-century England," *Comparative Literature*, 24, 1972: 193–215.

Steele, Richard, *The Tatler*, ed. Donald F. Bond, 3 vols, Oxford: Clarendon Press, 1987.

——*The Tatler*, Philadelphia PA, 1844.

Sterne, Laurence, *The Life and Opinions of Tristram Shandy, Gentleman*, ed. Ian Campbell Ross, Oxford: Oxford University Press, 1983.

Stewart, Larry, *The Rise of Public Science: Rhetoric, Technology, and Natural Philosophy in Newtonian Britain, 1660–1750*, Cambridge: Cambridge University Press, 1992.

Stigler, George J., *The Economist as Preacher and Other Essays*, Chicago IL: University of Chicago Press, 1982.

Straka, Gerald M., "1688 as the Year One: eighteenth-century attitudes towards the Glorious Revolution," in Louis T. Milic (ed.) *Studies in Eighteenth-Century Culture*, vol. 1, Cleveland OH: Case Western Reserve University Press, 1971, 143–67.

Stubbe, Henry, *Campanella Revived, Or an Enquiry into the History of the Royal Society, Whether the Virtuosi there do not pursue the Projects of Campanella for the reducing England unto Popery*, London, 1670.

——*Legends No Histories: Or, A Specimen of Some Animadversions Upon the History of the Royal Society*, London, 1670.

Stumpf, Thomas A., "*Tom Jones* from the outside," in Howard M. Harper Jr and Charles Edge (eds) *The Classic British Novel*, Athens GA: University of Georgia Press, 1972, 3–21.

Sundstrom, Roy A., *Sidney Godolphin: Servant of the State*, Newark DE: University of Delaware Press, 1992.

Swearingen, James E., *Reflexivity in* Tristram Shandy*: An Essay in Phenomenological Criticism*, New Haven CT: Yale University Press, 1977.

Swift, Jonathan, *The Prose Works of Jonathan Swift*, ed. Herbert Davis, 14 vols, Oxford: Oxford University Press, 1939–68.

Syfret, R. H., "Some early critics of the Royal Society," *Notes and Records of The Royal Society of London*, 8, 1950: 20–64.

Tave, Stuart, *The Amiable Humorist*, Chicago IL: University of Chicago Press, 1960.

Tavor, Eve, *Scepticism, Society and the Eighteenth-Century Novel*, Houndmills: Macmillan, 1987.

Temple, William, *Essays on Ancient and Modern Learning and Poetry*, ed. J. E. Spingarn, Oxford: Clarendon Press, 1909.

Thomas, Keith, "Women and the Civil War sects," in Trevor Aston (ed.) *Crisis in Europe 1560–1660: Essays from* Past and Present, London: Routledge and Kegan Paul, 1965, 317–40.

Todd, Janet, *Sensibility: An Introduction*, London: Methuen, 1986.

——*The Sign of Angelica: Women, Writing and Fiction, 1660–1800*, New York: Columbia University Press, 1989.

Touchwood, Jack, *Quixote Redivivus: Or, The Spiritual Knight Errant, in a Letter to Isaac Bickerstaff, Esq.*, London, 1710.

Traugott, John, *Tristram Shandy's World: Sterne's Philosophical Rhetoric*, New York: Russell and Russell, 1954.

Tribe, Laurence H., "Policy science: analysis or ideology?" *Philosophy & Public Affairs*, 2, 1972: 66–110.

Tuveson, Ernest Lee, *The Imagination as a Means of Grace: Locke and the Aesthetics of Romanticism*, Berkeley CA: University of California Press, 1960.

Upham, A. H., "English femmes savantes at the end of the seventeenth century," *Journal of English and Germanic Philology*, 12, 1913: 262–76.

Van Sant, Ann Jessie, *Eighteenth-Century Sensibility and the Novel: The Senses in Social Context*, Cambridge: Cambridge University Press, 1993.

A Vindication of the Conduct of Capt. M—N and of the Court-Martial. By a SEA-OFFICER, London, 1745.

Viner, Jacob C., *Essays on the Intellectual History of Economics*, ed. Douglas A. Irwin, Princeton NJ: Princeton University Press, 1991.

——*The Role of Providence in the Social Order: An Essay in Intellectual History*, Jayne Lectures for 1966, Philadelphia PA: American Philosophical Society, 1972.

Voitle, Richard, "The reason of the English Enlightenment," *Studies on Voltaire and the Eighteenth Century*, ed. Theodore Besterman, 27, 1963: 1735–74.

Ward, Ned, *The London Spy*, ed. Paul Hyland, East Lansing MI: Colleagues Press, 1993.

Warren, Leland E., "Of the conversation of women: *The Female Quixote* and the dream of perfection," *Studies in Eighteenth-Century Culture*, 2, 1982: 367–80.

Wasserman, Earl R., *The Subtler Language: Critical Readings of Neoclassical and Romantic Poems*, Baltimore MD: Johns Hopkins University Press, 1959, 169–72.

Waszek, Norbert, "Two concepts of morality: a distinction of Adam Smith's ethics and its stoic origin," *Journal of the History of Ideas*, 45, 1984: 591–606.

Watt, Ian, *The Rise of the Novel*, Berkeley CA: University of California Press, 1957.

Weinsheimer, Joel C., *Eighteenth-Century Hermeneutics: Philosophy of Interpretation in England from Locke to Burke*, New Haven CT: Yale University Press, 1993.

Welsh, Alexander, *Reflections on the Hero as Quixote*, Princeton NJ: Princeton University Press, 1981.

——*Strong Representations: Narrative and Circumstantial Evidence in England*, Baltimore MD: Johns Hopkins University Press, 1992.

Werhane, Patricia H., *Adam Smith and His Legacy for Modern Capitalism*, New York: Oxford University Press, 1991.

West, Edwin G., "Adam Smith on the cultural effects of specialization: splenetics versus economics," *History of Political Economy*, 28, 1996: 83–105.

Westfall, Richard S., "Robert Hooke, mechanical technology, and scientific investigation," in John G. Burke (ed.) *The Uses of Science in the Age of Newton*, Los Angeles CA: William Andrews Clark Memorial Library, 1983, 85–110.

Whig and Tory: Or, Wit on Both Sides, London, 1712.

Wilson, Kathleen, "Empire, trade and popular politics in mid-Hanoverian Britain: the case of Admiral Vernon," *Past and Present*, 121, 1988: 74–109.

Winch, Donald, *Adam Smith's Politics: An Essay on Historiographic Revision*, Cambridge: Cambridge University Press, 1978.

Winn, James Anderson, *John Dryden and His World*, New Haven CT: Yale University Press, 1987.

Wolin, Sheldon, *Politics and Vision: Continuity and Innovation in Western Political Thought*, Boston MA: Little, Brown, 1960.

Wood, P. B., "Methodology and apologetics: Thomas Sprat's *History of the Royal Society*," *The British Journal for the History of Science*, 13, 1980: 1–26.

Woodward, C., "'Feminine virtue, ladylike disguise, women of community': Sarah Fielding and the female I am at mid-century," *Transactions of the Samuel Johnson Society of the Northwest*, 15, 1984: 57–71.

Ziolkowski, Eric J., *The Sanctification of Don Quixote: From Hidalgo to Priest*, University Park PA: Pennsylvania State University Press, 1991.

INDEX